The Politics of Working Life

PAUL EDWARDS
and
JUDY WAJCMAN

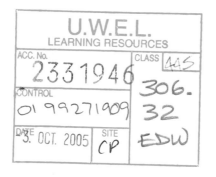

OXFORD
UNIVERSITY PRESS

OXFORD
UNIVERSITY PRESS

Great Clarendon Street, Oxford OX2 6DP

Oxford University Press is a department of the University of Oxford.
It furthers the University's objective of excellence in research, scholarship,
and education by publishing worldwide in

Oxford   New York

Auckland Cape Town Dar es Salaam Hong Kong Karachi
Kuala Lumpur Madrid Melbourne Mexico City Nairobi
New Delhi Shanghai Taipei Toronto

With offices in

Argentina Austria Brazil Chile Czech Republic France Greece
Guatemala Hungary Italy Japan Poland Portugal
Singapore South Korea Switzerland Thailand Turkey Ukraine Vietnam

Oxford is a registered trade mark of Oxford Univeristy Press in the UK
and in certain others countries

Published in the United States
by Oxford University Press Inc., New York

© Paul Edwards and Judy Wajcman 2005

British Library Cataloguing in Publication Data
Data available

Library of Congress Cataloging in Publication Data
Data available

Typeset by SPI Publisher Services, Pondicherry, India
Printed in Great Britain
on acid-free paper by
Biddles Ltd., King's Lynn, Norfolk

ISBN   0-19-927190-9   978-0-19-927190-0

ISBN   0-19-927191-7(pbk.)   978-0-19-927191-7 (pbk.)

1 3 5 7 9 10 8 6 4 2

PREFACE

The world of work is a complex and confusing place. This book is intended to provide a critical perspective on the dramatic changes that are occurring in what work now means. Such a perspective requires not only an assessment of empirical evidence but also an analytical framework through which to understand a potentially bewildering set of facts.

Many studies of work respond to this complexity by focusing on one key issue or development. Some have a positive emphasis, as in accounts of 'empowerment', the 'new economy' or the rise of the 'knowledge worker'. Others have a negative tone, as in studies of stress and insecurity. Still others focus on broader trends, such as globalization, but have little to say about their implications for the experience of work. These approaches attract criticism for being 'grand narratives'.

In many respects, we side with those who are sceptical about the possibility of identifying a single trend and we provide a critique of such views. But we aim to do more than highlight myths. Our emphasis is on the presence of forces that are inherent in the operation of an organization but that also pull in opposite directions. Organizations are riven internally by tensions between autonomy and control: they have to find ways to respond to employees' expectations of material rewards and to provide at least a degree of participation while at the same time ensuring that they have a focus and sense of discipline and purpose. They also have to respond to conflicting pressures from outside, for example in relation to social responsibility while meeting financial objectives.

Thus a central theme of the book is that of contradictions. This both helps make sense of the empirical evidence and provides us with a valuable analytical tool. We highlight many of the downsides of modern work experience. These include: the undercutting of career ambitions; pressures on family life; great difficulty in living up to ambitions for participation and empowerment; and a propensity to generate risk and to take decisions in irrational ways. We emphasize these issues because they are not brought to light in many accounts. Reasons for these characteristics are long-term and short-term. Long-term reasons include fundamental aspects of organizational functioning, notably pressures to control subordinates' behaviour and an inability to change existing structures of power despite stated beliefs in such new developments as gender equality, empowerment, and corporate social responsibility. These have been strengthened by short-term developments around the rise of shareholder value and the working of modern market economies.

But it is also true that organizations need the commitment of their employees and legitimacy in the wider society. Demands for participation and responsibility have increased, for example as a result of the actions of environmental and human rights groups. Responses to these have offered some genuine progress. Such responses have not *resolved* the tensions of organizational functioning, but they have altered the ways in which these tensions are managed.

The analytical strength of the notion of contradictions is that it helps us to grasp *why* organizations have a dual character. It also helps to cut through debates as to whether the present is different from the past. Organizations and the social structure in which they are embedded are necessarily dynamic as the working through of contradictory forces leads to new sets of arrangements. Yet such change is the result of unplanned responses to events and reflects enduring features of social organization. Finally, the idea gives emphasis to the active role of people within organizations, as they negotiate their way through the pressures to which they are subject. No organization is monolithic: there are spaces within the structure that people can use to create meaning and dignity in their working lives. We aim to examine the mix of forces that shape the world in which they work and in so doing indicate the ways in which it may be changed.

Chapter 1 serves as an introduction to the book's main themes. It argues for the importance of the study of work, explaining and illustrating the core concepts and frameworks that we have adopted for our study. Over the course of the subsequent chapters the discussion moves from the 'micro' to the 'macro' level. Chapters 2–4 address the immediate work experience of individuals, showing for example how meaning and significance are created even in unlikely places. Chapters 5–8 consider the functioning of organizations, including the management of performance and the nature of decision-making. Chapters 9 and 10 turn to wider forces shaping organizations, in particular the structuring of markets and the impact of globalization. Chapter 11 confronts key ethical questions and the degree to which existing structures are changeable through action. It argues that individuals have more power to change their working lives than they might realize. Because of their contradictory qualities, organizations are open to change. Yet the structural developments of markets and organizations set limits. By understanding these limits, people may realize (in both senses of the word) their potential.

The book is not a catalogue of workplace issues or an assessment of particular policy options. Rather, it provides a way of thinking through issues of organizational life in the context of contemporary capitalism. The concepts and analytical tools that we use are illuminated with numerous examples. While telling stories that are important in their own right, they also illustrate wider issues of the politics of working life.

In many ways, our purpose is captured by the rhetorical question posed by the social theorist Albert Hirschman (1982: 1483), 'after so may failed prophesies is it not in the interest of social science to embrace complexity, be it at some sacrifice of its claim to predictive power?' We do not promise predictive power, but we hope to have captured and clarified the complexity of life in organizations.

ACKNOWLEDGEMENTS

The origins of this book can be traced back to Judy Wajcman's appointment as a Principal Research Fellow at the Industrial Relations Research Unit (IRRU), Warwick Business School, between 1992 and 1995. We identified shared interests and intellectual approaches that have matured in the writing of this book. The stimulating scholarly environment of IRRU has continued to be important to both of us as we have moved into substantive issues not usually considered to be 'industrial relations'. We feel that this field is broader and richer than might first appear, and its distinct approach to the world of work has deeply informed this book.

Many universities claim that teaching and research are mutually reinforcing. This book exemplifies such claims. Many chapters draw on our teaching in a variety of places, but two specific examples should be mentioned. Chapter 8 in particular draws on teaching by Edwards on the Critical Issues in Management, an undergraduate module at Warwick, and he acknowledges more generally the contributions of colleagues and students on this innovative and challenging programme. Chapter 5 reflects MBA teaching. Chapter 3 draws on Wajcman's ongoing research with Michael Bittman and Chapter 4 on research conducted in Australia with Bill Martin.

The early stages of writing were carried out while Edwards was on sabbatical from the University of Warwick, and he is grateful for the university's maintenance of its sabbatical leave arrangements, which were once relatively standard but are now notably generous. The latter stages were completed during his fellowship in the ESRC/EPSRC Advanced Institute of Management Research. The unusually broad remit of the fellowship allowed time that more traditional research grants would not; equally importantly, interaction with colleagues helped to strengthen the analysis.

Similarly, Wajcman heartily thanks the Research School of Social Sciences, Australian National University, for the increasingly rare opportunity to focus on research. She is also grateful to the London School of Economics for a Centennial Professorship that enables her to maintain ties with British colleagues in the field of work and employment.

During the course of writing the book, we have received constructive help and encouragement from, in particular, Paul Adler, Jacques Bélanger, David Collinson, Dan Cornfield, Jenny Earle, Steve Frenkel, Marek Korczynski, and Donald MacKenzie. Ceridwen Roncelli provided excellent research assistance. David Musson, together with Matthew Derbyshire, at OUP provided advice and support throughout the project.

CONTENTS

LIST OF FIGURES

LIST OF TABLES

LIST OF BOXES

LIST OF ABBREVIATIONS

BR	British Rail
BSC	British Steel Corporation
CBI	Confederation of British Industry
CME	Coordinated market economy
CSR	Corporate social responsibility
DBS	Digital Broadcasting Satellite
FDI	Foreign direct investment
GATT	General Agreement on Tariffs and Trade
GII	Global income inequality
HRM	Human resource management
HROT	High Reliability Organization Theory
IMF	International Monetary Fund
IRRU	Industrial Relations Research Unit
IT	Information technology
LME	Liberal market economy
LTCM	Long-Term Capital Management
MBO	Management by objectives
MIC	methyl isocyanate
MMD	Man-made disasters
MNC	Multinational company
NAT	Normal Accident Theory
OECD	Organization for Economic Cooperation and Development
PMS	Performance management system
PRP	Performance-related pay
TRIP	Trade-Related aspects of Intellectual Property
WTO	World Trade Organization

1

Introduction: Why and How Should We Think about Work?

This book is about working in a modern market-capitalist economy, taking the point of view of the questioning observer. We first set out some core propositions about capitalism and the meaning of working within such a system. We then explain the 'questioning observer', and the value of taking such a perspective. The bulk of the rest of the chapter then introduces three sets of ideas that structure our argument. These are: *connections and contradictions*, that is the mix of forces shaping organizations; *structures and choices*, the ways in which people can influence their working lives; and the *economic, political, and ideological processes* by which organizational life is managed. At the end of the chapter, the outline of the book is explained.

Work, Organizations, and Capitalism

In thinking about who they are and how they make sense of their lives, many people—including a good proportion of the intended readers of this book—will not immediately start from work, still less an abstraction such as capitalism. They may think about a mixture of things including: the immediate and day-to-day issues such as fashions (be they to do with dress or the latest electronic equipment) and personal relationships; and the less immediate questions of national and international politics.

Indeed many social commentators argue that we are living in a post-industrial society, focused on information, consumption, culture, and lifestyle. It is true that some of the characteristics that used to be associated with 'work' are now less obvious than they were. Coal mines and factories employ fewer people than they used to, trade unions have lost members and influence in many countries, and so on. Yet the fact that the impact of work on everyday life may be less obvious than in the past does not deny the force of that impact. And the lack of obviousness makes it more, not less, important to reveal what is going on. In the nineteenth century, Karl Marx used the now famous phrase the 'hidden abode' to refer to what went on inside the production process. This abode is now in some ways more hidden than it was then.

Production has not disappeared, but is being carried out in strikingly novel forms on an increasingly global basis. For a young woman in the West, her silver mobile phone is experienced as a liberating extension of her body. The social relations of production that underpin its existence are invisible to her. As material objects, however, mobile phones have to be mass-produced in factories. Furthermore, along with other electronic devices, such as laptops, they require the scarce mineral Coltan. One of the few places where this can be found is Central Africa, where it is mined under semi-feudal and colonial labour relations to provide raw product for Western multinational companies (MNCs). Box 1.1 contains more details.

Box 1.1 Coltan and the global production chain

The sharp rise in the price of Coltan on global markets has local effects, accentuating exploitation and conflict among competing militias, with the very specific consequences for women that military conflict brings, including rape and prostitution. For example, Coltan is implicated in the civil wars in Democratic Republic of Congo and Rwanda that are usually assigned to 'ethnic conflict' and, thus, seen as remote to Western lives. (See, UN Security Council Report of the Panel of Experts on the Illegal Exploitation of Resources and Other Forms of Wealth of the Democratic Republic of the Congo 12 April 2001, listed on the website of the Mineral Resources Forum <*http://www. natural-resources.org/minerals/ law/conflict.htm*>). The severe food shortages that this has given rise to have forced people to seek bush food, thereby threatening the local population of gorillas and raising serious environmental concerns. In a postmodern twist, fans of Leonardo Di Caprio can join a letter-writing campaign to support the gorilla population at his website as part of his commitment to environmental awareness. Finally, the disposal of mobile phones and other modern products can pose serious health hazards in the (poor) communities near which they are often buried. A mobile phone then is a very different artefact depending upon a person's situation.

Why, then, is understanding the world of work important?

- Without work and production, consumption is impossible. And what goes on inside the hidden abode of the productive system says a great deal not only about people's dignity but also about their exposure to risk and many other things.

- A large part of the population still depends for its livelihood on largely mundane jobs. Making a living is a fundamental fact of existence here, and the questioning observer who wants to know about the world around him or her needs to know about such jobs even if they do not directly impinge on his or her own existence.
- It is a commonplace that many jobs impose major demands on workers in terms of working hours and pressure; work-related stress became a standard image from the 1990s onwards.
- There are some jobs, in some accounts of growing importance, in which the demands of work impinge directly on personal identity. They include customer service jobs, in which workers are expected not just to perform a task but to do so with enthusiasm and personal engagement. Here, work and identity become intertwined.

Beyond the immediate work itself lies 'the organization'. In the past, the organization could be comfortably equated with large bureaucracies that seemed to dominate the private sector as much as the public. And the requirements of conformity to the demands of the organization seemed equally clear. With the reduction in the size of the public sector in many countries and the apparent eclipse of large firms by newer and smaller ones, the organization may seem less important. But work is still subject to expectations from employing organizations. These expectations may in fact increase, as individuals are required to take on more responsibility, as they have to respond to more than one set of demands, and as pressures from 'outside' (the market) increasingly intrude within organizations.

And beyond the organization lies the operation of the capitalist economy. Its impact on working lives can often be profound, as when an economic crisis in one country has knock-on effects elsewhere. According to the scholar of international finance Eichengreen (2002*b*: 6), currency crises are endemic to capitalism and they are more common now than in the late nineteenth century. Elsewhere he documents a total of 168 crises in the period 1973–98 and estimates that *each* crisis led to a loss of output in the relevant economy of 5 per cent (Eichengreen 2001: 24). How capitalism works has important effects on day-to-day existence.

There are two potential objections to our focus. First, the collapse of state socialism means that capitalism is the only feasible economic system under current conditions, so that debating what is or is not capitalist is of little value. There is, however, a flaw of logic here. Even if we assume that capitalism is dominant, it does not follow that it is fixed, unchanging over time and place. It is, on the contrary, a uniquely dynamic mode of production, and hence identifying its different patterns and rhythms, and their consequences, is more pressing than it was when one might hope that a wholly different alternative might be found.

In understanding the nature of a capitalist economy attention has turned to Marx. This is ironic since he supposedly foresaw the early overthrow of capitalism, and the failure of this prediction might be expected to render his work obsolete. Yet an investment banker told *New Yorker* magazine in October 1997, 'the longer I spend on Wall Street, the more convinced I am that Marx was right', for he provided 'the best way to look at capitalism' (quoted in Wheen 1999: 5). Desai (2002) provides an analysis of Marx's thought appropriately titled *Marx's Revenge*, for its core argument is that Marx did not hold the views commonly ascribed to him. Hence the irony of turning to him is indeed only apparent. Desai argues that Marx saw capitalism as a dynamic and creative system that was not doomed to immediate collapse. Given the strength of the system and its novelty at the time when Marx was writing, it would have been perverse, notes Desai, to argue that it was about to disappear in short order.

Capitalism would not go away until after it had exhausted its potential. The information technology revolution has just begun. What more may come we do not know. . . . The limits to capitalism will be reached when it is no longer capable of progress, but it will be in the daily practice of the people working the machinery of capitalism that its limits will be felt, and it will be overcome by them. (Desai 2002: 9–10)

In this book, we focus, as explained below, on what Desai calls 'daily practice'.

The second objection is that the ownership of the physical means of production (capital) is no longer crucial and the key mode of production is now knowledge (popular statements of this view being Handy 1995 and *The Economist* 2001). We should be debating the knowledge-based economy and personal skills and careers, not 'old' bureaucracies. Yet ownership of the means of production means not mere possession but the capacity to put them to work. Knowledge has to be put to use in the generation of goods or services that will command a position in the market. It is true that firms using new kinds of knowledge have developed, and that is part of the dynamism of capitalism. It is also the case that knowledge workers will have different concerns from those of semi-skilled workers. But their presence does not negate the basic ways in which the economy works.

There is one key point that emerges from this example — the danger of reducing history to simple stages. The story that large organizations and hierarchies have been replaced by independent knowledge workers contrasts a new world with the old. Yet many new developments are not that new, and breaks with the past are rarely sharp. The historian Charles Tilly (2001) neatly captures this point, in contributing to a book of the twenty-first-century firm a chapter entitled 'Welcome to the Seventeenth Century'. We address the continuing dynamics of work and how it is organized.

Work Experience and Institutions: Making the Links

Capitalism's two core economic institutions are the market and the firm. It is true that markets and enterprises existed before capitalism. Yet capitalist markets are different from those of, say, feudalism in many respects including their extent and taken-for-granted nature. The feudal economy was shaped by notions of a 'just price', whereas in capitalism the language of 'supply and demand' is barely questioned. The fact that health care is a commodity much like any other would seem very curious to the pre-capitalist mind.

The firm, as an organized body having legal status and the goal of making profits for shareholders, is also taken for granted. Its emergence was, however, the result of a historical struggle. Even in the home of free-market capitalism, the USA in the nineteenth century, the legal standing of the firm emerged through a process of contest. The US constitution made no reference to corporations and the power to issue corporate charters was seen as a matter for the citizens of each state. The influence of corporations over citizens and independent farmers and artisans grew slowly, and was not sealed until a Supreme Court ruling in 1886 that the corporation was a natural person under the constitution, acquiring all the protections extended to individuals (Korten 1995: 55–9).

Capitalism is not a single entity, and it is resilient precisely because it is so flexible, variable, and creative. A large bank in Frankfurt, a clothing workshop in the back streets of Los Angeles, an electronics factory in an export processing zone in Malaysia, and a hi-tech software firm have many obvious differences but they are all capitalist organizations, and they are all shaped by the global nature of capitalist production. To illustrate briefly in relation to each case:

- The bank is powerfully influenced by the fact that there is a world financial system with the free movement of capital, a situation which did not exist at other times. It is also affected by the fact that it operates within an economy, the German, whose economic institutions differ from those of other countries and which may be in a state of 'regime competition' with these other systems. Pressures to meet profit targets may develop from these two influences, with implications for the ways in which people in the bank are managed.

- The clothing workshop will be threatened by competition from firms in lower-wage economies, so how does it manage to survive, and what are the implications for people concerned with the welfare of workers? For example, a minimum wage will improve pay, but will it further endanger jobs?
- The electronics factory exists because of global demand for computers and because, apparently, it is cheaper to use labour in Malaysia than in Germany or the USA. Yet cheap labour is a long-established feature of many economies, so what additional conditions were needed for the creation of the factory? And what are the links between global forces and the way of life of workers, both within the factory and outside it?
- Hi-tech software firms increasingly organize themselves internationally. The boundaries between 'the firm' and other firms are also often fuzzy. Some workers work on the firm's premises while being employed as independent contractors, and with links to subcontract organizations being at least as important as those within the firm's formal boundaries. How are such 'boundaryless' firms managed, and how far can employees develop their skills and knowledge?

The first, third, and fourth examples have in common that MNCs play a direct role while they do not in the second case, though such companies may feature in the commodity chains of which it is part. The first three will also be numerically dominated by women employees while having clear divisions of labour on gender lines, though the specific details of the latter will vary. Workers will also face differing demands on their time in the workplace and on the linkages between paid work and other activities. The relatively high-paid woman manager in the bank, for example, may find herself working long hours and hence respond to family demands by employing an immigrant worker from Eastern Europe as a domestic help. This worker has in turn been drawn into such employment as an indirect result of the functioning of capitalist markets. The worker in the electronics factory may rely on kin in her local village to care for her children.

At least four types of analysis can be distinguished.

- The first examines capitalism as a world system, including debates on globalization.
- The second compares different 'national business systems'.
- A third studies the operation of the firm within its market context.

- And the fourth looks inside firms at the working conditions of employees and structures of power and authority.

To say what it is like working under capitalism would in principle entail attention to all four levels. We attempt to make some linkages across these levels. To claim to offer anything like a synthesis would, however, be fool-hardy. We indicate below how we have tried to contain the task. One way in which we do so relates to the 'questioning observer' to whom we now turn.

The Questioning Observer

In broad terms we define this notional person as living in one of the core capitalist economies of the USA, Western Europe or Australasia and as having an intelligent but not necessarily tutored interest in the world of work.

- The first set of issues likely to concern our observer are those related to his or her own work situation in a firm, for example the satisfactions and pressures of day-to-day work and the kinds of career that he or she might expect.
- The second set covers the structure of organizations and such issues as the forms of power and authority that exist. Related questions include why are democracy and participation within firms proving so difficult to attain, since democracy is a long-established political principle, and why, if organizations are rationally organized and goal-seeking bodies, do things go wrong so regularly.
- The third set is about the wider capitalist system. Why is there now a global financial market, and what are the key principles that govern the world economy, and how has the current definition of the firm as a body in pursuit of 'shareholder value' come to take hold? Under the last, shareholder value means that the aim of the firm is purely to maximize returns to shareholders but, as we will see in Chapter 9, this can create problems even in its own terms, it was not historically the objective of many firms, and it ignores the costs for other stake-holders, notably those arising from restructuring and rationalization.

Our prime goal is to explore these issues in a way that can be grasped by someone without specialist knowledge. But there are two ways in which this is not an introductory text.

First, we assume a reader willing and able to engage with complex issues, and we do not stop to offer exercises or learning points. We think that there are many places where reflection may be called for. In our own reading and writing, we continue to be struck by new ideas that challenge assumptions or throw a new light on a familiar subject. We invite the reader to interrogate the text in this spirit.

Second, we cover a number of fields without doing so exhaustively. For example, the field of 'organizational behaviour' or 'organization studies' deals with such issues as the structure of organizations, social group dynamics, motivation, and organizational learning. We cover some of these issues, but not all of them. Another field is 'international political economy', which examines the world economic and financial system. We draw on some of this work in arguing about the development of capitalism, but do not pretend to be comprehensive.

This is because we are interested in a set of questions about the real world, not in starting from lines of academic inquiry. It is evidently the case that a standpoint implies a focus on some issues and not others. We claim that our approach helps to identify meaningful questions that can be addressed in sensible depth. But the reader should also interrogate the text by asking the following:

- In what ways does this give me new factual information?
- What expectations or views, if any, did I have before, and does this change them? In short, what is this telling me, and why do I agree or disagree?
- In terms of the material itself, what general lessons can be learned? If we have an example of a US insurance company, what is particular to that company, what is specific to the US insurance industry, what is true of the insurance industry in any country, what is true of all industries in the USA, and what is applicable to modern capitalist countries?

In asking the last question, evidence may be available either from research or personal experience. In other cases, direct evidence may not be to hand, but it is still possible to ask what might be distinctive in a particular case and where, in principle, we might look for new information. The reader is invited to use this book to think actively about the issues it raises and how better knowledge might be produced. We now develop analytical themes relevant to this task.

Connections and Contradictions

Much literature on transformations in the world of work tends to operate at a high level of abstraction. Three well-known interpretations are those of the US, German and British sociologists Sennett (1998), Beck (2000*a*, 2000*b*) and Giddens (1999). Each identifies a current condition that is contrasted with that of the past. For Sennett, it is 'the corrosion of character' in the USA: the decline of past certainties and the emergence of a sense of rootlessness and doubt. Beck would locate such feelings in economic change, notably the decay of systems of mass production and consumption, and the rise of flexible and precarious employment. Giddens identifies globalization as the culmination of a process of modernity that began in the sixteenth century.

Such views are considered in detail at various points in this book, for example in discussions of whether careers are more precarious (see Chapter 4) and of globalization (see Chapter 10). Here, we use them to signpost a different approach.

1. *History.* In these accounts, the past tends to be rendered as an unproblematic age, with the present being a uniquely uncertain time. This device is also very common among management pundits who identify shifts towards 'empowerment' or 'portfolio careers'. Is historical development ever so clear-cut or uniform? Though these writers identify certain aspects of contemporary work experience, they overgeneralize their insights into a thesis of radical breaks from the past. Historical continuities as well as breaks are central features of capitalism, which is a distinct system with lasting features.

2. *Agents.* The writers tend to see certain forces emerging almost inevitably. Yet globalization is a result of a struggle between different social actors and the projects that they promote. We will argue that such a grounded view is necessary to understand why globalization has taken the shape that it has, and hence to grasp what is changeable.

3. *Evidence.* The three writers offer essays rather than cases backed with evidence. None uses the now extensive survey information on labour-market structures and career paths. Sennett uses a set of conversations, which are not claimed to be in any way representative, to illustrate a view rather than to establish their wider relevance. Beck offers a set of possible scenarios but does not try to say what conditions produce each scenario or how common any given scenario is. Giddens operates very largely at the level of ideas.

4. *Contradiction.* Capitalism has at its heart contradictory processes. We need to try to understand how these work through at the level of concrete experience, rather than see the world as shifting from one approach to another.

The core framework of the present book is an argument about *connections* and *contradictions*. This argument is most commonly labelled as one based in a political economy approach. For the moment, we can indicate the meaning and value of these terms by illustration, rather than extensive definition.

Connections within an organization are illustrated by links between careers and changing structures of organizations (see Chapter 4). The opportunity for a career has been reduced as a result of downsizing and delayering. These are not automatic or inevitable processes, but reflect a particular conception of the organization that emerged with particular force in the 1980s. This example also illustrates connections between organizations, for firms behaved in similar ways. Though some accounts see this as a common response to common conditions (the 'invisible hand' of the market), it is preferable, as shown in Chapter 9, to explain it as a result of choices made by organizations: markets are created, to a considerable degree, by firms, not the reverse.

Connections between organizations and the environment include responses to global change. These responses are, however, *organized* in that the forces of 'globalization' are often defined and driven by organizations (of the state and corporations) and they reflect structured choices rather than the automatic effects of markets (see Chapter 10). Yet the idea that markets are natural and efficient dies hard. For the reader accustomed to thinking of markets as natural (primarily, those with backgrounds in economics), we add some comments in Box 1.2. Readers coming from the opposite position (most commonly, derived from sociology or organizational behaviour), of seeing markets as *no more* than social constructions, should not feel superior. There are senses in which markets are efficient, and social constructions need a base in reality if they are to have any real force.

The idea of a contradiction is less common, but in many ways more powerful, than that of connections. According to Bell (1996: xvi), 'the contradictions of capitalism [lie] in the antagonistic principles that underlie the technical-economic, political, and cultural structures of the society', that is between these different 'realms'. A much stronger argument is that each realm has its own contradictions: sets of principles that are inherent within it, and yet are opposed in their working. A central example within any one capitalist organization is the need to exercise control over its workers while also persuading them to exercise their skills and creative ability. This contradiction runs through debates on participation. One simple story line argues that control has been replaced with participation, involvement, or even empowerment. As we will see, research suggests that the picture is highly inaccurate, but this particular evidence needs to be seen in wider terms. Empowerment does not mean the abandonment of control. Indeed, a now routine result is that workers experiencing the

---

Box 1.2 Markets and the invisible hand

The metaphor of the invisible hand is the work of Adam Smith. The idea is that signals from the market bring forth a response from firms without any conscious direction. So if there is a glut of corn, the price will fall and less will come on to the market. This image has always had problems when it has been probed at all closely. How do people learn what the price is, what happens to the corn that is no longer needed but which has presumably been produced, and what happens to the people whose livelihood is threatened by the fact that corn is no longer in such heavy demand? A neat illustration of the point comes from the celebrated economist Stiglitz: 'One of the great achievements of modern economics is to show the sense in which, and the conditions under which, Smith's conclusion is correct. It turns out that these conditions are highly restrictive. Indeed, more recent advances in economic theory . . . have shown that whenever information is imperfect and markets incomplete, *which is to say always*, . . . then the invisible hand works most imperfectly' (2002: 73, emphasis added). The invisible hand is a fiction that even economists seem to have given up believing.

---

greatest autonomy are often also those reporting the strictest controls over their work. Empowerment reflects one strand of organizations, and this strand is connected with that of control in a state of inherent tension.

The contradictory nature of market societies is underlined in Hirschman's (1982) identification of four long-established views of market society, as follows:

- the market is essentially a civilizing force, an idea developed in the eighteenth century idea under the label of *doux commerce* (gentle business);
- the market is destructive of social order;
- the market's potential civilizing effects are moderated by feudal traditions; and
- such traditions are in fact an important basis on which market principles rest, and which promote the civility that markets tend to erode.

Hirschman then argues that these views need not be opposed, since markets can be, at the same time, self-reinforcing and civilizing and yet also self-destructive. It is difficult, he goes on, to think in terms of such contradictory processes because this makes it hard to proclaim a clear set of results. However, he advocates that social science embraces complexity, albeit 'at some sacrifice of its claim to predictive power'

(1982: 1483). We agree, adding only that predictive (or explanatory) power is not wholly lost and that the idea of a contradiction is not a deus ex machina. One needs to be able to say why forces in society contain contradictions and what their effects are. Chapter 4, for example, explains that contemporary careers are marked by mutually contradictory processes.

Seeing the world in this way helps with another source of confusion. Periodizations in terms such as 'Fordism' and 'post-Fordism' have become commonplace. They are not always clear in their reference points or definitions. Fordism is generally taken to refer to the period from the 1940s to the 1970s. As Crouch (1999: 38) shows, the term embraces variously:

- a particular system of manufacture (mass production of standardized products),
- an (alleged) 'class compromise' between capital and labour within the enterprise,
- a policy of economic management based on Keynesian principles, and
- the welfare state.

To argue that these elements fit into a coherent, indeed planned, whole is to claim far too much, and Crouch himself rejects the term. We might also add that if Fordism is an unclear concept, then post-Fordism must be even more obscure. But analysis in terms of contradictions suggests that it may be more a matter of emphasis (in this case, relative stress on the side of involvement) than of shifts, and that, rather than a decisive shift on one direction, the pendulum can swing back.

We have asserted that control and commitment are inherently contradictory principles. A substantial body of writing on 'the labour process' has established why this is so (e.g. Hyman 1987; Thompson 1989). Contradictory principles are not opposite ends of a continuum. Control and commitment can go together, and they are principles that are likely to be combined in distinct ways. The fundamental tension between control and commitment is also likely to produce specific policies that run across each other. For example, management may need close supervision to monitor and control behaviour, but this is costly and it discourages the use of skill and discretion. Consequently, alternative policies of autonomy may be pursued, but these make it hard to ensure that performance standards are reached and increase uncertainty for managers. Managers will be constantly juggling between these competing logics.

In Chapter 7, for example, we show that there are competing logics about industrial injuries, one stressing 'profit at any cost' and the other 'safety is the prime concern'. Both these logics will operate, and the analytical task is to show when they might be consistent, when they are in tension, and the concrete reasons why they lead to specific dynamics in specific circumstances. We give certain examples. The test is whether these examples *illustrate the theme* and offer *analytical implications* that can be applied to other situations.

The contradiction between control and commitment is not the only one shaping capitalist firms. Though they are about control of employees, they are also about many other things. Crucially, they have goals of growth, profit, and survival, and control of employees is not an end in itself. These goals are not clearly specified. As one substantial study of large US firms says flatly, and surprisingly for those who take it for granted that there are clear objectives, 'managers and entrepreneurs were not optimizers or satisficers. Instead, they constructed new courses of action based on their analyses of the problems of control they faced' (Fligstein 1990: 2). (Box 1.3 explains these terms.) Goals are also contestable by different groups within an organization, with the result that organizational life is more messy and uncertain than models of rationality and efficiency, or of control and exploitation, can grasp. As a result, attempts to redesign work processes may be confused and unclear in their aims, and they may leave space for people to define their own views of the organization.

If any single capitalist organization has to manage contradictions, an economy of such firms faces further contradictions. For, except in the world of the invisible hand, the pursuit of the goals of each firm will not result in a lasting equilibrium. There is, for example, no reason to expect that the number of jobs generated by firms will match the number of people seeking work. Capitalist markets are not only shaped by firms. At minimum, firms need states to establish the political and legal environment in which they can do business. The behaviour of the state will in turn affect how markets are structured, for example determining what forms of market control are legal (e.g. cartels) and what forms of employment practice are forbidden (e.g. setting minimum wages). States regulate markets, and the more that markets take on a global character the more important become supra-state bodies such as the International Monetary Fund. We examine the main institutions of the global economic system in Chapter 10.

Structures and Choices

If we wish to understand how people in organizations behave, however, a fundamental question is: what weight we should place on structural or institutional forces and what influence should we attribute to social

Box 1.3 Optimizing, satisficing, and control

Optimizing means achieving the best set of returns available under given conditions. A self-seeking individual is assumed. The term 'optimizing' is used instead
of profit-maximizing since the individual may have goals other than profit, such as
a certain amount of leisure. (How individuals come to have such goals is left out of
conventional economic analysis even though it is arguably the most important
question.) The concept of satisficing was introduced in an attempt to reflect the
fact that people typically do not have explicit 'utility functions' that they strive to
maximize. Firms may instead seek some conventionally defined set of satisfactory
outcomes. The idea of 'courses of action' underlines the point that what firms try
to do varies over time and space, with appropriate action being defined as firms
interact with each other and with legal regulation. A conception of control is 'a
totalizing world view of managers or entrepreneurs that causes them to filter the
problems of the world in a certain way' (Fligstein, 1990: 10). Note that from our
point of view control embraces issues of relations with workers, as well as the
market relations analysed by Fligstein's economic sociology. Firms face contradictions in the management of labour, in relations with markets, and in the
interplay between these two sets of contradictions.

choice? The obvious practical corollary concerns how far people can
shape the world in which they live. Stated thus, the only possible answer
is that structure and human agency are both important. A much more
interesting issue concerns how they are connected and how they influence
each other. In this book we emphasize the enduring social arrangements
that shape the world of work.

A good illustration of what we mean is the work of the social anthro-
pologist Mars (1982), detailed in Chapter 5. Mars studied occupational
crime, and was at pains to stress that certain illicit practices were shaped
by the occupation rather than being the result of the personal predilec-
tions of people practising it. (Reasons to reject the selectivity argument are
given in Box 1.4.) Mars showed that in occupations with strong collective
cultures, social norms are imposed on individuals, whatever their previous preferences.

Three other points may be highlighted. First, Mars detailed just what it
was in the structure of an occupation that made it prone to crime (or
'fiddles', to use his word, an important shift of terminology discussed in
Chapter 5). Analysis in terms of structure calls for concrete illustration of
what it means. Second, structure and action reinforce each other. Struc-

Box 1.4 Choosing a life of occupational crime?

The selectivity argument states that people choose their occupations, with criteria including the ease of practising fiddles. Any observed association between occupational position and proneness to fiddle (or any other characteristic) would thus be due to choice and not a hypothesized aspect of an occupation. But:

1. The evidence on occupational choice indicates that most 'choice' is strongly conditioned by the opportunities available, expectations of friends, and so on, with much that is not structurally shaped being due to chance or drift rather than deliberate choice.
2. The practices in most occupations are known only by insiders, so that free choice is limited by lack of knowledge.

Finally, what of sorting over time, that is a tendency, as people move through the labour market, for occupational features and personal preferences to become more closely matched? Yet much movement is involuntary, reflecting retrenchment by firms and job losses or a need to move geographically for family or other reasons. People will also change their preferences in the light of occupational experience. Self-selection may be part of the story, but it is far from being the dominant one.

tures do not directly 'do' things: it is individuals who act. People behave in the light of conditions as they find them, and in doing so help to reinforce these conditions. A supermarket worker 'fiddling' a customer puts into practice the structural opportunities available, and in doing so perpetuates the relevant cultural expectations. Third, actions may, intentionally or not, change structural conditions. A deliberate action in the foregoing case would be a decision to increase the amount of fiddling, perhaps because of discontent over wages or to get back at a particular manager. This might or might not provoke further actions by others, with one possible outcome being a change in the structure (e.g. the use of new monitoring devices to cut down fiddling opportunities). Note that the outcome is open but is none the less shaped by the existing structural conditions. Different conditions (e.g. if the workers involved act through a trade union rather than individually) will produce different outcomes.

Economic, Political, and Ideological Processes

It might be appealing at this point to identify what the structures of work are, and hence to show how structures X, Y, and Z affect actions P, Q, and R. Marx offered one of the most famous attempts, in distinguishing between four modes of production, each of which was expected to generate distinct patterns of social relations. Yet, as Runciman (1999: 110–39) argues, this is at best a very rough start. Why are there four and only four modes? On what theoretical basis are they identified? What are their key features? And what other structural features would we have to add to take account of the evident differences between societies characterized as capitalist?

Runciman's conclusion is that seeking a taxonomy of types of society (or, in our case, types of organization) is an activity doomed to failure. This does not mean that a category such as capitalism is meaningless. Such categories help to 'pose questions about the relations of different "feudal", "capitalist" or "socialist" practices, roles and institutions to one another in a manner which will (perhaps) generate some illuminating hypotheses about the workings of societies to which these labels can be more or less convincingly applied' (ibid.: 114). We are interested in processes and connection and hence with understanding how organizations work. But this activity does not render itself into neat taxonomies.

Relations of domination and subordination are embedded in societies, and formal organizations in capitalism reflect these relations particularly clearly. Following Runciman, these relations can be analysed as: economic (to wit wealth, income, and goods); ideological (esteem, honour, and privilege); and coercive (physical force and political authority). A particular social institution will have certain combinations of these factors, and apparently very different societies may have striking similarities.

We say more about these three concepts in Chapter 6. Our present purpose is to indicate an analytical approach. Establishing closed categories is impossible because societies change continually, and because they have many features which interact with each other. Some organizations may appear to be the archetypes of a bureaucracy, but they will differ between each other in important ways. The analytical purpose is to be able to offer convincing accounts of particular cases, not to reduce them to examples of the operation of mechanical forces.

We need to comment a little further on the ideological dimension. Burawoy (1979) examines ideology in the light of the work of the Italian Marxist Antonio Gramsci. Imprisoned from 1928 until his death in 1935, his prison notebooks provided major inspiration to scholars through such concepts as hegemony (Gramsci 1971). Hegemony refers to the ways in which certain sets of ideas become established as natural and in which a dominated group actively consents in and helps to reproduce its own domination. Burawoy's question was why workers consent to their own exploitation, and his answer turned on the ways in which they helped to generate an ideology that legitimated and reproduced their position.

Ideology was not something outside experience in the workplace but was produced as part of economic relations: it was not a free-standing set of ideas, but a material product of social relations.

We will use these ideas at various points, in particular to show that the ways in which people think about organizational life (ideology) is shaped by economic and political factors. The concept of hegemony has 'attracted increasing attention from scholars of organization' (Humphreys and Brown 2002: 421). The popularity of the concept does not always mean, however, that it is deployed in Burawoy's sense. Much writing in organizational behaviour is concerned with 'narratives' and 'deconstruction' (e.g. Knights and Willmott 1999). In our view, this approach has tended to study narratives with little or no reference to their economic or social context, neglecting explanation of why things happen as they do. This not being a text in organizational behaviour, we do not argue out the point but simply identify the danger of the approach.

Structure of the Book

The rest of this book falls into three parts. Chapters 2–4 focus on the direct experience of the individual, looking in turn at what is happening to the types of jobs available in modern societies, the relationship between paid work in the labour market and home and leisure, and what is now meant by the idea of a career. We highlight the contradictory forces at work and the ways that people can actively respond to them. For example, many low-skill and low-wage jobs not only continue to exist but are also newly created by the dynamism of market economies. Workers in these jobs are often portrayed as highly exploited, and in a way they are; but they also display commitment and engagement. We unravel this paradox.

Chapters 5–8 turn to the functioning of organizations. Chapter 5 links to the first group of chapters by examining a key element of individual experience, the appraisal of performance; it then examines how this process is managed in organizations. This management necessarily entails power and political bargaining. These themes are examined directly in Chapter 6, through consideration of what 'empowerment' and 'participation' mean. Chapters 7 and 8 turn to why things go wrong, and what aspects of the ways in which large organizations function can explain such events. A key theme running through these chapters is the inherent tension in organizations between the efficient pursuit of goals and political processes defining the goals and how they are to be pursued. As indicated above, politics are not an addition to what would otherwise be an efficient machine; they define what that machine is.

The final three chapters address the context in which organizations are embedded. Chapter 9 examines markets and the ways in which they are constructed through social processes, looking in effect at what we termed above the political and ideological aspects of economic life. Chapter 10 moves to the global level, asking how far the world economy is now global, discussing the political and ideological aspects of economic integration, and indicating linkages with individual experience.

We should stress that we have chosen topics on which we think that we have something to say and that these topics are not the only possible ones. One major issue is how capitalism continues to generate poor quality jobs in the Third World and how workers respond to such employment. We do not directly address this theme (on which Cohen and Kennedy 2000: ch. 8 offers a good introduction) though it is mentioned in the analysis of corporate social responsibility and of globalization. Any book on broad themes such as ours cannot be *substantively* comprehensive. Consider studies of international variations in capitalism, for example, the important works by Whitley (1999), Coates (2000), and others. These can cover the main cases but they demonstrate that each 'national business system' is a complex whole that also has to be grasped historically; in addition, the main trajectory in any country will have variants in different economic sectors.

What such studies do when they work well is to offer key *real-world examples* backed up by *methodological and theoretical* frameworks. We insist on the importance of such frameworks. We offer numerous examples in this book. They are not only important in their own right, but also for the ways in which they help us think about how to understand the world. An account of the US national business system can be used, for example, as a template to address other systems, or to improve the template. We thus use historical as well as contemporary examples, not because we are writing a book on history but because they offer ways of thinking about the nature of evidence. In speaking of methodology, therefore, we are not referring to the techniques or methods of inquiry. We mean a way of thinking about a phenomenon as an example with wider lessons.

Our goal throughout is not to offer a compendium of evidence but, rather, to think through some key issues and dilemmas of work in modern economies. Tools such as the idea of contradiction and the distinction between economic, political, and ideological processes aid in this task. As noted above in discussing Hirschman, these tools do not offer neat classifications, and they require engaged effort from the reader. We hope that the effort proves worthwhile.

2

What Is Happening to Jobs?

Who we are is profoundly affected by what we do for a living. But, for most individuals, feelings about work are characterized by ambivalence. On the one hand, work seems synonymous with promise. It is the means by which we nourish a sense of achievement in the world. Through work we shape our ambitions and our talents and develop our social selves. Simultaneously personal and social, work is a crucial source of meaning and satisfaction in our lives. On the other hand, work can be a source of persistent dissatisfactions, a realm of necessity and constraint. If the idea of work contains a promise, then for many the obligations and experiences of work life bring disappointment. A similar ambivalence runs through much academic writing about work, as we shall see.

The issue of what individuals expect from work and how those expectations are shaped is the theme of this chapter. What are the circumstances in which work is experienced as fulfilling, and when is it experienced as dissatisfying? The chapter begins with a discussion of some broad historical trends that help locate more contemporary debates about how employees experience autonomy and constraint in organizations. Has the experience of work changed as a result of new types of jobs and the rise of new industries? What sort of rewards do people seek from work in the twenty-first century and how are these mediated by the different subjectivities they bring to the workplace?

With industrialization, a major historical shift in the organization of work took place. Prior to capitalism, household production was generally for domestic consumption with only small surpluses brought to the market. In this way, work was integrated with other aspects of social life. With the rise of industrial capitalism, this gave way to an arrangement whereby household members worked for employers in exchange for wages. Rather than producing goods to satisfy their own immediate needs, most people became employees at places separated from their homes.

The rise of this new system of employment for wages developed in a slow and often piecemeal fashion, with working arrangements in some early factories mirroring earlier forms of work. For example, family members might be employed as part of a single wage bargain with the male head, who would divide the proceeds according to conventions of age and gender. Even now, there are forms of employment where a 'gang master' is paid a contract for labour undertaken by all the members of a gang and the distribution of wages among the gang is left to the 'gang master'. (In the UK today, for example, there are upwards of 3,000 gang masters employing 100,000 workers, mainly in seasonal work.) While earlier forms of gang labour were frequently governed by conventions derived from the norms of the communities from which the workforce was drawn, contemporary gang labour frequently uses marginal and migrant workers who are unprotected by social norms that would limit their exploitation.

Notwithstanding such arrangements, the dominant image is that the capitalist market economy is organized in terms of an individual wage bargain between an employer and employee, where the employee contracts his or her labour under the direction of the employer (or his or her agent; that is, a supervisor or manager) in return for a wage. Indeed, all factors of production—labour, land, and capital—come to be treated as commodities that can be competitively bought and sold on markets with a view to reduce costs and increase profit. Labour is a commodity like any other and it finds its own price in the wider market for labour. Just as labour is something that employers might wish to purchase, so it is something that employees might wish to invest in, to improve their skills and, thereby, their price in the labour market. Hence in contemporary management literature, labour is discussed in terms of 'human capital'.

Work is a highly complex phenomenon that is at the heart of contemporary social organization. It seems to be delimited to its own separate sphere—the economy—distinguished from other spheres of life, such as the household, the polity, and wider public sphere of friendship and leisure. Yet, at the same time, as we shall see in this section of the book, it is thoroughly intertwined with them. Employment and the labour market are the predominant means through which social resources are produced and distributed. Paid work is both a crucial source of personal identity and central to the discourses of fairness and justice that seek to legitimate modern forms of inequality.

Market Individualism

The institutional separation of paid employment from other spheres of social life has affected how contemporary social science conceptualizes work. For mainstream economics, the transition to a capitalist system brings into being a distinct object for study, an economy driven by market principles. Pre-modern life is characterized as having been governed by values largely derived from outside the economic order, such as status, lineage, kinship, and religion. These are communal social forms that extend over time and generations. By contrast, emerging market spheres of action are seen as both rational and oriented around the choices and decisions made by the individual. The market is therefore paradigmatic of new principles of action and order in which individuals rationally pursue their own interests, unrestricted by received social obligations.

The role of money is crucial in this kind of relationship. Not only can any good be sold, but it can be translated into formal terms of calculation by being given a price. Money is the medium that facilitates the many decisions and choices of individuals that when aggregated together make up a market system. It is both the medium in which employers and employees negotiate the labour contract, as a purchase of labour in return for a wage, and the medium through which wages are spent on commodities according to individual preferences. Alongside the 'sovereign' individual, capable of entering into contracts to dispose of his or her labour, there emerges within capitalism the idea of 'consumer sovereignty', where the individual is held to be the best judge of his or her preferences. These preferences are also seen to be best secured through market exchanges.

As might be expected, the complexity of advanced capitalism has given rise to arguments that a more multifaceted conception of the individual is necessary. For example, psychologists have pointed out that human beings have more diverse needs than those captured in the standard economist's model. As the economic system becomes more productive, these needs have to be addressed by employers and organizations if they wish to derive the most from their workforce. The influential neo-human relations school, associated with Maslow (1943), Hertzberg (1966), and McGregor (1960), recognized that human needs include psychological growth and advocated job enrichment schemes to motivate employees. These ideas were to influence work design techniques and practices into the latter half of the twentieth century, and arguably were the precursors of contemporary human resource management (HRM) (see Chapter 5).

In this way, industrial psychologists have argued that the contract or 'effort bargain' between employer and employee is more complex than suggested in standard economic theory. Employers seek to gain the maximum productivity or effort from their workers in return for the wages they pay, but the motivation of workers cannot be expressed simply in monetary terms. Employers require not just maximum effort from their workforce, but also their commitment and the two may not be entirely compatible. The economist's contract is essentially short-term and almost infinitely negotiable, while the psychological model of human needs emphasizes longer-term requirements of human personality.

Important though the contribution of psychologists is to the understanding of work and employment, for sociologists it shares a limitation with the approach of economists. Both approaches are individualistic and lack an appreciation of the importance of social groups and the wider relationships in which individuals are embedded. Sociologists, for their part, see work as quintessentially a social phenomenon not just an individual activity—even those who work on their own do so within a social context. The world of work cannot be adequately explained by reference to market forces and economic rationality alone. Nor can it be explained by reference simply to the dimensions of human personality. Work encompasses symbolic representations, meanings, values, and interpretations. Employees typically seek more than purely economic rewards from their employment; their attitudes to and behaviour at work are influenced by a diverse set of social and cultural factors. The potential contradictions in the 'effort bargain' where managers have to maintain control and secure the commitment of workers, then, are sociologically complex. We go on to discuss this in more depth below.

Alienation and the Division of Labour

At its most basic, employment represents the exchange of pay, and possibly other rewards, for work—the buying and selling of labour power. Unlike the buying and selling of almost all other commodities, however, the exchange does not and cannot take place instantaneously. Employment, as distinct from self-employment and some other ways of providing labour services under contract, necessarily involves a continuing relationship between employer and employee. What the employer secures by employing someone is their capacity to work, and this potential can only be realized over time. This is at the heart of the sociological approach to work in capitalist societies.

Given the nature of this exchange, is there a necessary conflict between employer and employee? Are work relationships inherently antagonistic, such that capitalist organizations will always face a problem in securing the motivated compliance of their workforce? This is what Marx suggested and his theory has proved very influential, even for those who have not accepted all of his conclusions about the transformation of capitalism and its replacement by social and work relations that are intrinsically cooperative. Alternatively, there are sociologists, such as the human relations school, who have suggested that employment relationships could become embedded in a more solidaristic work ethic. While some areas of employment seem to conform with Marx's view of work in capitalist societies, others seem to be closer to the solidarism outlined by human relations writers. For some, recent developments in the world of work have prefigured the overcoming of conflict in the workplace and the greater integration of employees within their organizations. For others, these same developments have the opposite implication. As we shall see, the circumstances of contemporary work relationships are both complex and diverse.

In this book, we take the view that the employment contract is best understood as one involving inherently unequal partners. The basic institutions of a capitalist economy include the employment relationship, in which workers are paid a wage in exchange for entering into an open-ended relationship with employers, or their agents, namely managers, who have the authority to direct workers; and shareholder primacy, whereby owners of capital have exclusive decision-making rights regarding its use. Unilateral management power combined with the drive for profitability suggests that there will always be contestation over how workers' labour power is utilized. This is not to say that conflict in the workplace is reducible to a struggle between capital and labour over control of the labour process. Workers' activities and interests are highly diverse and cannot be characterized simply in terms of either cooperation or resistance to capitalist control, as we shall see in later chapters. At this juncture, however, we stress that 'structured antagonism' between employers and workers is embedded in the employment relationship, shaping how everyday relations are handled and lending organizations much of their dynamic (Edwards 1986).

Studies of work have traditionally been concerned to describe the conditions and experience of manual labour that was the result of industrialization and the rise of the factory system. Here Marx's analysis of alienation casts a long shadow. According to Marx's classic account, the exploitation of workers arises from the fact that the capitalists own the means of production and treat labour as if it were another inanimate factor of production. Workers are alienated from the product of their labour since what they produce is appropriated by others and consequently they have no control over its fate. At the same time, they are alienated from the very act of production. Work becomes an alien activity because it allows no intrinsic satisfaction. Marx's definition of alienation in the *Economic and Political Manuscripts* is given in Box 2.1.

Box 2.1 Alienation

In what does this alienation of labour consist? First that the work is *external* to the worker, that it is not part of his nature, that consequently he does not fulfil himself in his work but denies himself, has a feeling of misery, not of well being, does not develop freely a physical and mental energy, but is physically exhausted and mentally debased. The worker therefore only feels at home in his leisure, whereas at work he feels homeless. His work is not voluntary but imposed, *forced labour*. It is not the satisfaction of a need, but only a means for satisfying other needs. Its alien character is clearly shown by the fact that as soon as there is no physical or other compulsion it is avoided like the plague. Finally, the alienated character of work for the worker appears in the fact that it is not his work but work for someone else, that in work he does not belong to himself but to another person.

Source: Bottomore and Rubel (1963: 177–8).

Although the concept of alienation is widely used to describe the subjective experience of work, in Marx's vision alienation is essentially an objective condition; it is not only reflected in job dissatisfaction or frustration, it is something intrinsic to the employment relationship that includes a structural antagonism between employer and employee.

To a large degree, Marx's analysis of alienation derives its force from his view of the developmental tendencies of capitalist production. The impersonal market processes of capitalism, he argued, will remove traditional limitations on labour contracts. The competition among workers for jobs serves to depress wages as higher-paid labour is substituted by the labour of those who work for less. A further consequence of these competitive pressures is to produce a surplus population, surplus, that is, to the needs of capital for labour. This 'surplus population' operates as a 'reserve army of labour' available for work during periods when the demand for labour is high and returned to its ranks when demand is less. At the same time, capitalists strive to reorganize production techniques in the drive to cheapen commodities. According to Marx, these changes have the consequences of transferring skills from human beings to machines and so increasingly skilled labour is replaced by less skilled labour and the workforce becomes increasingly homogenous and mere 'appendages to machines'.

Braverman's influential *Labor and Monopoly Capital* (1974) was an attempt to bring Marx's analysis of the division of labour to bear on modern work. For Braverman, scientific management as exemplified in Fordism is the management system whereby the division of labour is pushed to the extreme. It involves the simplification of work to its most basic components. The assembly-line type of automobile manufacturing is a system of control based on the monopolization of knowledge by management and its use to specify each step of the labour process. The separation of conception and execution removes brain work from the shop floor resulting in the increasing fragmentation and cheapening of labour. The deskilling of craft workers, leading to the increasing homogenization of labour, was the dominant reference point for his analysis.

It is now widely recognized that a major problem with Braverman's approach was his deliberate exclusion of class consciousness and organization in the labour market. This resulted in his neglecting how labour can influence the production process through compliance and resistance. Machines do not run themselves. The form of jobs is always the result of a *social* process, involving choice and often negotiation between management and labour. The threat of deskilling precisely led to defensive actions on the part of workers, particularly labour organized in craft unions. The history of strikes and industrial sabotage in car factories around the globe indicates the extent of workers' opposition to management in workplaces where Fordist conditions prevail.

Even the most menial of jobs require the discretion and cooperation of employees. The open-ended nature of the employment contract means that the work that the employee actually does, the 'effort bargain', can only be finally determined in the ongoing interaction between employer and employee. In *Manufacturing Consent* (1979), Burawoy uses ethnographic evidence to capture the experience of workers on the shop floor, countering a simplistic depiction of the complete subjugation of labour under management control. While the organization of work or 'rules of the game' are externally imposed, the art of 'making out' is continuously to negotiate with other machine operators over tasks and tools in order to maximize production and hence earn incentive pay. For Burawoy, the active involvement of the workforce in 'making out' generated a particular sense of work-based identity that compensated for the negative features of wage labour. Workers were involved in a 'game', and that involvement generated a subjective sense of autonomy and freedom.

When one is trying to make out, time passes more quickly — in fact, too quickly — and one is less aware of being tired. The difference between making out and not making out was thus not measured in the few pennies of bonus we earned but in our prestige, sense of accomplishment, and pride. Playing the game eliminated much of the drudgery and boredom associated with industrial work. (Burawoy 1979: 89)

As a rich portrayal of shop-floor culture, showing how people give meaning and dignity to work in harsh conditions, Burawoy's narrative is appealing. However, his analysis is not attuned to differences between workers, such as age, ethnicity, and gender. As feminists have pointed out, male working-class solidarity has often operated as an exclusionary strategy. While successful at securing job control, craft unionism played an active part in creating and sustaining women's subordinate position in the workforce. Printers, for example, perceived clashes over technological innovation as not only affecting the power relations between capital and labour, but also as an aspect of gender power (see Box 2.2). The compositors' craft involved the construction of an identity both as skilled workers and as men. The two elements were inextricably linked. They experienced the move to computerized typesetting technologies as an affront to their masculinity and they organized against it as though their virility depended on it.

Box 2.2 Sex, skill, and technical competence

In her book on the history of typesetting technology in Britain, Cockburn (1983) reveals the sexual politics involved in a workplace culture based on technical skill. Compositors are described as an archetypal group of male craft workers, whose ease with technology is integral to their masculine identity. The industrial power of craftsmen was derived from their knowledge and competence with machines. The control over this type of industrial technology has traditionally been the province of men, and women workers have been excluded from these technical skills. The technical change from Linotype to electronic photocomposition, however, literally made the compositors feel emasculated. Because the work of composing now resembles typing and involves working with paper instead of metal, that is, a shift from factory work to the office, the compositors no longer consider it to be real work. Traditional craft culture was associated with hot metal, dirt, and physical work and the elimination of this not only diminishes their control over the work but it also represents a threat to their masculinity. The move to a 'feminine' white-collar environment is perceived as negative by male manual workers precisely because it is seen in terms of a loss of masculine status. Thus the gender relations of work and technology shape people's experience in the workplace.

More recently, traditional working-class identity, based on a white, male breadwinner working full-time in manufacturing, has been undermined by developments such as the expansion of services, the increasingly global organization of production and exchange, and the feminization of the labour force. Moreover, Braverman's neo-Marxist thesis of the proletarianization of white-collar work, according to which the modern office would become the new factory, is belied by the dramatic growth of highly skilled technical, professional, and managerial jobs. Rather than any overall trend to deskilling and the homogenization of work, labour has become much more differentiated. 'As a result, what it means to be a worker is no longer as certain as it once was' (Du Gay 1996: 3).

A New Workplace and a New Worker?

It is now widely claimed that we are living in a post-industrial, information, or knowledge economy, with manufacturing and factory production being displaced by information- and knowledge-based work. Instead of requiring physical work, organizations are opting to engage with minds instead. As a consequence, the old hierarchies of manual work will be replaced by more open and negotiated networks. The conditions enjoyed by white-collar workers means that they are more likely to be integrated into solidaristic work relations, in contrast to the conflictual work relations of manual labour. Hence the erosion of class consciousness as the basis for workplace identity. For example, Castells (1996) argues that rapid developments in information and communication technologies are revolutionizing the economy and the character of employment. In the new 'informational mode of development', labour and capital, the central variables of the industrial society, are replaced by information and knowledge. In the 'network society', organizations can decentralize and disperse, with high-level decision-making remaining in 'world cities' while lower-level operations, linked to the centre by communication networks, can take place virtually anywhere. Information is the key ingredient of social organization, and flows of messages and images between networks constitute the basic thread of social structure (ibid.: 477). For Castells, the information age marks a whole new epoch in the human experience.

Such futuristic scenarios all predict a trend away from routine work towards more creative, problem-solving, and people-focused activity. The old style command-and-control management will be increasingly inappropriate, as knowledge work requires management to give employees more control over their work. Even at the bottom, empowered production and service employees will be working smarter not harder.

Moreover, with the shift to lateral networks, knowledge workers may choose to opt out of organizations, offering their skills to a collection of clients and customers, and leading flexible lives between home and the workplace. The emergence of 'portfolio workers' implies the loosening of organizational ties and the increasing individualization of people's lives. For management gurus such as Handy (1995), the demise of the traditional stable career is to be celebrated rather than mourned. Rather than planning single, linear careers, and identifying with and being loyal to organizations, people will be much more autonomous and independent. As individuals have more choice about how to live their lives, work may become less salient for their identities.

So are the structures of employment and the pattern of jobs changing in line with the predicted transition to a new knowledge economy? Is the work that employees do assuming a radically different character and are they more or less satisfied than in the past?

Claims about the transformation of work are both quantitative (more work is becoming information work) and qualitative (information work is profoundly different from manufacturing work). Certainly, major occupational shifts have been taking place, with a long-term rise of non-manual employment. However, quantifying the expansion of information work is problematic given that 'informational and service occupations' encompass a wide range of very diverse kinds of work. For example, it includes 'symbolic analysts' (who trade globally in the manipulation of symbols, such as engineers, consultants, and advertising executives) who are seen as typical of knowledge workers, but it also includes hairdressing, the fastest growing occupation in the UK in the past decade. It is a very different subjective experience to be involved in high-level professional services compared to working in personal services, such as cleaning or gardening.

Sifting the British evidence, Nolan and Wood (2003) conclude that reference to the service, rather than the knowledge, economy better encapsulates recent changes in employment patterns. De-industrialization and the shift to service work has been dramatic, as has the growth of new occupations like software engineers and management/business consultants. But much of the growth of employment in professional, scientific, and technical grades has been driven by the expansion of the established professions (education, law, and medicine), which account for two in five of the total increase in higher status employees. In other groups, the most significant growth has been in three areas: (*a*) hairdressers, sales assistants, data input clerks, and storekeepers; (*b*) state-dominated education and health services; and (*c*) care assistants, welfare and community workers, and nursery nurses. 'Employment growth, in short, has been concentrated in occupations that are not, in the main, associated with the shift from an old to new economy' (Nolan and Wood 2003: 170).

Indeed, the spread of 'bad jobs' within Anglo-American capitalism as a result of the rapid growth in non-standard forms of employment (part-time, temporary, and fixed term) is well documented. McGovern et al. (2004) identify four measures of bad jobs: low pay (half of the median for full-time men); no sick pay; no pension scheme; and no recognized career or promotion ladder. Between one quarter and half of the working population in Britain are in jobs that have at least one bad characteristic. Approximately one quarter of all employees are low paid, just over one-third have no pension and no sick pay, and half are in jobs that do not have a recognized promotion ladder. In the USA, Kalleberg et al. (2000) similarly estimate that one in seven jobs are bad jobs, as defined by low pay and without access to health insurance and pension benefits.

Rather than a new egalitarian era of knowledge work, a more accurate description of employment trends is the growing polarization of jobs. Over the last twenty-five years in the UK, there has been a large rise in the number of well-paid jobs (MacJobs — professions, computing, and information technology (IT)), but also a rise in the number of badly paid jobs (McJobs — fast food, shops, and personal services) (Goos and Manning 2003). The 'middling' jobs of craft and clerical workers are disappearing, the casualties of automation. The growing disparity in the incomes of rich and poor in the advanced economies has in turn fuelled the revival of paid personal services. In the UK, for example, levels of wage inequality are higher than they have ever been during the twentieth century, rising sharply in the 1980s and continuing through the 1990s (Machin 2003; for US figures see Box 9.6). An integral feature of this widening gap in the last quarter century is the increasing wage disparity between workers with high levels of education as compared to those with low education levels. Certainly in terms of pay, technological changes have benefited more skilled and educated workers.

Given that there has been an upward shift in the occupational structure and that the average skill level of jobs has been rising, we might have expected to see an overall rise in job satisfaction. In fact, job satisfaction declined among workers in the UK during the 1990s. Green (2003) explains this in terms of changes to the *quality* of work. That workers are now more highly educated does not necessarily indicate a higher level of knowledge inherent in the jobs in which these people are employed. Jobs are more skilled than in an earlier era, but the workers that fill them have qualifications whose levels have risen somewhat faster. Workers who are 'overqualified' for the jobs they do tend to express lower levels of job satisfaction. Despite predictions about a new world of work, the *content* of much contemporary clerical and white-collar work, as well as service work, remains highly specified and repetitive, requiring little skill or discretion.

As for the quality of work relations, loyalty is often said to have decayed, as a result of changing attitudes to work. There is in fact little evidence for the empirical claim, as detailed in Box 2.3. Any lack of engagement reflects a natural response to the employer's inability to offer rewarding work, rather than any positive choice from 'post-materi-alist' employees (Ladipo 2000). We might speculate as to why a picture of individuals with new expectations has arisen. One important reason is confusion between what is new and what is typical. New practices attract interest, but they are often in a minority. It could then be argued that what is new is on the increase and that it is *prototypical* of the future. Yet past assertions, for example on the spread of telework, proved to be wildly inaccurate, so that we would need concrete evidence that new things are indeed the way of the future. The dangers of stereotyping the 'old' are also evident.

More generally, however, Green argues that increased working hours and workloads have reduced job satisfaction. With nearly a third of workers, especially men, working more than fifty hours a week, long working hours are a dominant issue for employees. The consequence is that an increasing proportion of employees report that they are dissatisfied with the balance of their working and non-working lives, a central

Box 2.3 Has loyalty perished?

Ladipo (2000: 187) neatly identifies an 'unholy misalliance' between what he terms left-libertarian sociologists and right-libertarian business gurus and political scientists, 'each of whom would have us believe that the workers of the twenty-first century no longer share the same work-related attitudes as their parents and grandparents'. These authors, he goes on, start with the changing expectations that employers place on their employees but then assert that it is individual choice that is the driving force. The three key claims are that: job security is less important to people than it was; the work ethic has decayed; and organizational commitment has fallen. Using data from across the advanced economies, Ladipo shows that none of these claims is supported by the evidence.

theme of Chapter 3. Not only are people spending more time at work, they are also working harder. Throughout the 1980s and 1990s, the intensity or pace of work intensified in British workplaces, with the greatest intensification being in the public sector. 'Comparing 2001 with 1992, an increasing proportion of workers are experiencing work at high speeds, report that they are "working under a great deal of tension", and agree strongly that "my job requires me to work very hard" ' (Green 2003: 143). The extra skills and responsibilities required in more challenging and rewarding jobs may well produce high workloads that are in turn associated with stress and lower job satisfaction.

Clearly the quality of work experience is highly variable, depending on the nature and content of the job. In Chapter 4 we will consider professional and managerial occupations and assess the nature of contemporary careers. For the remainder of this chapter, we will focus on the experience of those at the lower end of the labour market.

Hand, Heart, or Head: The Changing Character of Labour

Although manual work may be declining as a proportion of overall employment, it remains a significant part of the employment scene. The total number of manual workers in the UK, for example, has remained remarkably stable, at around 10.5 million or 40 per cent of total employment (Nolan and Wood 2003: 170). The conditions that Braverman and Burawoy describe remain significant for many workers in advanced capitalist countries, even if they no longer seem to capture the future trajectory of work. At the same time, with the globalization of capitalism, a local workforce's first experience of capitalist production is frequently closer to such neo-Marxist accounts than anything postulated by writers who identify the emergence of new work relations with post-industrialism. Assembly-line work is still typical of automobile manufacturing, food processing, and many other types of manufacturing work and it is here that the most concerted efforts to intensify work occur.

In *Dignity at Work* (2001), Hodson describes the typical conditions of an assembly-line as severely restricting workers' freedom of movement, skill, and autonomy as they perform a limited and repetitive range of activities. The intense pace of work leaves workers exhausted and drained at the end of the day. How, he asks, do workers achieve a sense of dignity under these conditions? Trade unions are the obvious expression of a collective voice enabling workers to negotiate over their pay and conditions. Workers who lack union representation are almost 50 per cent more likely to have substandard employment conditions than those who are unionized

(McGovern et al. 2004). Moreover, unions have provided a key source of identity and meaning when the work itself offers little intrinsic satisfaction.

However, 'for the many employees who do not have the benefit of a union, and even for many of those who do, the most common reaction may be a grinding acceptance of their working conditions as an inescapable fate. In many assembly-line jobs, workers are expected to turn off their minds when they enter the factory gate. Such workers must seek life satisfaction through their off-hours activities instead' (Hodson 2001: 119).

While trade unionism and industrial militancy associated with assembly-line work has been in decline in advanced industrial societies over the last few decades, less formal modes of resistance to management remain. High rates of absenteeism and labour turnover are still more common in assembly-line work than in other contexts. Moreover, as mentioned earlier, groups of workers resist attempts to control the pace of work by 'effort bargaining', that is, withholding full work effort, as illustrated in the example in Box 2.4 from South-East Asia, where much manufacturing has been relocated. (See Chapter 10.)

As a strategy of labour control, the assembly-line is an efficient production system at one level. However, as Hodson argues, it is at the cost of human dignity. More profoundly, however, opportunities for worker

---

Box 2.4 Effort bargaining in contemporary manufacturing

An example of effort bargaining is provided by an ethnography of small manufacturing shops in Taiwan. The ethnographer describes a group of female employees whose jobs entail painting designs on drinking glasses before the glasses are glazed and fired. The women are engaged in a constant battle over the piece rate for the work. In one episode reported by the ethnographer, the owner stresses the importance of taking extra care with the work and the workers offer their rebuttal.

'In principle, you shouldn't rush. Don't let the dye get outside of the lines. The flowers should look natural. They should be painted nicely,' Mr. Lai said.

'In principle? How dare you business guys talk about principle? Your conscience has long been eaten up by the dog. How can you talk about principles? (Hsiung 1996: 136–7)

The motivation for this running battle is to ensure the workers' earnings while keeping expectations for the effort at reasonable levels. 'We [wrangle over piece rates] a lot. It's just a way to make sure that they don't think we are living at their mercy' (ibid.: 136).

Source: Hodson (2001: 128).

initiative and creativity are squandered in highly rationalized forms of assembly-line work. Parallels have been drawn between industrial assembly-line work and the highly routinized service work in telephone call centres. These represent one of the most rapidly expanding forms of business organization of recent years. Strict performance targets, measurement of all aspects of call handling in fractions of a second, scripting and fragmentation of tasks into simpler and more repetitive jobs, together with extensive electronic monitoring and surveillance, represent new forms of managerial control.

While for some writers, such service work is an extension of industrial labour that cannot offer meaningful work or any positive identity, for others it represents a fundamentally new kind of work and establishes new forms of work-based identity. Whereas in manufacturing, employees only need to be controlled at the point of production, in the service economy, workers are brought into direct contact with the final product at its point of consumption. This raises two issues: the management of the relation with the customer as one that keeps the customer happy, and the need to prevent antagonisms intrinsic to the employment relation spilling over to impact upon the customer relation — hence the issue of a heightened need for the employee's emotional identification with the employer alongside customer relations. Let us consider the implications of this in more detail.

Perhaps the starkest difference between assembly-line work and call centre work is that the former involves manual, physical labour and the latter involves more mental and psychological work. Some of the contradictions inherent in the employment relationship in these kinds of service work are illustrated by the debate on 'emotional labour'. Hochschild (1983) identifies emotional *work* as an activity conducted by everyone in their private lives. Emotional *labour* occurs in the public sphere and is distinguished by three features:

- Feelings become commodities, to be bought and sold.
- Emotional labour occurs in the context of an unequal relationship between the powerful customer and the relatively powerless provider of the service.
- Rules for the display of feeling are laid down by management. Moreover, managers demand that workers do not merely 'act out' emotions but that they internalize the feelings that they are expected to display.

Hochschild's work struck a chord in academic analysis and also in relation to everyday life: with the rise of new service sectors based on telephone call centres, and with the standardization of routines in such established fields as restaurants, interactions between customers and workers around scripted performances have become commonplace. For these writers, there is a new commercialization of feelings.

Building on Hochschild's analysis, much has been made of the fact that the skills required by call centre work are aesthetic and social, rather than technical. For example, Thompson et al. (2001) stress how banks increasingly compete with each other in terms of the ability of their call centre staff to 'smile down the telephone'. Accordingly, in assessing applicants, managers focus on personality traits and communication (especially verbal) skills. Such skills are crucial to interactive service work. See Box 2.5 for details.

Box 2.5 Call centre work in 'TeleBank'

Call centre operators in Telebank take on average 120 calls a day with each call lasting around 180 seconds. Calls are split into two main parts: talk time (160) seconds and post call wrap-up time (20 seconds). Most of the calls are similar, relating to simple requests such as bank balances and charge queries, with scripts and screens determining what employees can see and do. Telebank managers stress that they want people who can continually communicate with energy and enthusiasm, who can recognise nuances in conversations with customers and vary their voice accordingly.

The operators also place emphasis on the ability to survive stressful and repetitive work:

> In my opinion the main skill you need is patience in abundance. You can get some people on the phone who are a bit vague about what they want, you get people who are very angry, obviously you've got to be patient with them. The main thing is definitely patience, to give them time to get the information over to you, and sometimes to give them time to let them let off stream. If you've not got patience you get in an awful state working in a service centre.

Such predispositions are built upon and formalized during Telebank's six-week full-time training programme. The main emphasis is on communication skills, which are split in two parts—managing a conversation (techniques of conversational control) and managing yourself (control over energy and enthusiasm). Together these begin to give trainees an awareness and influence over the regulation and management of feelings—categorized as acting:

> Tone gives away just about everything that's going on in your mind . . . if a customer is stupid you need to become quite clever in your acting abilities . . . enthusiasm and tone give away your mood, if you are five minutes for the end of a shift, or having a bad day . . . you'll have to fight these reactions, shut them out, push them out. The good thing is if you can do this eventually you will be able to change yourself. Or on the 'bad days' unless it is very serious, you put up with it.

Source: Thompson et al. (2001: 936).

Such research emphasizes the extent to which service sector employees are encouraged to 'deep act', that is, to actively work on and manage their feelings to match the display required by the job. Contradictory performance demands and pressures are thus placed on staff, who experience a tension between the repetitive and routinized character of the work and the requirements to actively engage with the caller and to project a particular persona. In other words, there is a tension between acting and acting naturally, and having to project themselves as a 'real person' while not engaging their private self.

Hochschild's analysis has affinities with that of the present book, for we, too, aim to connect what goes on inside work organizations to wider structures of power and, indeed, to distinctive features of capitalism. For her, there is a relatively direct link between the commodity status of emotional labour in capitalism and workers' own experiences of the workplace, and workers are harmed by this commercialization. Yet, as Korczynski (2002: 143) points out, this conflates the subjective experience of emotional labour and the objective condition of workers in capitalism. Significant analytic weaknesses flow from this, notably the neglect of the satisfactions that service workers gain from their relations with customers. As Korczynski (p. 77) argues more generally, a wide range of research on service work demonstrates the satisfaction to be derived from helping customers; in some cases, this means that the worker has established a degree of control of the interaction. Workers can be subservient to customers, but they are not necessarily or wholly in this position, and a wealth of research addresses the ways in which workers control the relationship.

It is important to be clear in these discussions about what we mean when we contrast the subjective with the objective. We do not construe the subjective as purely a matter of personal feeling or preference nor the objective as being hard truth. In particular, it is not the case that there is an objective truth about emotional (or other kinds of) labour that is separate from experience. An evident difficulty concerns the analysis of deep feelings, for how do we know whether someone has internalized managerial rules, as Hochschild would have it, or whether she 'genuinely' likes working with customers? There is no satisfactory way out of this dilemma if the subjective and objective are defined in the way that we are rejecting. The solution is to say that the subjective relates to concrete lived experience while the objective pertains to the surrounding conditions such as the structure of an organization and the competitive context in which it operates. The subjective and the objective are equally based in fact, and equally open to empirical analysis.

The problem with Hochschild's project, for example, is her idealized, universalist model of emotional labour. The contradictory relations between subordinate and superordinate are features of non-capitalist as much as of capitalist relations, with the feigned obedience of the servant to the feudal master, or the slave to the slaveowner, being a familiar theme. It is not only capitalism that calls for emotional labour. What would service work without emotional labour look like empirically, and how would we know whether we had found it? Relevant issues include:

- What are the specific conditions leading, say, an airline to call for workers to display emotional labour? As Hochschild herself notes, her informants argued that in the past they could be more genuine in their relations with customers, so what are the changing commercial (objective) conditions leading to a change of emphasis?
- Do all airlines work in the same way, or do some allow workers the space for 'genuine' engagement with customers (for example, in the first-class cabin), while others expect the performance of a script (the 'average' situation) and yet others (perhaps the budget carriers) expect no emotional labour at all?
- How much power do workers have in the interaction with customers? Even call centres are heterogeneous on this score. At the high-end, for example those selling complex financial products, there is more space for operator discretion and an emphasis on the quality of customer service (Taylor et al. 2002). To take another example, Leidner (1993) studied fast food workers and insurance sales agents. She found that the latter were often in control of relations with customers because of their expert position, while the former found standardized scripts to be useful ways to manage customers' expectations. (This does not of course mean that the workers were in complete control, for they had to meet sales targets and performance standards as specified by senior management.)
- Does the meaning of emotional labour vary between different kinds of service interactions, for, as Korczynski (2002: 84–103) argues, work in a field such as health care necessarily entails more empathy with the customer than is the case in a call centre?

Addressing such questions is the way to avoid a universalist model.

The wider point of these examples is that people's experience of work has to be addressed at the 'subjective' level. Objective developments shape this level in powerful ways. We have argued that the emotional labour process cannot simply be treated as equivalent to the physical labour process, resulting in alienation from emotional labour. Unlike the case of the factory worker, in a sense employees own the means of production (or the means of emotional engagement) and actively make choices about how they will behave in relationships with management and customers. While the interaction between the service provider and the customer is an unequal exchange, it is still the emotional labourer who weighs up how much authentic feeling to invest in the performance. As Bolton and Boyd (2003: 294) point out, 'the indeterminacy of labour is further exacerbated within the contested terrain of the emotional labour process'. Thus growing pressures to meet financial targets may mean that firms monitor workers more closely, cannot afford promised training, engage in unannounced downsizing exercises, and so on. The impact of such developments are, however, mediated by employees' past experiences and their future expectations. These in turn are informed by people's sense of themselves as gendered beings, and the making of masculinity and femininity at work.

Subjectivity, Status, and Satisfaction

Nowhere is this better illustrated than in relation to the labour of paid care. In a recent attempt to revive much-maligned studies of job satisfaction, Rose (2003) presents new comprehensive data showing that a fairly stable 'league table' of occupational job satisfaction exists. The core of his argument is that sociologists have mistakenly given undue weight to affective and intrinsic (quality of work) job-facets, while understating the effects of cognitive rationality and extrinsic (instrumental, material) job-facets. For him, the latter predominate and the 'intrinsic' job satisfactions typically seem to be consistent with the extrinsic reward. It is the latter — material inequality — that is the most sociologically compelling feature of the occupational system. While he sees his data as supporting a rational actor approach, he is surprised to find that 'poorly paid childcare workers with low negotiable skill have higher overall job satisfaction levels than sales managers enjoying fat bonuses' (Rose 2003: 526). Indeed, childcare and related work come top of the job satisfaction table.

How can we begin to make sense of this if, as Rose notes, it cannot be explained in terms of standard measures of social stratification? Could it be that childcare workers are genuinely committed and identify with their work even though the job lacks the pay and status that would ordinarily lead to such investments? Might this indicate the limits of the idea of *homo economicus*, of men and women as exclusively rational maximizers of their own (economic) self-interest, when positive human attributes such as altruism, generosity, and loyalty are shaping workplace behaviour?

Care work in particular differs from the provision of other services in being the development of a *continuous* personal relationship. The product of care is not separable from the person who delivers it and the emotions of the person performing it affect the quality of their product. Carers are supposed to want to care (and certainly not to give any indication that they do not). Thus caring is both caring about (a motivation) and caring for (an activity) — in this sense it is not alienated labour. It is meant to be 'work' not mere 'labour' (Radin 1996).

This means that who performs caring matters. The skills involved in caring are largely, though not entirely, person-specific, and people learn through personal experience. Because women are more caring than men they appear to have, and may in practice have acquired, a greater ability to develop the skills that are learnt through the development of relationships. Certainly, childcare work and personal care work are highly feminized occupations. In Australia, for example, women are 96 per cent of employees in private childcare organizations and 93 per cent of employees in community childcare organizations. They account for over 95 per cent of employees in public and private nursing homes and around 80 per cent of employees in other aged accommodation facilities (Australian Bureau of Statistics 1998). These jobs are also characterized by low pay, insecurity, part-time hours, and deemed to be 'low-skilled'. Indeed, in this classic case of the gendered evaluation of skill, jobs that require nurturance are paid less, all else being equal, than other jobs (England 1992).

Care workers thus experience their work as both highly pleasurable and extremely stressful at different times (see Box 2.6). Although men also do these jobs, women are still seen as 'naturally' suited to care work as they take primary responsibility for these duties in the home. Indeed, gender identity is an intrinsic part of how these jobs are both defined and experienced. Heterosexual femininity provides much of the cultural meaning for the performance of caring emotional labour. 'Real' men don't do 'women's jobs': it does not sit well with traditional masculinity. The paranoia about the presence of gay men in childcare demonstrates the extent to which they pose a threat to the stereotype of the feminine care. Care work is a good example of the way that the emotional labour of the service encounter is a gendered cultural performance.

This is not to imply that women form a homogeneous group: their experience of work is mediated by age, class, religion, sexuality, and, importantly, by ethnicity. Indeed, one of the marked increases in inequality at work has been between white middle-class women, who have made

---

Box 2.6 The work of care

Franzway's study of (mostly female) care demonstrates that they are not simply the victims of greedy organizations. Rather, it is the nature of the work itself that evokes commitment, and in that commitment there is satisfaction, identity, and even pleasure to be found. People gain real satisfaction from putting their values into practice.

> 'It's a very, very stressful industry . . . you really have to love this job to stay in it and the positive stuff is all the teaching of children. I know this sounds really corny but it's like, it's a special breed of people who do it. It's people who really love children and want to be with them because you don't do it for the money, you really don't, and I can honestly say that with everybody that works here, particularly this centre, it's the love of the children and wanting to see them learn and stuff like that.' (Childcare worker)

Similarly, an aged carer describes her motives:

> 'It's not for the money. The majority of carers you'll find put in probably a minimum two hours extra a week that they don't get paid for . . . they hang back, they finish feeding a resident or they'll finish doing their bookwork just to make sure that resident gets the best care she can . . . My job's to look after the resident, but you know what the centre of my job is? It's the resident, if the resident's not there I don't have a job.'

Source: Franzway (2003).

---

significant inroads into professional occupations, and the limited opportunities afforded to women from ethnic minorities. For example, four out
of ten West Indian women in the UK work in hospitals and medical care,
areas that have seen a rapid growth of low-paid workers over the last two
decades.

This is twice the proportion of white women, who are more concentrated in retail and finance. Ethnic minority men have fared even
worse, being much more likely than comparable white men to be
employed in the secondary labour market or to be unemployed. Average
pay among West Indian men is some 20 per cent below the average of
British-born white men (see Modood et al. 1997 and Wadsworth 2003 for
details of the large differences between ethnic groups; for the USA see
Heckman et al. 2000). Once again, the experience of work cannot simply
be read off from the 'external' characteristics of jobs; it is mediated by the
diverse 'subjectivities' associated with differences in class, gender, and
ethnicity.

Box 2.7 Why do low-paid workers accept bad jobs?

Why do workers tolerate low-wage jobs, even in times of economic boom? The investigations of Ehrenreich (2001) in the USA, and Toynbee (2003), in the UK, who both took a series of low-wage jobs, provide surprising answers. Key points include the following:

1. Searching for a new job is expensive and time-consuming. Jobs advertised may not in fact exist, and it can take two or three journeys to an employer to land a job; public transport to reach these jobs is often highly inconvenient.
2. Employers do not advertise the pay, and its exact level (plus any bonuses) may become apparent only after a job is accepted. There is no negotiation as to the acceptable wage.
3. In the USA, drug testing is a further barrier.
4. A new job may require moving home, which is very costly.
5. Jobs offer rewards of sociability and of being known. Even 'unskilled' jobs have substantial demands in knowing work routines and learning the ropes. A satisfactory job in terms of its demands, and relations with co-workers, is worth a lot.
6. Exercising 'voice' to demand better pay in the present job is limited by extreme secrecy around earnings and the lack of any tradition of organization that could express workers' grievances and lead them to mobilize around them.

Why do workers continue to accept low pay? The fundamental reason is that the labour market is very different from that of economics textbooks. Information on other jobs is hard to obtain, and moving jobs entails financial and other costs. These are detailed in Box 2.7.

A further key element is the satisfaction from work, and the investment of time in social relationships that produce this satisfaction. In her book about life on low pay in Britain, Toynbee (2003) describes working as a porter at the Chelsea and Westminster Hospital and compares it with her experience there thirty years earlier. The bleak and neglected Victorian hospital building has been replaced by a gleaming piece of modernity, 'vast, bright and airy' with glass lifts, splendid walkways, and walls decked with modern art. In many ways it is unrecognizable, yet the low pay and high turnover of staff have not changed nor has the use of ethnic minority labour. In the earlier period, many ancillaries were Maltese, Italian, or Spanish; now many are West Indian, Asian, or East European. Then, cleaning, catering, portering, technical, and other non-medical staff were employed directly by the hospital and had some security. Since privatization, the hospital has subcontracted all its ancillary staff — everyone below the rank of nurse. Employment agencies now provide the labour, typically in the form of casual and temporary workers. Even the porter's pay of £4.35 an hour has actually fallen in real terms since the author's earlier foray into this work. 'The words are "outsourcing", "subcontracting", "market testing", "best value", "externalization" — for people working on the bottom rungs of the public sector, all these words have meant just one thing: lower pay, worse conditions, less security' (Toynbee 2003: 75). In *Making Gray Gold*, Diamond (1992) similarly describes a highly privatized and profitable US healthcare industry, paying minimum wages to poor women of colour, either from the USA or Third World countries such as the Philippines.

Hospitals are places of strict status hierarchy and the workers described are not only poorly paid but are also treated with little respect. Their daily working lives are worlds apart from that of the mostly white doctors who rarely even acknowledge them while they perform their tasks. The job description of a porter denies any role in caring for patients. Moreover, the employment agency specifically rules out touching or lifting patients for fear of insurance claims if the patient should fall. These are dead-end jobs with no training and no prospects. Yet these invisible hospital porters are the 'lifeblood of the place' as they wheel patients around hospital corridors. They do take risks, breaking the rules in order to help patients when they can, and providing much-needed conversation and kindness to patients. And, across a myriad of ethnic differences, these ancillaries cooperate to exert some control over how their work is done, making the most of the meaningful aspects of their work. As Toynbee (p. 75) comments, 'the surprise is that the staff give so much anyway'. Despite the narrow specification of their job contract, the camaraderie among the porters and the satisfaction they obtained from helping patients made the job purposeful and rewarding.

Conclusions

This chapter has explored aspects of the contemporary experience of work and employment. We have sought to capture how individuals live the contradiction between employers' need to exercise control over workers while at the same time securing their cooperation in the performance of their work. We would argue that there is little evidence that people are less concerned about, interested in, or committed to work. Indeed, the notion that work is a purely instrumental activity and that people work simply in order to consume is difficult to sustain. Financial rewards have always been the principle reason for undertaking employment but work is an important source of identity and a means of self-actualization.

While classic accounts of alienation still have considerable purchase, they concentrate on the objective aspects of the labour process. Here and throughout the book we emphasize the interconnections between the defining structures of work and how individuals make sense of them. Work is a social relationship and workers actively shape their own work practices and cultures within those material contours. Crucially, we have stressed the multiplicity of social relations, such as those that revolve around gender and ethnicity, that mediate the subjective experience of work.

Such an approach is particularly important as jobs are becoming more, and not less, polarized and unequal. While for some groups, such as middle-class white women, their education and hence job expectations have risen sharply, for others, low-paid, dead-end jobs are still the norm. We have challenged generalizations about a wholesale move to an information or knowledge economy, but recognize that service employment does represent different kinds of working relationships and products. In service delivery the quality of work is intimately related to the characteristics of the service providers, which was not the case with the older model of the industrial workplace. These new contexts generate new forms of alienation, solidarity, and resistance. Individuals continue to strive for dignity and respect through the work they do for a living, however degraded the conditions in which they find themselves.

Here, we have focused on the continuing prevalence, both in manufacturing and services, of jobs that apparently require little skill or initiative on the part of employees. We argue that, on the whole, employees are eager to be active participants in their organizations but the nature of jobs and the way management power is exercised can leave them little scope to demonstrate their commitment. The phrase 'meaningful work' has been used in a variety of contexts, but it generally specifies work that is 'interesting, that calls for intelligence and initiative, and that is attached to a job that gives the worker considerable freedom to decide how the work is to be done and a democratic say over the character of the work process and the policies pursued by the employing enterprise' (Arneson 1987: 522). The quality of work for many people in contemporary capitalism falls far short of this ideal. Yet we have seen that, for the most part, people work hard despite the managerial controls to which they are subject. They do this through involving themselves in their jobs, by resisting managerial authority, and most importantly through forming social ties at work. The workplace thus remains a central location for the realization of employees' personal identity, their sense of autonomy and their will to connect with society.

This is not to deny the significance of non-work, domestic, and family activities. Indeed, as we will see in Chapter 3, the spatial and temporal boundaries between work and home are increasingly blurred, especially given the ubiquity of information and communication technologies. It no longer makes sense to try to understand economic life in isolation from the home.

3

Has it Become Harder to Balance Work and Family Life?

Until the mid-1990s, most studies of modern organizational life treated work in isolation from home and family life. It is increasingly recognized, however, that organizations cannot be separated from the societies in which they are embedded. At the same time, seismic shifts in the structure of both the labour market and the family are having a profound impact on the lives of individuals. There is much talk of the 'time-squeeze' as people juggle the often competing demands of their jobs, relationships, and family responsibilities. Work-life issues have come to the fore as women have entered paid employment in unprecedented numbers.

The rise of dual-earner families poses a whole new range of questions for employees and organizations. How are men and women negotiating the balance between work and family commitments? Are women, and increasingly men, having to choose between a career and parenthood? How can work be fitted into modern family life when women's responsibility for the domestic sphere can no longer be taken for granted? Are new information and communication technologies making the work/family boundary more permeable as work becomes a task that can be carried out in almost any location? Or does the answer lie in new forms of workplace flexibility, new working time regimes, and a revaluing of care work over market success?

Time and Life

Contemporary debates about work-life balance are, in large measure, about how to manage time—time for work, time for caring for family members, and sufficient leisure time. Since the publication of Schor's *The Overworked American* (1991), the politics of working time has become a central issue in economics, industrial relations, and the sociology of work and gender relations. Schor's argument, echoed by many others (Hochschild 1997; Galinsky 1999), that US workers are logging more time at the workplace than their parents and grandparents, touched a chord in the popular imagination. Whereas economic progress and increased prosperity were supposed to deliver more leisure time, time scarcity and the lack of leisure time are at the centre of the growing concern about the quality of contemporary family life.

That time pressure is now a common experience is evidenced by the fact that an increasing proportion of the population report feeling short of time. Starting in 1965, the US time-use researcher John Robinson and his collaborators have been asking respondents: 'Would you say you always feel rushed, even to do things you have to do, only sometimes feel rushed, or almost never feel rushed?' The proportion of 18–64-year-olds who reported 'always' feeling rushed rose from 24 per cent in 1965 to 38 per cent in 1992; it then declined slightly in 1995 (Robinson and Godbey 1997: 231). Time poverty is a particularly widespread experience among women who juggle work, family, and leisure.

In the past, time was managed in the context of the traditional division of labour between men and women. This separation of the public sphere from the private sphere was the foundation on which both marriage and work organization was built. Women's primary responsibility was for domestic duties, while men specialized in paid work. Men were seen as the breadwinners, working full-time outside the home, and therefore doing little domestic labour. Whereas men's identity was primarily derived from their job, women's was said to be based on their roles as wives and mothers. There was a symbiosis between these work patterns and the patriarchal family form.

A career in management is a case in point. Male managers, for example, typically required a stay-at-home wife for their careers to flourish. Kanter's classic *Men and Women of the Corporation* (1977) describes how men's success was predicated upon the services of a corporate wife (see also Pahl and Pahl 1971). She describes the way in which large organizations assumed a 'two-person single career' in which wives were incorporated into their husbands' careers. Value was attached to the wife's role in sustaining her husband's motivation and commitment to the job, leading to the preferential treatment of the 'stable and mature family man'. Although only the man was officially employed by the company, the corporate wife also had a role, that of shadowing her partner. According to the bureaucratic theory of the modern corporate organization, 'men were presumed to leave their private relationships at the door to the company when they entered in the morning', but as Kanter (1977: 104) shows, husbands and their employers benefit directly from wives' unpaid social and domestic work.

While Kanter's description is of continuing relevance today for senior managers, such marriages, consisting of male breadwinners with full-time housewives, are now relatively uncommon. Since the 1950s, with the growing proportion of women in employment, the 'dual earner' has become the usual arrangement for couples. For example, in Australia, while in 1984 more than half of all Australian couple families with dependants lived in male-breadwinner households, now less than a third do (Pocock 2003: 31). In the UK, almost three-quarters of married/cohabiting families are now supported by two earners compared with 65 per cent a decade ago (Harkness 2003: 152). Most children live in families where both parents are employed. Women comprise nearly half the workforce, with many working full-time especially in the USA. More mothers are in employment than in previous generations, most returning to work soon after births. In many countries, such as Britain and Australia, the more common pattern for mothers is part-time work. At the same time, fathers are working longer hours, especially when their children are young.

To a large extent, these changes are part of overall changes in capitalism. In most capitalist economies, but especially in those like the USA and UK where neoliberal policies of deregulation have predominated, there has been an intensification of market pressures over the last few decades. Shareholder values have been emphasized, with increasing requirements on companies to restructure and derive maximum productivity from their workers. Increasing numbers of people are on part-time, casual, or limited contracts. The experience of unemployment has also risen. In sum, the overall picture, detailed in Box 3.1, is one of an increasing polarization of working time, between those who work very long hours or overwork, and others who work few or no hours.

Although some commentators maintain that working-time arrangements also reflect choices about the organization of the family, there is reliable evidence that many people are not working the number of hours they would like. Results from a recent European survey indicate that nearly two out of three employed women and men would prefer to work a different amount of hours to their present arrangement (Fagan 2001; for US data, see Clarkberg and Moen 2001). The overall picture is that many full-timers would prefer substantially shorter hours, reducing their wages accordingly, and many part-timers want to increase their hours. UK data also shows that, during the 1990s, there was a dramatic decline in satisfaction with working hours. The proportion of men at work who said they were completely satisfied or very satisfied with the number of hours they worked dropped from 35 to 20 per cent between 1992 and 2000, and from 51 to 29 per cent for women. Today this dissatisfaction is more equitably distributed among the workforce, being most marked at the top, among managers and professionals, and, at the bottom, among

Box 3.1 The dispersion of hours—the work-rich and the work-poor

Increasing proportions of the British workforce are working long hours: whereas 17 per cent of the employed workforce worked at least forty-eight hours a week in 1983, by 1998 the proportion had risen to 20 per cent. Although at the end of the period, many more workers were doing long hours, this was balanced on average by the introduction of other workers doing relatively few hours. The proportions working fewer than twenty hours a week rose from 10 per cent in 1983 to over 14 per cent in 1998. Four out of five of those doing long hours are men while British women work fewer hours than all other European Union (EU) countries bar the Netherlands. Nevertheless *both* sexes have been increasing their long hours *and* their short hours working. In the case of males, the proportion doing at least forty-eight hours rose from 25 to 30 per cent, while the proportion working fewer than twenty hours rose from 2 to 6 per cent. Equivalently for females the long-hours proportions rose from 5 to 8 per cent, while the short-hours proportion rose from 22 to 25 per cent.

Source: Green (2001: 59–60).

manual workers. Growing insecurity among full-time employees is believed to lie behind the trend to very long hours of work among full-time employees and a reluctance to take time off for holidays for example. 'The disgruntled manager has joined the disgruntled manual workers, at least in complaints about the long hours culture' (Taylor 2002).

Surprisingly, there is little empirical evidence supporting Schor's claim that the average length of the work week has changed appreciably in recent decades. Indeed, Robinson and Godbey (1997) argue that between 1965 and 1995, leisure time actually increased (see also Gershuny 2000). So how do we account for this mismatch with people's experience of a rising deficit of family time?

What happens to individuals' average hours of work is not the same as what happens to households. As Jacobs and Gerson (2004) have pointed out, discussions about average working hours masks a dramatic redistribution of paid work between the sexes (see also Epstein and Kalleberg 2004). While the contribution of prime-age men has significantly declined, the hours that prime-age women contribute to the labour market have significantly increased. It is as if much of the paid work has been transferred from men to women. The resulting dual-earner *households* are supplying more working hours to the labour market than ever before. Time pressure is especially strong in couple families with dependants, where both husband and wife are in full-time employment.

The perception that life has become more rushed is due to the real increases in the combined work commitments of family members, rather than changes in the working time of individual workers. This transformation in family composition and gender relations over the last few decades is the key to explaining the family time deficit.

Modern Marriage and the Consequences of Work

The emergence of the dual-earner family and the perception that family time is being squeezed are in tension with contemporary expectations governing marital partnerships. A standard assumption of current sociology is that modern Western personal relationships are based on the central value of egalitarianism. Writing on love and intimacy, social theorists such as Giddens (1992) and Beck and Beck-Gernsheim (1995) draw a strong connection between the general emancipatory thrust of modernity and the new democratic politics of the private sphere. The recasting of traditional gender roles and a reshaping of the family are said to be the result of women's increased labour force participation, combined with the profound cultural shift brought about by the women's movement. Although pioneered by women, the search for self-identity through the pure relationship, characterized by an emotional openness and intimacy associated with social and sexual equality, is now being pursued by men as well. There is also a new model of fatherhood unfolding, with men striving for a new balance between work and family, and seeking satisfaction in 'pure relationships' rather than commercial or professional ones.

Certainly there has been a significant shift in ideas about equality in modern companionate marriages. For example, the notion that traditional ideas governing domestic divisions of labour are unfair is now quite widespread. According to the British Social Attitudes Survey (1992), normative preferences concerning domestic tasks heavily incline towards egalitarianism and the desirability of sharing household work. The proportions saying that tasks should be shared have grown steadily over the period 1984–91. Contemporary ideas about companionate marriage also involve raised expectations about intimacy built through talk and self-disclosure as playing a key role in consolidating trust between couples (rather than physical or sexual intimacy). Although these issues are too complex to verify by surveys, when people have been asked, both men and women overwhelmingly rate companionship and affection as the most important part of any marriage relationship.

Intimacy cannot be conjured out of the air; it must be built up and sustained over time. Indeed the key to the practice of intimacy is time, but time is often what is at stake in work/life conflict. Not all men and women experience these conflicts in the same way, and class and occupational differences are of particular importance to the changing dynamics of family time. There has been a decline in the relative sufficiency of average male earnings and an increased importance of female earnings across the life course of individuals and families (Harkness 2003). As a growing proportion of the population rely on two wages for sufficient household income, people on low incomes have little choice about the hours they work.

Family life has been affected not only by the number of hours people spend at work. There is now much greater variance in the structure and pattern of the working week. Standard working hours, that assumed a forty-hour week over five working days, are no longer the norm. The fastest growing sector of the economy, the service sector, is now commonly referred to as the 24/7 (twenty-four-hour, seven-day working week) economy. Employment growth in this sector has been disproportionately concentrated in casual and part-time jobs (Bosch 1999). It has also been accompanied by a significant increase in the number of people working unsocial hours, including a higher proportion working on weekends, and this is especially true for women. According to Presser (2003), one in five employed Americans works evenings, nights, or rotating schedules. The presence of children increases the likelihood of working non-standard schedules. Many fathers would like to be more involved with their children and are themselves hitting the brick wall of demanding work practices. Long hours, weekend working, and inadequate and outdated leave provisions make family time harder to achieve.

These economic changes have seen the development of the '24/7 family' (La Valle et al. 2002). A Rowntree Foundation report, based on interviews with over 1,000 families, found little trace of traditional family suppers and Sunday outings. Instead, 88 per cent of dual-income parents and 54 per cent of lone mothers and fathers 'frequently' worked at traditional family times, that is, before 8.30 a.m., after 5.30 p.m., and at weekends. The report also describes 'shift-parenting', where parents do back-to-back shifts, passing the children between them. While parents, especially mothers, in professional/managerial jobs could often arrange their hours flexibly to maximize time with their children, 'people on low incomes, particularly fathers, just didn't have that kind of bargaining power, and neither did lone mothers. They expressed a strong sense of unfairness, especially if they had to work on Sunday, which is still seen as a special family day'. *The Work/Life Collision* (Pocock 2003) similarly concludes: 'relationships with children are also casualties of time poverty and low energy in many households'. Pocock found that many Australians say that intimacy, sexual activity, and physicality are at a low ebb in their relationships. Indeed, there is good evidence that working non-standard schedules, particularly nights and rotating shifts, significantly increases the odds of marital instability for couples with children (Presser 2000). The unexpected ways in which these issues impinge on the world of paid work are illustrated by the events described in Box 3.2.

However, the story is not the same across the occupational spectrum. Although most people who work long hours say that they do so because it is a requirement of the job, two-thirds of higher level professionals and managers admitted that they worked long hours because they found their job interesting (Taylor 2002). Moreover, it appears that for managers and professionals, working overtime hours is increasingly rewarded: 'average yearly earnings for managers and professionals who worked additional hours increased from 10–20% of their counterparts working full time to about 36% [between 1986 and 2001]' (Fligstein and Shin 2004: 31). For those who occupy prestigious jobs and occupations, the joys of worldly success as portrayed by Kanter (1989) are seductive. She argues that the post-entrepreneurial corporation has increased the lure of work. Indeed,

---

Box 3.2 The work-life balance enters the bargaining agenda

The importance, but also the widespread neglect, of work-life issues was brought into focus by a strike of British Airways customer service staff at Heathrow in July 2003. Five hundred workers, three-quarters of whom were women and one-quarter of whom worked part-time, walked out over plans to introduce an automated swipe card system to record attendance. The strike surprised managers and also the trade unions, who had agreed to the system in other parts of the company. But these employees were concerned that the system would interfere with their ability to manage their lives. It threatened to reduce the predictability of their working rotas and also to make it hard for them to continue to juggle work-life responsibilities by swapping shifts with their colleagues. The strike was resolved through agreement to introduce the system along with the establishment of a working party to handle issues of hours, shifts, and staff deployment. According to Kevin Curran, General Secretary of one of the unions involved, this was a 'twenty-first century dispute' reflecting demands for 'dignity, respect and consultation', and work-life issues would become a key part of the future bargaining agenda.

Source: European Industrial Relations Observatory, 'Strike Grounds British Airways at Heathrow': www.eiro.eurofound.int/2003/ 08/feature/uk0308103f.

she explicitly criticizes psychological theories that see workaholics as pathological victims of the 'greedy organization'. Managers' jobs are increasingly complex, requiring high discretion and creativity to seize the new opportunities that are available. Such work is intellectually absorbing and immensely exciting, offering 'the exhilaration of living on the edge'. When work is so consuming, particularly in mixed-sex settings, the workplace becomes the site for intense personal attachments. It can easily become the centre of emotional life. In this context, the attractions of staying at work may well outweigh the attractions of going home.

This is particularly problematic for professional women who become mothers while in full-time employment and fall prey to a new form of maternal guilt. Numerous studies of dual-career couples document the shifting of gender roles and norms and the dilemmas that this shift poses for family life (for example, Brannen and Moss 1991). These mothers have multiple responsibilities and struggle with the burden of managing the dual-earner lifestyle. Research suggests that middle-class educated women are now subject to a new, oppressive ideology about mother-hood – the 'supermother' – whereby they are supposed to excel in their careers and simultaneously fulfil all the demands of full-time exclusive mothering, without sacrificing the demands of either role. While the culture of competitive materialism offers parents the opportunity to assuage their guilt feelings with consumer purchases for the children, from electronic toys to brand-name clothing, it also feeds the need to work long hours.

Similar themes have been taken up by Hochschild in *The Time Bind* (1997). But whereas Kanter stresses the joys of work per se, Hochschild's emphasis is on the interaction between work and home. Her argument is that people are not necessarily or wholly 'forced' into long hours and that the contrast between the pressure of work and the 'haven' of the family can be overdrawn. She contends that a shift in the relative values attached to home and work has led many workers to place more emphasis on the rewards of work and to view the workplace as a respite from the difficul-ties of contemporary family life. In some respects people choose to focus on work because it offers satisfactions and is more manageable than the messy personal relationships of the home. Thus, home has become work and work has become home.

One of the ironies Hochschild describes is how efficiency techniques from the workplace are increasingly being applied to the home. While corporations have introduced total quality systems to produce a strong culture of commitment and make the workplace more homely, harried parents are adopting Taylorist techniques to manage the constant demands of family life. Even 'quality time' with children is compartmentalized and rationalized, lived in a quasi-industrial way.

An increasing number of career-oriented women are, like men, spending less time at home. However, Hochschild tends to neglect the constraints on personal choice, stressing the strong motivation to do jobs offering autonomy and discretion. As we argue in Chapter 5, high performance management practices combine high commitment *and* tight managerial control. Indeed these techniques are associated with high work intensity or work pressure, which may result in fatigue, anxiety, or other adverse psycho-physiological consequences that can affect the quality of home life (White et al. 2003). Moreover, it appears that working mothers in all social classes are increasingly using medications, both on themselves and their children, in order to minimize work absence due to illness (Vuckovic 1999). Americans have less holiday entitlements than workers in any other industrialized country, yet few take their full amount. By comparison, Swedish and German workers average six weeks of paid vacation a year, and Dutch workers have five weeks. When employers associate time spent on the job with high motivation, it is difficult for individuals to reduce their working hours.

Doing Time at Home

For all the differences between women, a shared aspect of feminine gender identity is the primary responsibility for the domestic sphere (West and Zimmerman 1987). The daily doing of housework continues to be pivotal to being a wife and mother. How this is managed is a key aspect of the way work and family commitments are reconciled.

The issue of how households allocate time to paid work and its interrelationship with unpaid domestic labour has become the subject of serious academic debate. While the separation of public and private spheres made non-market household production invisible in conventional measures of economic activity, it is now regularly included in satellite national and international accounts (Goldschmidt-Clermont 1991). Modern economists consider unpaid work to be work because it is an activity that combines labour with raw materials to produce goods and services with enhanced economic value. Indeed, the industries of the household economy are collectively larger users of labour than the combined sectors of the market economy (Ironmonger 2004). Consequently a book such as this, about work and employment, would be seriously amiss if it failed to deal with a key aspect of production, that is, unpaid domestic production.

The most accurate way to document household labour is through time-budget surveys, and there now exists an extensive international comparative literature on this subject (Gershuny 2000; Robinson and Godbey 1997). Overall, this evidence shows that, although men's contribution has increased substantially, albeit from a low base, women's labour still accounts for over 70 per cent of the total time devoted to unpaid work. For example, time-diary data on housework, excluding childcare, show that, in 1992, Australian husbands averaged eleven hours per week, while their wives averaged twenty-three hours. The most comparable data from the USA show husbands doing thirteen hours per week, while wives do eighteen hours (Bianchi et al. 2000). Even amongst young couples, where there is greater sharing of household work, more traditional patterns emerge after they have children.

Many authors (Gershuny et al. 1994) have optimistically argued that women's greater financial independence would enhance their bargaining power within the household, and inevitably lead to an increase in men's domestic labour. However, rather than a radical transformation in men's behaviour, the greatest change has come from women themselves. Women's increased labour force participation has led to a significant reduction in the time they spend in unpaid work. For example, in the UK and Australia, the average hours that women spend on housework has fallen by three hours per week over the 1990s. Any convergence in men's and women's time spent in housework has occurred because women are doing less rather than because 'new' men have discovered how fulfilling housework can be.

Moreover, the traditional gender specialization of domestic tasks has remained remarkably resilient. Men spend more time on home, car, and garden maintenance, the outdoor jobs, than on laundry and cleaning put together. Indeed, laundry remains the touchstone of sexual segregation — it is a task predominantly done by women. While men have increased their cooking time since the 1970s, the more significant change has been the reduction of women's cooking time. Both male and female parents, however, devote more time to childcare. There are clear indications that men are taking greater fatherly interest in very young children. However, mothers typically remain much more emotionally and practically involved with their children than fathers. Moreover, in addition to performing more household tasks, women tend to have the management of, and responsibility for, the main elements of family life.

Thus, there is an apparent disjunction between beliefs about the value of sharing domestic duties in modern marriages and the reality of men's resistance to household work. Qualitative research shows that when women attempt to raise issues such as who is going to clean the floors, male partners typically either use a variety of strategies to avoid discussion, and even if they do talk, they generally fail to alter their behaviour (Backett 1987). Perhaps this generates less resentment than one might expect because of women's low expectations about their partner's practical contributions and their own acceptance of most domestic responsibilities. There is an evident reluctance on the part of many women to confront the fact of inequality within the home (Brannen and Moss 1991), because women do not straightforwardly judge the asymmetrical division of family work to be unfair. Moreover, most women compare their husbands with other men, who may do even less around the house, and thus judge that their own circumstances are not so bad (Thompson 1991). Women would have a stronger sense of injustice about family work if they compared themselves to their husbands.

The public rhetoric of domestic equality also tends to obscure the uncomfortable issue of how men's higher earnings translate into greater marital power. Economic inequality between husbands and wives persists and this may help explain the continuing imbalance in men's domestic contribution. A study by Arber and Ginn (1995) compares the occupational status and earnings of marital partners. They demonstrate that, although at a macrolevel professional women have made major gains in earnings relative to men, gender inequalities between marital partners in terms of pay and occupational level are proving more intractable. While they identify a trend towards equality within couples in terms of occupational standing, very substantial inequalities in earnings between partners remain. Only 11 per cent of married women who work full-time have higher earnings than their husband, compared with the 63 per cent of husbands who earned more than their wives.

Despite a quarter century of equal pay legislation, wives who earn more than their husbands are rare. Frequently, this is a consequence of the unemployment of the male partner. Studies show that in these households the gender division of labour tends to be more marked. Unemployment threatens masculine identity and it is unlikely to result in men taking on 'female' housework. Until men and women have more equitable earnings, it is unlikely that the patriarchal domestic division of labour will be seriously challenged, and perhaps not even then (Bittman et al. 2003).

Is Technology the Solution?

In the absence of a radical redistribution of the domestic workload within families, what strategies suggest themselves for balancing home and work? Domestic technology is often seen as the eventual solution to the problem of housework. As with other forms of production, the future is often conceived of in terms of automation or robotization eliminating the need for heavy and time-consuming labour. Indeed, many commentators attribute some of the recent reduction of women's routine housework time to 'time-saving features of new household appliances' such as the dishwasher and the microwave (e.g., Gershuny and Robinson 1988: 539).

Certainly the technological argument has intuitive appeal. The 'industrial revolution in the home', with the diffusion of electricity, gas, hot water, indoor toilets, refrigeration, and heating has made housework much less burdensome. However, the mechanization and automation of the household has not followed the Fordist system of large-scale production and a cooperative application of labour. Instead, as Cowan (1979: 59) aptly puts it:

Several million American women cook supper each night in several million separate homes over several million separate stoves—a specter which should be sufficient to drive any rational technocrat into the loony bin.... Out there in the land of household work there are small industrial plants which sit idle for the better part of every working day; there are expensive pieces of highly mechanized equipment which only get used once or twice a month; there are consumption units which weekly trundle out to their markets to buy 8 ounces of this nonperishable product and 12 ounces of that one.

Experiments in Britain in the 1930s in social housing with communal restaurants quickly faded (Wajcman 1991). Rather than mass production and specialization, or social cooperation, the privatized nature of the single-family household requires housewives to have multiple skills and often to exercise them simultaneously. While some tasks have been abandoned as a result of market-based substitutes, such as restaurant meals, takeaway food, and almost-ready-to-eat goods from the supermarkets, shopping time has grown as has the standard of living.

One of the great paradoxes about domestic technologies is that, despite being universally promoted as saving time, these technologies have been singularly unsuccessful in lessening women's domestic load (Bittman et al. 2004). Indeed, it is ironic that such emphasis has been placed on technology when much of the growth of housework during the late twentieth century derives from the care of children. Childcare is perhaps the activity least amenable to technological solutions. In this area, the effect of technology has been peripheral and the effect of cultural changes profound.

What about the electronic home of the future? Will this finally eliminate household drudgery? The smart houses occupied by the very affluent display what high-technology dwellings might offer the family of the future. Magazines like *Wired* and films like *The Matrix* present home networking as the backbone infrastructure of the twenty-first century-lifestyle. But it seems that the designers and producers of the techno-logical home, such as the MIT 'House of the Future', have little interest in housework (see *http://architecture.mit.edu/house_n*; and Wajcman 2004). Home informatics is mainly concerned with the centralized control of heating, lighting, security, information, entertainment, and energy con-sumption in a local network or 'house-brain'. Prototypes of the intelligent house tend to ignore the whole range of functions that come under the umbrella of housework. The target consumer is implicitly the technically interested and entertainment-oriented male, someone in the designer's own image. The smart house is a deeply masculine vision of a house, rather than a home, somewhat like Corbusier's 'machine for living'.

While there would certainly be a commercial market for smart tech-nologies that reduce housework, such as the robotic vacuum cleaner, the variety and complexities of household labour impose limits on its mech-anization. Even in the differently ordered world of paid work, robots perform only routine tasks in manufacturing, and personal service work has proved impossible to automate. However, even the most visionary futurists have us living in households that, in social rather than techno-logical terms, resemble the households of today. The space-age design effort is directed to a technological fix rather than envisioning social changes that would see a less gendered allocation of housework and a better balance between working time and family time. The wired house may have much to offer but democracy in the kitchen is not part of the package.

Perhaps more significant than the wired house per se are the wider possibilities afforded by new information and communication technolo-gies. Personal computers, the Internet, and mobile phones have made the boundaries that once separated the public world of work and the private home more permeable. However, this is almost always in such a way as to facilitate the transfer of work into the home rather than the transfer of home concerns into the workplace. Those who belong to the flexible workforce, especially managers and professionals, increasingly work from and at home, and when they are on the move. It is hard to gauge the long-term impact of the diffusion of these new technologies, but they already appear to have complex and contradictory effects. On the one hand, they can lead to the intensification of work, allowing employees to be constantly available, and interrupting and diminishing the quality of family time. According to a recent estimate, over 80 per cent of Americans check in to the office while on vacation (*Guardian Weekly*, August 2003: 32). The idea that the preoccupations of work can 'spill over' into non-work life is a familiar one, but it may be that new technologies are exacerbating this tendency and could make pure, uninterrupted leisure time a thing of the past.

On the other hand, by transcending the link between time and space, information and communication technologies may offer greater control over the location and scheduling of tasks. This could make the organization of both paid and unpaid work time more manageable, as production no longer requires personnel to be concentrated at the place of work (Handy 1995; Castells 1996). Computer-based homework or telework offers the freedom of self-regulated work and a reintegration of work and personal life. Moreover, an expansion of teleworking may lead to more sharing of paid work and housework, as men and women spend more time at home together. Mothers are particularly seen as the beneficiaries of this development as working from home allows much greater flexibility to combine employment with childcare.

Futurologists commonly assume a dramatic increase in teleworking, but the term itself suffers from a lack of clarity. If one adopts a narrow definition of teleworkers, as those employed regularly to work online at home, the figures are rather small, perhaps 1–2 per cent of the total US labour force (Castells 1996: 395). Nevertheless, it has important implications for the way work is understood. First, we need to distinguish between skilled or professional workers who work from home and the more traditional 'homeworkers' who tend to be semi-skilled or unskilled low-paid workers. The former certainly do have more choices about how they schedule their work to fit in with the rest of their everyday lives. However, these teleworkers, who tend to work in occupations like computing and consultancy, are typically men. Women who telework are mainly secretarial and administrative workers. So a rather conventional pattern of occupational sex segregation is being reproduced in this new form of work (Felstead et al. 2002).

Indeed, women and men are propelled into teleworking for very different reasons. While women's main motivation is childcare and domestic responsibilities, men express strong preferences for the flexibility, enhanced productivity, convenience, and autonomy of such working patterns. The common media image of a woman working while the baby happily crawls across a computer is misleading. There is an important difference between being at home and being available for childcare. Women continue to carry the bulk of responsibility for domestic work and childcare and, for them, telework does not eliminate their double burden.

Even among the minority of professional women who work from home, few are able to separate the demands of motherhood and domesticity from paid work (Adam and Green 1998). For men, who can more easily set up child-free dedicated 'offices' at home, telework often leads to very long and unsocial hours of work. These long hours tend to militate against a more egalitarian and child-centred way of life.

Is Outsourcing the Solution?

Increasingly, it is not just paid work that is brought into the home, but paid workers too. The contracting out of housework is a growing trend in advanced industrial societies, especially among dual-career middle-class households. The feminization of the labour force has greatly increased demand for the types of services that housewives traditionally perform, such as cleaning, cooking, and childcare.

This phenomenon has received relatively little attention, largely because sociological research on housework has concentrated on the sexual division of domestic tasks. Feminist researchers have been reluctant to confront inequalities between women, and to address the contradictory interests that women have as employers and employees. After all, it is largely women who hire and fire other women to do housework and substitute mothering, as paid domestic servicing usually involves labour substitution for men in the household (Gregson and Lowe 1993). For all women's anxieties about hiring other women to do the housework, it is a way of gracefully accommodating men's continuing resistance to domestic work, and preserving their marriages, as the evidence in Box 3.3 illustrates.

Box 3.3 Time for leisure

In a paper given to the Royal Geographic Society conference in 1997, Rosie Cox revealed from her survey of Hampstead, London, that many domestic workers were employed, not because people did not have the time to do their own domestic work but because they 'merely wanted to avoid doing the chores themselves and therefore gain the time for extra leisure'. Her work suggests that the cash-rich, time-rich, and not just the cash-rich, time-poor, will employ domestic workers. Those who were doing the work, on the other hand, were 'the poorest 10 per cent', often women with heavy childcare responsibilities (scarcely 'time-rich' themselves), or with uncertain immigration status.

Source: Anderson (2000: 87).

While the rich have always hired domestic servants, there is now a mass importation of caring labour from the Third World. There is a growing trend for immigrant women from the Third World to leave their own children in order to work as nannies, cooks, and cleaners for families in the First World. From Hong Kong to the USA, for example, Filipina domestic workers are employed for low pay and long hours. Indeed, countries such as the Philippines have become economically dependent on the remittances women domestic workers send home. As we shall see in Chapter 10 women make up an increasing proportion of the millions of people who migrate, both legally and illegally, around the globe.

What is distinctive about this form of labour is that it straddles the boundaries of public/private and of free/unfree labour. In the case of live-in domestics, for example, what the employer is buying is not just the worker's labour power but their *personhood* (Anderson 2000). Thus migrant women workers take on a servant role in a quasi-familial setting that may deprive them of normal employment rights, including the right to a private personal life. This increasingly internationalized trade in emotional labour, 'the global care chain' (Ehrenreich and Hochschild 2003), is based on intersecting hierarchies of sex, class, age, race, and nation.

This trend is also evident in the food industry. Today about half of the money used to buy food in the USA is spent in restaurants—mainly at fast-food restaurants such as McDonald's. The billions of hamburgers that Americans now eat every year rely for their production on a migrant workforce (Schlosser 2002). The fast-food industry exemplifies the way in which the capacity of more affluent households to buy time through utilizing consumer services is made possible by the supply of cheap labour.

Discussions of the move to outsourcing household work tend to criticize professional women for employing other women as low-paid, casual workers. What they overlook is that greedy organizations, with their long-hours culture, make it impossible for women to compete and still be mothers. As we have seen, gendered family relationships still allocate domestic responsibility to women (rich or otherwise). One of the consequences of the inadequate work/care regime is a globalized service economy reliant on the exploitation of Third World women. However, it is not just men's refusal to take an equal share in everything domestic, but the lack of change in the nature of work that lies at the heart of this problem.

Family-Friendly Workplaces and the Future of Work

Individuals and families have adapted in various ways to the changing pressures of reconciling work and life. Up to this point, we have been considering responses at the level of the household. Indeed most workers experience the incompatibility between work and home as their own individual problem, requiring them to juggle competing demands on their time. Perhaps, however, much of the answer lies elsewhere, in the institutions of work and the reorganization of working practices.

Changes in the profile of the workforce and in the shifting expectations both of business and the employee are prompting the introduction of 'family-friendly' policies to help people combine their care commitments with participation in the labour market. Specific initiatives fall into four main groups: leave provisions (such as parental and family or carer's leave); flexible hours provisions (including part-time work, job-sharing, flexible start and finish times); childcare provision or assistance; and support measures (counselling and referral services) (Glass and Estes 1997). Such policies do not only apply to people with children. With the ageing of the population, increasing numbers of people are caring for sick, elderly, or disabled relatives. In 1995, this was the case for 13 per cent of British adults and, within this group, two-thirds were in full- or part-time employment (Yeandle et al. 2002). An Organization for Economic Corporation and Development (OECD 2002) review of family-friendly policies noted that the importance of the reconciliation of work and family life lies not only in the well-being of families and the promotion of gender equity, but also in its capacity to increase aggregate labour supply and contribute to the sustainable development of societies.

Indeed, there is now a high level of support for work-life balance policies among some employers, who appreciate the business benefits of helping employees strike a satisfactory balance between work and the rest of their lives. Of over 1,000 large US companies that offered various forms of flexible work arrangements, three-quarters considered the arrangements to be cost-neutral or worth the cost (Galinsky and Bond 1998). Employers have an interest in offering family-friendly provisions to their workforce for a number of reasons. In the first instance, they can help in recruitment, attracting talent and skills from a wider pool than is available if people with caring responsibilities are excluded. Such an 'employer of choice' strategy is being pursued by companies seeking highly qualified or skilled employees in a competitive labour market. The challenges and rewards of initiatives to enhance work-life integration are illustrated in a study of major US corporations (see Box 3.4).

Box 3.4 Looking at work through a 'work–family lens'

The Ford Foundation entered into research partnerships with three major US corporations during the 1990s—Xerox, Corning, and Tandem Computers—to examine and restructure conventional work practices (for example, long working hours and early morning meetings) that assumed 'ideal workers' with unlimited commitment to the job. Although these companies boasted an array of work–family benefits on paper, access to these benefits was often limited or constrained in practice. For example, at one administrative centre, flexible work hours and part-time work were available only at management's discretion. Managers tightly controlled the number and type of requests granted, fearing that productivity would suffer. As part of this action-research project the controls were lifted, giving individuals more autonomy to work out their own schedules and leading to the development of self-managed teams. The result was a 30 per cent decrease in absenteeism in this part of the company. More generally, the authors demonstrated that connecting business issues with work–family concerns benefits both the company and the employees.

Source: Rapoport and Bailyn (1996).

Several surveys have shown that work-life balance is important to contemporary graduates. It was identified as the second top career priority in a survey of 1,000 young professionals in North America, Europe, and Asia. Forty-one per cent said they would value more choice over working hours and 20 per cent said they would like to work part-time (*Financial Times* 8 May 2000). Work-life balance came either first or second in a survey of what 10,000 workers in Europe, the USA, and Japan think is important in a job. Imbalance was found to be one of the main problems with their current job. A PricewaterhouseCoopers study (1999) of graduates worldwide found that work-life balance was key to choice of employer for 45 per cent of graduates compared to salary for only 22 per cent. In fact, most employees believe their employer has a role to play in helping their employees to balance work with other aspects of their lives (Stevens et al. 2004).

Linked to recruitment is the issue of staff retention. Family-friendly provisions can reduce staff turnover. Employees are more likely to stay in a job that provides them with the flexibility and support that they need over the life cycle. At the World Economic Forum in Davos in 2000, Deborah Holmes of Ernst & Young was named a 'global leader for tomorrow' for her initiatives to retain staff including developing a database for flexible work arrangements. Reducing staff turnover results in direct and major savings in training and other labour costs. British Telecom, for example, estimates saving 180 million pounds a year as a result of its flexibility policies that cost less than 1 million to implement (Industrial Relations Services 2002). At a more general level, companies adopt work-life practices to strengthen employee loyalty and commitment, and increase productivity.

Indeed, in many OECD countries, arguments about the positive dividends to organizations of implementing work and family policies have become the dominant discourse. They are advanced as being in the self-interest of business rather than, for example, as part of the social responsibility of business or primarily a responsibility of government to manage. However, voluntary business-case-driven initiatives can be an insecure foundation for a widespread improvement in access to family-friendly work arrangements and the associated increase in equal employment opportunities (Dickens 1999).

For one thing, business is often responding to short-term market pressures rather than operating in what may be its long-term strategic best interests. Individual organizations may find it in their immediate interests to treat workers with family responsibilities as a cheap flexible workforce rather than to fully integrate them by accommodating their needs. Narrow cost–benefit analysis may block work and family initiatives rather than promote them. Working arrangements that may collectively benefit employers and the economy on the long-term may not present as immediately beneficial to an individual enterprise. Indeed, the financial gains to companies can be hard to quantify (Dex and Smith 2002).

Certainly, business case arguments have greater salience for some organizations than others. While some businesses report remarkable rates of return for providing family-friendly work practices, the 'business case' is stronger for highly skilled employees. Workplace flexibility is not necessarily made available to those who need it (e.g. parents) but rather to those whom the organization most values. Family-friendly provisions are therefore unlikely to become universally available if left to voluntary business initiatives.

In any event, what purport to be family-friendly working arrangements can further entrench inequalities between women and men in the labour market. For example, while part-time employment can be valuable to employees with children by reducing hours, it is often associated with irregular schedules, insecure tenure, and poor training and promotion prospects. For managers and professionals, part-time work is known as the 'mommy track', the point at which a career goes downhill. There are often hidden barriers to the take-up of family-friendly work options, which can be associated with the exercise of management discretion and the workplace culture in which it is operating. Changing organizational culture to be both family-friendly and gender neutral is a much bigger challenge than some of the rhetoric in this area admits.

It was to speed up progress in this area that the UK government introduced a legislative scheme entitling employees with children under six to request flexible working arrangements. Employers have a statutory duty to consider such applications seriously, and must have genuine business reasons for refusal. In the first year of the scheme's operation, almost a quarter of eligible employees requested some kind of flexible work arrangements, a large majority of which were accepted by employers (Palmer 2004).

Conclusions

Any analysis of work and employment that treats them as separate from family and home life is deeply flawed. Traditional studies of organizations, while overtly ignoring the home, implicitly assumed that unpaid domestic work would be performed largely by employees' wives. Times have changed and organizations can no longer rely on women fulfilling their traditional roles, thereby freeing men to be fully committed to work organizations. Young men and women in particular desire a new model that allows them to be involved in both parenting and paid work (Brannen et al. 2002).

A new paradigm of work and care would be one in which women and men share good jobs and the work of care, assisted by community and public institutions. As Appelbaum et al. argue (2001: 12), this is necessary alongside a 'set of social norms that structure behaviour by workers and firms, that temper employers' demands on employees, and that shape the aspirations of both women and men for the type of employee and the type of parent or family member they can strive to be'. This 'Shared Work/ Valued Care' model would properly recognize and value the productive work of care, and more equally distribute the cost of children who are, after all, a public good on whom a sustainable economy depends.

While Anglo-Saxon countries, with their neo-liberal policies, make this hard to achieve, Scandinavian countries have more extensive regulation of family-friendly work regimes — with statutory provision of maternity, paternity, and parental leave, options for reduced hours working, and time off to care for dependants. These societies place a different value on children and have a more extensive commitment to gender equity, hence providing a better environment for combining parenting and work. It is an environment that is also consistent with the high-productivity economy that globalization seems to require.

4

Is the Organizational Career
an Outdated Concept?

Popular management literature and business journalists tell us that we are currently witnessing the demise of the predictable career. The story goes that large corporations have restructured, merged, flattened, and down-sized to the extent that managerial and professional jobs are constantly under threat. At the same time, there is an emerging model of a 'portfolio career' whose advocates declare that it provides managers and professionals with new opportunities for autonomy and control in their working lives. To survive, we must come to terms with turbulent environments, thrive on risk, and adjust to a high degree of uncertainty. The discourse of constant change is particularly pronounced in accounts of the occupational and organizational realities inhabited by managerial and professional employees.

This chapter unravels some of the apparently contradictory claims about the pattern of contemporary careers. Is the organizational career headed for extinction? Is it being superseded by new post-bureaucratic career pathways? How have the changed conditions and expectations about employment influenced the ways in which managers and professionals approach and perform their work? Do men and women share the same experience and success in their careers? Indeed, are women managers more suited to post-industrial corporations that increasingly are argued to require communicative and cooperative styles of management in which women are said to excel?

The Changing Career Contract

Careers have traditionally been seen as providing a set of organizing principles around which white-collar employees within bureaucracies have been able to structure both their professional and private lives. The 'psychological contract' between employer and employee was based upon loyalty and commitment to the organization in exchange for the incremental increases in authority, status, and financial remuneration associated with a corporate career (Rousseau 1995). The combined promise of job security and personal advancement within corporate hierarchies constituted the major rewards of the twentieth-century middle-class career.

The typical organizational career from the 1950s to 1980s consisted of a series of related jobs through which a person moved in a sequential manner. The term 'career' designated occupations located within organizations expressed in terms of hierarchical, bureaucratic career structures. The notion of progress within an organization meant regular successive stages of development with increasing responsibility and more highly paid posts. The criteria for advancement were associated with length of service, ability, and performance. Personal success tended to be closely related to various age-related stages, with careers being consolidated in middle age. An internal labour market could deliver lifelong employment in a single organization.

'Organization men' identified with and were deeply loyal to the organization in which their career was made (Kanter 1977; Mills 1953). They might internalize its norms, values, and goals, becoming the living agents of its existence and future (Riesman 1950; Whyte 1956 – see Box 4.1). Or

Box 4.1 The organization man

This is the title of Whyte's classic book published in 1956, which describes how a new type of man has been created—the organization man—who not only works for the organization, but also *belongs* to it as well. According to Whyte, this new generation of organizational workers had been moulded by the needs of the corporation through the propagation of a new bureaucratic 'social ethic' of loyalty, security, and 'belongingness'. With the rise of the large corporation, US business life had abandoned the old virtues of individualism, self-reliance, and entrepreneurship in favour of conformity. Young men of ambition submerged themselves in the organization, adopting what Whyte described as a standard litany: 'Be loyal to the company and the company will be loyal to you'. They identified their own well-being with that of the company and assumed that they would be with the organization for their whole careers: 'They have an implicit faith that The Organization will be interested in making use of their best qualities as they are themselves, and thus, with equanimity, they can entrust the resolution of their destiny to The Organization' (pp. 124–5). And whereas once it was conventional for young men to resent group life and the loss of individualism, it was now seen as a positive boon. At the senior executive level, Whyte described men who worked long hours but did not feel that it was a burden. They worked fifty or sixty hours a week, as well as after hours in work-related entertaining, conferences, and reading. They promoted those who followed their example. 'We have, in sum, a man who is so completely involved in his work that he cannot distinguish between work and the rest of his life—and is happy that he cannot' (p. 142).

they might outwardly emulate this ideal employee, playing the bureaucratic politics required for career success, while inwardly resisting full internalization of organizational aims (Jackall 1988). (The ethical issues raised by Jackall are discussed in Chapter 11.) In either case, managers' orientation to the organization was built on an understanding that service would be rewarded with security and progression. This generated loyalty and commitment to the organization's goals and interests, sustaining it as well as the manager. In sum, the image of 'organization man' pictures the manager as developing an identity around a series of intra-organizational processes — the internal managerial career structure, the work of managing, and the formation of organizational values and goals.

The limited applicability, indeed mythical elements, of this linear view of career has been noted (Cohen and Mallon 1999). For a start, the model was premised on the exclusion of various groups, primarily women. Organization man has now been joined by organization woman, the implications of which are discussed below. Moreover, for many white-collar workers the career path proved a dead end, rather than moving inexorably upward and onward. In reality the bureaucratic career has never been the dominant organizing principle of white-collar work. Nevertheless, the perception that it was is deeply embedded in our consciousness and forms the backdrop against which claims about recent changes are made.

There is now broad agreement that traditional bureaucratic patterns of work organization have given way to more flexible organizations which entail more ambiguous authority structures, less predictable career pathways, and less employment security (Cappelli 1999; Neumark 2000; Osterman 1999). One stream of literature emphasizes the negative effects of organizational change, especially for managers. The loss of large numbers of managerial jobs, along with flatter structures, is said to have caused significant loss of morale, lowered career horizons, and produced a quantum leap in general uncertainty among the managers left in organizations (Heckscher 1995). Scase and Goffee's (1989) landmark study of British managers in the 1980s produced evidence of a rather dour managerial middle class, worried about its future, with sharply curtailed career expectations, and strong tendencies to displace commitment away from work to family and leisure pursuits. More recent research has identified a distinct trend towards the decline of the internally promoted manager (Blair and Kochan 2000; Osterman 1999). A study of eight large organizations in Britain by McGovern et al. (1998) describes the frustration of managers at a perceived loss of the career opportunities and job security associated with the traditional 'organizational career'.

They express considerable suspicion of their organization's commitment to enhancing their skills and 'employability' (Gratton et al. 1999). Not only do they perceive declining opportunity to mobilize organization assets, but also an unwillingness on the part of companies to assist them in converting these assets into cultural resources valued in external job markets. As a result, many managers have become less attached to their company (Worrall and Cooper 2001).

The overall picture that emerges from these accounts, then, is not one of employee empowerment, but a rather pessimistic view of the predicament many middle managers are in. And if the foundations upon which an organizational identity is built are being undermined, this in turn poses new problems for managers in forming and sustaining viable identities, and new challenges for organizations in generating and maintaining commitment. Indeed, some commentators go so far as to argue that the uncertainty and unpredictability of the 'new capitalism' erodes people's very moral character and is a fundamental threat to fully responsible social action (Sennett 1998).

Virtually the opposite view has been propounded by business school academics who see the removal of bureaucratic structures as ultimately freeing employees to chart their own course through work, popularized in the notion of the 'portfolio career' (Handy 1995). New flatter, more flexible organizational forms are viewed as the environment within which portfolio careers can flourish. In this model managers, much like professionals, accumulate skill and personal reputation as key career resources by frequent movement between firms and in and out of self-employment. Advocates emphasize the personal rewards available in these 'post-entrepreneurial' (Kanter 1989) or 'boundaryless' (Arthur and Rousseau 1996) careers, where managers are able to adapt their career paths to their own interests and special abilities. As they search for personal fulfilment, thus focusing on the intrinsic rewards of their work, managers reduce their loyalty and commitment to any particular organization (Heckscher 1995). They are thus freed from the constraints of organizational life that confined their predecessors in the bureaucratic age.

Neither of these approaches can fully capture the complex mix of change and continuity that characterizes contemporary careers. For this we need to consider a broader range of empirical evidence. First, it appears that predictions of massive downsizing and job loss of managerial employees were overly pessimistic. In the UK and the USA, employment levels have been rising and the fastest growing jobs have been professional occupations like managers or engineers. This trend is so marked that Goos and Manning (2003: 74) describe it as a 'managerial epidemic' that has swept Britain in the past twenty-five years. Similarly, Gordon (1996) shows that most US companies actually employ more managers and supervisors than ever before. Indeed he argues that the threat and practice of downsizing has been most effective in squeezing the wages of average workers (see also Baumol et al. 2003). So while there is clear evidence of extensive delayering of occupational hierarchies in US and UK labour markets during the 1980s and 1990s (Hudson 2002; Jacoby 1999), new layers and new functions have been added. In many cases, like the British National Health Service, managerial and supervisory bureaucracies have burgeoned.

Second, overall job tenure rates, a key test of the thesis that the career is dead, have remained almost constant over the past twenty years. Moreover, there has been no aggregate rise in job insecurity (as measured by the fear of job loss) over the last two decades in either the USA or UK. What there has been is a very significant redistribution of insecurity between blue-collar and white-collar workers. No doubt this change accounts for the sharp increase in attention that job insecurity has received. During the post-war boom years, job insecurity remained low and stable, but the proportion of male blue-collar workers feeling insecure was, at all times, approximately twice as high as the proportion of male white-collar workers. When job insecurity rose in the late 1970s, it especially affected blue-collar workers. While the period between the mid-1980s and mid-1990s saw little aggregate change, 'the most marked changes were that the professionals and workers in the financial services, previously the most secure occupations and services, were now the least secure' (Burchell 2002: 68).

Third, it may be that the most dramatic effect of the dismantling of internal labour markets has been on the career development of low-skilled employees. In a study of four large service sector organizations (telecommunications, banking, retail, and local government), Grimshaw et al. (2001, 2002) found that in all of them, the intermediate grades in the job hierarchy had disappeared. The result was a widening gap in the job ladder between base-grade employees and the first step on the promotion ladder: 'the most direct effect of the flattened jobs hierarchy has been to remove the architecture necessary for career progression' (Grimshaw et al. 2001: 38). Employers and managers introduced a number of strategies, including multiskilling and teambuilding, in attempts to offset the adverse impact of delayering on workers' expectations. However, these had not been particularly successful and there was little evidence of firm-based training that linked skills development with incremental career advancement. The authors conclude that it is likely that workers entering the contemporary large organization with few educational or vocational credentials will face major obstacles to pay and career paths.

For those groups of workers on the upper rungs of organizational job ladders, case-study research indicates more continuity in both the pattern of managerial careers and the structure of organizations than was anticipated. One quite common finding is that of considerable persistence of upward intraorganizational careers, suggesting that managers' opportunities to exploit their organization assets have been less devalued than many predicted (Halford et al. 1997; Storey et al. 1997). There are many large firms where, despite some changes, managers' lengths of tenure, frequency of intercompany movements, and rates of career progression remain rather similar to those of thirty years ago (McGovern et al. 1998; Newell 2000). Indeed, Jacoby (1999: 135) argues that it is 'the reallocation of risk—not the decline of career-type jobs—[that] is the central dynamic driving today's internal labor markets'.

Research on the impact of external restructuring on careers is likewise equivocal. Many large companies have restructured their operations externally across a network of firms through arrangements that include subcontracting, outsourcing, and partnerships. The nature of these new 'networked' organizational forms has been much debated. Many have pointed out that the delayering process associated with teamwork and horizontal linkages has not dispensed with the vertical hierarchies of control that remain the backbone of organizations. For example, a study of a widely proclaimed alternative organizational form, open-source software communities, concludes that: 'despite all the enthusiasm with which management scholars have greeted ideas of self-management and distributed leadership, the basic fact is that, for all their novelty and radical ideology, open-source software communities are organized along similar lines of hierarchy and adopt similar mechanisms of coordination as giant corporations' (Grant et al. 2003: 235). Reviewing the evidence for the eclipse of bureaucracy in favour of post-bureaucratic organizations, Alvesson and Thompson (2004) judge that structural changes have been relatively modest.

Overall, then, the empirical literature leads one to conclude that restructuring has eroded the traditional career model, rather than transformed it. Furthermore, such changes as have occurred in employment policies and practices are not unidirectional and vary considerably between companies and sectors. In some companies, the psychological contract has shifted away from stable careers; in others, there has been little change; and in others new managerial careers are appearing. Crucially, however, these different trends are producing contradictory

outcomes, as employers attempt to capitalize on changing external conditions often at the expense of meeting internal organizational demands.
For example, network relations designed to enhance the learning capacity
of the organization rely on the skills and motivation of 'empowered'
workers. Yet the development of high-trust, high-commitment relationships, both between the organizations, and between those employees
whose task it is to establish such networks, is not easy in the absence
of stable employment and internal career paths. While employees are
encouraged to be self-reliant, innovative, and make their own career
choices, at the same time they are expected to be good team players, to
conform to company norms, and to be subjected to ever tighter financial
and operational accountability. Under these conditions, there is no guar-
antee that employees can be trusted to pursue the interests of their current
employer. As we shall see below, these conflicting pressures create tensions
and present new dilemmas both for employers and employees, 'often with
no obvious or sustainable long-term solutions' (Grimshaw et al. 2001: 51).

An important caveat needs to be registered at this point. It was never a
realistic prospect that bureaucratic careers would be completely supplanted during the decade or so of organizational turmoil that began in
the early 1980s. Various forms of institutional and psychological 'sticki-
ness' militate against such a possibility, especially amongst older managers. Older managers, particularly those whose careers were already
well established, are likely to remain more 'bureaucratic' in outlook and
career patterns. But they are also the ones who have few prospects: 'the
combination of delayering, the changing nature of the business, and early
retirement incentives (i.e. pension payable at 50) resulted in the development of an unwritten rule that "few here survive past fifty" ' (McGovern
et al. 1998: 467). It is the younger generation of managers and professionals, who began their careers after the wave of organizational restructuring, who may be the pioneers for the new career pattern. Some
evidence is emerging that the key structural features of the portfolio
career—frequent intercompany movement, the importance of external
marketability, and an environment of flat, flexible organizations—are
tending to characterize younger managers' experience of corporate employment (Wajcman and Martin 2001).

While career patterns themselves have not been revolutionized, the
nature of the job has changed, and with it employees' view of themselves
and their careers. Work intensification, heightened supervision, and
more responsibility, combined with increasing fears about job security,
have produced a culture of long hours. Incremental salary systems,
automatically linked to career progress, have declined with the rise of

individualized payment and reward systems. Performance-related pay means that the rewards of a job are at least partly detached from seniority and status, so encouraging all staff to be single-minded in pursuit of their targets. We consider the nature and impact of performance management schemes at length in Chapter 5, arguing that there has been a growth of bureaucratic control mechanisms alongside the erosion of the traditional career. In Chapter 9 we examine the wider context in which these changes are occurring, such as the considerable pressure on companies to achieve shareholder value. What we go on to consider here is how these changed conditions have affected the meaning of careers and work cultures over the past two decades.

Career as a Project of the Self

How then do managers and professionals understand themselves and their careers in an uncertain world of corporate restructuring, reinvigorated market competitiveness, and the decline of secure employment? Has the move towards market-based forms of employment, shifting more risk onto central employees, changed the culture of organizations and careers?

Certainly there has been a significant shift in management theory and practice over this period. Enthusiasm for 'cultural' strategies was widespread during the 1980s within organizational analysis and in popular business texts, such as the best-selling *In Search of Excellence* (Peters and Waterman 1982). The management of culture was identified as one of the principal objectives of HRM, and a key element of competitive advantage. The prescription for enhanced performance required senior managers to create strong corporate cultures to win the commitment, and not simply the compliance, of their employees. There was a move away from narrow, bureaucratic roles, in favour of normative rules and internalized emotional controls, that seemed particularly well suited to knowledge-intensive companies requiring high degrees of employee autonomy. Kunda's (1992) ethnography of a US hi-tech company ('Tech'), described in Box 4.2, was frequently cited as an exemplar of successful cultural management (see also Casey 1995). The function of management was not only to monitor the behaviour of employees but also their thoughts and feelings.

There have been lengthy debates about what is variously called cultural management, new wave management, or soft HRM — about the extent to which it is actually practised, its effectiveness, and whether the ethos was internalized by employees (Legge 2000; Sisson and Marginson 2003). Some dispute the claim that it is even new. They point out that managerial efforts to eradicate conflict in organizations, through the production and

Box 4.2 Engineering culture

In *Engineering Culture*, Kunda (1992) describes managerial efforts to design, articulate, and impose an explicit corporate culture in a leading computer firm. This enormously successful firm gained its reputation not only for its technical prowess but also for its social vision. Considerable efforts were undertaken to codify and disseminate the corporate culture, through publications, ritualized group meetings, training sessions, and many other 'bonding' activities. The following excerpt from the company's *Culture Handbook*, for example, specifies the appropriate mindset and desires of the 'people we hire in this company':

'You have to be a self-starter. An individual who takes chances and risks and moves ahead. The expectation is that everyone is going to work hard, not for hard work's sake, but for the fun of it, and enjoy doing what they are doing, and show commitment no matter what it takes. A core of the environment is individual commitment, a lot of integrity, and a very high level of expectations from yourself. Hassle is the price of the organizational structure. For those who don't like it, it's very frustrating. You can wrap those three or four things together (openness, honesty, success, fairness) and you can sum it all up in one word and that is caring. Caring about your job, the people who work for you, yourself.' (Kunda 1992: 73)

This was a working environment designed to be challenging but safe, characterized by a strong rhetoric of autonomy ('be your own boss', 'show initiative', 'talk back') combined with security ('lifetime employment', 'organizational tenure', 'a career, not a job'). It was supposed to be the kind of workplace that would relieve employees of the constraints of bureaucracy and encourage them to take risks, while at the same time fostering a sense of community and company loyalty.

regulation of particular work-based identities, mirrors earlier approaches such as the 'neo-human relations' school. In any event, these new management strategies continue to rely on the traditional psychological contract of employee commitment traded for organizational careers.

Contemporary flexible organizations challenge these models by breaking down the organizational side of the bargain. This weakens the link between normative corporate cultures and managers' appropriation of them through identifying their interests directly with those of the organization. The problem becomes how to ensure that employees will act optimally when the practices of governing organizations are constantly in flux. According to one influential school of thought in the Foucauldian tradition, the shift from bureaucratic to entrepreneurial styles of management is accompanied by attempts to forge new forms of subjectivity among employees. For example, Du Gay (1996: 119) argues that the aim of the new enterprise culture is to produce 'self-regulating, productive individuals whose sense of self-worth is inextricably linked to the "excellent" performance of their work and, thus, to the success of the company employing them'. Organizational cultures now require employees to take responsibility for the diligent and dedicated monitoring and improvement of their own work performance. The ideal employee becomes the striving, self-improving individual who regards unthinking conformity as an indicator of insufficient initiative and a moral failure to take responsibility for one's own destiny. Crucially, they do this in relation to ideals that serve the interests of the organization, but are framed in terms of an abstract 'good' person *unconnected* to any particular firm.

Precisely this transformation in management discourse occurred in 'Tech', as Kunda and Van Maanen (1999) discovered when they returned there in the 1990s. As a result of declining financial performance, 'Tech' had undergone a series of upheavals, ending its costly no-lay-off policy and carrying out large-scale downsizing. At the same time, the rhetoric of organizational communities and cultures was being replaced by talk of markets and entrepreneurs. In this context, managers and professionals are expected to regard their work (or business unit) as a product or service to be sold to others within the firm. Employees are urged to take ownership of their jobs, and responsibility for the design and development of a career itself shifts from the employer towards worker-owned 'employability'. Kunda and Van Maanen (1999: 75–6) conclude that the 'loyal subjects of the 1980s may have become the entrepreneurial agents of the 1990s ... [whose survival] depends not only on the usefulness or value of the services they offer but also on their sales skills, communication abilities, and image-building talents'.

This literature on the culture of control is extremely valuable in highlighting the role of the entrepreneurial ethos in 'individualizing the middle-class career' (Savage 2000: 139). The cultural meanings of work, employment, and career have been fundamentally recast over the past two decades. While we would not want to represent organizational culture as determinant in the formation of employees' identities, the character of the managerial and professional career has been redefined. Organizational loyalty and commitment are inevitably eroded when the substance of company cultures is no longer grounded in de facto employment guarantees and protection from external competition. Employees come to view their particular firm more instrumentally, as providing the right opportunities for them at the time. The organization may then be viewed as offering resources and scope for self-development, rather than the basis for allegiance and identity formation. A career thus becomes a more individualistic project designed for oneself.

An analysis of managers' career stories found that they were indeed dominated by such a 'market' narrative. As detailed in Box 4.3, managers placed themselves as strategic actors making choices in a social world constituted by market-like interactions.

This 'individualizing' of the career can be understood as part of a wider societal change, as the sociologists Beck (1992, 2000*a*) and Giddens (1990, 1991) remind us. They emphasize that the sharp decline in both the power and legitimacy of authoritative norms, and in the capacity of social

---

Box 4.3 Contemporary managers' narrative identities

In an Australian study, Martin and Wajcman (2004) explore the work identities of a group of middle managers in the private sector, arguing that 'market' narratives have become key to managerial careers. When presenting themselves to significant others, managers no longer focus on positioning themselves primarily in relation to the demands of strongly enforced company norms or bureaucratic politics. Instead, they focus on constructing and presenting marketable images of themselves in universalistic terms. One interviewee, reflecting on how things had changed and on his view of loyalty, drew a contrast with career patterns of the fairly recent past to explain how he imagined his career. He emphasized his perception of the contemporary firm's approach:

'How companies become best in class now is no longer . . . you strap six of your best managers into a harness and just drive them . . . 60 hours a week for five years. You no longer do that. You're looking for innovation, flexibility, people fast on their feet with good ideas . . . [Companies] don't want puppy dog loyalty . . . What a company needs is a high level of innovation, aggression and ideas that they couldn't have got from a loyal guy who has been here for 20 years. You get that from a guy who walks through the door and who is prepared to leave another organization.' (Business development manager, male, mid-30s) (Martin and Wajcman 2004: 252).

The managers in this study maintained a critical distance from company cultures, while being able to strategize around the new risks of more marketized career paths. A central motif was their ability to control their work and satisfy their preference for interesting, challenging, and pleasurable work. Explanations for taking particular jobs were commonly presented as active choices so that expected roles were reversed: employees became consumers of jobs and their employers sellers of workplaces. The authors conclude that, while companies may once have unequivocally supported the cultural supply of this identity, it has now taken on a life of its own that firms are clearly incapable of controlling.

institutions to dictate people's biographies, gives rise to a new form of identity formation oriented around the lifelong 'project' of constructing and exploring the self. While these changes represent a kind of 'freeing' of individuals from institutional and normative constraints, they also make people much more susceptible to the risks of their life decisions, notably in the labour market. At the heart of the individualistic career is people's capacity to *choose* how they will respond to new work circumstances, and to what extent they will play the game or try to adapt the rules to suit themselves.

Employees' ability to successfully negotiate the risks of market-based careers will vary considerably according to their resources (such as cultural capital), as will their self-image. As we noted above, there is ample evidence that the demise of stable career structures associated with delayering has produced many disillusioned, demoralized, and emotionally detached middle managers, suffering from 'survivor syndrome' (Littler et al. 2003). For others, however, the new work cultures provide opportunities for shaping their own career trajectory.

Indeed, those at the top of the skill distribution, in contrast to those at the bottom, have reaped large benefits from the changes in employment relations wrought by the shareholder value society. Drawing on the 2001 California Workforce Survey, Fligstein and Shin (2004) report that, during the 1980s and 1990s, the effect of downsizing was to intensify work for managers and professionals, lengthen their work hours and lessen their job security. But the financial rewards were very high. Managers and professionals also report higher job satisfaction and fulfilment from their work. They enjoyed the workplace and their colleagues, and had more opportunities to make a difference in the workplace. For workers at the top, the intensification of work has increased their sense of personal efficacy at work. Fligstein and Shin find this ironic, but it makes sense if people in this position think they are more able to take control over their careers and trade their skills into higher incomes. The real irony is that career structures have not been revolutionized, but managerial and professional employees view their careers as if they have been.

Gendered Career Paths

While the impact of organizational restructuring on work and careers has been the focus of much management literature, an equally significant change has been the remarkable movement of women into professional and managerial jobs. This development has received much less attention in standard management texts and, we believe, warrants more extensive consideration in a book on the modern workplace.

Sex equality in employment is now enshrined in the law as well as in equal opportunity and diversity policies at company level. In the UK, for example, 64 per cent of workplaces surveyed in 1998 had equal opportunity policies (Cully et al. 1999). Moreover, the framing of the contemporary career model around performance and merit should displace selection processes based on ascriptive markers such as social background, age, race, ethnicity, and sex. Some even claim that new models of portfolio careers, and the nature of the post-industrial corporation, are especially suited to women. So are women now taking their rightful place alongside men at all levels of organizations, and if not, why not?

A cursory look at the statistics reveals that although women now comprise equal numbers with men in many professions, such as law and medicine, and are very evident in junior to middle management, the top rungs of most professions and organizations remain heavily male dominated. Although there has been an overall increase in women working in management jobs, women still comprise less than a quarter of executives and only one in ten company directors in the UK (Equal Opportunities Commission 2002). In the Fortune 500 companies in the USA, the percentage of women holding corporate officer positions nearly doubled, from 8.7 per cent in 1995 to 15.7 per cent in 2003 (Global Information Network 2002). Reviewing global data covering women in professional and managerial roles, Wirth (2001) concludes that women are still segregated into sex-stereotyped management functions such as HRM and administration. Such data indicate that the glass ceiling has not disappeared. In considering possible explanations for this we will explore the implications for the notion of the individualized career, which may after all be a gendered construct. We will argue that the very idea of a career is grounded in masculine organizational cultures.

Historically, the formation of the white-collar career was built on a gender division of labour in both the public and private spheres. The development of large bureaucracies around the turn of the twentieth century drew large numbers of women into low-grade clerical work, allowing middle-class men to gain rapid promotion. Most organizations operated a strictly gendered segregation of occupations in which women and men were recruited into different grades of employment, with different salary scales and promotion prospects. Many imposed marriage bars on their female workforce, forcing them to retire on marriage and to become full-time housewives. The bureaucratic career in various institutions, such as the British Civil Service, the Post Office, and Lloyds Bank, was defined in male terms (Savage and Witz 1992). Until the last third of the twentieth century, then, sex-based ascription was standard practice for filling managerial positions.

Equally, there was a significant association between men's life course and their career prospects. For men, acquiring a family was desirable for the move into management and represented long-term stability and responsibility. Typically, a wife was expected to carry out a range of duties for her husband, freeing him to devote more time to the organization's affairs. The traditional model of career was based on a gender contract that privileged men as workers and defined women who entered the workplace as family-oriented persons. 'The attributes and activities of the "worker" are constructed together with, and as the other side of, those of his feminine counterpart, the "housewife" ' (Pateman 1988: 135). The organizational career has its origins in these sexual divisions.

It is increasingly recognized that the very concept of a career, with its hierarchical model of continuous service and regular promotion progress, is gendered (Dex 1987; Evetts 1996). As we noted in Chapter 3, there has been a profound cultural shift in gender norms, with new generations of women more strongly oriented to employment than their mothers. While many feminist authors (for example, Fraser 1997; Walby 1997) would agree that a new gender regime has been established, the structure of a career in management remains at odds with women's life-cycle patterns of work and childbearing. The career stage when the workload and commitment necessary to succeed are most intensive coincides with peak childrearing years. The developmental trajectory of a career is still designed to fit men's life course. Women's careers, which are generally 'broken' or 'interrupted' in order to have and to care for children, are thereby rendered not just different but deficient.

This career break is crucial in explaining the relative absence of senior women managers in, for example, the British National Health Service where the 'golden pathway' to rapid career progress requires both continuous commitment and the ability to be geographically mobile. A survey of their top managers (NHS Women's Unit 1994) found that most senior managers had to be very mobile during their careers. A lack of geographical mobility was understood by respondents to be a barrier to career progress. Multiple relocations were a feature of these managers' careers. In the context of careers in MNCs, geographical mobility assumes even greater significance. The globalization of national economies expands the demand for managers available for posting to positions all over the world. Several studies argue that international experience is an increasingly important step along the career path to senior management, a requirement that has negatively affected the opportunities for women in management (Adler 2002). The number of women sent on foreign assignments is extremely small.

In the face of these structural barriers, many women have adopted an alternative strategy for their careers. One can distinguish between linear organizational careers, which involve promotion to positions of managerial responsibility, and professional occupations, where doing the job may include taking breaks and part-time employment (Crompton and Sanderson 1990; Crompton and Harris 1998). For example, a career in medicine readily accommodates flexible hours and career breaks, in contrast to more managerially driven areas like banking. However, while the professional option does offer women a way of combining family and career, it nevertheless still bars women from the higher reaches of professions. In the USA, the 'mommy track' describes a variety of organizational arrangements that allow women in management the opportunity to spend more time at home with their young children (Schwartz 1992). Although part of the career strategy of many women involves such breaks from their paid work, as Evetts (1996) notes, activities other than paid work do not contribute positively to their promotion prospects. Indeed, they damage them, as evidenced by figures on the 'mother gap', which represents the difference in lifetime earnings between equivalently educated women with and without children: for a woman with two children these figures are £285,000 for the low-skilled, £140,000 for the mid-skilled and £19,000 for the high-skilled (Rake 2000; for the USA, see Budig and England 2001; Waldfogel 1997).

Marriage and fatherhood do not present serious career dilemmas for men seeking promotion in professional and managerial occupations. In their study of sex discrimination in employment, Collinson et al. (1990: 193–4) provide extensive evidence of the way employers' preconceptions about gender roles in the family affect decision-making. 'For men, real, imagined or potential domestic responsibilities were usually evaluated as a positive indication of stability, flexibility, compatibility and motivation, while for women, they were often viewed negatively as confirmation of unreliability and a short-term investment in work'. This discrepancy is not a matter of favouring men over women in all circumstances, but simply reflects the perception of jobs themselves as gendered. Indeed, employers positively discriminate in selecting women 'homemakers' for jobs linked with low pay and low status in female-dominated workforces (Curran 1988). But where a job such as that of a manager is sex-typed for men, the 'ideal candidate' is a family man. There is even evidence that managers with working wives are paid less than their counterparts with full-time housewives (Hotchkiss and Moore, 1999).

Much of the literature on gender and careers thus focuses on women's difference: the way women's experience of a career differs as a result of their family circumstances. However, many women have adapted to the predominant male model of a successful manager or professional and are pursuing the same organizational careers as the men. They have made a conscious choice either not to have children, to defer having them, or to organize childcare and domestic life so as to be able to dedicate themselves to their careers. A high proportion of successful women in senior positions are not parents, in sharp contrast to their male counterparts. Hewlett's (2002) survey reports that 49 per cent of women over forty who earn more than $100,000 a year in the USA are childless compared to 19 per cent of men in the same category. This has led to talk of a fertility crisis among educated professional women, as they reject motherhood in favour of employment. For such women, there is an increasing convergence between their career orientations and men's. For example, the study referred to in Box 4.3 found that the career aspirations of a comparable group of men and women managers hardly differ, with them being equally likely to see their work as central to their self-identity. They adopted similar individualized market narratives to describe their prospective careers and work lives, placing themselves as gender-neutral market actors in their career stories. These women are as ambitious as men and have embraced a similar lifestyle in which career commitment and ambition for advancement are central life interests. However, for all the similarities in career patterns and attitudes, this study, like many others, found that women remain disadvantaged with regard to pay and promotion prospects.

The Gendered Culture of Organizations

How then do we account for continuing sex discrimination in an environment of gender equality? Explaining the disjunction between discourse and reality requires a shift in focus from the formal character of organizations to more subtle inhibitors of women's achievement. There is a growing literature, known as gender and organizational analysis, that argues that gender relations are integral to the structure and practices of organizations and this is key to understanding how men define and dominate organizations (Hearn and Parkin 1987; Acker 1990; Mills and Tancred 1992; Halford et al. 1997; Wajcman 1998). Gendered processes operate on many institutional levels, from the open and explicit to more subtle discrete forms that are submerged in organizational decisions, even those that appear to have nothing to do with gender. They include the way men's influence is embedded in rules and procedures, in formal job definitions, and in functional roles as well as in everyday interactions. Through such cultural representations and meanings, people build their understandings of the gendered structure of work and opportunities. Indeed, organizations are one area in which widely disseminated images of gender are continuously invented and reproduced.

The historical legacy of men's virtual monopoly of the first management jobs is important in explaining the continuing predisposition of organizations to staff managerial jobs through sex-typing. 'For most of the twentieth century a "masculine ethic" of rationality dominated the spirit of managerialism and gave the manager role its defining image. It told men how to be successful as men in the new organizational worlds of the twentieth century' (Kanter 1977: 25). As a result, management was equated with masculinity. When women tried to enter management jobs, the 'masculine ethic' was invoked as an exclusionary principle. This labelling of manager as male gave men's entitlement to management jobs the sanction of custom, and once institutionalized, organizational practices resist alteration.

Take the example of recruitment. Research has shown that people tend to appoint in their own image. Powerful groups clearly have an interest in institutionalizing their privileges so that the fact men try to maintain their status is no surprise. However, even without conscious efforts, people have an automatic propensity to favour members of their own group. As Kanter (1977) pointed out long ago in her discussion of 'male homosociability', male managers tend to share a common language and understanding and so may feel most comfortable in each other's company. After all, filling management positions entails risks, and men's preponderance in management makes male choices appear as less risky. Practitioners often refer to this cultural dynamic as a 'men's club' which serves to perpetuate women's exclusion from power and influence. This is no doubt why a major US study found that 'open recruitment methods are associated with women holding a greater share of management jobs, while recruitment through informal networks increases men's share' (Reskin and McBrier 2000: 210). Formalized, rigorous and systematic approaches to assessment in selection appear less potentially discriminatory than more informal methods, especially in large establishments.

Assessment remains, however, a social and subjective process. Bias can occur in the identification of criteria against which assessment will be based. Jenkins (1986) has drawn a useful distinction between decisions based on specific job-related qualifications or experience (known as suitability criteria), and assessments about whether a person will fit in with the organization, other workers, or customers, known as acceptability criteria. During detailed observations of interviews, Collinson et al. (1990) found that managers used different (gender-based) criteria to assess whether applicants were able to meet the job requirements. For example, a form of behaviour described as 'showing initiative' and assessed as desirable when demonstrated by a male applicant, in a woman applicant was seen as 'pushy' and undesirable. Similarly, Curran (1988: 344) shows that managers often find it hard to separate the assessment of a quality such as leadership from the concept of masculinity. What is important about these findings, as Liff (2003: 434) stresses, is that they show that for some managers at least, gender becomes part of their assessment of suitability criteria. As with related findings on ethnicity, this raises questions about claims that recruiters can avoid discrimination by assessing only on those criteria necessary to do the job: 'If these criteria themselves embody gendered or race-based assumptions then this may be a necessary but not sufficient condition.'

Gender bias in judgements about the way jobs are performed is evident in the now ubiquitous performance management systems (PMSs), detailed in Chapter 5. It has been noted that 'impression management' may count for more than actual performance in obtaining good ratings in performance appraisal and in achieving success within organizational hierarchies, particularly for managers (Bowles and Coates 1993). There is some evidence to suggest that men are better players at this game than women, having and taking more opportunities to ensure high and appropriate visibility. The differential ability and willingness of men and women to engage in successful impression management is likely to be affected not only by their gender but also by the fact that their managers — the appraisers — are generally men. There is also considerable evidence that women tend to rate themselves less positively than do men (Fletcher 1999). These assessment systems are a key component of the move to individual performance-related pay. While the move to performance pay may have some advantages for gender equity, for example, by shifting pay away from automatic increments based on seniority and status, Rubery's (1995: 651) review of the evidence points 'to an overall deterioration in gender pay equity under performance-related pay'. This is due both to the highly discretionary character of the payment system and to the unfavourable context in which it is being implemented, one in which collective regulation and social norms of fairness and equality in labour markets are being dismantled.

Changing Modes of Management?

The individualization of careers and the rise of performance management have thrown a spotlight on the nature of managerial style and qualities of leadership. While the criterion of acceptability, including the possession of appropriate cultural capital, has always been important for a management career, in bureaucratic organizations greater emphasis was placed on formal credentials and technical expertise. The move to flexible corporate structures places a higher premium on attitudinal, behavioural, and personality factors. According to the rhetoric of management gurus, the post-bureaucratic organization requires managers with less hierarchical, more empathetic, and cooperative styles of management. Questions of gender difference have been at the forefront of these debates. In particular, are the qualities generally attributed to women especially suitable for the post-industrial corporation?

Certainly there has been much discussion of the need for a more open style of management as part of the new human resource/cultural management model. Successful firms are described as people-oriented and decentralized, networks uncluttered by bureaucratic layers of management. Leadership is now concerned with fostering shared visions, shared values, shared directions, and shared responsibility, requiring a softer edge, a more qualitative approach. In contrast to the command-and-control leadership style associated with men, it is suggested that women have a more consensual style of management and that their seemingly feminine skills of communication and collaborative working will be at a premium. Some feminist writers in management schools have also been emphasizing women's difference, arguing that women executives are making it to the top 'because of—not in spite of—certain characteristics generally considered to be "feminine" ' (Rosener 1990: 119–20). The conclusion drawn in this literature is that the norm of effective management will be based on the way women do things. This discussion of women's different style mirrors a shift in the language of equal opportunities from a concern with equality to 'valuing diversity', in this case, a valuing of diversity in management styles (Liff and Wajcman 1996).

Echoing the research on service work discussed in Chapter 2, the management literature considers the advantages women have, because of communication and social skills, to be natural attributes. Certainly a large number of studies confirm that there are definite gender stereotypes of leadership, with the male style typically described as directive, aggressive, and task-oriented, while women are seen as more participative, team-oriented, and supportive of their colleagues, bosses, and subordinates. It is striking how the copious literature on leadership style is permeated by stereotypical dualisms, such as that between hard and soft, reason and intuition (Helgesen 1990; Fagenson 1993). Instead of questioning the gendered nature of these dichotomies, they are simply inverted. Leadership traits that correspond with male traits, like dominance, aggressiveness, and rationality, are now presented more negatively, while formerly devalued feminine qualities, like soft and emotional, are presented positively. Although these portrayals have intuitive appeal, the extent to which they correspond with actual management practice is questionable (Powell 1993; Vinkenburg et al. 2000).

Tellingly, a study of senior managers in five high-technology MNCs found that while a high proportion of both female and male respondents believe that there are sex differences in management style, there is remarkable similarity in the way they describe *their own* management style (Wajcman 1998). The majority of male managers, like the women, claimed to manage in a cooperative, consultative manner. Rather than concluding that men are managing like women, the author suggests that their endorsement of the people-centred approach reflects the current vogue for soft HRM. Moreover, the study revealed a major discrepancy between this feminized management discourse and the reality of managerial practice. Both women and men stressed that the harsh business context of continuous restructuring has precipitated a return to a more traditional hierarchical structure, requiring both sexes to conform to the 'hard' macho stereotype of 'managing like a man'. This finding is reinforced by Billing and Alvesson's research review (2000: 154), which concluded that there is little evidence for the existence of a distinctive feminine leadership 'as an empirical phenomenon'. The similarities between the attitudes and behaviour of male and female managers far outweigh the differences. How women manage depends far more on the organization and the task in hand than on their gender. How women are judged is another matter.

Managers of both sexes must present themselves so as to project an image of the authoritative manager. Yet Eagly et al. (1992) found that females and males in leadership roles are evaluated similarly by their subordinates except when behaving in an authoritarian manner, when females were evaluated more negatively. As Acker (1990: 152) has argued, the sexualization of women's bodies presents a particular problem for women managers: 'women's bodies—female sexuality, their ability to procreate and their pregnancy, breast-feeding, and child care, menstruation, and mythic "emotionality"—are suspect, stigmatized, and used as grounds for control and exclusion.' Without constant vigilance regarding self-presentation at work, women run the risk of not being treated seriously as managers. Much feminist literature has stressed that senior women walk a tightrope between presenting as feminine enough and at the same time as authoritative enough. Some organization theorists have also identified the ways in which male sexuality underpins the patriarchal culture of professional and organizational life (Hearn et al. 1989 Cockburn 1991; Gherardi 1995). It is men's bodies that are inscribed in the managerial function and women's bodies that are defined as problematic.

Self-presentation and style have become key elements of the job performance of managers (Kunda 1992; Casey 1995), and men in corporations are also increasingly self-conscious about their image. This is consistent with the emergence of new forms of marketplace masculinity that display entrepreneurialism and risk taking (Cheng 1996; Kerfoot and Knights 1996). The adaptive organization requires managers with charismatic personalities, displaying flexibility, dynamism, and interpersonal skills. As a result, the criteria for advancement across a broad range of management jobs become more intangible and implicit, more a matter of personal compatibility and perceptions. The appropriate 'personality package' is becoming more salient for career success. According to Brown (1995), the current hyperbole about the flexible, communicative, and entrepreneurial manager may paradoxically be producing a narrowing of the social backgrounds of senior managers. McDowell's (1997) study of merchant banks in the city of London supports this view, noting that while the rules of entry and promotion have become increasingly personalized, recruits from elitist backgrounds, schools, and universities have retained their dominance. The increasing significance of cultural capital, albeit cast in a new form, disadvantages individuals from working-class origins, women, and ethnic minorities. Confidence, personal authority, and skill—the embodied dispositions of class—come to be seen as the prerogative of those destined to rise up the organizational ladder (Savage 2000: 146).

Conclusions

This chapter has considered the contemporary character of white-collar careers. We have argued that while there has been substantial corporate restructuring leading to a reduction in the opportunities for promotion, predictions of the demise of the bureaucratic career are exaggerated. Downsizing and delayering do not necessarily spell an end to hierarchy. The rungs on the ladder may be fewer and further apart, but many traditional career ladders remain intact. At the same time, however, organizational pressures to achieve shareholder value and greater labour market flexibility have increased risk and uncertainty. So too has the competition for access to careers intensified, due to the influx of women into professional and managerial jobs. These trends have radically ruptured the psychological contract between organizations and their employees about reciprocal obligations at work. Employers not only want their employees to be flexible and work harder but also to accept responsibility for managing their own careers. As a result, organizational loyalty has declined and people have come to view their careers in more individualistic terms. On balance, changes to the structure of organizations have been far more modest than changes in career identity and orientations.

Yet some of the new features of the contemporary organization may turn out to be mutually contradictory. Many of the changes in employer strategies reflect market pressures from outside the firm, rather than being in direct response to internal requirements. While the new flattened structures have provided novel opportunities for multiemployer careers for a select group of managers, they have also created problems of high staff turnover, low morale, and absenteeism. Organizations rely on the commitment and corporate loyalty of their employees to function effectively and policies that encourage individualism, while efficient in the short term, present major problems in terms of retaining experienced staff and training costs. Moreover, it is not clear that the current enthusiasm for outsourcing and contracting out many of the activities that are not considered central to the corporation have in practice reaped the promised productivity gains. Whether the current mix of internal and external restructuring will be sustainable in the longer term is still an open question.

By way of a postscript, it is important to note that arguments about a shift from bureaucratic to flexible firms with charismatic leadership have more relevance in some sectors than others. The focus of much research, including that on gender equity, has been on large organizations, but signs of change may be found among knowledge-intensive firms in the new economy where interfirm alliances and network organizations are thriving. Studies of high-technology sectors show that firms governed by networks are more conducive to speed, innovation, and learning than are hierarchies. Smith-Doerr (2004) argues that they are also more conducive to women's career success (see Box 4.4). She found that women scientists working in small, biotechnology companies are eight times more likely than their university counterparts to head a research laboratory. Perhaps the new flexible network structures, which are said to be the key to the future world economy (Castells 2001; Powell 2001), represent a genuine move toward employee empowerment and will produce a new model of career in the twenty-first century.

Box 4.4 Network careers

Smith-Doerr (2004) analysed the careers of 2,062 life scientists in the USA by gender for two patterns: early entrance into the biotechnology industry and promotion within network versus hierarchical organizations. She found that gender does not affect when a scientist enters the biotechnology industry, but that men are more likely to attain early supervisory-level positions across different organizational settings. Comparing careers in large universities and pharmaceutical corporations with those in biotechnology firms, she argues that the two organizational forms—hierarchy and network—provide different employment experiences for female scientists. Contrary to the standard view that the formal rules of bureaucracy can promote equity, women's career prospects are much better in small, biotechnology firms. They have project-based teams, flatter organizational structures, and multiplex relations with external collaborators. This flexibility translates into gender equity for the following reasons: it increases transparency in organizations, the project-based nature of work allows greater choice in forming collegial relationships, and collaboration rather than individual competition is fostered. Although part of the explanation may lie in the relatively small size of the firms, and the relative youth of the sample, the author's study points to the significance of variation in organizational form.

How Is Performance Defined, Measured, and Rewarded?

Chapter 4 considered the meaning of careers. We now show the ways in which individual career choices are constrained by requirements to hit predefined targets for performance. Ever since the emergence of large, formal organizations, the issue of how work expectations are established, and of how performance is assessed against them, has been a central theme. Performance management is a key indicator of how organizations establish employees' obligations and hence of how life in organizations is experienced. A sharp illustration of the spread of its ideas is provided by a study of a Norwegian hospital, where even the priest had performance measures that included the number of last rites performed (Modell 2001: 456).

One story line says that, as a result of long experience, obligations can be specified with reasonable precision and that employees are likely to be rewarded for their achievement and penalized for failure. A commonplace in discussions of performance management is the acronym SMART, meaning that objectives are specific, measurable, achievable (sometimes 'agreed', an important difference discussed below), realistic, and time-bound. This chapter addresses the extent to which the management of performance is a less technical and clear-cut process than the SMART acronym implies. In doing so, it considers the uncertainty and negotiability of apparently hard numbers. Such numbers either specify performance (e.g. a target to sell X units) or, more subtly, define its achievement (the employee produces figures to show that the figure was equal to or more than X). We do not restrict ourselves to the specifics of PMSs, pursuing some broader links with studies from accounting, and consider the negotiability of performance standards, drawing on studies of bargaining about organizational rules and of symbols and rituals in organizational life.

The issue of performance came into particular prominence from the 1980s as the result of a series of connected events including:

- the rise of the market for corporate control (see Chapter 9): firms were increasingly assessed on their ability to meet financial objectives, with takeover as the penalty for failure;

- the development of the strategic business unit, with each such unit (numbering hundreds in large firms) being held accountable not just for doing a set task but also for the efficiency with which the task was performed;
- in the public sector, the arrival of the new public management, with its stress on performance against targets and its explicit copying of (what were believed to be) private sector models of efficient capitalism; and
- a drive to control the performance of individual employees, which was encouraged by the above trends and facilitated by the decline of institutional structures for setting pay. In the UK, it is estimated that 75 per cent of employees were covered by collective bargaining in 1980, a figure that had fallen to 40 per cent by 1998 (Brown et al. 2003).

The process of PMS is something to which many more employees are subject than was the case in the past. In 1998, formal performance appraisals were conducted in 79 per cent of British workplaces (Cully et al. 1999: 71).

In addition to material on PMSs themselves, there is a much wider literature. At its broadest, it addresses the question of how employees are led to obey organizational expectations as to their behaviour and how far, and why, they challenge these expectations. There are two main traditions on which we draw. One looks at budgetary and other standards set down for managers, and addresses how far managers manipulate accounting data. There appear to have been rather few studies here. The second is much larger, addressing routine employees and the 'games' that they play in, for example, pilfering goods or bending payments systems to their own advantage. It is notable that a study of 'organizational misbehaviour' focuses almost exclusively on the latter (Ackroyd and Thompson 1999). The emphasis is important, for example in developing the argument of Chapter 2, that even the lowest-level employees have means of making their work meaningful. Yet it also needs balancing with a view of the, arguably more costly and significant, practices of other groups. Some reasons for this emphasis on low-level employees and the neglect of other groups are given in Box 5.1.

Broadly, there are three critical views on these issues:

1. Performance management is part of a 'disciplinary society'. The presumption here is that the systems work as intended to regiment individuals. In some accounts, the systems are indeed seen as designed to meet the purposes of their controllers. But increasingly

> **Box 5.1 What about the managers? Why managers' 'fiddles' are neglected**
>
> 1. Managers are more likely to permit access to study worker behaviour than managerial malpractice.
> 2. It can easily be assumed that managers generally act in the interests of the firm (because they are part of the managerial class, or for other reasons) so that fiddles are rare and the action of atypical individuals, whereas workers are on the other side of the fence and are thus more likely to practise fiddles on a large scale.
> 3. Researchers with a broadly radical perspective think that workers are more interesting than are managers.
> 4. Managerial fiddles may be buried in financial reports, whereas workers' fiddles are more directly observable.

    common have been arguments that rules and discourses control everybody and that they have grown up without conscious action.
2. Performance management is indeed a performance, that is, a negotiation or in the terms of Power (1997) a 'ritual'. Power stresses that we are in an 'audit society' but he sees the auditing as involving a negotiated acceptance that measurement has been carried out, rather than a hard and objective process. A strong statement would be that it is all about performance with no real substance. A weaker position is that rituals and performance are important but that these are part of a definition of reality.
3. Performance management varies in its meaning and extent between societies and organizations. Its effects are neither all-embracing (as suggested under argument 1) nor negligible (as strong versions of argument 2 suggest) but depend on how it is interpreted and how it relates to other aspects of an organization's operations. In some circumstances, clear targets are welcomed by employees.

Stated thus, the approaches are caricatures, but they have a role nonetheless. In particular, scholars who have stressed either of the first two views tend to underline only one aspect of the situation. The first argument implies that rationalization is the dominant social force and that people are powerless against it. The second argument often implies that the idea of an audit society is a game or ritual, an important one but separate from any real outcomes. According to the third argument, everything is contingent and context-specific, and thus it fails to adduce any common lessons. A perspective that draws from all three is needed.

The chapter has five main sections. After discussing the growth and operation of PMS in the first, it addresses the themes of appraisal as discipline and as ritual in the second and third sections respectively. The fourth section considers the meaning of rules in organizations, while the fifth examines the negotiation of budgets.

Rise and Operation of PMS

As studies of performance appraisal regularly note, definitions of performance measurement are far from exact (Bach 2000). The basic idea is that there should be formally prescribed standards, with the goal of giving workers clarity as to what is expected of them. The reason for this, though much of the PMS literature is curiously silent on the point, is that the employment contract is inherently imprecise. The industrial sociologist Baldamus (1961) was one of the first to develop the argument: the labour contract may be able to specify some details, such as the number of hours of labour required, but it cannot define the level of care and effort that is put in; still less can it specify such things as loyalty and commitment that firms increasingly expect. Looking at the matter from the worker's point of view, nor can the contract establish in any detail the employer's obligations in such areas as workplace safety, the degree of job security, or opportunities for autonomy and skill development. A PMS is one means of managing this uncertainty.

It is thus not surprising to find proponents of one particular approach tending to contrast it with alternatives in ways that may be sharper than is justified. The standard account is that PMSs evolved through four stages. First came early ratings scales, where employees were evaluated against desired attributes. This was felt to focus too much on personal traits, with the problem that it is very hard for managers to identify personality attributes and that links between these and work performance are tenuous. The approach was moreover one of measurement against defined standards so that it tended to be seen as a negative, control-oriented system with no emphasis on helping the employee to develop skills. Second came performance appraisal, which tried to use more objective criteria but which left the manager in the uncomfortable role of, as a celebrated critique put it, 'playing God' (McGregor 1957). Third was management by objectives (MBO) that tried to be less evaluative and more developmental. But critics argued that it neglected subtle aspects of performance that were hard to pin down as objectives and that it tended to encourage a focus on the process (saying what an objective was, and producing detailed evidence to say that it had been obtained) rather than meaningful performance (Armstrong and Baron 1998: 36). Finally, came the full PMS. This term was first used by the US firm Corning Glass, and it combined MBO, performance appraisal, and a process of salary review (Beer and Ruh 1976). Later refinements stress the importance of treating performance management as a process of development which is continuous rather than being based on formal annual reviews. There is also growing emphasis on 'competencies', a stress which tends to bring back in the interest in personal attributes as opposed to purely outcomes-based assessment.

A story of progressive development is undermined by the perpetuation of critiques. The tone was set by the analysis of McGregor who became famous for his distinction between Theory X and Theory Y styles, the former being based on command-and-control ideas and the latter on ideas of human relations and tapping unrealized 'human potential'. McGregor's hope that social science would offer a scientific solution to the problems of people management foundered on the difficulty (or indeed, impossibility) of finding a 'durable formula that can transform the conflicting, albeit complex, interests that lie at the heart of the labour process and employment relationship' (Thompson and McHugh 2002: 53) — transformed, presumably, into a tractable process based on agreed principles. McGregor's hopes that firms would adopt Theory Y and that all would then be well have plainly not been met. At best Theories X and Y reflect competing emphases that will characterize any organization and that will be in permanent tension with each other. This point was implicit in the critique of performance appraisal.

The alternative, based explicitly on MBO, involved the subordinate rather than the manager identifying performance goals and writing a plan, an emphasis on analysis rather than appraisal, and giving the subordinate an active role instead of being 'a pawn in the chess game called management development' (McGregor 1957: 91). Yet similar claims have continued to run through the literature ever since. The idea of a PMS as a developmental tool that allows the subordinate to address skills and training needs expresses just the same themes, and runs up against familiar problems.

These problems have been laid out in a series of later critiques (Grint 1993; Newton and Findlay 1996). These argue that the tensions in traditional systems continue to exist. They include the following:

- There is the problem of the superior acting as both evaluator and coach: is the process evaluative or developmental?

- The assumption that appraisal can meet the needs of both the appraisee and management is based on a highly questionable model of the organization as having unproblematic shared goals.
- The choice of whether to fix a rating to the end of a process of appraisal (which raises issues of fairness and consistency) or to have no specific rating (which makes comparison across individuals impossible) has proved very hard. (Witness the fact that about half of UK organizations using formal processes of performance management have overall ratings, while half do not: Armstrong and Baron 1998: 105.)
- Managing the process entails numerous problems of the criteria to be used. These include excessive formalization, the fact that judgements can be contaminated by a tendency to avoid extremes of any scale, by the 'halo effect' (evaluation on one criterion influences evaluations on others) and by an 'affinity effect' (giving favourable ratings to people like oneself). Issues of subjectivity, fairness, and consistency continue to loom large. Note here also that affinity effects are highly likely to sustain gender and ethnic inequalities (see Chapter 4). Bevan and Thompson (1992) report, from a study of four UK organizations, that managers tend to rate men and women against different criteria and that the use of qualitative assessments rather than quantitative measurements is likely to allow gender bias to creep in.

The concrete purchase of these issues may be illustrated by firms that claim to be at the 'leading edge' of management practice and that thus might have succeeded in minimizing problems. Yet, in three such firms, appraisal was felt by managers to be bureaucratic and inconsistent. Though the firms claimed to use appraisal to develop skills and 'employability', downsizing meant that there was little time for training and that career development opportunities were restricted (Stiles et al. 1997). In these firms, the management process was largely top–down in nature, which meant that any real chance for employees to shape objectives (under the 'agreed' element of the SMART acronym) was limited. The result was that employees either responded passively or withdrew any degree of commitment.

The most substantial effort to measure the impact of PMSs is the study by Gallie et al. (1998) of 3,500 British employees, conducted in 1992. They start from a model of 'bureaucratic control', meaning a system of individual career progression, assessment of performance against standards, and formal appraisal; such systems 'are now referred to' as PMSs (ibid.: 60). More than half the professional/managerial and lower non-manual employees in the sample worked under bureaucratic control. Among skilled manual workers, the proportion was one-third, while it fell to a quarter for semi- and non-skilled employees. Comparison with a previous survey in 1986 underlined an increase in the use of appraisal and growing use of 'the chief instruments of bureaucratic control even in a period when chances of progression were in decline' (ibid.: 69).

One key point warrants emphasis. This analysis suggests that work is not now of a 'post-bureaucratic' kind, meaning that formal bureaucracy has been supplanted by systems based on trust and autonomy. It reveals instead a growth of bureaucratic control mechanisms, albeit alongside the erosion of the traditional career. Recent evidence supports this interpretation (Nolan and Wood 2003).

What does a PMS do to workers? The thesis of a disciplinary society would expect that it will reduce employee discretion. Yet Gallie et al. (1998: 71–2) demonstrate exactly the reverse pattern, of rising task discretion with higher usage of a PMS, and several other investigations within specific organizations confirm this finding (e.g. Edwards et al. 1998).

How can we explain this apparently paradoxical result? We may discount arguments to the effect that employees are misled and are in fact being subject to more and more insidious forms of control. Case studies that have inquired into this possibility have concluded that employees are perfectly capable of understanding systems of control to which they are subject. The core of the answer is that there is no opposition between control and discretion: the ability to decide how to do the specifics of the task is wholly consistent with being appraised on the results. Indeed, the control of the worker may be heightened because responsibility is now passed on to her.

Research suggests that this may well be the case. There is clear evidence of a growth in the number of control mechanisms to which employees are subject. Green (2001) reports on seven possible sources of pressure to work hard, and shows that the prevalence of six of them increased in the UK between 1988 and 1997. 'Reports and appraisal' remained at a relatively low level, however (mentioned by 24 per cent of employees in 1997, up from 15 per cent in 1988). Their effect seems to have been indirect, for example through fellow employees, rather than strongly direct. There is also evidence that the rising use of performance measurement is associated with a fall in commitment and satisfaction (Gallie et al. 2001).

What, though, is control of employees intended to achieve, and does it work? Solutions to this puzzle turn on either its disciplinary or its symbolic functions.

Appraisal as Discipline

A clear statement of the disciplinary elements of appraisal schemes can be found in the work of Townley (1996: 571, 1999). Drawing on the work of Michel Foucault and using the example of the language of such schemes in British universities, she argues that 'as systems of accountability they act as disciplinary technologies, imposing an order on a series of events and also act[ing] on the individual to give both a sense of identity and to construct what it is to be accountable'. Writing more generally on accountancy, Hoskin and Macve (1994: 68) state that accounting is a form of power and knowledge because 'it disciplines behaviourally even while it provides expert disciplinary information, and it does both by the way as a practice it turns events into writing and subjects them to examination'.

Formal systems at a UK petrochemicals company were found to have 'freed, rather than constrained, dominant power groups to define and deal with reality in their own way' (Barlow 1989: 513). Career development, for example, depended more on social contacts and 'having the ear' of top management than on the formal appraisal system. As a manager told Barlow, 'if we were asked for a good man [*sic*], we certainly wouldn't go hunting through appraisal forms' (ibid.: 507).

Though having a common focus on the hidden meanings of appraisal, the emphases here are different. The last study stresses the ways in which it suits dominant interest groups. Townley makes the broader argument that it is the system of rules itself that has certain effects, with no one necessarily gaining from the process. If we take this stronger approach as a starting point, there are some clear benefits. Any organizational practice can have unintended consequences. It is also important to recognize that rules and procedures can define how people should behave, creating a terrain of language and assumptions that makes some practices acceptable and others illegitimate.

Yet there is a worrying tendency here to assume that the consequence (the establishment of a certain language and set of assumptions) is immanent in the cause (the invention of appraisal schemes or of accounting standards). This is often termed a teleological approach. As critics of Foucault-inspired writing point out, there is a deep irony here: the writings stress the creation of individual identity and criticize 'meta-narratives' and analyses in terms of cause and effect, and yet they tend towards a meta-narrative of their own, namely, that practices have determinate effects. A PMS can shape language and assumptions, but how far it does so will depend on other influences. Numerous studies now show that people are not tightly disciplined in standard ways. For example, Cowton and Dopson (2002) report that branch managers in a UK automotive distributive company responded to a new computerized accounting system in very different ways. We might add that they did not seem to express particular disquiet at any disciplinary 'gaze' to which they were subject, treating performance metrics as an unremarkable fact of organizational life.

Is it the case that people are led to conform, or that they learn to play the game? If the latter, is this game-playing wholly disconnected from day-to-day realities or does it have real consequences? Instances concern responses to targets. A standard aphorism is 'what gets measured gets managed'. So do people in fact focus on what gets measured to the neglect of other things, and in doing so do they manipulate figures in order to put their own behaviour in a good light? The evidence to give a decisive answer to these questions is not available. Examples can certainly be produced to show that games are played and rules are bent. But such examples are not decisive: we also need to know how common the relevant behaviour is, and where it is more or less common. To judge whether the disciplinary society has led to conformity, one would need evidence over a reasonable period of time to show that conformity had increased. Such specific evidence is generally lacking, not least because the relevant practices (bending figures and so on) will not be revealed through surveys.

Indeed, a long-established strand of writing has shown that rules and institutional processes help to define what is seen as possible. Batstone et al. (1977) for example draw extensively on such concepts as the 'mobilization of bias' and 'vocabularies of motive' to argue that some possibilities can be ruled out of order by the use of certain vocabularies and by mobilization around some themes and not others. Yet they also rendered these possibilities in precise form. They asked, for example, why workers do or do not develop collective attitudes. Their answer turned on the traditions on which different groups of workers could draw and the degree to which worker representatives aimed to mobilize around collective ideas.

A related study showed that what workers thought feasible depended on context. As opposed to those who expected that all workers everywhere would try to bargain about performance standards, it was shown that the boundaries of bargaining were defined by unquestioned rules (Edwards and Scullion 1982). For example, workers in some workplaces took it for granted that they could bargain over workloads and effort—negotiating with, and trying to pull the wool over the eyes of, the work study department was, as one worker memorably put it, 'the working man's birth right'. Yet, in other workplaces, the ability of managers to set performance standards went unquestioned. It was the politics of rules in particular places, and not any inherent tendency of the rules themselves, that was critical.

Some of the technical issues of appraisal are also pertinent here. The conventional literature on appraisal systems is full of the practical problems. What are the appropriate objectives, and how are they to be measured? Should rating scales be used, and if so what is to be done about the tendency of appraisers to avoid extremes of the scales and to suffer halo and other effects? If appraisal were a successful expression of a disciplinary society, these problems would be limited, whereas, as assessments of the technical literature stress, they are extremely widespread. As Newton and Findlay (1996) conclude, appraisal systems are part of a continuing contest over the terrain of work, not the successful creation of disciplined selves.

Performance Management, Ritual, and Symbol

Before addressing ritual in relation to performance management, it will be helpful to introduce the approach, social constructivism, that informs much of the analysis. We also draw on this approach later in the book, for example in discussing how the meaning of safety is socially constructed (Chapter 7) and how projects are created around 'globalization' (Chapter 10).

The core proposition of social constructivism is that people are active agents who create systems and institutions (Berger and Luckman 1967). The point was to argue against the 'functionalism' of much sociology of the 1960s, which saw people as slavishly following the norms of society and which tended to see society as a self-sustaining and equilibrating system. Social construction means that an institution such as a school is seen, not as having rules defined by 'society', but as the creation of the people within it. The core processes of social construction are:

- *externalization*: a pattern of behaviour is made external to the day-to-day interactions that create it; it is given a name and a tangible identity;
- *objectification*: this is the phase of accepting socially created institutions and practices as inevitable; and
- *internalization*: the phase when socially created rules and conventions come to be seen not just as objective facts but as legitimate.

The illustration given in Box 5.2 shows that the process of social construction can make what are in fact political issues seem natural and

> ## Box 5.2 Social construction of a job evaluation scheme
>
> Quaid (1993) studied a job evaluation scheme in the government of a Canadian province during 1980–5.
>
> *Externalization* involved the Hay job evaluation system, which was presented as scientific (thus discrediting the old system) and which helped to socialize people into the new approach.
>
> *Objectification* meant that social constructions were accepted as immutable, for example how points were awarded for job attributes.
>
> *Internalization* entailed acceptance of the new arrangements.
>
> According to Quaid (1993: 259), job evaluation 'beams back to employers and workers the notion that the current structure of inequality is right and just'.

inevitable. In this case, a way to measure performance was presented as objective when in many ways it simply reproduced 'subjective' understandings.

The core idea has many strengths. For example, a functionalist account of the breaking of school rules might say that the rules exist to promote order and that infractions are in some way deviant. A social constructivist would ask what the rules are in practice (e.g. why only some of the rules written in a rule book are enforced) and how pupils and teachers interact to 'negotiate order', wherein some infractions are tacitly tolerated. As soon as one makes such a statement, however, one shifts from a pure constructivist view to recognize that some groups are more powerful than others in making their social constructions effective.

The central value of a constructivist approach is then twofold. First, it stresses that people have choices and that the process of interaction will generate rules that may, in practice, run counter to formally stated rules. Such tacit rules can fill in the spaces of formal rules and help organizations to work, or challenge and undermine the formal rules, or do both at the same time. This is a fundamental feature of life in organizations. Second, questioning what seems to be inevitable or natural is a key part of thinking critically.

These themes are reflected in the idea that a performance or ritual reflects the 'magical' qualities of organizations as systems of beliefs. Before the rise of the PMS, Behrend (1959) neatly made the point by asking why firms persisted with incentive payments systems when there was no hard evidence that they met their goals of motivating workers. (Reasons why the systems do not work are listed in Box 5.3.)

Box 5.3 Why payment-by-results systems do not work

A set of studies of manual factory workers in the USA (Roy 1954; Burawoy 1979) and the UK (Lupton 1963; Brown 1973) established why payment-by-results systems do not succeed in tying workers to the goals of the firm and thus promoting commitment and efficiency. Note first that it was often not clear in the systems what the goal was: simply to relate pay to effort, or to generate efficiency, or even tie the worker to the long-term profitability of the firm. Their findings are as follows:

1. A focus on the quantity of output undermines the quality of the product.
2. Fixing the rate for a job is far from being an exact science, depending on judgements by the rate-fixer and continuous bargaining as to how hard a given job is.
3. The systems generate anomalies, as workers paid by the piece may earn more than relatively skilled workers paid by time, and as earnings in one department may outstrip those in another.
4. Workers commonly develop collective norms of output, for reasons including fear that pay rates will be adjusted downwards if workers maximize their short-term earnings as individuals.
5. Bonus systems can have perverse effects, for example where workers judge that a given job does not offer sufficient incentive to work hard and therefore reduce their levels of effort ('goldbricking').
6. 'Effort' is a highly uncertain and contested concept; for example, a frustrating and complex job can entail a great deal of effort and yet generate little by way of measurable output.

Her answer was that the systems fitted into common-sense theories about workers, notably that they are motivated largely by money. Paying people in relation to the effort they expend or their contribution to the firm seems axiomatic. Such common-sense theories continue to be attractive even when, as discussed further below, evidence for their accuracy is questionable.

The common-sense principle was for example enunciated by the then director-general of the main UK employers' body, the Confederation of British Industry (CBI) 'the framework for rewards needs to reinforce the steps that many employers have already been taking to link pay to individual, team and company performance, so that there is a clear link between wealth creation and pay rises' (Turner 1996). But putting such an abstract principle into operation is far from simple. Indeed, if reasonably simple payments-by-results systems do not work then more complex merit-based arrangements will face even larger problems. Yet Behrend's point is not about whether a system works in relation to stated goals. It is, rather, that the systems fit comfortable structures of belief. Moreover, introducing a system will be one way in which a management can show that it is managing actively. A system may thus serve purposes other than its stated aims.

How do these belief systems survive in the face of a lack of evidence for them? First, they are not necessarily tested against the evidence. Their goals are often ambiguous, so that achievement is not measured against one criterion. Second, a very common device is to blame operational difficulties rather than the fundamental design of a scheme. Nor is this necessarily wrong, for just as scientists do not abandon theories on the basis of a single experiment so managers may be right that a scheme might in principle have worked. Third, if everyone else has the same belief system then there is no external challenge (for further details, see Chapter 8). This is where the powerful concept of isomorphism is useful (DiMaggio and Powell 1983). The idea is that organizations adopt similar structures because any one of three processes pushes them in the relevant direction. Two processes are pertinent here: mimetic and normative isomorphism, meaning respectively that organizations copy each other and that there is a shared structure of rules and values that promotes similarity. Firms in a given market sector will tend to be alike, and once a belief in a given pay system or anything else takes hold, it will be hard to change.

The theme of 'management and magic' is also useful here. Gimpl and Dakin (1984), for example, start by quoting the aphorism of the well-known management writer Henry Mintzberg: 'it is not the decision-making under *certainty*, *risk* or even *uncertainty* of the textbook that the manager faces, but decision-making under *ambiguity*'. We address risk and decision-making in Chapters 7 and 8. The present point is that performance management is about handling ambiguous signals. How then do people in firms do this? Gimpl and Dakin identify several aspects of managerial behaviour that may be described as rituals because they are performed according to established and respected scripts and because they do not produce their ostensible effects. Examples include forecasting and long-range planning, areas where intended out-comes are generally absent. Yet the rituals are not without purpose. They encourage some sort of action rather than leaving people feeling helpless. Moreover, in a random world the best action may be random, and magic may give meaning to randomness (see Box 5.4). Magic gives justification for actions that would otherwise not fit a discourse of rational decision-making.

Box 5.4 Randomness and functional explanation

Gimpl and Dakin (1984) draw a parallel with some North American peoples whose rites to determine the best hunting grounds gave essentially random answers. Such answers were in fact useful since they counteracted the natural tendency to hunt in areas where prey had previously been found that would lead to the overhunting of these areas. Note also that this is what is called a functional explanation: the rites remained in existence in part (but only in part; they may have had other benefits) because they sustained a rational hunting policy. They thus contributed to the continuance of the society and were *functional* to it. This is quite different from illegitimate *functionalist* explanations that say that the rites existed *because* of the need to sustain the society. The rites cannot be explained in terms of effects that they happened to have; they emerged for other reasons that are in principle discoverable. (See Cohen 1978: 249–72.)

If approaches to performance management can survive because belief systems about them are not challenged, the story of recent performance-related pay (PRP) schemes adds a further twist. Part of the story is familiar. The schemes were introduced to link pay to performance, and in some cases the explicit language was about tailoring pay to the attributes of each individual. Yet research showed, first, that this rhetoric masked the fact of what Evans and Hudson (1994) identified as 'standardized packages individually wrapped'. Second, a series of studies set out to measure whether worker motivation was improved, generally returning a negative result (see Kessler 2000).

The twist is that the schemes had real effects on how organizations work. In other words, managerial beliefs about worker motivation did not just exist self-referentially as a set of ideas; they also impinged on the politics of the organizations and the pursuit of the control of employees. Kessler and Purcell (1992) show that PRP schemes are not to be assessed primarily in terms of measurable impacts on motivation. Instead, they have wider effects, such as sending messages about the need to perform and underpinning various initiatives aimed at changing organizational cultures.

These authors are careful not to overstate the case, and they do not argue in terms of a disciplinary society. Workers are well aware of what PRP schemes try to do, and they do not passively become captives of them. In some cases, they also recognize benefits. Healy (1997) studied performance appraisal of school teachers, examining a group (members of the National Union of Teachers) who might be expected to be particularly opposed to managerial initiatives. In line with other studies, she found that although motivation and the quality of classroom teaching had not been improved, there was a better identification of individuals' developmental needs. In other words, the system had some, limited, benefits in the eyes of the teachers while serving to change the language and assumptions about behaviour.

Understanding Workplace Rules

Where do such assumptions come from? We may turn here to studies of the concrete rules in practice that people develop. Gouldner (1954), in a classic of industrial sociology based on detailed fieldwork in a US plant producing gypsum, famously identified three types of rule. These are:

- representative (accepted by all, for example safety rules);
- punishment-centred (in which deviations by one party are punished by the other, for example managerial sanctions against absenteeism); and
- mock (formal rules, neglected in practice by everyone).

To the extent that a PMS operates according to one of the three rules, it will have different features; mock bureaucracy, for example, equates with a pure ritual.

Why are there are only three types? Implicit in Gouldner's account is a view of the value of rules. For example, where managers and workers both place a high value on a rule there is a shared perspective, which produces the 'representative' pattern. Where managers value a rule but workers question it, a 'punishment-centred bureaucracy' exists. And where neither side values rules, we have mock bureaucracy.

If value to the two parties is cross-classified as in Table 5.1, these three cases can be clearly located. The missing cell is then neatly filled with Gouldner's other noted invention, the indulgency pattern. This pattern refers to a situation in which workers develop customary standards and

TABLE 5.1 Types of workplace rules

| | | *Value of rules to management* | |
		High	Low
Value of rules	High	Representative	Indulgency pattern
to workers	Low	Punishment-centred	Mock

are 'indulged' in their exercise by management. Here workers place a high value on the informal custom and practice rules that they generate, and managers tacitly tolerate the situation. Gouldner (1954: 187) seems to have conflated mock bureaucracy and the indulgency pattern, for the former had no important rules whereas the key to the indulgency pattern was a set of customary rules that were of central importance to workers.

It should be noted that this is a classification of types of regulation, and not of substantive rules. Gouldner's example of mock bureaucracy was a 'no smoking' rule, which in the context of that time and place was seen as a dead letter. In a chemicals factory, by contrast, the dangers of smoking would put this concrete example in the representative category. And many organizations now have 'smoke free' policies, reflecting a shift in general social expectations to which organizations have responded.

A final elaboration concerns the degree of variability within any one category of rule and indeed between rules. Consider no-smoking policies. These could be representative in the strong sense that they are introduced after consultation throughout an organization. More likely is a much weaker sense in which management decides on a policy, which is then accepted by workers as inevitable and as something about which they do not become exercised. There may also be variations in the degree of legitimacy of a rule. One case that we studied was of a factory where shop floor workers had to obey the rule, but where (so they claimed) office workers escaped it (Edwards et al. 1998). Rules may be broadly representative in nature, but still contested in detailed application. Any rule also plainly needs sanctions for its breach, so that there may be punishment-centred actions if the no-smoking rule is broken. The question then concerns the response to the actions. At one extreme, punishment of an acknowledged rule-breaker may be generally accepted, with the representative nature of the rule being reinforced as a result; at the other, punishment may be felt to be excessive; and, in between, responses may depend on how far a particular exercise of a sanction is felt to be fair.

These ideas, based on a study (conducted over fifty years ago) of male semi-skilled manual workers, still have wide relevance. First, the contrast between management and worker can readily be extended to any situation in which one group attempts to control another through rules and targets. This is taken up below.

Second, Gouldner operated with a contrast between management and a group of workers who had a strong collective ethos, and he thus treats rules as the product of bargaining (both formal and informal) between groups. But his ideas can readily be extended to take account of different forms of authorship of rules. An intriguing illustration lies in the work of

Mars (1982). His focus was workplace 'fiddles' by low-level employees, a fiddle being any practice through which workers illicitly turned material rewards to their own benefit. The obvious example is the pilfering of goods or stealing cash, but Mars's examples also include fiddling time by bending the rules to do less of a task than is formally prescribed or manipulating the timing of tasks to earn leisure at the end of a particular assignment (an example of the latter being bus drivers who run ahead of schedule, thus earning time at the end of the journey). Where work groups have strong collective norms, an injury against one is an injury against all. Mars's example is the male dock worker and his group (labelled 'wolves'). Here, in Gouldner's terms, there will be a clear indulgency pattern (e.g. acceptance of the pilfering of cargo) plus mock bureaucracy. Where workers have weaker norms, management is more able to exert sanctions, and in some cases workers act wholly as individuals. Finally, there is a group of powerful individualists ('hawks') who use their professional or technical knowledge to confuse the customer, for example garage mechanics who overcharge or who charge for work not in fact performed.

Third, Mars's approach gives explicit and foresightful attention to relationships involving customers as well as managers and workers. He speaks of two parties within this triad fiddling the third, for example where managers and workers collude to cheat customers (e.g. by short-changing) or where a worker and a customer fiddle the firm (e.g. where goods are passed through a supermarket checkout without being billed). With growing interest in customer relations, this approach complements the current emphasis on the customer as a force for control by showing that relations with customers are negotiated. In fast-food outlets, for example, workers manage the encounter to contain any demands by customers for non-standard items or any attempts to engage personally. Here, the worker's job is made easier and the firm's targets for the time to serve a customer are met (Leidner 1993). How far customer concerns are met is less evident, and indeed the point is not to respond to such concerns (e.g. for personal attention) but to school the customer into what to expect and demand in a given setting (here, fast food means standard products provided rapidly, and little more). (Note the illustration of the wider argument about ideology made in Chapter 1: practice in fast-food stores creates the ideologies, that is sets of beliefs, through which customers and workers understand their positions.)

Fourth, a key point about fiddles is that they embrace a blend of practices, rather than simply shifting resources from one party in an exchange to another. Lupton (1963) in particular stressed the integrity of a set of practices that workers put together under the head of 'the fiddle'. Some practices (e.g. negotiating the rate for the job) shifted resources to workers; others (e.g. not booking all work done and recording it later, so as to even out earnings over time) had no effect; and others (e.g. finding new ways to do the job) improved returns to management and to workers. Using this way of managing workers, rather than imposing tight performance standards, also saved in supervisory costs and, according to Lupton, reduced other costs such as absenteeism.

The value of some organizational slack is also neatly illustrated in a study of refuse collectors in the UK whose old work practices had been transformed by tighter performance measurement. As a worker put it, 'we used to have time to chat to the old folks. . . . *We used to have customer care.* Now you are lucky if you see anyone, let alone talk to them' (McIntosh and Broderick 1996: 425, emphasis added). Here is an example where performance management cut down one part of service, which was not measured and probably scarcely recognized, which had been provided under a previously 'inefficient' system.

It seems probable that the celebrated fiddles of the past have been reduced in scale, in part through the use of performance management (aided by new technologies that assist in measurement) and in part because the sectors where they flourished (notably docks) have seen sharp falls in employment levels and the rationalization of work systems. Yet the negotiation of rules continues. Noon and Blyton (2002: 244) cite supermarket van drivers delivering orders placed via the internet; drivers reportedly take illicit breaks, do errands for friends, and neglect to explain to customers when a delivery does not match the order — practices plainly recognizable from Mars's earlier analysis of delivery drivers. A PMS will operate in the context of such rules in use. It may be able to change behaviour if it is sufficiently supported by its designers. But the more that it runs against the grain of an organizational culture, and the more that managers treat it as a piece of 'magic', the more it will become a mere ritual.

Negotiating Budgets and Rules

The negotiability of rules is sharply illustrated in the case of auditing, where one might expect hard numbers and accuracy to be particularly emphasized. Box 5.5 indicates some of the issues. Note in particular that different interpretations of the same figures seem common (point 1) and that this permits processes of social construction as reflected in the other points.

Box 5.5 Why good accountants do bad audits

Bazerman et al. (2002) list six sources of bias in auditing:

1. Ambiguity of definitions. For example, when the records of a hypothetical firm were sent to different auditors, estimates of the tax that the firm should pay varied by 83 per cent.
2. Attachment: auditors depend on clients for business.
3. Approval: self-serving bias increases when people are endorsing others', already biased, judgements.
4. Familiarity with the firm being audited.
5. Discounting: potential bad news is postponed.
6. Escalation: acceptance of minor lapses makes it hard to challenge these later.

(The processes involved in categories 3, 5, and 6 are examined in Chapters 7 and 8).

The possibility of bargaining over performance standards arises whenever one group sets objectives for another. The head office of a large firm and the managers of its operating units would be one such case. Jackall (1988: 26) analyses the processes involved, drawing on detailed observational inquiry in three US firms. A division of one firm was prosperous for a time and thus met its commitments to its owners; this was 'the crucial coin of the realm to purchase continued autonomy'. But, when economic difficulties arrived, profit targets were adjusted downwards and in the case of one subdivision figures were made only just acceptable 'by remarkable legerdemain with the books'. Jackall does not detail what was involved here, but familiar practices include delaying capital expenditure, cutting down on maintenance, anticipating earnings on goods not yet delivered, and revaluing stocks of work in progress.

We have observed cases where targets laid down by head office were simply ignored. This is the extreme end of the 'mock' category. In one such case, the manager of the Italian subsidiary of a UK pharmaceuticals firm, when asked what he did with the targets that he received from the UK, simply opened a desk drawer, placed a piece of paper inside, and closed it: he treated the targets as largely irrelevant to him. This was possible because the subsidiary was profitable and was the sole producer of a key product, so that there were bargaining resources at the manager's disposal (Edwards et al. 1996). A study focused directly on the negotiation of budgets found, in the case of a Spanish subsidiary of a US firm, that on one occasion the budget was changed in Europe without consultation with the head office and that figures were manipulated to create a good impression. Geographical location was among the political resources deployed in this case: 'the corporation persists with the ritual of achieving legitimation through "tight" budget negotiation and target setting and apparent under-achievement in performance' (Peres and Robson 1999: 406).

Representative patterns are exemplified by the now common pattern for the performance targets of business units to be agreed through a process of discussion, rather than by straight imposition from above. Note, however, that there will be degrees to which there is genuinely free negotiation and also that, as indicated above, there are commonly shifts towards punishment. One UK survey found that targets were commonly set by negotiation but also that a business unit seriously underperforming was likely to be sanctioned, in particular through dismissal or other penalties for its manager (Armstrong et al. 1996).

The accounting literature contains a small number of studies on this point. An early study by Hopwood (1973) examined a large US manufacturing firm. It found that several practices were common, for example, putting the wrong cost codes on invoices so that materials were charged to cost centres other than one's own. The key point, however, was that this practice was far from universal, and indeed some other practices occurred only under certain conditions. These conditions reflected the budgetary regime in place. Fiddles were most common under 'budget constraint' systems, those where meeting short-term budget targets was the primary performance measure. A later study (Merchant 1990) confirmed that the manipulation of figures was most common where pressures for financial performance were greatest.

Given growing emphasis on financial performance (see Chapter 9), a reasonable expectation is that manipulation of budget data will have increased. Two important qualifications must be made, however. First, the above studies addressed fiddles within a company. These are very different from the cases of corporate fraud that exploded on the late 1990s and early 2000s and that involved, as discussed in Chapter 9, now celebrated examples such as Enron, WorldCom, and Parmalat. These latter cases involved systems of management in which misrepresentation was encouraged from the top–down. Second, there is likely to be a tendency towards fiddles, but this may well be counteracted by closer monitoring.

In respect of workers' fiddles, studies at one time gave great attention to the effects of new technology, testing the hypothesis that in clerical work, for example, the opportunity to measure key strokes per minute would heighten managerial control and tighten performance standards. More recently, a minor industry has grown up studying telephone call centres. The results of the first set of studies generally point to the absence of any overall logic of the kind hypothesized. The second set show that, though performance standards are often specified in exact detail such as fractions of a second to complete a call, workers can to a degree evade some standards. Mars's (1982) idea of a triad is useful here: workers and customers can collude, by engaging in unscripted discussion, and there is a limit to how far managers can crack down, for fear of alienating the customer who is, as other parts of corporate rhetoric often proclaim, sovereign. It is also increasingly stressed that call centres vary in the intensity with which they aim to standardize worker behaviour. All that said, it is also true that the adoption of a given technology does tend to set limits on social behaviour. Control implications are not inherent in the technology, but work in a call centre has disciplines and routines that constrain behaviour.

Several factors seem to affect the real impact of performance measurement. Some are listed below, but research to date has not produced wholly convincing evidence either on the 'dependent variable' (how far standards change what people do, and whether such change is seen by them as positive or negative) or on the causal influences.

Organization of Work

A concrete contingency embraces a set of factors connected to the organization of work. Several research studies have shown that firms that produce relatively standard goods and services across several locations have a greater need for targets, and a greater ability to impose them, than others. Car firms, for example, have developed coercive comparisons between sites making comparable products, and with the international spread of the industry these comparisons have gone beyond national borders (Mueller and Purcell 1992; Marginson 2000). Banks, supermarkets, and fast-food chains are other examples of firms producing services that can be measured on standard metrics.

The space provided by difficulties of measurement is one resource that subordinates can use to negotiate performance standards. We have noted above in relation to managers that tight budget standards tend to promote financial manipulation. Mars (1982) showed, in relation to workers' traditional fiddles, that difficulties of measuring quantity and quality left room for fiddles to emerge. The numbers of bricks delivered to a building site or the number of meals served in a restaurant are highly negotiable measures. The same point applies to the very different context of managers in MNCs: where a firm produces non-standard goods, it may be unable to enforce coercive comparisons. In addition, as long as the goods are important to the firm's strategic plans, plants making them have political resources. For example, Bélanger and Björkman (1999) summarize the results of a series of studies of sites across the globe owned by the multinational ABB. They found that there was strong central coordination, which they characterize as 'programme management': a system embracing process control and benchmarking across plants. But at the same time the influence of any one plant was shaped by its own success, the degree to which it had few direct comparators within ABB, and its strength in its local market. 'Metrics', the authors comment, ' can be denied, subverted, or corrupted' (ibid.: 251).

Product Market Conditions

This example points to another key contingency, the nature of the product market. Even where metrics might be technologically feasible, they may not be used if the firm can tolerate a few fiddles. One of the most lasting results from traditional industrial sociology was the tendency of oligopoly to allow managerial leniency of fiddles. Because the cost of the product was not central, controlling labour costs was not important. Moreover, firms learned that there were some hidden benefits in a lenient approach, notably the facts that they did not have to spend money on monitoring and that allowing workers some slack reduced potentially costly activities such as quitting and going absent (Lupton 1963).

The idea that organizations will reflect their context is a simple yet powerful one. The basic thesis is that the structure of the organization, and hence the ways in which it manages its workers, reflects environmental contingencies. Fast-food chains produce a standardized product and also a standardized 'service encounter'. This market context encourages a highly formalized internal management system and the routinization of tasks, which in turn leads to the employment of interchangeable workers, many of whom are students. The implication for performance management is that workers are evaluated against detailed standards and that monitoring is close and frequent. Expensive restaurants, by contrast, emphasize personalized service and are likely to have much more diffuse performance standards for their workers. Between these extremes, researchers have increasingly found, lie restaurants and hotel chains practising 'mass customization': the well-known upmarket chains offer a largely standard service, and that indeed is a key part of their marketing strategy for the customer knows what to expect, but the customer is also treated as an individual and employees, it is claimed, are 'empowered' to meet customer needs rather than follow detailed scripts. Performance management in these last cases would entail a mix of measures: knowledge of standard procedures, but also flexibility.

The Determination with Which a Political Project is Driven Through

Performance standards and league tables are now an accepted part of the scene in schools and hospitals in the UK. One press report among many, on hospitals, cites an employee as complaining about 'being performance managed to death' (*Sunday Times* 8 February 2004). There was widespread complaint when targets were introduced, but this has not led to their removal. Both major political parties adopted the use of targets, and increasing efforts were made to refine them, for example by seeking 'value added' indicators in schools as opposed to crude output measures that took no account of the quality of the 'inputs' (children's social background and so on). There remains debate as to the specifics of targets, and there is evidence that their number and complexity may be reduced in some areas. Indeed, there seems to be something of a cycle, with tight standards being seen as too onerous and complex, so that there is a shift towards what in UK universities is called a 'light touch', no doubt followed by a further round of hard standards. (Note that the lightness of the touch is negotiated according to the political resources of institutions concerned, so that in the university example, the old universities have been able to use their reputation to build a case for the light touch.) Yet, despite such qualifications, the audit model remains dominant. This is a reflection of the political strategies of certain groups, and not the result of the 'disciplinary society'. The model fits some of the aims of the strategies, but at the same time it has direct costs (more time is spent in auditing than in doing creative work) that may undermine the strategies and there may be unintended consequences.

A political project may well be successful not only in the sense of meeting the sectional goals of its promoters but also the wider aim of organizational performance. This is clearly illustrated by the following comments of a senior operations manager in the UK water industry after it had been privatized:

There was a much more integrated and co-ordinated business planning process.... [T]he new Director or Water Services stood up and said, 'I'll be setting targets for you managers to agree and then achieve and primarily they will all be headcount based'...We all came out and said...'the service will collapse'. But within a year we were focusing, not just on manpower headcounts as such, but where we can improve service. (Ogden 1995: 205)

A sufficiently determined project can drive through a PMS. It will have clear costs, and in the case of privatization there is substantial evidence that the costs fell on workers, in terms of lost jobs and worse wages and conditions. But there may also be benefits, identified here as improved service. A further set of questions might be whether the service had really improved, whether the benefits outweighed the costs, and whether the benefits might have been obtainable by other means. These are proper, but hypothetical, questions. Political projects have complex goals and need to be understood accordingly. Box 5.6 gives a related example.

Issues of contingency and fit are neatly illustrated by a study of telephone call centres (Kinnie et al. 2000). This starts from the observation that there is great diversity in this sector: it is not all based on standard scripts. A telling statistic is that in the UK starting salaries vary by almost 100 per cent. A contingency model begins to make sense of this. Three patterns of interaction with customers can be identified, each with a distinct approach to employee relations.

- Short-term transactional interactions imply a cost minimization strategy.
- Broader longer-term relational interactions imply a 'high-commitment' strategy.
- In between lie 'pseudo-relational' interactions, leading to a mix of the two employee relations strategies.

But the authors go on to argue that the environment is not a simple thing. Any one firm is likely to face the three different patterns of interaction, reflecting different market segments. However, one case study organization chose not to segment its activities to fit these external contexts because it had a strategy of customer service: the market did not determine a response. Technical change further complicates the nature of interactions with customers. And a third element of the environment is the labour market, which may or may not map onto the patterns above. For example, fluctuating demand may suggest a labour market strategy of using short-term and temporary contracts, but this may conflict with training and involvement if market signals suggest a high-commitment strategy.

'Best fit' models thus fail because: they assume that there is a clear corporate strategy with which an employee-relations strategy can be aligned; they assume that managers know what is happening in the product market; they neglect the speed with which the context changes; they assume that

---

Box 5.6 A political economy of contingency and performance standards

Ferner (1985) studied the then nationalized railways in Britain, British Rail (BR), focusing on managerial strategies of modernization and, in particular, a decision to suffer a damaging strike. He provides a clear illustration of three points: environmental signals are more than neutral forces; the interpretation of the signals within an organization is a political and contested process; and chosen courses of action may have more to do with political legitimacy than with hard performance objectives.

1. The British government had a clear policy of reforming public enterprises and introducing market principles. The signals sent to BR management derived, not from an asocial 'environment' but from a particular political strategy and model of how enterprises should work. In this case, a long-standing concern about productivity received new emphasis in the light of tight controls of public sector finances and government antipathy to previous, more cooperative, approaches towards the trade unions.
2. These signals did not in themselves define what BR management should do. They were themselves negotiable, for example in terms of just what performance targets should be met. And there were varying positions as to how they were to be met.
3. BR managers chose to take on the trade unions in a series of industrial disputes. Ferner demonstrates that the costs of lost revenue were greater than the likely benefits to be derived from concessions by the unions. Why then was this policy pursued? The answer was that 'taking on the unions' demonstrated managerial purpose and that this purpose was consistent with the general thrust of government policy at the time. The policy was in Ferner's word a 'symbol' of determination to make changes. This symbolic action had real goals, notably aiming to persuade the government that BR was to be trusted with public funds for a new investment programme.

This analysis has lasting value. Even after waves of privatization, the public sector remains a significant employer, while many private organizations providing public services, including not only railways in Britain but also water and airline companies, are subject to detailed government regulation. Ferner argues that politically defined targets are different in kind from the performance standards of private firms. The process of juggling different demands will therefore be a particularly complex one.

firms do one thing, rather than trying to be good at several; and crucially, they assume that all firms in a sector will cohere around the same model, washing out any distinct pursuit of competitive advantage and change.

PMSs thus contain different elements that may well contradict each other. The tension between meeting fixed standards and developing skills and autonomy is the most obvious.

Conclusions

The spread of performance management has plainly had effects on how organizations work. Measurement is more common, and it has defined standards of performance in new ways. Yet the standards also have elements of ritual, in that meeting a set target becomes important even though other things may be neglected and meeting the target may entail producing appropriate data rather than any substantive performance. How far performance measurement is imposed on people depends on a wide range of contingencies.

Performance measurement also has clear costs, both direct monitoring costs and indirect costs in terms of activities now abandoned and the displacement of activity onto that which is measured. In some cases, there can be counterproductive results. Some are discussed above, and a further example is given in a different context at the start of Chapter 8: what is measured as 'bad' performance may in fact be good because the people involved are able to admit errors and do not manipulate figures in their own favour. There are therefore strong counter-currents against performance measurement.

But this does not mean that it is either bound to fail or, by contrast, able to entrap workers. Armstrong and Baron (1998: 99–100) criticize 'academic' critiques of PMSs on two grounds. First, a focus on hidden forms of power implies that organizations are not entitled to a sense of direction, and managers do not always renege on promises or merely go through the motions of making a PMS work. Second, organizations have moved on from performance appraisal and crude judgemental approaches; evidence suggests that performance management is taken seriously and that it can work. The first argument is fair comment on some studies that overplay proper critique to suggest that a PMS is about nothing but tightening discipline. However, the second argument is based more on hope than experience. The hope itself rests on a contrast between what a few 'good practice' schemes may now promise and the messy realities of performance schemes in action, a dangerous basis for analysis. New schemes, whatever their sophistication, cannot escape problems of fairness, subjectivity, and unintended consequences.

Our approach in this chapter has been to suggest that a PMS is a way of managing the inherent ambiguities of the effort bargain. Some may be better than others, however (a point taken up below). We have stressed that a PMS is not only about managerial control: it is part of a wider process, which can include benefits such as precision and clarity.

It is not part of our purpose to identify good practice. Books on the design of a PMS provide examples (Armstrong and Baron 1998: 388). But there are some overall principles that such books tend to neglect. The first and most important one concerns employee participation in the design and management of a PMS. The tendency in many texts is to treat management as the main actor. Managers may now be urged to have schemes that are transparent, to use appraisals from several sources rather than top-down judgement of one person by a single rater, and even to take account of ethical principles. But the approach is still one that is managerially defined and led, with the assumption being that the organization is indeed a unitary body. If firms really believe in a PMS that reflects shared values, why not have systematic employee involvement in it? As we will see in Chapter 6, there are reasons why participation is hard to achieve, but at least organizations might be more open than most are. In other words, conventional texts discuss the PMS as a technical tool, and critics then 'deconstruct' it. A more sensible engagement is desirable.

The second related point is that the core principles of a PMS, such as defining goals, monitoring progress, and promoting personal development, are scarcely controversial. The issue is that these broad concepts have varying meanings, and that firms too readily move from acceptance of ideas to the assumption that employees have 'bought into' the whole process. A more realistic and less ambitious approach may be preferable to complex systems that have little purchase in reality. A third point relates to the direct costs and the unintended consequences of a PMS. It is desirable to recognize such issues rather than assume that there is a technical fix. Fourth, performance management has elements of mimetic isomorphism and ritual about it. A certain amount of self-awareness may assist in limiting the purely imitative and ceremonial features here.

As for employees under a PMS, one question concerns how far its beneficial aspects can be sustained. For example, can the promised personal development be secured? There is a degree of taking a policy at its word here, and seeing how far one can take it, rather than necessarily retreating into cynicism. It is likely that there are sectional interests as well as common ones at work, and some of these may not be apparent. The discussion above helps in thinking about what they may be and how they can be brought to the surface. However, there may be circumstances where a PMS is simply inevitable, and then the best policy may be to tolerate it as best one can.

6

Why Is Empowerment Hard to Achieve?

A key question that anyone taking a job is likely to ask is, apart from the pay and other benefits: What opportunities are there to influence decisions about the work itself and the policies of the organization as a whole? Terms such as participation have a long history, while from the 1980s the even more engaging-sounding concept of 'empowerment' became popular. The importance of employee participation and involvement is widely stated across most of the advanced economies, for example in an influential paper of the Commission for the European Communities (CEC 1997). One US scholar remarks that participation is the 'new conventional wisdom' (Osterman 1994: 173).

Part of this wisdom concerns the reasons why participation is popular, which include demand and supply aspects. Demand for participation comes about as jobs call for new skills and the active use of creative capacities, as distinct from simply following orders. Workers possessing increased skills and education provide the supply of people seeking participation. As Walton (1985: 76) put it in a much-cited review, 'workers respond best—and most creatively—not when they are tightly controlled by management...but instead when they are given broader responsibilities [and] encouraged to contribute'. There is also evidence that participation can bring benefits to workers and to employers.

This popularity was not merely an academic one. Major firms, such as BP, have used the word empowerment explicitly. Two leading UK employers' organizations have stated flatly that 'employee participation is critical' to firms' success (EEF/CIPD 2003: 5). Empowerment was even adopted by the then CEO of GE, Jack Welch, whose previously ruthless approach to the interests of employees had earned him the sobriquet of 'neutron Jack'. In an apt comment on the measurement systems discussed in Chapter 5, Welch argues that measurement interferes with understanding: the three important things to measure are customer satisfaction, employee satisfaction, and cash flow, and employee satisfaction delivers 'productivity, quality, pride and creativity' (Welch 1993). Is it the case that capitalist firms have come to believe in workers' control?

We can begin to answer this question by considering the core social science concept, power, embedded in the term empowerment. One curiosity is that debate on the latter developed largely independently of discussion of the former. To be empowered means to have the ability and resources to take key decisions. Yet there is an immediate and important slippage of language, as acutely pointed out by Fenton-O'Creevy (1995: 154): empowerment was initially used by radical social movements to mean giving the disadvantaged the tools and resources to further their own interests, whereas managerial uses of the term mean that managers remain in overall control and grant a certain amount of authority to subordinates. This tension also runs through older debates on participation. At one extreme, the term can embrace specific and often paternalistic managerial initiatives and, at the other, radical workers' movements associated with revolutionary transformation.

A second curiosity is that discussion of participation and empowerment has developed at the same time as accumulating evidence (discussed in Chapter 2) on growing wage inequality, the rise of precarious employment, work intensification, and, as discussed in Chapter 5, an emphasis on measurement and control. Does this second trend mean that the language of empowerment is simply a delusion?

This chapter aims to help thinking about such questions as it (*a*) reviews debates on power and turns to participation more directly; (*b*) provides some conceptual tools; (*c*) shows why participation matters; (*d*) considers evidence as to the extent and meaning of participation; and (*e*) addresses the reasons for the limited and patchy progress revealed in (*d*).

In one sense, it is easy to anticipate the answer. Organizations are, as Section 1 shows, structures of power. People at the top rarely give up power voluntarily. As one lengthy review concluded, achieving collaboration between different groups is never easy, collaboration readily breaks down with a reversion to (command-and-control-based) type, and the idea of managerial prerogative is deeply embedded in law (so that the board of directors is defined as the ultimate decision-making body and its duty is to make returns for shareholders) and concrete practice; participation exists at best on the edges of a system structured in very different ways (McCaffrey et al. 1995).

Yet an absolutist view of participation would be too simple. Such a view, from the side of capital, treats participation as a minor activity, or as something that could interfere with organizational functioning, or possibly as a useful tool to mislead workers. From the side of labour, the same view treats it as a sideshow or an effort to mislead. But participation is not an all-or-nothing thing. There are degrees to which it can work. The important question for a worker concerns the conditions under which it works and what it might in fact deliver. This point reflects a wider theme. As argued in Chapter 1, capitalism rests on efforts to balance control over workers with the generation of active cooperation, and to treat participation in absolutist terms is to address only the former aspect. Marx did not take such a simple view, seeing capitalism as a dynamic and creative system (Adler 2001). In short, power is intertwined with control, and we need to understand such complex linkages, rather than assume that power is simply a thing.

How Does Power Work in Organizations?

Organizations are hierarchical and those at the top have more power than those at the bottom. If organizations are viewed as rationally constructed entities pursuing the common goals of their members, then this fact is of little consequence: power resides where it should, and is deployed for shared purposes. However, even relatively conventional organization theory recognizes that organizations comprise different groups with different goals and hence that politics and bargaining are inevitable (see Thompson and McHugh 2002: 117–21 for elaboration and criticism). More radical theories locate the exercise of power more deeply in the structuring of organizations.

Debates on the nature of power are necessarily complex. But a useful starting point is the definition of power as 'the capacity to control patterns of social interaction' (Bradley 1999: 31). Power is thus an ability, and is to be distinguished from its exercise. Crucially, powerful individuals and groups can secure their objectives without having to use overt means, for other groups are often aware of the capacities of the powerful and adjust their behaviour accordingly.

This approach avoids the problems of 'zero-sum' and conventional 'positive-sum' models. Many standard views of power are zero-sum in that the powerful actor is said to gain what the powerless lose. The problem with zero-sum views is that the positive contributions of the exercise of power (e.g. the carrying through of a new and difficult project, in which the 'capacity to control patterns of social interaction' will loom large) are ignored. This can then lead to the conclusion that the powerful always win and that capitalism systematically works against the interests of subordinate groups in all circumstances. Positive-sum views had the opposite problem of treating power as a generalized capacity that necessarily met collective goals (see Giddens 1977). Controlling patterns of interaction is a process in which common and conflicting goals are intertwined.

Capacities are not always used skilfully, and their exercise can have unintended consequences. Powerful groups, moreover, are not usually unified. There are divisions of interest between, for example, large and small firms. Within large ones, divisions exist between levels and functions of management. To take a well-attested case, in the nineteenth-century in Britain laws restricting the hours of factory and mine workers were intro-duced. This reflected in part the powers of trade unions and campaigners against excessive hours; note in passing that such groups were far from unified, but that they came together on this issue. But some large employ-ers actively promoted the legislation because it would help to drive out smaller firms that relied on sweating labour, whereas the large firms were more capital-intensive and had other means of securing profits. Note also the ambiguous implications of the legislation for workers: it brought protection, but also consciously aimed to buttress the gender division of labour whereby women were restricted to the home, and it thus helped to underpin a particular set of power relations between men and women (Humphries 1977; Fox 1985). The exercise of power is dynamic, and the outcomes of overt contests have unintended consequences.

In a search for tools to grasp different ways in which power is exercised, it has been common to list 'bases' of power, meaning the resources that people can use. Bradley (1999) lists nine such bases, and a celebrated list widely used in management studies named five (French and Raven 1959). It can be a useful exercise to ask on what a claim to exercise power rests. For example, the IT department of a firm may be influential because it has technical knowledge. We might then ask how far the expertise is 'real' and how far it stems from a professional mystique. What happens if claims to expertise are challenged?

But such exercises have two problems. First, why are there five or nine or some other number of bases of power? Second, are these bases hard object-ive things, or simply claims that can be challenged? The result of these problems is that in practice analysts do not organize discussion around bases of power: one would expect an identification of the bases, and then a demonstration of how power resting on one base had certain effects, but this has not been the way in which power can best be understood.

A more fundamental approach asks not about the bases of power, but about the underlying dimensions on which these bases may be mapped. Runciman (1999: 64–9) identifies three kinds of power:

- economic power, involving the capacity to provide or withhold wealth or income;
- ideological power, entailing control over the resources of social esteem and privilege; and
- coercive power, involving physical force.

An element might seem to be missing from this list, namely, political power. But later Runciman (1999: 71) refers to 'economic, ideological and political [not coercive] power'. His main theoretical source here, the sociologist Max Weber, famously defined the key political institution, the state, as that body that claims a monopoly on the right to use physical force in a given territory. So coercive power, though rooted ultimately in physical force, is likely in most circumstances to be embedded in political relationships. Bradley similarly speaks of 'positional power' gained by virtue of the authority of certain positions, such as manager. But on what does this authority rest? It rests ultimately on rights that are expressed in laws or conventions. So the right of a manager to dismiss a worker, evidently a form of power, is a political right which can if one so wishes be traced back to coercion (the right of the employer physically to exclude a sacked worker from the workplace). Physical and positional power are parts of the same basic kind of power.

Ideological power merits further comment. Belief systems and ideas are significant fields of social interaction. Burawoy (1985) captured the point neatly when he argued, on the basis of detailed participant observation in a US engineering factory, that he and his fellow workers produced not only parts of engines but also ideology, that is sets of beliefs which expressed and reinforced a particular set of power relations. Ideology is not only something that is created by the powerful and imposed on others, though of course it can have that quality. It is also produced in the process of social interaction, as in rituals and ceremonies and also in day-to-day life. Not all rituals and ideas imply power. Artistic ideas for example address human aesthetic sensibilities. But they can entail power, most obviously where architecture is used to embody images of the might and majesty of rules; not for nothing did Girouard (1980) commence his discussion of the English country house with an account of the statements of power that the building of large castles and palaces expressed. The relevant question is: what resources are being used to influence what social interactions? Applying this question allows us to examine ideological power.

There are in essence two approaches at this point. The first, building on the tradition established by Lukes (1974), asks which individuals or groups exercise power over others in the sense of affecting them in some way that would have been absent had power not been there, or, second, in the terms used by Lukes the powerful are able to act against the 'real interests' of the (relatively) powerless. Lukes identifies three 'faces' of power as laid out in Box 6.1.

Box 6.1 The faces of power

First face

Focus: Concrete behaviour and the making of decisions. There must be some observable conflict as expressed in preferences and choices. Power occurs where one group's expressed views come into opposition with those of another, and power is the ability to secure one's own aims.

Comment: Note the emphasis on clear, expressed views. Groups are assumed to be able to organize to identify their interests and mobilize around them. Note also the absence of a distinction between *interests* and expressed *wants*.

Example: A company wants to build homes on agricultural land. Analysis will identify other power-holders (the local council, environmentalists, etc) and how these power-holders interact in observable efforts to influence each other.

Second face

Focus: How potential issues are handled to prevent their being matters of open decision. The making of a non-decision is still a form of concrete behaviour. Conflict may not be overt in the sense of a direct clash such as a strike, but it is still observable in behaviour, for example vocalized grievances.

Comment: Lukes says that this is only a partial critique of the first face focus on behaviour: the concern is still with concrete behaviour and observable action.

Example: Mechanisms to keep decisions off the agenda, especially what is termed the *mobilization of bias*, are identified. For example, the company may highlight the jobs that the building of the homes will bring, or offer other inducements such as road improvements paid for by it, or work on the local authority through bribery or other less obvious actions.

Third face

Focus: The second face merges into the third the more that it sees the mobilization of bias as covert and not open to direct observation. The third face defines power as the ability to act against the interests of the powerless. There may be a '*latent conflict*, which consists in a contradiction between the interests of those exercising power and the *real interests* of those they exclude. These latter may not express or *even* be conscious of their interests' (Lukes 1974: 24–5; italics original, underlining added).

Comment: If people are not conscious of their interests how do we know what they are? Power is seen here as some people acting against others, and shares the 'zero-sum' approach of Faces 1 and 2.

Example: Residents faced with a housing project may fail to realize that they may have an interest in opposing it, perhaps because they cannot grasp the possible dangers, or because they lack any tradition of collective discussion and organization.

In his reassessment of this approach, Lukes (2005: 109, emphasis original) notes several limitations:

it focuses entirely on the exercise of 'power over' — the power of some *A* over some *B* and *B*'s conditions of dependence on *A* . . . [I]t equates such dependence-inducing power with *domination* . . . neglecting . . . the manifold ways in which power over others can be productive, transformative, authoritative and compatible with dignity. [And] it treats an actor's interests as unitary, failing to consider differences, interactions and conflict among one's interests.

We can take the three-dimensional view as addressing some, but not all, issues to do with power.

The second approach thus treats power as a resource. Whereas in the first approach power is zero-sum, here it is an ability to secure common goals. A highly skilled group of software designers, for example, might be said to have power because their skills enable them to achieve ends that are unattainable to other groups. Yet, in promoting a new solution that does indeed help the organization in the market, they may also be competing with other groups for personnel and capital and may, to the extent that they are successful, defeat alternative projects and establish their own definition of what the organization is trying to do.

Developments of this approach have accordingly attempted to treat power more as a feature of the structure of organizations than as a property that can be possessed in the same way in which a skill may be possessed. Power resides in networks and 'discourses' and the powerful and the powerless are equally 'prisoners of prevailing discourses' (Hardy and Leiba-O'Sullivan 1998). This view makes several useful points, including:

- attempts to exert power are not necessarily successful, and the use of resources may lead to unintended effects;
- real interests are impossible to operationalize in a meaningful way;
- organizational rules and routines inscribe assumptions that may well reflect prior overt attempts to exert power but can also simply be taken for granted as legitimate; and
- the way in which power works is embedded in social structures and relationships (which is what the term 'discourses' may be intended to signify) rather than being reducible to a capacity of a particular actor. (Whether or not these insights are in any way new is not of present concern, though in our view many of them are not: see Edwards and Collinson 2002: 275).

The difficulty is that it claims too much. Are 'discourses' so all-pervading as to make everyone their prisoner? Such a view may even excuse the powerful from any responsibility for their own actions and imply that power serves a mysterious system rather than real people. The irony is that there is a leap from an emphasis on discourse and the ways in which people negotiate their own worlds to an assertion about what discourses do, with active agents seeming to have little freedom of choice. In the case of the article cited, which is an assessment of 'empowerment' schemes, the result is that it is asserted as a matter of fact what results these schemes have, whereas an array of empirical studies points to highly contingent and varied outcomes (Wilkinson 1998).

A useful illustration of these issues is the analysis by Wilson and Thompson (2001) of sexual harassment in the workplace as an exercise of power. The authors review evidence against the models of power discussed above.

Face 1: Complainants of harassment often find themselves subject to counter sanctions, including dismissal (a fact also noted in relation to other challengers to organizational order, notably 'whistle-blowers').

Face 2: The issue is kept off the agenda by processes including weak sanctions against perpetrators of harassment, the absence of policies about it, and cultural definitions as to what is acceptable behaviour so that people are expected to tolerate harassment or seem weak or foolish.

Face 3: Socialization of people and processes of internalization mean that harassment is not even defined as such. Yet the authors also note ambiguities here, in that women, plainly the group most likely to suffer harassment, may enjoy sexual banter in the workplace, which may be for its own sake, or to relieve boredom and generate fun, or as a bargaining counter (as when groups of women mock male supervisors in order to create social space and autonomy: Pollert 1981).

This last point leads to a discourse view, stressing that power is ambiguous and that the harassed need not be eternal victims and can use their own resources to change the ways in which acceptable behaviour is defined.

The value of the discourse view notwithstanding, the authors, rightly in our view, stress that power can be possessed by sovereign individuals rather than being lost in language and meaning. Consider for example a harasser: he may be trapped by existing discourses in so far as he feels that harassment is acceptable or even expected (as in strongly 'macho' cultures, for example), yet he plainly exercises choice, and his behaviour is also an assertion of power over others. The interesting question then is what social conditions define harassment as acceptable and under what conditions it may be challenged.

This example helps us to see the complex and embedded nature of power. It is not that there is a fixed entity called harassment but rather that what constitutes harassment is defined through social processes, in which power plays a central part. The very identification of a distinct form of behaviour with this label constitutes an exercise of power by the relatively powerless, for before the term was defined it was much easier than it is now for the powerful to engage in Face 2 and 3 forms of power. By contrast, many other labels are imposed by powerful groups, for example 'restriction of effort' or 'restrictive practices'. Note here an interesting ambiguity. Armstrong et al. (1981) set out to study practices so labelled in firms (relatively small ones) where they were usually felt to be absent, and were asked by managers whom they approached not to use the term to workers lest it 'give them ideas', that is, lest it release workers from Face 3 or discourse-based acceptance of the existing order. These researchers identified many subtle ways in which power was exercised and accepted as legitimate. Managers, for example, were able to persuade workers to forego their formal rights to 'waiting time' payment if there was no work to do, on the grounds that workers would prefer to go home rather than sit in the factory. Through such complex processes does power work. Box 6.2 gives a further illustration.

Box 6.2 Are power and exploitation ever transparent?

Burawoy (1979) has argued that capitalism is a distinct form of exploitation because there is no clear observable distinction between that part of production which is socially necessary (roughly, the part needed to pay wages and cover the costs of raw materials and depreciation) and that which is 'surplus' and generates profits. In feudalism, by contrast, necessary time was spent by serfs tilling their own land, and surplus labour was provided to the feudal lord, working his land. This distinction is useful analytically, in indicating that the wage form under capitalism has some distinctive features. But it does not imply that feudal lords were transparent in their assertion of exploitation. Their rights to the labour of serfs were legitimized in many ways, such as the lord's military defence of his serfs, family tradition, and the feudal theory that land rights derived from the monarch and ultimately from God. In day-to-day terms, moreover, acceptance of these rights was maintained in that those who were employed directly by the lord were dependent on him and thus reluctant to challenge his authority, while others were bound up in a system of legal rights and obligations which seemed to have a natural order to it. Where power operates solely on the basis of stark force, it is at its most vulnerable.

Conclusions are as follows. First, power may be zero-or positive-sum or a mix of both. Second, it may be held by individuals but can also be inscribed in rules and assumptions. Third, it is not helpful to describe such structures as discourses, as though they were infinitely malleable or alternatively so deeply embedded as to be beyond direct comprehension; in the case of the latter, moreover, if power is so deep how can the analyst claim to know what it is? Fourth, it is possible to ask what effects rules and assumptions have on people and how easy it is to change them. No rule can directly cause behaviour since someone has to decide to apply it, and in this decision the rule can change. Fifth, power is a resource. Worker participation is an engagement with patterns of power, and not a discrete activity. It is about using rules and resources, and not a question of absolutes.

Mapping Participation

Before we can use these ideas directly in relation to participation, we need to be clear as to what it is. Three conceptual devices help us address claims about trends in empowerment. First, empowerment relates in some way to the rights of employees and their recognition by their employer. The alternative approach is one of 'hire and fire' in which the employment contract is reduced as far as possible to a market exchange.

These two tendencies are captured in Streeck's (1987) distinction between status and contract. 'Contract' refers to a relationship based on the principles of hire-and-fire and individual responsibility. 'Status' covers longer-term relationships and the treatment of the employee as an investment rather than a cost. For current purposes, we include the provision of means for employees to participate in decision-making. A purely contractual relationship will give no space for such 'voice' and will treat employees simply as hired help, whereas in a more lasting relationship members of an organization may be expected to engage in its key choices.

Streeck's summary of moves towards contract and status is given in Table 6.1. This listing anticipated several developments in relation to both contract (e.g. temporary and agency work) and status (e.g. teamwork) that have become more salient since 1987. A particularly foresightful point was the highlighting of 'the possible contradictions inherent in a *simultaneous pursuit of restored contract and extended status*' and the fact that employers will 'find it exceedingly hard to formulate a consistent strategic approach to building a more flexible system' of employment relations (Streeck 1987: 295, emphasis added).

The next step is to perceive that status and contract are not logically opposed. Though it is normal to assume that the one runs counter to the

TABLE 6.1. Two routes to organizational flexibility

	Return to contract	Extension of status
Employment status of workers	Temporary	Permanent
Numerical flexibility	Hire and fire	Flexible working time
Functional flexibility	Hire and fire	Self-regulated job rotation
Work organization	Taylorist	Teamwork
Qualifications sought	Narrow	Broad
Wage determination	Industrial engineering	Payment by ability
Management style	Unilateral prerogative	Consultation, participation

Source: Taken from Edwards (2003: 20), which is abbreviated from Streeck (1987: 294).

other, it is possible for them to go together. Figure 6.1 lays out the possible relationships between the two. The main combinations have labels attached to make the following points. The key overall theme is that this is a model of status and contract, and not directly of participation. *Hire and fire* is the simplest case, where the employment relationship is treated as a market transaction.

The opposite case is in the top left of Figure 6.1. One example is *paternalism*, where the employer relies on diffuse obligations and usually offers significant job security. A second is labelled *responsible autonomy*, a term introduced by Trist and Bamforth (1951) to describe a small group of coal miners who were responsible for the whole of a work task. In the

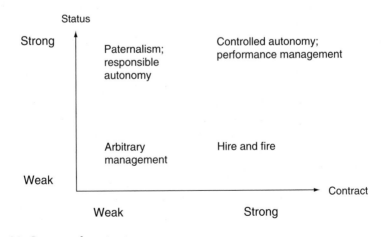

FIG. 6.1. Status and contract

latter case, contractual requirements are not absent, and indeed in the case described the miners were paid mainly by the piece so that in some respects contract was particularly salient. But they had discretion in the task and were not subject to direct managerial control of their day-to-day behaviour. The term has also been used to refer more generally to a situation in which management grants considerable discretion at the level of the job itself to workers. Note, however, that words like autonomy are often used loosely (see Box 6.3).

The top right of Figure 6.1 reflects the combination of status and contract. Its labels indicate that autonomy is likely to be controlled by the need to reach specific performance targets and that a 'performance management' system necessarily sets rules and procedures that contain empowerment or at least shape the context in which it is practised.

Box 6.3 Meanings and dimensions of autonomy

1. Autonomy can be defined in terms of the amount of freedom given to the worker as an individual to carry out work tasks or more broadly to decide what those tasks should be. The British Skills Survey asked a random sample of employees 'how much choice do you have over the way in which you do your job?' Overall, 46 per cent said 'a great deal', with high proportions among managers and professionals (63 and 56 per cent respectively) and the lowest proportion among sales occupations (33 per cent) (Felstead et al. 2002). What respondents meant by this is plainly open to debate. What choice means for professionals is very different from workers in routine tasks. Perceived autonomy for the latter is most likely to reflect some comparison of what a particular job normally means, with whether in practice it permits a degree of choice as to the order in which tasks are performed and the frequency with which behaviour is monitored by supervisors.
2. Autonomy can also mean that a work group has authority to make its own decisions, as in teamwork. The importance of this is that individuals are not isolated and hence some active discussion and participation is possible.
3. Autonomy may be granted by management, which is the emphasis of many current models of teamwork, or developed independently by workers (the latter being the case for Trist and Bamforth's miners). Under the latter head, it may entail specific work group-level efforts to shape the work task or wider collective projects for workers' control, or intermediate strategies.
4. Autonomy can refer only to the specifics of a work task, and is probably best defined in this way. Participation means engagement with wider questions of work design, and can itself vary in extent as discussed below.

Finally, a potentially puzzling situation is one where status and contract are both weak. It might be argued that this is a logically incoherent case, because a management must manage using status or contract or both. The dimensions of weak or strong emphasis on the two principles are better seen, however, as measuring the degree to which management has explicit and clear policies on the principles. Some cases are clear on contract. In large accountancy firms, for example, the principle of 'up or out' is well-established, meaning that junior employees either develop their skills and proceed upwards or they leave. Other large firms have set out to 'manage out' those at the bottom of measured contribution. By contrast, a reliance on hire and fire can be left highly implicit. For this reason, we use the label 'arbitrary management' to identify cases where status and contract lack coherent bases. Such bases may derive from formal strategic choices by firms, or they may reside in the tacit but still clear assumptions of a job. People taking casual jobs on construction sites, for example, will know that contract is strong even though there need be no formal statement to this effect.

Areas towards the bottom of Figure 6.1 will tend to have little or no empowerment because work relations rest on established forms of hierarchy. (There is one important qualification to this point, which is pursued below.) Anyone wishing to assert that empowerment is a general trend in a modern economy would need to examine the changing structure of jobs, assess the likely balance of status and contract, and show that there was a tendency towards the former. Yet much job growth in modern economies is either in established professions (where degrees of empowerment have probably not changed much) or in low-skilled jobs in the service sector (Nolan and Wood 2003).

As we move up and to the left, the possibilities for empowerment increase because workers are treated as investments rather than costs. But particularly notable is the area at the top right, where status and contract go together. Here, firms may 'empower' workers through autonomy but also expect them to deliver on specified performance targets. As discussed below, substantial empirical evidence now exists to show that this pattern is a common one.

The qualification mentioned above is that a hire-and-fire style embraces two distinct situations. The first is the obvious one where workers are treated as hired hands and empowerment is not contemplated. But it is also possible for workers here to have influence over their work situation precisely because they are independent contractors. A large firm which externalizes its IT provision to independent firms has clearly decided to manage the relevant relationships through contract (as the label of contracting out stresses). But the workers concerned may well have substantial autonomy in their work, and there are examples of such contractors who are better paid than equivalent in-house employees, and even instances when firms have decided to bring the work back in-house, only to find that it is hard to place the former contractors within their existing pay and grading structures. This case leads to the following conclusions:

- In terms of substance, the contractors have labour market power. Though the term empowerment is sometimes used particularly loosely, to refer to any outcome in which workers are freed from hierarchical control, using the term here causes confusion. Participation means engagement within some collective activity, and not just the absence of hierarchy. Independent contractors have bargaining power, but this should not be confused with empowerment within participatory arrangements.
- The second substantive point is that not all contractors have market power, for many are highly dependent on large firms. The absence of formal hierarchy does not mean total autonomy, and in many ways market relations establish relations of control and subordination more effectively than do hierarchical ones.
- An important point of method in thinking about devices such as Figure 6.1 is that they are sometimes presented as a complete mapping of a phenomenon. In this case, any pattern of work relations can usefully be described in terms of its balance of status and contract. But it is important to be clear as to what is being conceptualized, in this case this balance, and not the wider characteristics of the work in question. To capture these characteristics will require at least one further dimension, here the degree of labour market power. Conceptual diagrams are essential tools for understanding empirical reality, but it is essential to be clear as to what they can and cannot do.

This last point applies to other features of status and contract. We said above that shifts towards status make empowerment more likely. They do not, however, entail this result. 'Status' at the height of Fordism meant formal job classifications and promotion ladders that gave workers job security and sets of rights, but that did not offer active participation. Indeed, these rights were part of a tacit deal in which managements continued to make all the key decisions, and workers and their unions were excluded from them. Other conditions are necessary before empowerment reaches the agenda.

A second conceptual device is useful at this point. Most models of organizations operate around the distinction between markets and hierarchies (Adler 2001). Market principles are familiar. Hierarchies are also well known through debates on bureaucracies and their formal rules. According to Adler, many accounts treat these two principles as opposed, so that a bureaucratic rule on, say, pay levels replaces pay determination through the market. Yet they can be combined in various ways. For example, some pay systems include labour market considerations such as the going rate for a given job as well as evaluations of the contribution of individuals to the goals of an organization; people who are not marketable outside may still play key roles that labour market relativities would not capture. In addition, he goes on, there is a third principle, that of trust. Coordination of economic activity can be secured not only through the market or through rules, but can also be achieved by trust between the parties. These three principles can also vary independently, so that, dichotomizing each into high and low, eight distinct types of organization can be identified. In Adler's view, there is also a secular trend towards an emphasis on trust, a point taken up below.

This framework is useful in suggesting that *participation becomes feasible only where hierarchy and trust exist above some minimum level and where market principles are contained to some level.* Where the market threshold is exceeded, the emphasis will be towards contract, and it will be very hard to allow participation to develop. Where there is hierarchy but little trust we have a standard bureaucracy in which jobs may be secure and desirable but in which rule-following rather than active engagement is stressed. Where there is little or no hierarchy, however, we have situations of very strong trust such as may obtain within some workers' cooperatives. This is a case of primitive communism which is rare in economies like the UK (see Box 6.4). It may be left to one side where more formal and structured participation is concerned. A combination of hierarchy and trust with contained market principles permits participation to flourish.

The third conceptual device addresses the meaning of precarious employment. Heery and Salmon (2000) identify three dimensions:

- properties of jobs, notably the length of tenure of jobs;
- properties of labour markets and welfare system, including the length of spells of unemployment and the ratio of unemployment pay to normal pay; and
- properties of individual experience, in particular perceptions as to how secure a job is.

These dimensions are very helpful in sorting out what is meant when jobs are described as insecure. It is, for example, not the case that mean job

Box 6.4 Workers' cooperatives and participation

- Cooperatives are rare in the UK. In the 1980s, they were estimated to number only around 900, with a total employment of 6,000 (Hobbs and Jefferis 1990: 296).
- Studies in the UK and other countries commonly report that principles of work organization are not very different from those observed in comparable conventional firms. One study notably identified 'disturbing' findings in the well-known case of plywood factories in the north–west of the USA (Grunberg 1991). In contrast to earlier studies, productivity was lower than in conventional firms and accident rates were higher. The author explains this in terms of trends over time: (a) workers under conventional capitalist authority lost power in the workplace (so that in our terms pressures based on market and hierarchy were sufficient to secure increased work effort), and (b) the cooperatives experienced degeneration, which included a growth in the number of hired workers who were not members of the cooperatives while members themselves worked less hard and sought the most desirable jobs.
- It does not follow that cooperatives are bound to fail. The most celebrated success is that of Mondragón in the Basque region of Spain (e.g. Whyte and Whyte 1988). But it would appear that success rested on a particular combination of factors including: a network of cooperative enterprises, not least a bank, as opposed to isolated cooperatives in a sea of capitalism; rapid economic growth; the fact that workers do not own stock directly, so that there are no problems of buying out those who leave; fixed limits to the number of non-members who can be employed; and perhaps the support of nationalist sentiment.

tenure has collapsed in countries such as the USA and the UK. But the costs of job loss have often increased, while perceptions of insecurity reflect the extent of restructuring. As Heery and Salmon point out, staying in a job may reflect insecurity and a fear of taking the risk of moving elsewhere at least as much as it reflects commitment to that job. For present purposes, the insight is that shifts towards status will reduce insecurity on the first dimension but will have no effect on the second (which is a feature of national labour markets rather than firms) and may increase the third if PMSs tighten expectations as to what workers must do and establish means of monitoring, reward, and sanction.

There is, then, no reason why empowerment and status cannot go along with work intensification and a stress on contract. The balance will depend on where in Figure 6.1 jobs are located. To treat empowerment as the sole trend of importance is seriously to misunderstand the dynamics of jobs in modern economies.

Why Participation Matters

But do workers expect to participate at work? In a study of US workers at work, Freeman and Rogers (1999) found that people want more participation than they currently enjoy. We discuss this below. But they were also led to consider why what workers want matters. Box 6.5 summarizes the objections that were put to them and their answers. We would underline the arguments under the second and fourth points.

The second point states that the dissatisfied can leave. This, in turn, relies on: a moral argument, that workers have no business seeking to

Box 6.5 Why participation matters	
Objection	Response
1. Long-term jobs are disappearing [and therefore participation in one job is unimportant or, even if important, largely impossible]	Typical workers still spend substantial periods with one employer; a considerable number also have responsible positions and are thus a key part of the firm's human capital; and many express loyalty to their employer.
2. Dissatisfied employees can take other jobs	The costs of changing jobs are substantial and the social security system gives only limited support to the unemployed.
3. The economy is growing [and workers will thus gain key material benefits]	Inequality has soared and real incomes for average earners have stagnated.
4. The experts know best	Workers know their own situations better than any expert can.
5. Job satisfaction depends mainly on pay and conditions; intrinsic job interest scores low	It is true that extrinsic features of work are crucial. But once jobs are chosen extrinsic benefits are set, and the degree of participation can make a big difference. Nor does it mean that workers can trade off pay for participation, for the two go together, and the 'compensating benefits' explanation for differences of pay between jobs is false.

Source: Rows 1–4: Freeman and Rogers (1999: 8–14); square brackets our own elaborations. Row 5 is our own addition.

change how a firm chooses to operate; and an efficiency argument, that quitting will mean that workers sort themselves into firms according to their preferences for a given amount of participation. The moral argument slides over the investments that workers make in their jobs, as reflected in evidence on loyalty and other substantial evidence on the psychological effects of job loss: jobs contribute to people's self-identities, and the employment relationship is a social as well as economic one. It also takes it for granted that the owners of companies should define how they function, ignoring the fact that ownership implies no real commitment at all, since shares can be bought and sold at will. Workers' investments of skills and commitments are in many senses greater. The efficiency argument assumes that workers have the information to sort themselves and has a naive view of the functioning of markets (see Chapter 9).

The fourth point, about expertise, ignores substantial evidence that workers use 'tacit skills' on the job, often in ways that help them to get round formal procedures that interfere with efficiency. Like the moral argument, it also assumes that authority resides at the top, a view that conflicts with democratic principles as they apply outside the workplace.

The broader arguments for participation are widely rehearsed and are laid out by Heller et al. (1998: 8–10). They identify three. The 'humanistic' view is that participation aids employees' sense of creativity and achievement. The power-sharing view argues in terms of fairness. The most common recent justification is a business case based on efficiency. Though the authors do not say so, there are plainly different conceptions here. Under the first argument, it is sufficient for workers to be granted some space and autonomy, whereas the second addresses issues of power and rights, leading to the conclusion that employees require more than managerial concessions. As for the third, it is a difficult position to uphold in universal terms, for the empirical evidence is at best mixed and it seems clear that there are situations, most obviously routinized operations, where participation is unlikely to bring efficiency gains. If such gains were in fact clear, then participative organizations would drive out others, an outcome for which there is no convincing evidence. Rights-based arguments are the most coherent.

Extent of Empowerment and Participation

Before considering the extent of empowerment and participation, we need to recall some core facts about the balance of status and contract in the UK labour market, outlined in Chapters 2 and 5. There has been a growth in both 'bad' and 'good' jobs. Pressures around contract, through such things as PMSs, have intensified. Job satisfaction in the UK fell during the 1990s. There will thus be many jobs where empowerment is absent or tightly constrained. The facts summarized in Box 6.3 suggest that the labour market has not been transformed in the direction of status or high trust. Many low-level jobs have been created, and across the workforce as a whole there have been significant trends towards work intensification and stress.

The relationships between discretion, control, and participation are complex. The most sustained effort to address them is the study by Gallie et al. (1998) discussed in Chapter 5. Gallie reports significantly increased skill levels and concludes that 'the most prevalent employer policy with regard to work organization has been a move towards "responsible autonomy"' (Gallie 1996: 156). Yet this last term was not used in the way in which it was introduced by Trist and Bamforth, to indicate a self-governing collectivity. For Gallie, autonomy meant delegation to an individual. As noted in Chapter 5, the survey also found that monitoring and control systems were growing in use and that work intensification was also rising. 'The structures of control of work performance are being modified but control remains pervasive and possibly more intense in the pressures it brings to bear on work effort' (Gallie et al. 1998: 316).

Control and discretion were both increasing, but there was no simple pattern of polarization whereby some workers experienced increased discretion and reduced control, while others suffered the reverse. In our terms, there was no straight polarization between the hire-and-fire and responsible autonomy fields in Figure 6.1. The authors also measured the intensity of work pressure and identified two apparently contrasting influences: people with discretion commit themselves to high intensity, but tight control systems also lead to high work pressure (Gallie et al. 1998: 79).

The result is surprising only if one takes either of two rather simple positions (both of which have been in evidence). The first sees hard work as the result of willing commitment and of the removal of assertive control. The second takes the opposite stance, seeing work effort as the outcome only of intrusive managerial control. Both tendencies are in fact in evidence, and most importantly they are often combined for the same individual, so that asking whether hard work is the result either of commitment or of control is to pose a false dichotomy. Under performance management, in particular, control and commitment are combined. It is important, moreover, to see them as linked, rather than as two separate forces that are in some way added together. A worker will know that she has to attain targets and that her performance is measured in defined ways, and yet also that she has freedom to decide how precisely to do the job; and she is likely to find that there is a sense of fulfilment in achieving goals.

The conclusions of Gallie et al. (1998: 85) clearly run against optimistic assertions of a long-term trend towards trust and discretion. Before reviewing the empirical conclusions the lack of historical evidence for such an assertion, by writers like Adler (2001), should be stressed. Many scholars have identified cycles of managerial control, with swings between responsible autonomy and command-and-control systems, rather than a unidirectional trend. Adler recognizes such arguments but suggests that there is also an underlying trend line towards high levels of trust. Quite how one would test this empirically is very unclear. In any event, the interesting issue is not whether capitalism has any single trend of this kind, but rather how different combinations of market, hierarchy, and trust are organized. While the empirical evidence suggests that some trend towards trust can be identified (in the recent past but not necessarily in the long term), the key point is that this is combined with other forces such as performance management, so that to analyse trust alone is not productive. As Gallie et al. conclude, predictions of a 'transformation of employment relationships' are inaccurate, and a picture of continuing and indeed increasing control by employers is more accurate. Advanced technology does not lead to 'an era of less coercion and more trust': it does nothing to check increases in supervision and it favours 'both technical and bureaucratic control systems'.

It is easy to point to the limitations of a rhetoric of empowerment. The term 'rhetoric' is important here, signalling that at this point the interest is in the largest possible claims that might be made about giving workers power over their working lives. To begin, it is useful to clarify the different dimensions involved, for participation takes different characteristics in different contexts. Four key dimensions are shown in Box 6.6.

Looking first at the *degree* and also the *range* of participation, a large comparative study in the 1970s asked individual employees about their involvement in decision-making, using a six-point scale running from 'I am not involved at all' (point 1) to 'I decide on my own' (point 6). In

a sample of nearly 8000 people in 134 companies in twelve countries, describing the influence they had over sixteen different decisions, the average for workers did not quite reach point 2, 'being informed beforehand', and for strategic decisions, like investments, was closer to 'not involved at all'. Even at the middle-management level, the average barely exceeded 'informed beforehand and can give opinion' [point 3]. (Heller et al. 1998: 159)

Box 6.6 Dimensions of empowerment

Marchington and Wilkinson (2000: 342–3) show that participation is not an all-or-nothing process and that it can vary on four dimensions:

- The *degree* of participation measures the extent to which employees can influence management, with the range running from the provision of information, through communication, consultation, and co-determination, to 'control'. Co-determination means joint decision-making as opposed to consultation, where employees' views are sought but the decision rests with management. The authors do not define 'control', but presumably mean that employees can decide on their own authority.
- Participation can occur at such *levels* as the work task, a department, a workplace, or the whole company.
- The *range of issues* covered can run from specific issues 'such as canteen food to more strategic concerns relating to investment strategies'.
- The *forms* of participation are: financial (e.g. profit sharing), representative (through elected representatives), and direct (face-to-face discussion either around the immediate work task or through off-line projects or problem-solving groups). In our view, the first is not about the process of participating in what an organization does but is simply to do with sharing the returns that it makes. We therefore say no more about it.

It is true that this study took place before the upsurge in interest in participation, which is usually dated from the 1980s. But similar results are reported from studies of the early 1990s (Heller et al. 1998: 160).

A survey of US workers conducted in 1994 asked how much influence and involvement they had on a range of eight issues and how important it was to have influence (Freeman and Rogers 1999: 47–50). These issues focused on details of work tasks rather than strategic decisions. The highest score for actual involvement was on 'deciding how to do your job and organize the work' (57 per cent reported a lot of influence) while the lowest were on deciding pay rises and what kinds of benefits (i.e. sick pay and the like) workers should receive (both at 6 per cent). On average, the proportion of workers with less involvement than they wanted was 53 per cent, with the largest gap in relation to benefits and the smallest on deciding how to do the job.

Other studies reveal significant national variations. Dobbin and Boychuk (1999) looked at reported job autonomy in seven countries from studies during the 1980s. Overall they found, in line with the above results, quite low levels of autonomy: the mean score on a 0–5 scale was 1.45. But scores were significantly higher in national systems stressing skill development, training, and employee responsibility (Denmark, Finland, Norway, and Sweden) than in those with a more traditional top-down approach (Australia, Canada, and the USA). This study also found that countries with high worker autonomy did not have low managerial autonomy: it was not the case that autonomy was a zero-sum phenomenon, and on the contrary worker and managerial autonomy tended to go together.

A survey in 1996 across ten European countries asked managers in 5,786 workplaces about the extent and depth of participation (see Edwards et al. 2002). The importance of this survey is that many others give apparently higher figures but are often based simply on the existence of a practice and not how intensely it is used. The number of issues on which employees were consulted and the extent of employee autonomy were measured and combined into a measure of intensity. To attain a significant degree of work group autonomy, approximating in our terms to responsible autonomy, a workplace would have to score high on the intensity measure, but in fact no more than 5 per cent of cases achieved this result, and even in the home of work group autonomy, Sweden, the figure was only 18 per cent.

Case studies of consciously advanced efforts at employee involvement also point to limited results. Witte (1980) studied an important case in the USA, for here there was a strong initiative from the president of the parent company, and it was possible for the experiment to be tracked over time. There were two autonomous work teams, together with an elected council at company level. Yet despite some successes, most of the experiments were abandoned, which Witte attributes primarily to the hierarchical ways in which companies are structured and the difficulties of developing alternatives. A more recent, and well-known, US case is the Saturn Corporation, as detailed in Box 6.7. The key conclusion here is that, in contrast to Witte's case, the experiment worked, survived, and contributed to the goals of workers and managers, but was not generalized to other parts of the company.

Particularly interesting information comes from Norway and Sweden, for in these two countries experiments in work redesign have a very long history and they are strongly embedded in the philosophies of trade unions (which remain strong and influential), political parties, and to a degree companies. As summarized by Heller et al. (1998: 180–6), slow diffusion was common despite encouraging conditions. The Volvo plant at Kalmar in Sweden is a well-known example, where despite rising productivity levels the plant was closed, and its experiments were not copied even in other plants in Sweden.

Box 6.7 The case of Saturn

Saturn was established as a General Motors subsidary in 1985 and produced its first vehicles in 1990. It is a critical case because the extent of employee involvement was greater than in other US companies and because the experiment was conducted with the active engagement of senior managers and the relevant trade union (Rubinstein and Kochan 2001). The key innovation was 'co-management partnering' in which union representatives and managers worked together actively in the making of shop-floor decisions. There were in addition more familiar devices including online work teams, off-line problem-solving groups, and joint labour-management committees.

Saturn achieved very high levels of quality and productivity as compared to other GM plants, though performance tended to erode over time. Wages were comparable to or better than those in the rest of GM. The experiment worked well at the level of work teams, but off-line problem-solving was less successful. The union demonstrably contributed to improving the management process, but there were tensions between involvement in decision-making and the desire to represent workers' interests as against those of management.

When a new facility to build Saturn-badged vehicles was established, it was run on conventional lines, with a conscious decision not to copy the experiment. Learning, the authors conclude, is very difficult.

As for *levels* of participation, surveys focus on the immediate work task, and it is at this level that most of the rhetoric of empowerment has been directed. Participation at higher levels necessarily entails some form of representative arrangement. Overall trends run counter to any tendency for participation to grow. In countries such as the USA and the UK, where teamwork and the like have been particularly popular, the presence of trade unions has fallen, especially in the private sector. Other forms of representation are either absent (the USA has no statutory works council system, while one will be introduced in the UK only from 2005) or weak. Countries with statutory systems have seen no notable increase in their powers, while union membership has generally been stable or in shallow decline. Box 6.8 summarizes the position in the key case of Germany. We also pick up on this issue in Chapter 8, in relation to past board-level worker involvement in the UK (see Box 8.3); the discussion is at that point to deal with tensions in group decision-making, but it also adds to the present evidence by pointing to difficulties of this type of representation in essentially adversarial structures of corporate governance. In more cooperative systems, such as the German, these difficulties appear to be smaller.

Box 6.8 Works councils and co-determination in Germany

- Works councils are mandatory in private firms with five or more employees, but in fact are estimated to cover only 24 per cent of eligible workplaces and 60 per cent of employees.

- Councillors are elected by the whole of the work force. They have rights to 'co-determine' some matters. This means that management must win their assent with any stalemate being resolved by binding arbitration. Councils are forbidden to strike, and are bound by a generic obligation to pursue peaceful agreement. Matters subject to co-determination include working hours, hiring and firing, and training. Councils have the right to be consulted on such issues as the reorganization of work. They receive information on such matters as financial plans. Generally, rights are weaker the more that strategic issues are concerned. Councils must be consulted about large-scale redundancies and may object to, but not prevent, individual dismissals.

- Research has focused on structure and organization rather than effects. There is clear evidence that councils are established and accepted parts of the system, and that managers welcome them for their help in negotiating potentially conflictual issues and for their provision of a coherent employee voice. They have been found to improve communication and increase the quality of decision-making, and also to ease the process of restructuring.

- Evidence on effects is limited at least in part because it is hard to find comparable firms without councils and because other factors influencing outcomes are hard to control. Research has also tended to look for the presence of a council rather than measures of effectiveness. Some economics-based research tends to cite negative performance effects, but weaker or zero effects tend to be neglected. Overall, negative effects seem small.

- In large German companies, workers also have elected representatives on supervisory boards. They comprise between one-third and one-half of board members, though the chair with the casting vote is nominated by shareholders. Supervisory boards select management boards that make day-to-day decisions. Because supervisory boards meet rarely and are at some distance from concrete issues, the impact of worker representation is often felt to be weaker than that of the works council system.

Sources: Frege (2002); Jacobi et al. (1998); Wever (1995).

In our view, a key feature of effective councils is that they act to stimulate managers to take more careful and considered decisions than would be the case without such checks. This picks up the point in Box 6.8 about measures of effectiveness. Not all councils will act as effective means of checks and balances, and measuring simply council presence may underestimate the potential positive effect. A long strand of research, mainly in the USA, also suggested that trade unions could 'shock' managers into acting in a more considered and professional manner (Freeman and Medoff 1984). It does not follow that all unions do this, and research never addressed the types of unions most likely to do so or the conditions necessary for the effect to exist. But the potential was certainly present.

These facts pose a puzzle, since evidence in several countries suggests that direct participation is most effective when it is combined with representative arrangements. This is acknowledged in Britain by the main employers' body, the CBI, which together with the Trades Union Congress has argued that 'optimal results are achieved where there is a mix of direct employee involvement *and* indirect participation ... through a trade union or works council' (CBI/TUC 2001: para. 31, emphasis original). Some case studies suggest that the reasons for this association include the value of representative arrangements in introducing teamwork and the fact that direct participation alone may lack the means to aggregate sets of concerns into overall modes of organized action. Heller et al. (1998: 122) cite research showing the association and offer the example of the handling of repetitive strain injuries in the car industry. In the unionized NUMMI plant in the USA, union pressure led to emphasis on this issue, while at non-union Isuzu little was done and this heightened 'employee disillusionment with an ostensibly participative teamwork system'.

Why, then, is representative participation unpopular with firms? One part of the answer may be that firms are simply unaware of the benefits. But more than intellectual awareness is required. We have seen that representative systems call for a change of thinking, away from hierarchical approaches. Such change may be hard to achieve, even if abstractly the benefits might be appreciated.

Even more fundamental is the way in which competitive advantage is achieved. Representative participation is likely to be one among a set of conditions that work together. Where it exists, benefits can be identified. But it will not work alone, and it has costs as well as benefits. Might it be, though, that firms with the relevant characteristics (direct and representative participation) perform better than others and thus drive them out? There are, however, many influences on the performance of firms, and evidence that it is representative arrangements in and of themselves that cause good performance is lacking. What then are the conditions under which participation works?

Conditions for Participation to Work

It is now a commonplace that participation 'works' but only when conditions are appropriate (e.g. Edwards et al. 2002; Heller et al. 1998: 190–216; Marchington and Wilkinson 2000). Among the key underpinning conditions are job security, for without such security workers may distrust management while management may be more concerned with handling a hire-and-fire system than seeking longer-term commitment. For such reasons, participation may never reach the agenda, and when it does it may be undermined by short-term cost minimization.

Job security can be promoted within an individual organization, for example US 'welfare capitalists' (Jacoby 1997). Or it can be supported through a national employment regime such as the Nordic countries discussed above, or Germany, where it was widely argued that security based on legal protections against dismissal encouraged workers to accept organizational change, which in turn promoted growth and promoted security. Whether such a virtuous circle has continued to exist after the heyday of the German system in the period from the 1950s to the 1980s is a contested point. Such a system has costs and limits as well as benefits, and in retrospect some of its virtuous aspects appear to have rested on economic growth that was not sustained in perpetuity. Nonetheless, job security seems to give managers an incentive to build long-term relationships and to give employees the confidence to engage in the necessary trust relations.

Job security is often encouraged by the economic context of a firm, so that large firms in stable and oligopolistic markets are likely to be able to afford status-based systems and to feel that developing employee commitment will have long-term business benefits. It has thus been found that sectors such as pharmaceuticals can sustain participative arrangements. It is also the case that such sectors, along with continuous process industries, have work organizations that generally lend themselves to teamwork because tasks tend to have a long cycle time and to involve group rather than individual activity.

A key issue is the existing pattern of work organization and the social relations that it encourages. Workers who have enjoyed a degree of responsible autonomy may well feel that participation schemes take away from, rather than enhance, their autonomy. Vallas and Beck (1996) studying workers in US pulp and paper mills found that these workers had enjoyed craft knowledge and that new computerized systems codified and restricted the exercise of this knowledge. A later study of teamwork experiments in the same industry makes a useful contrast, following the German social theorist Jürgen Habermas, between instrumental and communicative rationality (Vallas 2003). The former is a planned and formal approach, while the latter relies on shared understandings and collective debate. Managers in the workplaces studied overemphasized rational elements, and yet workers were willing to participate actively where they could draw on 'cultural patterns that were indigenous to production crews' (ibid.: 244). Managerial efforts to generate teamwork in fact reproduced existing hierarchies. In other conditions, for example the UK supermarket studied by Rosenthal et al. (1997), relatively modest efforts to promote participation can be welcomed when they mark a distinct break from previously hierarchical systems, though it also appears that substantial and real managerial commitment, rather than lip service, was also important.

Underlying such aspects of the workplace itself are larger systems of control. Vallas (2003) notes that a 'logic of standardization' was pursued by managements concerned at demonstrating the value of costly new investments, with this concern in turn stemming from a top-down corporate agenda. Appelbaum and Berg (1996) discuss wider trends towards the deregulation of financial markets and pressures for short-term shareholder value and argue that these make commitment to participation hard to achieve (see Chapter 9 for more details).

An important theme runs through such studies. The general principle of participation is often welcomed, but managements define it in terms of instrumental rationality and may do so increasingly. With the growth of performance targets and received notions of 'best practice', the tendency is towards such rationality in place of the less formalized approaches of responsible autonomy. New investments have to demonstrate a rate of return and managers are likely to be driven by the language of target achievement, even though this language undercuts the very participation that they wish to achieve.

The context of empowerment is also often unfavourable. Restructuring and job losses are familiar experiences. One survey of UK managers found that virtually all of them reported some significant organizational change, such as a culture change programme, delayering or outsourcing, in each of three years; and the figures imply that managers on average experienced three such changes each year (Worrall et al. 2000: 655). The study then looked in more detail at redundancies, which were reported by about half the managers, and at the impact on those who survived the job losses. The 'main consequence' was 'increased task overload and reduced role clarity' with the result being to 'reduc[e] trust and creat[e] a blame culture' (ibid.: 657, 665). There are two distinct implications here.

The first is the obvious one that workers losing their jobs will not be empowered by the experience. The second is that the process of restructuring is likely to lead to attention to the basics of organizational survival, with empowerment being a luxury of more expansive times. As another study found, it is not that managers dislike the idea of participation in principle (indeed a US study found that, in relation to the specifics of the work task, managers are as likely as workers to think that participation is a good idea: Collom 2003). The issue is more to do with the time and energy involved in promoting participation when other demands are more pressing (Fenton-O'Creevy 2001). Finally, empowerment means something only for employees in reasonably secure and well-paying jobs. It means little or nothing for the many workers in low-skill and insecure employment.

As cases such as Saturn suggest, to achieve a work organization that supports substantial participation requires intense managerial investments of resources, time, and personal commitment. Sustaining such a work organization is also a major task. Even though participatory systems work, then, they are not diffused widely. The conditions underpinning them are hard to reproduce elsewhere, and they entail costs as well as benefits.

Conclusions

This chapter began with social science debates about power, to inform the substantive discussion of participation and also the politics of decision-making as discussed in Chapters 7 and 8. The key analytical lesson was that power is about control of other people and the ability to achieve goals, some of which may be individual or shared with other people, while others may run counter to the goals of other people. Any organizational process is likely to entail a mix of these elements (though it should also not be forgotten that some may be only about power in the crudest sense of shifting rewards from one group to another). The practical lesson, as the case of harassment illustrated, is that power resources are not fixed and that structures that appear immovable may be open to challenge. People may have more resources than they realize, and challenging existing structures can show that they are more changeable than they may seem.

Yet change is also driven by corporate agendas, and 'empowerment' may be much less evident than some such agendas like to claim. It is generally limited in scope and depth. Its popularity waxes and wanes, and experiments to promote it tend not to survive and are rarely generalized outside their own contexts. Yet it works, in that both employees and firms gain benefits. The reasons for this apparent paradox are twofold. First, participation works under particular conditions, which are hard to generalize. Second, it entails costs, embracing direct financial costs and less direct risk for employers in giving up a degree of authority. Even if it is desirable, therefore, firms may not make the necessary investments. The implications may be considered as they apply to people exposed to 'empowerment' schemes, companies, and public policy.

For individuals, the key issue is not empowerment in the abstract but whether it fits with the context of the organization. By 'fit' we mean to what extent the conditions discussed above are present. For example, widespread job insecurity is likely to undermine participation. Then there is the nature of an initiative itself and the extent to which it, first, has clear managerial support, second, is consistent with other managerial practices and, third, is compatible with existing forms of work organization. An initiative that seems to come out of the blue and to lack engagement with current practice is likely to stall. This does not mean that change is impossible. There may even be circumstances in which radical change is desirable. But the evidence suggests that the difficulties are substantial and, crucially, that simply contrasting a current situation with some desired model of 'empowerment' is unlikely to be constructive. Engagement with current expectations is crucial, with new ideas needing to establish some direct connection with current models rather than being applied in an idealized and distant manner.

How, then, can individuals use the language of empowerment? There is some evidence that workers can take managers at their word, and use the 'language and concepts' of participation schemes to 'bring managers into line with worker expectations' (Rosenthal et al. 1997: 498–9). There may be ways in which a general participatory initiative can be shaped by workers to suit their own aims. A common model here is that of 'capturing' an initiative and turning it against itself, for example by taking a management-led approach and subverting it so as to pursue a different agenda. Though such a strategy may suit certain conditions, in general the evidence reviewed above does not suggest that participation is limited to this zero-sum agenda. Participation schemes are attempts to manage the contradictions between control and autonomy, and worker responses to the schemes are means to negotiate a particular way through the contradictions. For example, a teamwork experiment proposed by management may neglect needs for training; worker action on this front may rescue the experiment from itself by insisting on the missing ingredient, and may at the same time secure worker goals (more interesting jobs, more skills) even though in other respects the scheme places new pressures on workers. Worker responses are about negotiating the dynamics of essentially uncertain processes, and not (necessarily or wholly) fighting zero-sum battles.

In relation to companies, attention needs to focus on what is under their control and on how to deal with what is not. Matters open to choice include the design of participation schemes so that they have an affinity with existing work organization and worker expectations (so that, for example, a constant series of 'new' initiatives is avoided). Companies can also address the familiar problem of mixed messages: if they genuinely seek participation, is there evidence, as seen through workers' eyes, of specific commitments and of consistency? The evidence suggests that companies are not prisoners of their economic context, and that firms in similar positions can manage in different ways. Yet some factors, such as pressures for shareholder value, are inescapable. They may mean that some participation schemes are simply not appropriate for some contexts, for example 'teamwork' where work is low-skill and routinized. In other cases, they suggest a realism of ambition and a willingness to recognize that even well-intended plans may fail if the context changes.

A key part of the last point concerns communication with employees. We have over the years observed numerous instances where workers, faced with a change of plan by managers, either condemned apparent incompetence or argued that managers in fact knew what was going on and were devious in their treatment of workers. The uncertainties of the business environment, and the fact that managers are not necessarily incompetent or devious, were not accepted ideas. The nature of the uncertainties needs communication involving, crucially, not distant statements but an effort to provide a meaningful grasp of the context. To the extent that this is done, workers are likely to believe the message. Building the necessary relationships takes time, however, and a rush to see immediate results may well undermine a participation scheme. To the extent that it is not done, and the evidence here is far from encouraging, workers will reasonably retain scepticism about the depth and durability of participation schemes.

Perhaps the most important issue is the linkage between levels of participation. Direct participation has become popular while trade union influence has waned and firms have shown little enthusiasm for employee representation, particularly in top decision-making arenas. Many firms remain deeply suspicious of challenges to managerial prerogative because they fear a weakening of authority and because of fundamental distrust of those outside the managerial circle. Other forms of participation are not worthless, and we have shown that they bring real benefits, but these benefits remain tightly constrained.

As for public policy, participatory approaches are clearly more strongly embedded in countries such as Germany or Sweden than they are in the UK or the USA. If policy is to promote participation, then the conditions where it thrives need attention. Such an approach is very different from that of much public policy, which entails the identification of 'best prac-tice' and exhortation to emulate it. If conditions are not appropriate, emulation will be absent or will fail. One key feature of Germany is that institutions such as works councils are well established, which means that firms have to adjust how they behave: the institutional context shapes assumptions and the ways in which choices are made. By contrast, in the UK and the USA, assumptions about 'shareholder value', the need to retain commercial confidentiality, and the right and obligation of man-agements to take key decisions are equally strongly embedded. Public policy would need to find ways to shift such assumptions as well as to promote the economic conditions which sustain organizations that stress status over contract.

7

Why Do Disasters Happen?

Organizations are rationally designed systems pursuing defined ends. So why do things go wrong?

A familiar list of spectacular failures would include the *Challenger* shuttle disaster in the USA in 1986 (7 crew were killed), the Piper Alpha oil rig in the North Sea in 1988 (167 dead), and the explosion of the Union Carbide chemicals works at Bhopal in India in 1984 that left between 2,500 and 10,000 people dead (estimates vary widely as to the exact number; the catastrophe is probably the largest single industrial disaster, leading to more immediate deaths and illnesses than the Chernobyl nuclear disaster of 1985, which killed immediately only 30 people). Less spectacular cases of organizational failures include computer systems that fail to work: the Taurus electronic trading system at the London Stock Exchange was initiated in 1986 and abandoned seven years later having run substantially over budget. In none of these cases was there a deliberate attempt to destroy the operation, and they all occurred either in prestigious public organizations or in large MNCs.

There are two distinct processes at work here. The first concerns operational mistakes and miscalculations that can have catastrophic consequences. The second covers decision-making processes that lead to failure. In the first case, the goal is clear and unquestioned (running an oil rig safely) but the execution fails. In the second case, there is a choice of goals and in retrospect it appears that the wrong one ended up being chosen. These two issues are addressed, respectively, in this chapter and in Chapter 8.

The criminologist Box (1983: 26–8) put the issue of workplace danger in sharp perspective. He calculated the number of deaths in the UK between 1973 and 1979 from fatal accidents and occupational diseases. The number was 11,436, which he set against the number of homicides (3,291). Allowing for differences in populations at risk (occupational hazards apply only to those in employment), the ratio was of the order of 7:1. Box also argues that there may be serious underrecording of the occupational data. Box appears to have intended the comparison to be taken literally, as comparing different sets of avoidable deaths. The degree of intentionality and the social processes involved are, however, very different. Nonetheless, the data underline the extent of industrial injury and how little attention is paid to it.

Apart from its inherent importance, the issue of mistakes and errors is valuable for several reasons. First, it is rarely addressed in studies of organizations. Not only is it absent from many standard textbooks, but it is also not discussed in a volume aiming to lay out the key approaches to strategy, even though overcoming errors might be seen as central to strategy (Mintzberg et al. 1998). Nor is it mentioned in a book directed explicitly at what it terms organizational misbehaviour (Ackroyd and Thompson 1999). The reasons for this need not detain us here, but anyone using this book to study analytical approaches to organizations may care to think of some. Second, it throws light on many important themes of how people see the world and how they relate to each other in organizations. For example, it brings into very sharp focus what Weick (1993) calls false hypotheses: when we expect to see or hear certain things, we interpret evidence in the light of such expectations, and fill in gaps to tell a consistent story. This tendency can have severe consequences in certain conditions. Third, it helps us fill out and develop the themes of power and organizational negotiation introduced in Chapters 5 and 6. A key point about disasters is that they are attempts to keep organizations working, and thus illustrate power as a capacity. But they are also about struggles over different definitions of organizational processes, thus reflecting power in the sense of domination of one group by another.

One other remark is needed. Weick identifies a psychological process. Such a process is likely to operate anywhere. Indeed, as shown below, the need for interpretative schemes characterizes science as much as it does everyday life. They also need to be placed in the context of structural factors to do with technology and the distribution of power. A focus on psychology can lead to a tendency to 'blame the operator', whereas we also need to ask why the operator was placed in a certain position.

We thus begin by examining systems and then placing them in a wider political economy perspective. Our remark above, that there is a clear goal but a failure of execution, is a first approximation, for it is often the case that safety is much more contested and political than it implies. Analyses based on political economy often stress conflicts of interest almost exclusively, while more conventional approaches neglect them or treat them as unfortunate interferences with the pursuit of joint goals. Research that stops with the approximation is illuminating and often neglected, and it should be considered before wider issues are addressed.

We proceed as follows. First, some writers see science or organizational rationality as having run away from social control, with danger being inherent in modern society. We address two versions of this perspective in the first two sections of the chapter. We then turn to the opposite position, that high reliability is feasible. The rest of the chapter develops a more adequate analysis, first by placing disasters in the context of technology and then examining two specific perspectives, 'man-made disasters' and 'normal accidents'. The final section draws the argument together through a political economy of safety and risk.

Administrative Evil?

The broadest attempt to explain failures locates them in what has been termed administrative evil, which is in turn seen as an inherent component of the technical rationality of modern societies (Adams and Balfour 1999). Technical rationality is a key issue for large organizations, since they are the archetypical example of this approach. It embraces predictability, the following of rules, and formal procedures and standards of behaviour. Administrative evil is defined as a process through which outcomes causing suffering to others arise even though people may not be aware of these results because their actions are masked by technical rationality. Simply 'following orders' may entail evil.

For these authors, a critical case is the Holocaust. Along with others (e.g. Bauman 1989), they see the Holocaust, not as a dreadful aberration, but as inherent in modernity and technical rationality. For Bauman (1989: 17), it grew out of a bureaucracy true to its 'form and purpose' and was a central part of modernity and indeed could not have occurred under any other system. Adams and Balfour (1999: 167) stress that the administrators were following orders and procedures and that everything was legally sanctioned.

Explaining how it was that the Holocaust could happen and how 'normal' people were drawn to engage in it is an important activity. It is true that an administrative machine was put in place and that people who played their part did not ask why they were, for example, driving railway trains to extermination camps, focusing instead on the fact that they were 'just doing their job' or 'following orders'. Yet the causal chain here is too tight. Not all technical–rational organizations have inherent in them the risk of evil on a large scale. Much has been made of the 'following orders' argument, but under the exigencies of a repressive regime in wartime it is understandable why people would make such an argument, not least because refusal to follow orders could lead to severe punishment. In other conditions, it is reasonable to expect that people will be able to question orders. This is not to say that they will, as we discuss below. But any bureaucracy with formal procedures is likely to contain some means by which orders may be questioned and reservations noted. The whole point of professional authority is that there are standards of behaviour, and that professionals do not follow orders blindly.

Indeed, an ironic result of the model of administrative evil is that everything is explained by it and genuine evil is forgotten. Means and ends become confused. Administrative evil involves the rational pursuit of means without any questioning of ends. But the ends were prescribed by some people. This is not to say that the shape of the 'final solution' existed fully formed in prior plans; like any other complex process, its nature evolved over time. But there was nonetheless a stated end. The Holocaust surely needs explanation in terms of specific policies and choices, rather than being treated as the direct result of 'modernity'.

At this point, we should be clear what 'going wrong' means. One review of the literature observes that 'routine non-conformity, mistakes, misconduct and disasters are not anomalous events' (Vaughan 1999: 298). This is true, but it is unhelpful to lump different phenomena together. 'Misconduct' is deliberate flouting of rules or expectations, while mistakes and disasters are unintentional. Just how to identify misconduct is also much less clear than might appear, as we discuss below. This point has been made in respect of Vaughan's own analysis of the *Challenger* case (Perrow 1999: 379–80; the reference is to Vaughan 1996). The case is now widely used in studies of organizations. Its essence is simple and is set out in Box 7.1.

For Adams and Balfour, and for Vaughan, the disaster can be explained in terms of the social construction of reality (see Chapter 5), wherein a bureaucracy allowed the 'normalization' of deviations from safe procedures. Yet, as Perrow argues, to rely on social construction is to minimize the distinctive events in this case, and to treat it as an emblem of any form of organizational practice anywhere. The deviation from procedure (launch under cold conditions) was in fact unprecedented and not normal. And the launch was opposed by a group of engineers, who knew that conditions were outside parameters that they had investigated, rather than being deeply embedded in an unquestioned culture. What stands out for Perrow is the exercise of power by other people over the objections of the engineers: 'we miss a great deal when we substitute culture for power' comments Perrow dryly.

Let us pursue social construction in relation to data on industrial injury. It is true that all kinds of definitional processes are involved in deciding just how severe an injury needs to be before it is reported. And there are

Box 7.1 The *Challenger* events

The shuttle exploded soon after take-off. The immediate cause was found to be a failure of an 'O' ring that was meant to seal the rocket fuel; leaking fuel was ignited. Further investigation found that problems with the rings had been identified, and addressed by including two sets of rings. On this occasion, however, the launch took place in very low temperatures, which meant that the rings were less flexible than under standard conditions.

Reasons offered as to why the launch took place instead of being postponed include the fact that there had been several delays already and that this was the first flight to feature a civilian, which was important for establishing the political legitimacy of the shuttle programme, not least because the President of the USA was scheduled to speak to the civilian when she was in orbit.

Source: Vaughan, (1996). Adams and Balfour (1999).

convincing arguments that the weakening of trade unions in many countries reduces the strength of workers and hence their willingness to risk reporting injuries; the result is that reported declines in injury rates may be exaggerations (Nichols 1997). Yet it is also accepted that the more severe injuries will tend to be reported, and that figures on them are likely to be relatively reliable. An interesting illustration given by Nichols is summarized in Box 7.2: the nature of data can be explained and their value grasped, rather than being relabelled as mere exercises in social construction. (Box 7.4 provides another example.)

In short, to rely too much on social construction is to play down distinctive structural influences and processes. Disasters are neither unique nor direct reflections of the modern condition. The politics of their occurrence deserve attention.

Box 7.2 Interpreting injury statistics

In 1969 iron ore miners in Sweden went on strike to end the piecework pay system. Following their success, recorded severe injuries fell while minor ones rose. This can be accounted for by two effects. Piecework is well known to induce risk because it encourages the cutting of corners to raise earnings, and its ending cut the rate of severe injury. Workers now also had the time to report less severe injuries, since they would no longer suffer a pay penalty from being away from production. Statistics need to be questioned and interrogated but not rejected out of hand.

Source: Nichols (1997: 84).

Cultures of Fear

There is a widespread and often misplaced 'culture of fear' leading people to be 'afraid of the wrong things' (Glassner 1999). Scares about issues as diverse as airline crashes, medical procedures, and crime are often exaggerated; for example, fear of crime increases when the available evidence of crime rates suggests that the risk is falling. Glassner explains this in terms of the following factors:

- *Media hype and exaggeration.* Although some parts of the media correct the errors of others, in some cases a media frenzy can be identified. For example, cases of child abuse have led to possible solutions of unproven effect and unintended consequences such as mob violence against people suspected (often wrongly) of being abusers.
- *Self-interest.* People selling security systems, for example, have an interest in preying on fears of crime.
- *Preying on uncertainty and doubt.* A classic example is the *War of the Worlds* radio programme of 1938, in which a portrayal of a Martian invasion was taken by many people as being a real event. One reason for this was that the radio was perceived as an authoritative and reliable source. But Glassner also makes the more subtle point that some people saw the programme as an analogy: with fear of war at the time, the Martians were taken to represent Germany or Japan.
- *Scapegoating.* The point about analogies links to the attribution of blame. Glassner quotes an example from fourteenth century Europe when Jews were accused of poisoning wells. Impure water had been a long-standing problem, but when for some reason it came into focus it was desirable to find an explanation, and blaming a group such as the Jews was a convenient solution.

In developed countries, at any rate, various indicators (such as average life expectancy and numbers of deaths in road traffic accidents despite rising traffic densities) have improved. This is not a Panglossian view that everything is for the best in the best of all possible worlds: new technologies bring risks which need discussion and debate, and in many cases a specific innovation may have broad and unexpected effects that need to be taken into account. The point at present is to flag the danger of 'technophobia' (see Wajcman 2004) and to stress that our interest in disasters is not driven by the pessimism of such a position.

Risk takes on particular forms, and, crucially, there are hidden aspects of organizational functioning that help us to understand the sources of organizational failures. This point links to debates about the 'risk society', a concept introduced by Beck (1992). Beck does not claim that modern societies are necessarily more hazardous than those of the past. Instead, in pre-modern societies dangers were taken as pre-given. With the rise of instrumental rational control, unknown dangers become calculable risks. For Beck, 'risks always depend on decisions' (quoted in Elliott 2002: 295).

Given the popularity of Beck's ideas, we have here a clear rationale for the focus in this chapter and in Chapter 8 on decisions in organizations, for it is organizational decisions, rather than those of individuals, that shape the modern world. Yet Beck, like many writers identifying a shift from 'organized' to 'disorganized' capitalism or from 'modernism' to 'post-modernism', also argues that groups such as families and social classes are no longer stable sources of moral order. The individual is increasingly responsible for her actions and is able to reflect on the situation in which she finds herself and to act as a result. She is not the prisoner of structural forces but is able to act in relation to them. Hence the concept of 'reflexive modernity', meaning for Beck not just reflection on the state of the world but confrontation with oneself as to how one should act.

At this point, we need to be more precise about the meaning of 'risk'. There is a well-established distinction between risk and uncertainty.

- Risk refers to the probability of an event from a known distribution. A gambler on a roulette wheel faces a known set of odds. The chances of road traffic accidents can also be stated as one in so many thousand miles travelled, though here there is no defined probability distribution as there is in the roulette case. Similarly, it makes sense to estimate the probability that women, as compared to men, will attain top positions in organizations, or that a certain proportion of new businesses will fail within a year of start-up.
- Risk becomes uncertainty when the distribution is not known. The risks at roulette would be uncertainty if the table were fixed and the croupier could at will determine where the ball landed. Many aspects of organizational operation are stated in terms of risk, when they are in fact closer to uncertainty. It is, for example, common to estimate the probability of two events occurring as one in M million. But we would first need to be sure that there was reasonable evidence in relation to each event and, crucially, that there was an underlying statistical theory at work. If events are truly independent, the probability of them both occurring can be calculated by multiplying the two probabilities. But if the events are not independent

(e.g. if two safety devices are connected in an unexpected way, or even more broadly if there is an influence common to them both, they occur in a company with a poor safety culture) improbable events become much more likely. Even more fundamentally, the chances of some events are not known. The safety record of nuclear power is often stated in terms of numbers of years of accident-free operation. But power plants are not roulette wheels. There are many different designs, so that the life of any particular one may be short. They have parts which interact in complex and, as we will see, unpredictable ways. And they are subject to human intervention that can interfere with apparently objective odds.

As we will see, debate on safety often turns on treating uncertainty as risk. Whether this approach is defensible should be considered carefully. The ready translation makes safety assessment seem scientific when it may not be. The 'risk society' is more accurately termed the 'uncertainty society'.

While Beck's project may be a useful source of ideas for social theory, it is hard to make any judgement as to the accuracy or otherwise of what he says. As one commentator remarks in a matter-of-fact and routine way, writers such as Beck 'do not seek empirical support for their arguments' (Savage 2000: 105). Yet this is surely key. We would expect either evidence of long-term historical trends, to enable us to say how reflexive modernity differs from a presumed past, or a detailed anatomy of the current condition, indicating, for example, what countries or economic sectors are more or least prone to reflexive modernity. In one respect, what follows can be read as an attempt to apply Beck's ideas, in that we aim to examine in detail the nature of decisions and their political context. We addressed parallel issues in Chapter 4. But we will argue that there are very clear limits on individuals' power to comprehend and act on the world, precisely because it is structured by organizations and structures of power.

Reliable Systems

Complex systems are remarkably reliable: plane crashes and nuclear accidents are far from everyday occurrences. A line of theory, characterized usefully as high reliability organizational theory (or HROT to give it an unflattering acronym) by Sagan (1993) stresses four points:

- Safety is prioritized as a goal by leaders of organizations.
- There are high levels of 'redundancy', meaning that complex systems are designed with at least primary and back-up safety systems.

- A high reliability culture can be created, wherein decisions are decentralized to appropriate levels, people are trained, and an expectation of commitment to safety is established.
- Trial and error leads to the elimination of mistakes and to organizational learning.

Any critical organizational theorist could easily ridicule assertions stated this starkly. But Sagan does not follow this simple route. He carefully sifts evidence, and accepts that there are examples consistent with the theory. It is, for example, true that there has never been an accidental nuclear war and that safety systems in nuclear weapons programmes have functioned to prevent potentially catastrophic failures. A programme of research has demonstrated how high reliability systems can work (e.g. Roberts 1990). At a more mundane level, we have observed plants engaged in dangerous processes (aluminium smelters, where not only is the molten metal hazardous but also the raw material and some of the waste products are potentially carcinogenic, and chemicals factories) where there was a genuine safety culture. How one might identify such a culture is discussed when the reader has more evidence available.

The point of entering criticisms and qualifications is not to swing from complacency to panic. In many respects, work processes are safer than they were in the past. Yet they are not necessarily safe, and the purpose of a critical analysis is to help in thinking about what may be hidden, not to suggest that disasters are lurking wholly unchecked.

There is one key point in how we might think about failures. A thought experiment might entail a random sample of a set of a given 'type' of organization (however 'type' is defined). One might then assess cases where failures had occurred and investigate what they had in common. Yet the available evidence starts from the other end of the causal chain: cases that are big enough, or uncommon enough, to attract attention, or that simply happen to emerge because an investigator brought them to light. Committees of inquiry into disasters often tell a story of how one decision, perhaps inconsequential in itself, interacted with others to produce a chain of events that led to the disaster in question. This is perfectly sensible if we wish to explain a particular event, and indeed it is not just cool *explanation* that is sought, for those involved in a tragic event need to gain *understanding* (that is, embracing feeling and emotion as well as logic). But it can suggest, at the same time, two logically incompatible implications. The first is that this was a unique set of events. The second is that a similar set of conditions would spark off an identical chain reaction.

What is needed is an account of causal chains and appreciation that at various key points there were alternatives, together with consideration of why these were not taken. We may then be in a position to understand how people in organizations can recognize potential disasters and even do something about them.

Understanding Technology

Why things go wrong is often to do with the relationship between social and technical systems. Understanding disasters will be helped by considering the nature of technical systems, for these are often approached as though they are hard realities. The situation is more subtle and complex than is often thought.

There are two simple stories about the links between technology and society. The conventional one says that technology advances through its own logic: inventions occur as a result of the pursuit of scientific proof (and in the language of economics they can be treated as 'exogenous', with 'technological progress' being outside social science interest). A common corollary is that technology is generally beneficial, though a rather different position states that technology is socially neutral and that its uses in practice can vary between the good and bad. The opposite story sees technical progress as a battle between those using technology to advance their own interests. According to this version, for example, the introduction of computer-controlled machine tools and computer-aided design was a device for capitalists to wrest control of production from the skilled pattern-makers, toolmakers, and designers who used to perform the relevant tasks.

There is a substantial literature that moves beyond these two simple views. It shows that scientific discovery is itself a socially shaped process. For the purposes of this chapter we draw selectively from this literature, focusing on the politics of technical innovation. This enables us to extend the discussion of power in Chapter 6: the politics of technology is about the power to shape definitions, and not about directly opposed interests (as the second story above would have it).

MacKenzie (1996: ch. 1; see also MacKenzie and Wajcman 1999) summarizes the central conclusions to emerge from the field of science and technology studies. First, a technology that eventually emerges is not the 'best' in any clear sense, for we need to ask 'best for whom?' This question has also been refined, for it is not simply a matter of overt dispute: even 'homogeneous' groups have differing definitions of goals and of how to attain them. In the terms of the present discussion, there can be broad agreement on a final objective, but the goals needed to meet it may be unclear and thus open to different definitions; and what they are is likely to emerge only over time.

Second, technologies are often productive only when they are widely used. Particular technologies are 'best' because they won out in contests with others and therefore became generalized, rather than being best and therefore winning. It is an open question whether the benefits of a technology are intrinsic to it.

Third, belief in the potential success of one technology can lead to a concentration of effort on it. MacKenzie acutely gives the celebrated example of Moore's Law, which states that microchip processing power tends to double annually. This is not a fixed law of nature: because it became accepted, people invested heavily in new innovations in the belief that increased processing power would emerge.

Fourth, knowledge is central, and social science helps us understand how knowledge is produced and defined. We should stress that this argument is not that knowledge is simply socially constructed and relative, or that choices are wholly open. To say that technology is socially shaped is not to say that all processes of social definition are equally effective. It is to point to politics and negotiation as key processes through which technical possibilities were or were not put into practice.

These points are illustrated by MacKenzie's (1990) study of guidance systems for nuclear missiles. The key relevance here is that the systems were presented as offering more and more precise targeting of weapons; yet such claims had little basis in evidence, so that the systems were far from infallible. If things were to go wrong (and fortunately we have yet to find out) it would not be a question of people responding inappropriately to well-designed machines, but of how the machines were conceived.

- The invention of inertial guidance was not a question of scientific inspiration, for the method was widely considered impossible and it was only when a 'need' emerged from the military that scientific attention was directed at the problem.
- The ability of ballistic missiles to reach a target was never established. Test conditions are not indicative of what might occur under wartime conditions. For example, it was not possible to show conclusively that missiles would survive intense cold and then intense heat without exploding before reaching the target.
- And even if a missile survived, the accuracy of hits cannot be known, once varying trajectories and conditions and random error, together with differences between tests and real conditions, are allowed for.

A final issue here concerns technology and capitalism. We have drawn on some of Marx's ideas. Further elaboration for those interested in this issue is given in Box 7.3.

Box 7.3 Marx and machinery

A standard reading of Marx is that he was a technological determinist. What this means is a view that technical change determines social development. It matters because such determinism is faulty (though still not uncommon); hence if Marx took such a view much of his work could be dismissed. It also matters because, once the false reading is rejected, we can think about technology and society in more constructive ways.

The basis of the reading is the famous 1859 Preface to *A Contribution to the Critique of Political Economy*. MacKenzie (1996: ch. 2) offers a cogent alternative view (see also Cohen 1978: chs 2 and 6).

First, Marx's 'determinism' states that the forces of production determine the social relations of production. Yet the forces for Marx include labour and skills, and therefore cover much more than non-social technology. 'Determine', moreover, is best taken to mean 'influence' or 'set the conditions for', rather than directly cause. (Similar arguments that the forces determine in the sense of setting limits on the development of social relations, or facilitating some developments rather than others, are given by Katznelson (1986), and Edwards (1986: 61–2, 151–3)).

Second, Marx saw the linkage between machinery and the organization of work (the labour process) as follows. MacKenzie here highlights *Capital, Volume 1*, Parts 3 and 4.

- The origins of capitalism lie not in machines as such but in the emergence of a class of propertyless wage labourers. Simple cooperation within the labour process not only led to benefits of economies of scale but also tended to increase the capitalist's authority because of his central role in the coordination of production. (In the terms of Chapter 6, power to achieve goals and power over other people are intertwined. The many arguments as to whether the rise of capitalism was about productive capacity or intensified control of workers thus miss the point. It was about both. The two terms should, however, be specified more exactly.
- 'Productive capacity' does not mean simply 'progress' because there will be different preferences in terms of how the capacity is used, not only between workers and capitalists (e.g. preferences for labour-saving or labour-using technologies) but also between capitalists (development down one particular path rather than another). Capacities can be put to use in different ways, and choices between these ways reflect political struggles.

- 'Control of workers' should not be envisaged in terms of more or less. As capitalism evolves, new balances of control and cooperation are developed, and the question of whether any given form is more exploitative than another is strictly meaningless. The question is meaningful only when tight comparisons can be made, so that, for example, it does make sense to say that a given group of workers was working harder than previously and that, if other conditions were unchanged, it was more exploited than it had been.
- The further division of labour reinforced subordination, and this set of social relationships created the space for mechanization. The limits of organizational change possible under less mechanized systems created the *necessity* for this process of mechanization.

Marx's account is a theory, and not an attempt at a detailed history. The theory nonetheless broadly fits the historical evidence.

Man-Made Disasters

Two useful approaches to understanding why disasters happen, then, are Turner's (1976) model of man-made disasters (MMD; the gendered terminology is apparently unconscious, though in view of the masculine assumptions of correctness and unwillingness to listen to criticism revealed in the evidence, the label may be more appropriate than Turner intended) and Perrow's (1999) normal accident theory (NAT). They have much in common, though Perrow and other users of NAT refer neither to Turner nor to the examples used by him, and they thus need to be described in turn.

Drawing on three examples from the UK, Turner identifies a set of common features. The key ones are as follows:

- Rigid perceptions and beliefs: This includes inattention to warning signs and a lack of communication. For example, in the case of the disaster at Aberfan, South Wales in 1966 (in which 144 people were killed when a spoil heap from a coal mine slid down a mountain side onto the village) a memo of 1939 had anticipated the causal conditions but the document was restricted and people were unaware of its significance.
- The 'decoy problem': a focus on a well-defined but minor issue.
- Disregard of outsiders to the organization, who were written off as inexpert.
- Informational and coordination difficulties.

- Involvement of untrained people who behave in unexpected ways. For example, in the case of a fire parents of children who were trapped tried to enter the burning building.
- Failures to comply with existing regulations.

A key observation by Turner concerns the later official inquiries into the disasters:

[E]ach dealt with the problem that caused the disaster as it was later revealed and not as it presented itself to those involved beforehand. The recommendations, therefore, treat the well-structured problem defined and revealed by the disaster, rather than with [*sic*] preexisting, ill-structured problems. (1976: 93)

(Recall the quotation from Mintzberg in Chapter 5: much decision-making occurs under conditions of *ambiguity*, not risk or even uncertainty). For the understanding of why things go wrong, it is important not to fall into the same position as these reports. They have the benefit of hindsight and tend to imply that if certain errors were avoided — if, for example, communication had been less ambiguous — a disaster would not have happened. But Turner's point is that ill-defined situations necessarily exist. Plugging one gap will not necessarily resolve an issue. What inquiries discover are particular chains of events which are unique. They are certainly useful in dealing with particular classes of events so that, for example, spoil heaps in other Welsh valleys could be investigated, and action taken. But disasters can occur in any situations where two conditions hold: the background conditions render behaviour potentially dangerous and there is then a chain of events containing the features identified by Turner.

Normal Accidents

As to the relevant background conditions, NAT offers important insights. It is a subtle approach, throwing light not just on disasters but on many aspects of organizational functioning under more 'usual' conditions. We therefore discuss it in some detail.

Perrow (1999) begins with a homely example. You have an important job interview one morning and your housemate starts making coffee for you before leaving. But the coffee pot cracks; you make coffee again; and, now late, you shut the door with your car keys locked inside the house. You normally have a spare set but you have lent them to a friend (a design *redundancy* has failed, says Perrow). You seek a lift from a neighbour but he has to stay in today to have his generator fixed (this is a *loosely coupled* situation since the lost key and the generator are not connected). He tells you there is a bus strike, which means that when you try to call a cab none is available (the strike and the lack of cabs is *tightly connected*). You fail to make it to the interview on time.

It is the interaction of multiple failures that causes the problem, rather than a single event. Tightly coupled processes require special attention, whereas loosely coupled ones are more contingent and hard to predict. This framework establishes the core of the approach, except that, says Perrow, in this example the person involved can understand these inter-dependencies. In complex systems, the linkages are too many, and the possible ways in which parts affect each other too complicated, for an operator on the ground to understand them. The interactions cannot be seen and 'even if they are seen, they are not believed . . . seeing is not necessarily believing; sometimes, we must believe before we can see' (Perrow 1999: 9). Perrow here refers to many writers on organizations who stress that we understand the world through mental maps. Sense data are not simply received but have to be interpreted and rendered significant. In one neat experiment, subjects were asked to register at a desk. The 'receptionist' ducked behind the desk and appeared to emerge with a form to be completed. The majority of the subjects did not notice that one person ducked down and another, wearing a markedly differ-ently coloured shirt, appeared. This was because the details of the recep-tionist, though 'seen' literally, did not register as important.

Note that Perrow is using 'normal' ironically, to stress that accidents are embedded in organizational practice rather than being exceptional. As discussed below, he says that 'system accident' would be a more exact term, since the analysis turns on the structuring of systems. Some *common* accidents are not system accidents because they were simply the result of an individual failure. As we will also see, Perrow considers that the spectacular Bhopal case was not a system accident but simply a gross failure of attention to safety.

There are five main differences between tightly and loosely coupled systems:

1. Tightly coupled systems have time-dependent processes that cannot stand by until they are attended to. Reactions in chemicals plants cannot be delayed or extended.
2. The sequences in tightly coupled systems are relatively invariant. To produce a chemical entails a given sequence, whereas in an assem-bly operation the order of fitting parts can be varied more readily.
3. Tight coupling entails one way to meet a goal: an aluminium smelter can produce only aluminium, whereas in looser systems different

product mixes can be included and different elements can be included in the mix (e.g. using plastic rather than metal).
4. There is little slack in tightly coupled systems. A failure entails a shutdown of the process.
5. Safety calls for buffers and redundancies (alternative systems if a main system fails such as a reserve parachute). In tightly coupled systems these have to be deliberately planned whereas in looser systems there are more ways of replacing one operation with another.

Examples of tightly coupled systems include dams and nuclear power plants. Loosely coupled systems include post offices and similar agencies and universities.

Complexity is Perrow's short hand for interactions in an unexpected sequence. In complex systems, the state of an operation can be confusing, as for example when a monitoring device gives ambiguous data. A response to a signal can set off a series of events whose cumulative path is hard to follow. Operators, moreover, are likely to develop a mental picture of what is happening and to ignore disconfirming data. A ship's pilot, for example, may interpret a set of lights as indicating another ship moving in the same direction, and take other data to confirm this, even though in fact he has misread the lights and they indicate a ship moving in the opposite direction (Perrow 1999: 215–17 gives a real-world example of this). Other aspects of complex systems include the fact that one component can interact with one or more other components either by design (for example, when a heater serves two other components) or by accident (as when oil from a ruptured tank enters an engine compartment and ignites). Perrow gives several other examples of the nature of complexity and the problems that can arise as a result. A safety device can itself contribute to accidents. For example, in 1966 an engineer at the nuclear plant in Monroe, Michigan, introduced a new device aimed to add to redundancy, a zirconium plate; but the plate broke and blocked a coolant pipe. A further issue here is that the plate was added late in the design and was not included in the specifications, which made it hard to establish the cause of the problem (Sagan 1993: 160).

Complexity does not, in itself, render a system accident-prone. A university is a complex system because there are multiple functions which can interact in unexpected ways. But it is also loosely coupled because there is time for recovery when things go wrong and consequences of errors are not usually dangerous. Perrow's classification of his two dimensions is shown in Figure 7.1.

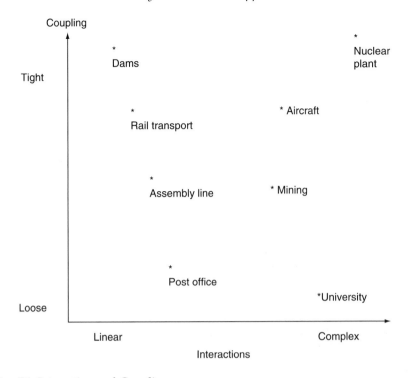

FIG. 7.1 Interaction and Coupling
Source: Abbreviated from Perrow (1999: 97).

One key implication emerges from this approach to disasters in terms of the structuring of systems. Perrow notes that, in inquiries into the causes of disasters, up to 80 per cent attribute a problem to operator error. Yet there is usually more to the story. Long working hours and tiredness are one feature. Another is the fact that operators are under pressure to save time or costs, and may thus be led to cut corners. Perrow cites one of the first oil tanker disasters, that of the *Torrey Canyon* in the UK in 1967; part of the context was pressure on the captain to reach port as soon as possible and he therefore chose a perilous route. But, perhaps most fundamentally, signals from the environment can be misleading, so that incorrect actions are encouraged. If systems are tightly coupled, this can set off a chain of events that is unpredictable and unmanageable, especially when operators have to respond in a short time to unfamiliar sets of events.

We can further elucidate NAT and compare it with HROT. Sagan (1993) considers the four elements of HROT and shows how NAT would see them.

- *Safety as a goal.* People in organizations have differing objectives, those at the top may not be directly exposed to some hazards (e.g. those in the inner workings of chemicals plants), there will be pressures to maintain production, and elites may be misinformed as to the prevalence of near accidents. Collinson (1999) provides a particularly sharp example of the underreporting of accidents (Box 7.4).
- *Redundancy.* Safety systems can interact in unpredictable ways, as in the Monroe case cited above.
- *Decentralization.* Can all events be anticipated and trained for, and can local decision-makers be given accurate information to allow them to make judgements, particularly when choices at one location interact with those at others?
- *Learning.* Causes of accidents are often unclear, politicized environments often lead to blame cultures, and some organizations are riddled with secrecy. In such contexts learning will be constrained.

Box 7.4 Hiding injuries on North Sea oil rigs

Several oil companies operate drilling platforms far out in the North Sea. Workers typically stay on them for two-week periods, working twelve-hour shifts. In 1990, Collinson (1999) studied two of these rigs owned by one firm. The company had a reputation for a safety culture, and had an accident rate of about one-tenth the industry average. There were safety committees, and each crew going through a year with no accident received a bonus. There were two key groups of workers, company employees, and contractors.

About half the company employees interviewed said that they had concealed accidents or near-accidents in order to protect their appraisal rating. (For analysis of performance appraisal, see Chapter 5). Attempts were also made to downgrade the recorded severity of incidents that could not be concealed.

The contractors worked for specialist firms and did the most dangerous work, notably drilling and erecting scaffolding. They suffered the most accidents but were under greatest pressure to conceal them: a feared system of reports meant that they could be refused further work, if 'Not Required Back' was recorded on a work report.

When these results were reported to senior management they were treated with disbelief, in line with Sagan's remarks. Several efforts were made to change the existing blame culture, but the contract bidding system remained in place.

Sagan goes on to examine the US nuclear weapons programme. The information is necessarily old, since much of it was originally classified (and Sagan was able to use the Freedom of Information Act to have documents released, using a degree of openness unknown in many other countries including the UK). But it is extremely detailed, since numerous reports were compiled and investigations held, such that similar information would not be available in much of the private sector. Though the examples are old, moreover, they reveal processes that are likely to continue to exist.

Sagan's initial expectation was that the tight discipline of a military organization, together with the lethal dangers of nuclear weapons, would lead to the confirmation of HROT. As he says, this is a very tough test for NAT. But he finds several results that cannot be understood without reference to NAT. In 1962, the USA discovered the construction of Soviet nuclear missiles in Cuba and during the ensuing crisis the defence forces were put on high alert. At the time, it was standard procedure to keep aircraft continuously in the sky, so that they could respond to any surprise nuclear attack. A very large number of missions was flown without mishap, as HROT would expect. Yet there were several false reports of missile launches that were potentially dangerous. Importantly the system was less tightly coupled than it was designed to be, with several cases where bombers should have been launched according to the information received but where other choices were made.

A particularly telling case occurred six years later. A B-52 bomber carrying nuclear weapons crashed near the Thule base in Greenland. (Among other things, the event influenced an election in Denmark, which administers Greenland, in that the presence of nuclear weapons on its territory had been kept secret.) The plane was flying a sortie around the base. The purpose was to add redundancy to the warning system, for if communication from the base disappeared there would be no way of distinguishing a Soviet attack from a systems failure; the B-52 sorties were designed to provide independent information. However, if the plane had crashed into the Thule base instead of near it, the crash would have set off false reports of an attack. The system added complexity and opacity as well as redundancy. A telling fact is that civilians in Washington did not know of the existence of the sorties: had they been faced with indications of an attack, they lacked the knowledge to consider the alternative possibility, of a B-52 crash.

The Politics and Economics of Safety and Risk Assessments

HROT was developed on US aircraft carriers and there is little or no reference to financial or budgetary constraints. In many other cases, however, costs and budgets loom large. The pressures in the *Torrey Canyon* case were noted above.

- Consider one example analysed from a basically HROT position. Weick (1993) studied an accident at Tenerife airport in 1977 in which two planes collided, killing 583 people. (This remains the world's biggest single airline disaster.) The planes had been diverted there and were much delayed. The crew of one of them was nearing the legal limits on its flying time, and was thus under pressure to leave as soon as possible. This economic pressure may have contributed to its decision to take off without proper clearance. Note also that very similar issues occurred in a collision of two planes on the runway at Milan's Linate airport in 2000 (BBC, *Horizon* programme, broadcast 10 August 2003). Here, standard procedures were changed without explanation, and the pilots became confused. Our point is that to explain such cases one certainly needs to understand how people make mistakes and misread information, but in addition what are the conditions allowing these errors to occur? Why were lessons from Tenerife not learned, why was ground radar bought but not installed at Linate (were financial constraints involved) and why was a new system designed in preference to using an existing Norwegian one (were organizational politics to blame)?
- In the case of the Union Carbide's Bhopal plant (see Box 7.5), Perrow (1999: 355–60) stresses that the disaster was not a case of a normal (i.e. systems) accident, for such an accident entails the unexpected interaction of small failures. Bhopal was much simpler. The plant had been starved of investment, maintenance workers were laid off, and safety systems were neglected. Alarms did not go off and evacuation procedures were not followed. Finally, whereas in other cases good luck reduced the number of deaths (e.g. the wind direction at Chernobyl took radioactive material away from the city of Kiev), here the effects were about as devastating as they could be. Perrow also notes the tendency of some observers to invoke Indian 'culture' as a convenient explanation, an explanation that appeared very hollow when a similar accident occurred only months later at Union Carbide's US plant. Rather than explain the accident in terms of culture,

Box 7.5 The Bhopal disaster

The best account of Bhopal, which is both analytical and moving, is by the journalists Lapierre and Moro (2003). The key facts are that on the night of 2–3 December 1984 there was an explosion in the Union Carbide chemicals plant. The explosion released toxic gases which killed immediately about 8,000 people, with the final death toll being in the region of between 16,000 and 30,000. The explosion was caused by a failure to manage the production of methyl isocyanate (MIC), a lethal and highly volatile substance that was intended for use in the pesticide industry. The reasons for the explosion lay in a catalogue of failures of safety procedures, which meant that on the fatal night forty tons of MIC were in storage tanks and all three safety systems were non-operational. Union Carbide no longer exists as an entity, many of its sites having been taken over by other firms.

[W]e might look at plain old free-market capitalism that allowed the Indian plant to be starved and run down.... [A]n economic system that runs ... risks for the sake of private profits, or a government system that runs them for the sake of national prestige, patronage or personal power, is the more important focus and culprit.... [T]he issue is not risk but power. (Perrow 1999: 360)

- Studying cases of injury, Nichols (1975) found that underlying them was pressure to keep up production. He reported that industry was estimated to spend 0.05 per cent of its research and development budget on safety. Is there any evidence that this proportion has increased? Much recent research has tried to measure 'human resource outcomes' of forms of work organization, but it is notable that safety performance is often excluded, for example in *The HR Scorecard* (Becker et al. 2001).

What, then, can be done to improve safety? Perrow begins by offering a critique of the apparently scientific approach of risk assessment (Perrow 1999: 306–24). This approach is essentially a cost–benefit analysis. It estimates the likelihood of an event, puts a monetary value on it, and then compares this with other events and selects the option which will maximize net benefits.

This thinking was exemplified by the widely discussed (and now dated: the company can reasonably claim to have learned from the case) Ford Pinto case. It was found that the fuel tank of the car in question was prone to explode; the company placed a dollar value on the number of liability suits it was likely to face and concluded that this cost was lower than the cost of recalling the cars and correcting the problem. In this particular case the issues are obvious: the callous equation of purely private monetary costs (of fixing the cars) with the emotional and other costs of death and injury borne by other people.

But there are broader issues from less clear-cut cases. Given that decisions have to be made and resources are finite, why not try to make decisions on a rational basis? Three points stand out from the answer given by Perrow.

- Risk analysis treats any death or injury as equivalent, whereas the collective costs of major disasters are shared and are greater than those of a similar number of individual events. How does one compare the 144 deaths in the small village of Aberfan with the same number in unconnected road accidents?
- Some risks involve choice and a sense of being able to exert a degree of control, for example driving a car. Numbers of injuries cannot be compared with numbers where the subjects lack any such control over their own futures.
- Risks are unevenly distributed across society, so that the poor and disadvantaged are subjected to relatively high technological risks. Moreover, the people judging what is an acceptable risk are not the same as those exposed to them. In some cases, it is also possible to externalize the risk (see Box 7.6).

The difficulty is that making decisions in this context involves very different kinds of rationality:

[E]conomic or absolute rationality, which requires narrow, quantitative and precise goals; bounded rationality, which emphasizes the limits on our thinking capacities and our inability to often achieve or even seek absolute rationality; and social and cultural rationality, which emphasizes diversity and social bonding. (Perrow 1999: 323)

Box 7.6 Externalizing risk

A study of the US petrochemicals industry found that widespread use of subcontract firms meant that the core firms could externalize the risk of accidents to subcontractors and their workers (Kochan et al. 1994; Rebitzer 1995). Training of subcontract workers was poor and was not seen as a responsibility of the core firms. Workers were also asked about their accident history. For those directly hired by the core firms, safety training cut accidents but this was not the case for contract workers, suggesting that these workers were relatively underprepared. This study did not, however, look directly at reporting, though it is consistent with Collinson's evidence (Box 7.4). Reported accident rates may not be accurate measures of the dangers of an occupation.

Cost–benefit analysis deals with the first. Risk assessment begins to move to the second. But what is also needed is the third. Social rationality recognizes the importance of *dread*: perceived risk shaped by a lack of control, inequitable distribution of hazards, high catastrophic potential, and a sense that technological fixes are not the solution (Perrow 1999: 328). Based on his analysis of the potential for catastrophe and the costs of alternatives, Perrow concludes that some technologies (primarily nuclear ones) should be abandoned, others (e.g. DNA research and experiments) restricted, and yet others subjected to more specific and narrow improvements.

Two observations are needed at this point. First, there is a danger of elevating social rationality above the others and implying that the kinds of false fears discussed at the start of this chapter have a reasonable basis. Yet it may be that some elements of dread are based on incorrect assumptions. It is true that 'expert', absolute, rationality needs to be questioned, for it too makes assumptions, and indeed has to do so since it is trying to estimate future probabilities of untried technologies, which are inherently unknowable. But the point is to encourage critical engagement between different ways of thinking. Indeed, the same people may use the different rationalities at different times. Perrow's analysis suggests that 'experts' engage in social rationality when they develop shared 'scientific' models. As we have already argued, even scientific judgements involve social rationality, and this will be especially the case where large profits are involved (e.g. biotechnology). A debate between different rationalities, and using the rationalities to throw different light on a given problem, is called for, not an argument that one rationality is superior to another.

Second, Perrow offers specific recommendations. These should not be seen as emerging directly from his social science. The science shows what the issues are and that safety concerns, for example, to do with dams, chemicals plants, and nuclear power are importantly different. What conclusions are drawn is a political question. A proponent of nuclear power might read the analysis as leading *inexorably* to the conclusion that nuclear systems should be abandoned, and hence dismiss the analysis as special pleading. Yet the underlying analysis remains central to how such a person might improve his thinking about risk and safety. The conclusion cannot follow from the analysis, though the analysis certainly shows that there are issues to be addressed.

The nature of the political argument about technologies needs clarifying. An early view said that technologies have necessary social effects. It was rapidly criticized for neglecting the choices that can be made, for example the very different social arrangements that grew up in different countries around assembly-line technologies. Yet choice is not limitless, and technologies are not simply neutral. Winner (1999) has identified two ways in which technologies are political. The first is where a given technology is chosen with a social aim in view, a reasonably well-attested case being forms of automation intended to reduce the power of skilled workers. The second theme is that some technologies are inherently political, in that they entail a particular form of social organization. The strongest form of this argument is that something like a nuclear power plant has patterns of authority built into it. A weaker argument is that there are strong tendencies towards one set of social relations and not another. Nuclear power in our view has strong implications for social organization, and that fact constrains the sorts of politics that can be pursued around it.

As this chapter has proceeded, we have moved from approaches based on 'safe' systems to a more critical account that locates injuries in the pressures of the production process. The most developed 'political economy' of injuries is provided by Nichols (1997), whose analysis may be introduced via his criticisms of Perrow and of Turner. In his view, the systems approach has the following limitations:

- It neglects normal, routine injuries in favour of large disasters.
- In doing so, the focus on particular systems may be relevant to their designers, but the analysis cannot address the major fluctuations of injury rates across time and space.
- It treats systems as equivalent, for example nuclear plants and universities, and it says nothing about one all-embracing system, that of capitalism (pp. 4–5, 11, 90–1).

In relation to our present purposes, the first two points are important but may be left to one side. It is true that small, routine events cause more injuries than do dramatic disasters. But we are interested in disasters for the clear light that they throw on organizational functioning, and not because they are to be equated with injuries. On the third point, Perrow's initial work did tend to abstract 'systems' from the social reality in which they are embedded, though his analysis of Bhopal would be consistent with the approach advocated by Nichols.

That approach treats injuries as one outcome of a work organization driven by profit. Workers are exposed to unsafe conditions when the drive for profit is particularly intense, when the work process is hazardous (mines or chemicals works) or prone to contradictory demands, and when countervailing forces are weak. A good example, which goes beyond the categories of normal accidents, is an accident on the Midland Railway in England at Aisgill in 1913 (Howell 1991). A train hit the rear of another after running through a signal at danger. The case became a cause célèbre when the driver was prosecuted and imprisoned, being released after widespread protests. Some aspects are consistent with NAT: railways are complex and closely coupled systems. But the degree to which the Midland Railway had these properties was worsened by its political and economic behaviour. The first train stopped because of the poor quality of coal it was using, and the driver of the second train was not watching for the signal because poor maintenance required him to check the lubrication of his engine so that he could not watch for the signal. These features in turn reflected financial pressures within the company to cut costs. In short, the system had the features that it did because of its political as well as its technological characteristics.

A neat way of capturing this, applicable to many issues other than accidents, is the question posed by W. G. Baldamus, 'what determines the determinants?' (quoted in Nichols 1997: 90). That is, specific causes can be located in a wider structure of influences.

A key point is that safety does not always suffer where profits are high. There is no direct trade-off. Nichols (1997: 104) gives several examples when the relationship may be positive:

- There is the threat of a major explosion, so that safety is taken seriously.
- Injuries are so common that production could be disrupted.
- Injuries are a worker–organization issue.
- An injury record leads to recruitment difficulties or customer discontent or the threat of state regulation.

Other examples could readily be given. A political economy view does not argue that safety is necessarily neglected, but sees the tension between safety and profits as one shaping how an organization will perform.

The tension between safety and profit is an example of the contradictions that run through this book: they reflect opposing *principles* that have to be managed, and in particular circumstances pressure for profit can be so intense that accidents are very likely. But how the principles work through in practice will reflect many other factors. It is not, moreover, the case that attention to safety is a cost necessarily to be minimized: a firm needs to attract and retain workers, and safety is important to business reputation and ultimately to the viability of the operation. The tension between safety and profit is a matter of degree, and the relationship will be different in different organizations. For example, firms pursuing a business strategy of innovation and 'high performance' would find their claims undermined if they took a callous view of safety. A considered approach to safety would reasonably be expected to be part of the strategy. Nonetheless, the contradiction has not disappeared.

In the UK an improved injury rate in the 1970s was reversed in the early 1980s, reflecting changes in numbers of hours worked but also a weaker ability of trade unions to challenge managerial control (Nichols 1997). This last influence illustrates the third bullet point above, and also the fourth (the threat of powerful state regulation was reduced at this time).

Numerous case studies have revealed the operation of the politics of safety. Grunberg (1986) showed that in a UK plant then owned by Chrysler a weakening of labour's position was associated with more work effort, while in a French plant a stronger position of labour at plant and national level reduced work intensity. As might be expected, direct links with injury rates were less apparent, for injuries reflect many contingencies, but there were trends in the expected direction. Novek et al. (1990) report similar evidence from the Canadian meat-packing industry, showing that mechanization of tasks and efforts to intensify labour led to reduced levels of safety. By contrast, it appears from Hall's (1993) analysis of a mine, also in Canada, that a new work process increased the impact of injuries on the whole production process and therefore encouraged a new and more systematic approach to safety. Wokutch and VanSandt (2000) argue in relation to Japan that safety has a high priority because the just-in-time lean production system cannot afford inefficiencies, and injuries are an important source of inefficiency. They argue that injury records in large firms are better than in similar US ones, a marked change from the past when injury rates were up to five times the US level.

Alongside such trends, there is evidence that in some countries the link between safety and profit remains inverse. Nichols reports his work on coal mines in Turkey, showing that productivity and injuries tend to move together because work is labour intensive. Sass (2000) notes that in Taiwan the injury rate is, despite health and safety protections, between five and ten times that in Japan or the USA. He also highlights a group of about 300,000 migrants (out of a work force of about 9 million) who work in the informal sector and lack legal protections.

We have come a long way from the disciplined safety systems of US aircraft carriers. The politics of safety continue to be fought out around the globe.

Conclusions

Accidents are a good illustration of the risk (or, better, the uncertainty or ambiguity) society. Processes for the individualization of risk include the putting of responsibility onto subcontractors and pressures on operators to disguise accidents. Wherever there is a blame culture there are likely to be such processes. Whether or not these processes are distinctively new, and hence whether they illustrate a risk society in the sense identified by Beck, is a different question. In our view, it is probably unanswerable: how do we know whether uncertainty has increased compared to some time in the past?

Several points are worth bearing in mind when thinking about the risk society. First, comparison of the present with a supposed stable or 'Fordist' past is unhelpful, since such an era was a relatively short one and was less coherent than might appear. The present may look uniquely risky only by comparison with a misleading picture of the past. Second, there is some evidence that long-term stability exists. Studies in the US textiles industry and the UK railways show remarkable stability of organizational processes over a period of approximately 100 years (Edwards and Whitston 1994). These sectors are, however, ones of limited technical and organizational change, so that when we look across society as a whole there may be more change, as the risk society thesis would suggest.

The key is to understand the organizational dynamics at work. What are the processes generating uncertainty and how are they distributed across society? To the extent, for example, that there is more subcontract working then we can expect an externalization of uncertainty. (See the discussion of status and contract in Chapter 6.) Yet there may also be limits on the process, for example tighter monitoring of contract compliance and legal regulation on the wearing of safety equipment. The 'risk society' is an element of social organization or one tendency, not a description of concrete social reality.

Lessons from the cold war, outlined above, have wider application. The particular context of two superpowers each capable of launching a devastating attack on the other has disappeared. But the growing number of nations with nuclear capability and the rise of regional tensions, as between India and Pakistan, suggests that the threat has not gone away. The issues of complex and tightly coupled systems, in particular problems of handling ambiguous data in times of tension, remain present. One of the key arguments of HROT is that high reliability organizations are capable of learning through analysis of experience and through structured training exercises. But new organizations will lack this experience: any learning in one organization will not generalize across all relevant organizations. Moreover, high reliability cases are not typical of all organizations, so that systematic attention to procedures and a strong safety culture are likely to be conspicuous by their absence.

In short, it is not the case that technological change has wrought unalloyed progress, but nor is it true that its results have been generally disadvantageous. Unexpected and contradictory implications often ensue.

The broader implication in thinking about organizations is: some organizations may stand as exemplars of 'good practice', but learning from them is never easy. There are many ways in which people in other organizations can find out that they are different so that the lessons are inapplicable. The point to consider is which aspects of practice are transferable, and which are not.

It is also useful to distinguish between the economic and the organizational context. The economic context establishes the degree of pressure to meet financial targets and may help some people to sustain arguments that certain safety procedures are too expensive. Yet the context does not wholly determine outcomes, and the arguments are open to challenge. Such questioning can be immediate or longer-term. In the immediate situation, it may be that cost pressures require completion of a project in a limited time, and that in practice this leads to the cutting of corners. But there may be other ways of organizing the work which make it safer and no less efficient. In the longer term the budget pressures can be challenged by finding genuinely better ways of organizing a task or by relieving the intensity of the pressures.

The organizational context covers the extent to which there is a 'culture of secrecy' or a tendency for work groups to take unsafe working practices for granted. These matters are pursued in Chapter 8. For now we can say that the salience of the culture will vary across organizations. The more a process is complex and tightly coupled, the more important it is that the people involved with it think about how they manage it and whether the purely social processes involved (e.g. are orders from above unquestioned, can people challenge authority?) heighten the dangers involved.

We have seen in this chapter, then, that safety is not a purely technical issue. The social organization of technical systems is a critical dimension. In thinking about why disasters happen, and what an individual in an organization can do, the contestability of views is central. Economic, bounded, and social rationality can be used as different perspectives to understand how we respond to uncertainty and risk. We can ask what kind of uncertainties exist in given situations and how they are managed. To what extent is there a safety culture, or how far do people feel that they cannot question existing assumptions? What can be done to change ways of thinking? Using the ideas in this chapter and in Chapter 8, it is possible to understand the causes of failures in organizations and the warning signs, as well as the ways in which they may be heeded.

8

Is Decision-making a Rational Process?

Chapter 7 focused on the particularly sharp issue of disasters and injuries and identified the social processes involved in them. We now consider decision-making of a less disastrous kind. Following the logic of Chapter 7, we begin with processes of social group behaviour, which are often analysed through a social psychological perspective that tends to see organizations as having shared purposes or as having 'politics' of a relatively minor kind. We then place this perspective in a wider critical analysis of the politics of organizations. As with Chapter 7, it is useful to take as examples cases where things go wrong. As we will see, however, many of the same processes underlie 'success' as well as 'failure'. We need to grasp how failure occurs but then aim to identify what is generic in the politics of organizations and what is particular to failure. With this approach in place, we can then ask how organizations might learn from experiences of success and failure and what organizational learning might mean.

A useful way to organize thinking here is the classic image of 'a garbage can model of organizational choice' (Cohen et al. 1972). What the authors mean by a garbage can is a choice opportunity into which problems and solutions are dumped. It exists because individuals and groups have their own projects and views on the ways in which an organization should develop. They are likely to have pet solutions that they put into practice when a new issue arises. Decision-making is often about the interplay of pre-existing solutions and recipes, which are looking for problems to which they may be an answer.

Social Group Processes

Normal Accident Theory discussed in Chapter 7 focuses on the properties of systems that produce 'accidents' and, if the technology is sufficiently dangerous, disasters. Yet how do we make links between organizational systems, which are relatively large-scale and which exist independently of people, and smaller-scale social group processes?

A study by Edmondson (1996) attempts an answer. It looks at errors in drug prescriptions, noting another study that found a huge range of errors between different hospitals (from 2.3 to 23.3 errors per 1,000 patient days); see Box 8.1. How can this range be explained? Edmondson examines the effects of good quality working relationships. As against the expectation that these will lower error rates, she shows that they were

Box 8.1 Lies, damned lies, and statistics

A key issue is the measurement of error. Edmondson cites a study showing a fortyfold increase in detected errors following new reporting procedures. This suggests that measured rates may be more to do with reporting enthusiasm than with the 'true' underlying phenomenon. Her conclusion is that in most cases of this kind the two are necessarily conflated: there is no way of establishing a true error rate independently of reports.

This is a more extreme example than that given in Box 7.2 in Chapter 7, where it was possible to offer an explanation of the trends of the data. Consider also figures for crime. A limited critique of crime statistics says that some crimes are not recorded because they are not reported to the police. But this assumes that there is a true figure which is in principle measurable. A more extended critique says that what is a crime depends on social definitions. A classic example in sociology is suicide. In some countries suicide was a crime, and some religions such as Roman Catholicism define it as a sin. In such a context people will try to define what may look like self-inflicted death as accidental. It follows that suicide statistics are social constructions that will not measure the rate of self-killing. Moreover, different social constructions will occur in different societies, so that comparing measured rates across space or time will be invalid. (See Downes and Rock 2003: 30–50 for discussion of crime statistics and other sources of data on crime.)

Yet it does not follow that organizational statistics are worthless. In the field of crime, murder rates are more likely to be reasonable indicators than are figures on 'mugging'. Downes and Rock also comment that some measures are useful in showing the *relative* extent of certain activities. For example, police figures on rates of crime by area correlate with other sources of information: though the police data will not record all crime, they can chart patterns of variation. In organizations, as noted in Chapter 7, figures of deaths due to accidents are more reliable indicators than those on less serious injuries. It is not, then, the case that all statistics are to be dismissed as social constructions. They need to be interrogated critically, and a view taken as to those that are reasonably *valid* (i.e. they measure what they purport to measure), those that may not be valid but which are collected consistently and thus offer reliable information on trends and patterns, those that may have limited validity but can still offer information as to relevant social processes (e.g. some industrial injury data), and those that are of little or no use for scientific purposes.

associated with high rates, which she attributes to a willingness to report and discuss errors. She suggests that 'true' errors may fall here, but cannot show this. Two conclusions are however clear. First, a high reported error rate need not indicate failures, and is perhaps more likely to illustrate success. This point is of obvious relevance to the performance measurement debate (see Chapter 5): poor measured performance may in fact mean that there is real success. Second, group processes are important in shaping how individuals behave.

Such results are consistent with a long line of studies of the effects of group solidarity. A classic study by Blau (1963) compared two groups of workers in a government employment agency. Workers were evaluated on their success in placing job applicants in employment. One group was highly atomized and competitive. In a further twist on the processes of manipulating data just discussed, each worker kept information on available openings to himself or herself rather than making the openings known to others. The second group was more solidaristic. Economic theory would expect that the competitive group should be more productive. It was certainly the case that individuals competed, but the inefficiencies are also obvious, and the solidaristic group in fact had the higher level of efficiency.

These points are reinforced by one of the studies discussed in Chapter 7, Weick's (1993) analysis of the Tenerife air disaster. Weick cites a large-scale attitude survey of pilots that asked whether they believed that their decision-making was as good in emergencies as it was in routine situations. This information was correlated with independent assessments of the pilots' skills. Contrary to (some) expectations, it was the best performing pilots who were most likely to say that they found decision-making in emergencies hard: they engaged in self-reflection. In relation to the Tenerife case itself, Weick highlights the group dynamics in the cockpit of the plane engaged in taking off. He notes that the pilot was a senior employee who had tested the co-pilot and given him his qualification. In this context, it was hard for the co-pilot to question the pilot's authority. Instead of a group working on a problem and sharing information, there were three (including the flight engineer) people behaving as individuals. One person's judgement was thus not openly scrutinized by the others.

'Groupthink'

Perhaps the best-known concept aiming to explain such processes is that of 'groupthink', developed by Janis (1982: 9) with conscious reference to the 'double think' of Orwell's *1984*. Double think is the capacity for holding two conflicting views at the same time. In the dystopia of *1984*, in which every aspect of society is controlled by an authoritarian force, the capacity is valued, not condemned. Language is controlled as much as behaviour, so that the word 'free' is reduced to a sense of 'lacking' as in 'this dog is free of lice' (Orwell 1954: 241). Orwell raises the question of whether an idea of freedom is conceivable without the language to go with it. Organizations are not (usually) *1984*s, but language remains a powerful way of defining debate, as wide usage of words such as performance, efficiency, and modernization testifies (see Chapter 5).

Groupthink is a mode of thinking in a cohesive in-group wherein the striving for unanimity overrides realistic appraisal of a situation. Symptoms include an overestimation of a group's power and morality, closed-mindedness, and pressures for uniformity. Underlying conditions include a group that is internally cohesive, insulation from other groups and social processes, and a lack of a tradition of impartial leadership. Janis developed the idea from examination of decision-making in the US government. Examples of groupthink were identified in the failed Bay of Pigs invasion of Cuba by the USA and the escalation of US involvement in the Vietnam war, while counter-examples are the handling of the Cuban missile crisis and the Marshall Plan (of post-1945 reconstruction in Europe).

The term groupthink has become widely adopted. It appeared in a dictionary only three years after it was coined, and it is treated as received wisdom in many discussions. For example, an otherwise profoundly thoughtful work states that organizations work by groupthink: 'a collective mind-set that protects illusions from uncomfortable truths and disconfirming information' (Cohen 2001: 66). An illustration of its reception is that this work cites a secondary piece for its evidence and misspells Janis's name.

Yet serious social psychological analysis fails to find support for the model of groupthink. The model identifies three elements:

- antecedent conditions (such as a group from homogeneous backgrounds, with strong cohesiveness and insulation from outside);
- symptoms of groupthink such as pressures for conformity; and
- consequences (defective decision-making and failure to consider alternatives) (Janis 1982: 244).

No research has supported these hypothesized links (Turner and Pratkanis 1998). Kramer (1998) has reanalysed the Bay of Pigs and Vietnam cases used by Janis and shows that the decision-making groups were not insulated and did seek information from a range of sources. The decisions were shaped by concerns about the respective presidents' images as leaders and their domestic political standing. It is thus true that the decisions were shaped by various considerations that may have swayed people's judgement (e.g. a wish to be seen to be showing decisiveness and firmness), and that this may have contributed to faulty analysis. But the process did not entail groupthink in any exact sense.

Groupthink could mean any of the following (Fuller and Aldag 1998).

1. An overreliance on concurrence seeking, which is nothing new.
2. The complete sequence shown above, which was Janis's meaning but for which no evidence exists.
3. The result of excessive cohesiveness, but there is little support here, and cohesiveness is, as we have noted above, often a positive feature of groups.
4. Any set of group processes preceding a poor decision, which is a tautology. We would add that, posed thus, the tautology is easy to spot but as shown below the danger of reading backwards from results to presumed causes is not always avoided. It is easy to find what appears to be an error of decision-making and then either assume that groupthink was present or read the data to stress groupthink and play down other features (the latter being itself an example of academic groupthink). These problems are particularly acute where, as in much research of this kind, the evidence is derived through the reconstruction of past events.

Janis 'simply selected a subset [of factors] and wrapped them in a metaphor', and the concept of groupthink has become an organizational myth (Fuller and Aldag 1998: 172). The authors also engage, however, in myth-making of their own that it is worth correcting; see Box 8.2.

In our view, the idea of a myth is useful, since it does not mean 'wrong'. Groupthink may be useful as a warning that may be uttered, that is to avoid becoming too inward-looking. It may also help people in that it seems to capture something of the way in which organizations behave. But like many myths it can be dangerous if people take it as literally true or use it as a lens through which to read real organizations.

A broader point about groupthink is that norms of appropriate conduct can often be deployed in organizations as part of an exercise of power (see Chapter 6). This is a kind of group process that illustrates, not failure to reach an agreed objective, but a political activity involving disputed objectives. To the extent that a powerful and cohesive group establishes assumptions and ways of behaviour, it can make it harder for other

Box 8.2 The myth of the myth of Tonypandy

Fuller and Aldag call their paper 'organizational Tonypandy'. In their view, there has emerged a powerful myth about events in the village of Tonypandy, South Wales, during a strike of coal miners in 1910–11. The myth was that miners were shot by troops; and it acted as a symbol of class repression and a rallying point, even though in their view no troops were involved and there was no bloodshed. The case is thus a metaphor for analyses based on myths rather than realities.

But the historical record does not support this view. Soldiers were present and on one occasion (21 November 1910) they used bayonets to press a crowd towards police lines. More generally, the policing of the strike was removed from the civil authorities and placed under the command of a general (Page Arnot 1953: 59–67). As the authors should be aware, myths do not develop out of thin air. In this case, stories of deaths may have been false, but they simply dramatized an intense struggle that certainly existed. In the same way, organizational myths should be interrogated for their accuracy and also for the ways in which they represent organizational reality, but not dismissed. In short, myths can be analysed either for their factual content or for how they are used to represent organizations and make claims of legitimacy.

groups to challenge this view. Two UK experiments in appointing worker representatives to the boards of directors illustrate the point. They are detailed in Box 8.3. They suggest that there is an inescapable dilemma. Either worker representatives accept managerial logics in terms of how issues are defined and the assumptions as to the goals of the organization; one group's set of definitions tends to hold sway. Such definitions are reinforced through frequent meetings, through the fact that members of company boards tend to be recruited from particular social groups, and so on. Alternatively, conflict is introduced into the board room, in which case the behaviour of the worker representatives is resented by management representatives and efforts are made to marginalize their influence so that their effects on concrete decision-making are minimal.

Escalation as Group Psychology

Along with groupthink, a key psychological concept is escalation. The core idea contrasts with an axiom of economics. The axiom states that 'bygones are bygones', that is, that once an irreversible choice has been made any future decisions should be made quite independently. Psychological studies, on individuals (Staw 1976) and groups (Bazerman et al. 1984), show,

Box 8.3 Worker directors in British industry

Two significant experiments with worker directors took place in Britain in the 1970s, in the then British Steel Corporation (BSC) and the Post Office. The two organizations have now changed beyond recognition but the experiments are of lasting interest because they were particularly ambitious. They were also the subject of detailed social scientific analyses that provide unique insights into group processes (respectively Brannen et al. 1976 and Batstone et al. 1983). The Post Office scheme was described as 'the "strongest" introduced in any western country' (Batstone et al. 1983: xi).

At BSC, worker directors were in a minority and they largely accepted managerial financial logics even when job losses were entailed. This was explained in part by the tradition of unions in the industry, which had always adopted a conservative approach that did not question the fundamentals of managerial strategy. But the structure of the scheme was also important, for the worker directors were in a minority on an advisory board and they had no continuing links with their trade unions. They were thus absorbed into managerial processes. The Post Office representatives were more critical of management but this reflected and did not resolve differences of definition as to the purpose of industrial democracy. Managers became increasingly hostile to the experiment when, as they saw it, conflict was being brought into the boardroom and they could not trust the worker directors.

however, that people tend to be swayed by past decisions; where, for example, a group was responsible for a past poor decision it is more likely to remain committed to it than is a group that was not so responsible. Explanations turn on notions such as dissonance, meaning that there is a tendency to assume that the first decision was in fact right or possibly also that future commitment to a line of development will reap rewards eventually. Like group cohesion, persistence in a stream of decisions is not necessarily false, for it may take time for an investment to pay off. But it can be one contributor to a path of escalation towards error.

An example of such a path is given by Ross and Staw (1993) in their analysis of the Shoreham nuclear power plant (Box 8.4). According to these authors, escalation is determined by four sets of processes:

- *Project issues* turn on the costs and economic merits of the project itself.
- *Psychological issues* include such processes as self-justification.
- *Social processes* entail interpersonal relationships.
- *Organizational issues* include political support for a project and its 'institutionalization' in organizational routines.

Box 8.4 The Shoreham nuclear power plant

The Long Island Lighting Company planned a nuclear power plant at Shoreham, fifty-five miles east of New York City. Construction was to begin in 1969 and finish in 1973, at a cost of between $65 million and $75 million. The endeavour was finally abandoned in 1989 after an expenditure of about $5.5 billion. A notable feature of the history was growing local opposition to the plant following the Three Mile Island incident of 1979 and the Chernobyl accident of 1986.

Previous research suggests that the first set of issues is important at the start of a process of escalation, the second and third take over in the middle, and the first and fourth are important at the end.

Applying these ideas to the Shoreham case, Ross and Staw highlight in relation to the project itself ambiguities in the economic data, the way in which cost increases occurred (with incremental increases being small in relation to what had already been spent and coming when the project was nearing completion), and the sheer size of the project both in absolute terms and in relation to the size of the company. Psychological errors in information processing 'may have influenced' (Ross and Staw 1993: 716) escalation. Social process included social bonding in the group (echoes of groupthink) and the fact that people had staked their jobs on Shoreham. Finally, at the organizational level, the company had placed all its hopes on nuclear energy, so that this one plant became in effect the whole of the firm's strategy. Linked to this, experts were recruited who could work in no other plant in the company, and they became a political force leading to commitment to Shoreham.

This is arguably an incomplete analysis. Some of the propositions, notably on psychological processes and the political role of experts, are plausible but do not seem to be buttressed by hard evidence. This is one reflection of reconstructions of cases. Escalation is, moreover, treated as a process internal to the organization. What is striking about Shoreham is the extent to which the company argued that the plant was safe and the degree of local political opposition, with the latter eventually winning the day. This case is made strong by Clarke (1999) who argues that closure of the plant reflected a local victory over not only the company but also the federal government and financial interests that gave the company very powerful backing. In the case of the government, for example, this included attempting to gain regulatory approval for the plant. Clarke makes the important argument that in a pure power struggle (that is, a fight of one set of economic interests against another) the opponents would have lost, since the plant's supporters had plenty of money and political strength. They used other resources to change

[T]he reigning vocabulary of risk, shifting the terms of debate from one about jobs, electricity prices, national security and *probabilities* of some remote incident, to one of *possibilities* that children and homes would be irreparably damaged. (Clarke 1999: 83, emphasis original)

The distinctions between risk and uncertainty, and between different kinds of rationality introduced in Chapter 7, are clearly illustrated here. The opponents were able to show that probabilities based on ideas of risk had little basis, and they deployed social rationality against economic and bounded forms. Importantly, the resources that they deployed were not fixed ahead of time but were generated through a process of mobilization. Power resources are not necessarily fixed, and the apparently powerless can reconfigure the terrain so that their resources have increased value and currency.

Studies of decision-making escalation tend to focus on the immediate circumstances. But there was also a related set of processes to do with the economics of the industry. The reason why plants like Shoreham were built were that the regulatory structure of the nuclear industry encouraged them: it was possible to make largely guaranteed profits on costs of capital expenditure, and nuclear plants had high capital and low fuel costs. But, when demand for electricity fell, inflation rose, and environmental concerns increased, the economics of the industry changed dramatically. Firms supplying finance to the industry were initially attracted and then repelled (Mintz and Schwartz 1990: 215). In the present context, we can say that they were engaged in escalation. The example also connects with the analysis of Chapter 9, in stressing that financial firms 'do not simply react to market conditions, even in constrained circumstances like those connected to nuclear power. Instead, they become important actors in the creation of conditions' (Mintz and Schwartz 1990: 216).

Escalation as a Failure of Rationality

A purer example of a process of escalation that had its own internal dynamic is the celebrated case of Taurus computer system at the London Stock Exchange, which fast became 'one of the most significant computer project disasters in the history of the financial services sector' (Currie 1997: 79). The key facts are set out in Box 8.5. Drummond (1996a, 1996b)

Box 8.5 The Taurus events

In 1986 the London Stock Exchange began a project to computerize its trading systems. Taurus is an acronym for Transfer and Automated Registration of Uncertificated Stock. The system was intended to shift from a paper-based to an electronic process for the registration of ownership of shares and their transfer from one shareholder to another. The move from paper to electronic systems was called 'dematerialization'. The project, intended to last three years and cost £6 million, was abandoned three years later. Though the new chief executive of the Exchange, Peter Rawlins, tried to stop the whole programme at that time, a new Taurus project was developed. It was due for completion in October 1991. During 1991, implementation was announced as May 1993. In March of that year, the project was abandoned with costs estimated at £80 million. Rawlins resigned, and 360 other jobs were lost.

Source: Drummond (1996*a*, 1996*b*).

in her extensive analysis of the case describes Taurus as a 'tragedy'. The term tragedy is appropriate, for according to Aristotle the plot of such a play should be such that 'he who hears the tale told will thrill with horror and melt to pity': the hearer understands and empathizes with the actors while still being horrified at their plight.

Two possible explanations of the tragedy are not convincing. First, in relation to groupthink, many groups were involved, so it was not a case of an enclosed group becoming locked into a social psychological view of the world. Second, 'decision dilemma' theory stresses the ignorance (bounded rationality) of the parties. Yet it was not a lack of knowledge that was the problem, for reports were commissioned and used. It was more an issue of organization and differing perspectives as to what the knowledge really meant. The reports were not ignored, but they were interpreted in different ways.

The start of Taurus also reflected processes that can be analysed in 'garbage can' terms (Drummond 1996*b*: 348). The idea of dematerialization had existed for twenty years. It was brought into focus by two events: deregulation of the financial services industry in 1986 threatened the role of the Stock Exchange; and the stock market crash of 1987 exposed the weaknesses of lengthy paper-based systems (where up to three weeks could transpire between agreement to buy and sell and the exchange of money and share certificates). Dematerialization was offered as the solution, but a large part of the problem was in fact the organization of investment houses, which had already begun to improve their systems.

Taurus was a solution to a problem, 'a large segment of [which] had already self-corrected'.

Drummond (1996a: 90–2) goes on to argue that the driving process was one of escalation. Escalation is to be found in the 'logic of the situation' and not mental processes. This idea is a powerful one; it is laid out in Box 8.6 so as not to interfere with the narrative of the case. The essential point here is that different groups approached the project with different requirements and expectations and that the interaction of these views allowed the project to evolve unchecked. No single group had a view of the whole project or sufficient authority to impose its own view.

Three levels of actors are identified by Drummond. At the highest 'macro' level, there were contradictory goals of key actors including the Bank of England and leading banks organized as the Group of Thirty. For example, the Stock Exchange wanted a central register of share owner-ship, which the banks opposed because this threatened their own regis-tration business. At intermediate ('meso') level, there was an interplay of different rationales. Crucially, it was not that people behaved irrationally but rather that a large group of people, trying to behave rationally and extremely committed to the project, took individual decisions on rational grounds but the decisions conflicted with each other. For example, in 1991 the government insisted on security arrangements and indemnities for private investors, which hugely added to the complexity of the project. Finally, at micro level, the project was in any event complex and was operating at the boundaries of existing knowledge.

Taking the analysis further, Drummond (1996a: 131–3) asks why the Stock Exchange Board did not abandon Taurus in 1991, when delays and cost overruns were clear. The answer did not lie in some social psycho-logical process of seeking to hide embarrassment or foolhardy persist-ence. There was, rather, a separation of responsibilities: any one party could show that it had exercised proper due diligence in relation to its own responsibilities and feel that it did not have to take ultimate respon-sibility. The rational focus on individual interest interfered with the wider objective.

Later, Drummond makes the point that persistence can be rational if it secures a group's long-term goals. This is a theme that she might have stressed, for the emphasis on escalation gives an air of inevitability to a process and can imply that persistence in the face of adversity is ir-rational. The logic of the situation is indeed the key. It would plainly be wrong to fault decision-making if the results are not as expected, for some beneficial outcomes can be the result of good fortune while failures can be unpredictable. It is necessary to ask what the balance of costs and benefits

Box 8.6 The logic of the situation

The concept of the logic of the situation was developed by Jarvie (1972). Drummond does not refer to his work, though it is very pertinent to her analysis. Rational people may produce irrational outcomes if they respond to the local rationality of the situation and neglect the wider objective. Jarvie's example is a collision between naval ships carrying out a routine manoeuvre (ibid.: 25–7). In 1893 the British admiral Tryon was in charge of two parallel columns of ships. They needed to reverse the direction in which they were travelling. The columns were close together and needed to coordinate a turn. According to the traditional story, Tryon, a very experienced officer, was attempting to move as in panel 1 of Figure 8.1. The impossibility of this led to his being seen as confused or mad. But a reconstruction of the logic of the situation suggests that his counterpart leading the other column, Markham, may have expected, having queried the order, the picture on panel 2, consistent with Tryon's order to carry out inward turns and preserve the order of the fleet. Tryon may in fact have intended the pattern as in panel 3. The conflicting interpretations led to the result in panel 4. Tryon went down with his ship.

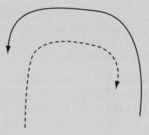
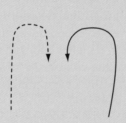
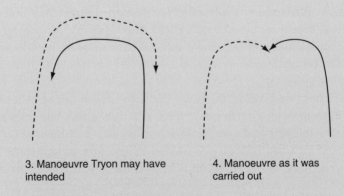

1. Impossible manoeuvre
supposedly attempted

2. Manoeuvre Markham
supposed that Tryon intended

3. Manoeuvre Tryon may have
intended

4. Manoeuvre as it was
carried out

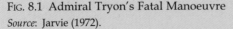

FIG. 8.1 Admiral Tryon's Fatal Manoeuvre
Source: Jarvie (1972).

One lesson is that instructions should not be combined into literally mixed messages. More important here is a point of *methodology*: though there is no evidence as to what Tryon was thinking, it is possible using knowledge of procedures in place in this context to reconstruct the logic of the situation as he saw it and thus to explain behaviour. Establishing plausible accounts of the logic of the situation as perceived by the actors is a key element in explaining why people act as they do.

was, as perceived at the time, and how salient the issue was to them. Like Shoreham, the project became elevated from the important to the vital, which also meant that potential critics tended to stay silent.

There are in fact two themes here. One is what Drummond terms institutionalization: when a venture is established as an end in itself, the processes surrounding it are taken for granted, so that Taurus became a goal in itself rather than a means to a specific purpose, namely, the modernization of the system of transactions. This is where there are some echoes of groupthink. The second theme is that of competing interests. For example, the Stock Exchange wanted to develop its own competitive position in the face of substantial changes in the market, while the securities industry aimed to reduce the risks that it faced (Drummond 1996a: 181). The Stock Exchange was not powerful enough to enforce its own definition and instead there was a destructive tension between the main parties (Drummond 1996a: 82). One possible resolution of the two themes is to argue that there were some shared assumptions, such as the centrality of Taurus, but competing definitions as to how the project should work in practice.

The 'whole saga can be viewed as a power struggle' (Drummond 1996a: 188). This must mean something more than a battle between two or more parties, for some views became institutionalized rather than being a source of overt struggle. Moreover, the language of a power struggle usually implies winners and losers, and here there were only losers. It is preferable to see 'power struggle' as meaning a struggle *for* power as well as *with* power resources: the resources have to be created, and part of the struggle was about how to mobilize resources to secure an end. The Taurus participants lacked the means to create enough power to secure their goals. As Drummond (1996a: 82) says, the Stock Exchange lacked the resources to impose its will, while other parties could insist on certain things without having the resources or the desire to control the whole project; thus retail stock brokers were able to insist on some attention to private investors, but they lacked the weight to force through full attention to the needs of private clients. The case is a good example of the dissipation of resources and hence of the fact that power struggles can have negative sum results (everyone loses).

The positions of the parties involved were too incompatible to generate the positive group processes indicated by Edmondson. Whether such processes would have been strong enough to have reversed other weaknesses in Taurus such as its move into uncharted technological territory is impossible to say. That is one theme of a tragedy: when could the key players have changed course and would it have made any difference? In respect of Taurus itself there seem to have been enough aspects of choice, for example the judgement that the project was vital and the unwillingness of various parties to step beyond their sectional interests, to suggest that a different decision path might have been feasible.

Drummond has used more than once what she terms the 'tragedy of the commons' to characterize Taurus. The thesis itself is considered in Box 8.7. Its wider significance is twofold.

1. A model such as the tragedy of the commons can be applied inappropriately. A given case may not in fact be an example of a larger class identified on theoretical grounds (such as groupthink, or a tendency for individual self-interest to be self-defeating, which is what the tragedy of the commons is intended to signify). In this case, the model of the commons overinterprets the evidence.

2. How far were the Taurus players maximizing self-interest in any exact sense (i.e. having a specific objective and deploying resources efficiently in its pursuit) as opposed to simply taking a narrow view and avoiding hard questions? The danger here is that of overinterpretation. The parties may have been self-interested but that does not mean that they had a clear set of goals. Indeed, a purely economically self-interested group, seeing its aims not being realized, will (having estimated the costs and benefits of the extra activity) try to cooperate with others. (This is the basis of cooperative games in game theory.) The problem for the Taurus participants was that they lacked a particularly clear view of what they wanted individually and the means to link individual and collective goals. The logic of the situation interfered with their reaching a position (i.e. one with defined sets of objectives) from which cooperative game-playing using rational principles could even start.

Box 8.7 More myths: the 'tragedy of the commons'

As rendered by Drummond (1998: 916) 'the commons were stretches of land offering free grazing rights. Logic dictated that each peasant would graze one more beast. However, the collective impact of each peasant maximizing his or her utility was to ruin the land'. The use of the past tense plainly implies a factual claim about really existing commons. The story is often reproduced (e.g. Buchan et al., 2002). One of Drummond's sources (Aram 1989) locates the issue in 'pre-industrial England' but offers no historical evidence. The origin of the story and her other source (Hardin 1968) makes no claim to historical truth, simply using the story as a parable to focus an argument about global population problems. There is no evidence that a tragedy of the commons ever occurred in a relevant historical case. As a matter of logic, if the tragedy had been a driving feature of behaviour, the commons would have survived for very little time. The reason that they did survive was that English peasants were not short-sighted individual profit-maximizers. There were limits as to who was allowed to use the commons, with rights often being proportional to the amount of land held, and in some cases there were explicit rules as to how many animals could be grazed (Bennett 1969: 57; Miller and Hatcher 1978: 99). More generally, life was ruled by customary standards of fairness (e.g. concepts of the just wage rather than a wage determined by supply and demand). As Aram (1989: 270) puts it 'the commons parable represents the expansion of the prisoner's dilemma game to n person settings involving a finite resource where property rights either are not or cannot be clearly defined and enforced'. Taken as a logically limiting case, the parable may be useful in helping to identify conditions under which self-serving behaviour can emerge. Its practical utility is otherwise low. It also has the effect, like many myths, of diverting attention from other stories: the obvious fact about the commons was that they were destroyed by landowners, who wished to enclose common land so as to practise proto-capitalist agriculture (so that, ironically, it was the ending of the commons and not their existence that reflected self-serving behaviour). Myths can thus have unintended results. The key point is that everyone at all times does not think like a neo-classical economist, and to tell a story of the commons can perpetuate such an error.

The sequel to the story of Taurus had a more successful conclusion. The Stock Exchange next implemented the Crest system that went live in 1996. According to Currie (1997), Crest succeeded for several reasons including the following:

- Responsibility was taken by the Bank of England, so that the Stock Exchange's problem of accommodating different interests was reduced. There were fewer stakeholders.

- The system was simpler in design, and it resolved some contentious issues; for example, Taurus would have required the relinquishing of paper holdings and was thus unpopular with small shareholders and their agents, whereas under Crest this was optional.
- Design of computer systems had evolved, so that there was more experience in the processes whereas much of Taurus was untried.

Currie also acknowledges that the contrast was not simply one of systems design. Several Crest software developers had worked on Taurus, and the lessons of overcomplexity and conflicting aims seem to have been absorbed.

Whether this means that there is a broader process of learning is more questionable. There have been several more recent failures of large-scale computer projects that have commonalities with Taurus in complexity and conflicting aims. It may be that the Crest team learned from Taurus because they were very close to it and the lessons came through lived experience. It is harder to draw lessons that are more abstract in kind.

Persistence, Failure, and Rationality

Persistence with a failing course of action can lead to people becoming trapped and to closed thinking. Yet in any large project there must be a degree of uncertainty as well as calculable risk, and some successful outcomes may have seemed unlikely. When is persistence rational?

Taurus and Shoreham became ends in themselves. The first issue, therefore, concerns the activity in which people persist. It may make sense to maintain an objective that is hard to realize. A problem arises only when a particular means is given undue status, and persistence to that means may be irrational.

A second theme from these two cases is that the means not only became ends but also became predominant ends: Taurus was deemed to be crucial, and it was also a complex step into the unknown. This made it hard for its rationale to be questioned. If an activity is less critical and less complex, the costs of persistence may be smaller.

These points may be developed by reference to a celebrated example of persistence that paid off: the entry of the Honda motorcycle company to the US market in the early 1960s. This case has become a business school staple for the light that it throws on different models of strategy formation (for assessments, see Mintzberg et al. 1998: 201–8; Mair 1999). We use it here to address the issue of persistence and rationality, then link this issue to pertinent parts of the strategy debate.

In the late 1950s, Honda had no position in the US market, yet by 1966 it had captured 63 per cent of the market (Pascale 1984). How did this come about? According to Honda executives interviewed some twenty years later, it was a story of persistence in the case of initial failure. The endeavour had simply been to see whether something could be sold in the USA. There was relative confidence in large machines, backed by a vague belief that, it was said, Sochiro Honda himself felt that the shape of the handlebars resembled the eyebrows of Buddha, which was a possible selling point. Some machines were sold, but they had a tendency to break down when driven long distances. The Honda representatives then found that there was interest in the very small machines that they used for their own transport. With this spur, and an inspired advertising slogan, they began to make substantial sales.

In this case, there was persistence in relation to ends, not means. Indeed, flexibility in relation to means (large or small bikes) was crucial. Nor was there an obsession with the particular mean of selling small bikes, which were, in relation to the Honda business at the time, a relatively minor part of its total operation. This latter point helps us to address some of the business school debates on Honda. The story was used by exponents of a 'learning' approach to strategy to criticize the approach in terms of planning. The debates unfolded as follows:

- The planning view was first laid out in a report commissioned by the UK government about the failures of its motorcycle industry. This argued that Honda's success was carefully planned: high market share in the Japanese market and a large and low-cost domestic production base allowed an attack on the US market through a new segment ignored by US (and UK) firms, small bikes for middle-class consumers.
- The learning view then laid out the Honda executives' accounts of what they in fact did.
- The planners' response was that trying something and seeing whether it works, even probable non-starters, is scarcely helpful advice.
- The riposte from the learning school came from Mintzberg (reproduced at length in Mintzberg et al. 1998: 205–7). The Honda managers did not perform a random experiment but exposed themselves to 'the chance to be surprised' by the market. They 'avoided being too rational' and were 'prepared to learn'. 'Sure they used their experience and their cost position based on production volumes in Japan. But only after they learned what they had to do'.

- A further intervention came from those stressing not planning or emergent strategies but 'core competencies'. These are deeply rooted abilities that may not be evident from the outside and will be hard to copy. Some firms' competencies may lie in marketing and branding, so that very diverse products can function under one label (the Virgin group, which embraces music stores, radio stations, airlines, and insurance, being one popular example). The competencies of Honda, it is argued, lay in the design and manufacture of small petrol engines, with evidence being the firm's later development into products such as lawnmowers.

Honda was, after all, simply selling an existing product rather than designing one from scratch. Its 'learning' was quite tightly constrained. The learning did not embrace how to design and build motorcycles, for this had already been done in Japan. According to Mair (1999), moreover, Honda already had a distribution network in Japan, so that the 'learning' in the USA was less novel than some of the learning school imply. It was simply to do with taking an existing ability and applying it in new ways.

A further lesson highlighted by the Honda case may be called 'overdetermination'. Just as accounts of escalation can imply a path to inevitable failure, so success stories can suggest that success is unlimited. If Honda had certain core competencies, why did these not permit it to dominate other industries such as small cars and why did it take so long to enter some sectors (Mair 1999)? There must have been limits on its competencies and on its ability to learn. How much information from a learning experience can really be absorbed and then transmitted? Honda's success in the USA in the 1960s can be explained in terms of shifts in market demand (that happened to be occurring and of which Honda executives seem to have been unaware), the possession of a product that fitted this demand, the willingness of the company to persevere, and luck. Yet such features may not be sufficient in other conditions. Firms face, moreover, internal limits: how much can they absorb, and what arrangements need to be in place to permit lessons to be grasped and then disseminated? There are also external constraints: other firms may compete, drawing on their own core competencies, so that success is neither predetermined nor set to continue into the future.

There may also be implications in relation to the conditions allowing such learning to take place. (These conditions are little discussed in the Honda debate.) How was it that the managers in the USA were given the space and time to experiment, rather than being sacked for failing to meet their sales targets? Though we have no information about the targets that were set or the place of these managers in the Honda hierarchy, they appear to have had a sense of what the company was doing (e.g. their ability to refer to what Honda himself thought, a personal link that would probably be unlikely in many US firms). It is also likely that as trusted people sent overseas they enjoyed substantial employment security. In terms of targets, Japanese firms relied (and still do so, though to a much reduced extent) on progression through the internal labour market rather than short-term targets. This is not to say that performance is not assessed. On the contrary, there are regular and detailed appraisals. And achievement in relation to one's peers, notably the speed of progression through the hierarchy, is a key aspect of a Japanese manager's view of himself (or herself, though in 1960 the managerial ranks in Japan were almost exclusively male). But this emphasis on achievement is against a broad set of measures, not short-term targets (see Box 9.7; Endo 1994; Storey et al. 1997).

If we suppose, to go back to the British industry that started the debate, that a group of British managers magically supplied with small motorcycles had been sent to bolster falling sales of large bikes, they might not have made use of the opportunity because they had been set specific targets, feared failure to meet them, and might well have been dismissed before any learning about small bikes could take place. The ways in which organizational rules create a climate of expectation shape the degree to which, and the form in which, learning can take place.

It makes sense, then, to say with Drummond and Mintzberg that rationality can itself be a problem. They are using 'rational' to mean 'the pursuit of narrow goals seen through the eyes of one particular party'. They are not advocating irrationality in the sense of illogical or arbitrary behaviour. The lessons are two. The simpler one is that when different groups pursue their own (rational) ends they interfere with the wider goal that they all claim to pursue. The more complex one is that, even in the absence of conflicting groups, rationality can lead to a focus on means rather than ends.

Learning

In this chapter and Chapter 7, we have seen numerous examples in which people do or do not learn from experience. But what does it mean to say that organizations learn?

The concept of the learning organization has become one of the most popular in the management literature. The reasons include the belief, now often stated as an axiom, that technologies are transferable and that it is the deeply embedded knowledge and 'idiosyncratic competencies' of organizations that gives them a competitive edge. Learning then becomes critical. A common, and useful, model is that of different forms of learning introduced by Argyris and Schön (1978) and summarized in Box 8.8.

We can see elements of single-loop learning in Taurus and double-loop learning in Honda. It is also possible to identify some of the conditions in the two cases that produced the respective results. Yet moving towards triple-loop learning is not an easy matter. Texts on these issues deploy models of learning loops and other devices. A popular one is the concept of the knowledge-creating company (Nonaka and Takeuchi 1995). They argue that Western organizations focus on explicit, formal knowledge while Japanese firms like Honda have also used less formalized and codified, or tacit, knowledge. They then cross-classify the origins and results of knowledge, as shown in Figure 8.2. Socialization involves the sharing of tacit knowledge; externalization converts such knowledge into formal kinds; combination is nothing but formal knowledge; and internalization involves people taking formal rules and procedures and developing them into practical routines. These authors argue that knowledge creation should entail a spiral through these different elements.

This is a very good example of the dangers of conflating description, analysis, and prescription. If this framework is offered as a descriptive taxonomy it may be useful to classify, for example, whether workers learn by purely tacit means or by exposure to formal routines. But in terms of analysis, have the categories been defined in measurable terms, and has work been done to indicate the antecedent conditions leading to different combinations and the possible results? Is it, for example, the case that in

---

Box 8.8 Learning loops

Single-loop learning focuses on errors in current processes. For example, if the quality of a product falls outside set parameters, corrective mechanisms will come in to play.

Double-loop learning might ask why the tolerances are set where they are and whether other approaches might meet the goal of producing a product to perform a given task: it entails questioning existing assumptions.

Developing from these ideas, the concept of triple-loop learning has emerged: it might ask why the product is being made at all and what the wider goals of the organization are. Rather than ask how to produce given widgets to set standards (single-loop), or how to produce widgets to meet existing market needs (double-loop), we would ask whether we should be in the widget business at all.

		Result	
		Tacit	**Explicit**
Origin	**Tacit**	Socialization	Externalization
	Explicit	Internalization	Combination

FIG. 8.2 The knowledge spiral
Source: Nonaka and Takeuchi (1995).

some standard organizations all that is needed is an appropriate mode of learning, with the spiral being redundant? We discussed above the hard time given to the idea of groupthink if it is to be a scientific concept. The same tests might well be applied to the model of the learning organization. Finally, is the model intended to apply prescriptively to all organizations, and on what grounds do we move from analysis of what is (or what might be) to what ought to be?

Thinking more broadly about such models, the first, and fundamental, issue concerns what amount of learning an organization might be said to 'need'. Though much is made of 'post-industrial' society, it remains the case that many organizations continue to operate on essentially Fordist lines (see Chapter 2). In the UK for example, half of manufacturing output in 1997 was classified as being of a 'low technology' kind (Nolan and Slater 2003: 75). The need for learning here is very restrictive. A second issue is the conditions permitting learning. A key aspect here is that each individual can have the time to learn from experience and that there is a group that is capable of developing some kind of collective memory. Many aspects of Anglo-Saxon organizations tend to undermine this condition.

- They include the prevalence of mergers and takeovers, discussed in Chapter 9, which generally mean that new management teams are put in place in existing operations and that many other operations are sold, so that new rounds of learning are needed.
- Also relevant here is a continuous and possibly increasing process of downsizing, delayering, and the introduction of new management systems. It has become a commonplace that scarcely has one innovation been introduced before it is supplanted by another. The rapid displacement of total quality management by business

process re-engineering is one frequently cited example. Organizational learning is about drawing lessons from experience and reflecting on them. This calls for time, which constant change may deny.

- Aspects of organizations also include an approach to management development based on short-term rewards and a lack of time for any learning to become embedded. A study of UK and Japanese firms found that the formal training systems in the two countries were often quite similar and that the amounts of training reported by managers were also surprisingly close; the difference was that in Japan there was a relatively stable structure of career planning into which training fitted, whereas in Britain arrangements were more haphazard and training systems were prone to be abandoned at short notice (Storey et al. 1997). In the British case, the opportunities for creating a 'corporate memory' were limited.

Third, who is learning what? A model of the learning organization often seems to assume that the organization is a single entity. But as we have seen with Taurus there are different groups with different interests. At its simplest, this means that knowledge in one group may not be communicated to another. More subtly, it can also mean that one group may not realize what another needs to know: information about product development may be of value to a marketing department, but the product development department may be unaware of this.

The fourth and last point assumes that groups would in principle share knowledge given the chance. But the existence of interest groups also means that knowledge may be withheld or produced in distorted form. Many of the models discussed above treat organizations as unitary bodies and assume that everyone will wish to share knowledge for the good of the whole. Organizational politics mean that potential lessons may not be learnt. A good example is the Saturn Corporation. As discussed in Chapter 6, this is the division set up by General Motors in Tennessee in 1985 with the explicit aim of being a 'learning laboratory' (Rubinstein and Kochan 2001: 2). In many ways the experiment was a success, for it combined participative work organization with high levels of productivity. Yet Rubinstein and Kochan (2001: 131) see 'the failure to learn from the experiences at Saturn as the biggest missed opportunity' of the experiment. They attribute this primarily to isolation of Saturn from the larger company and trade union structures, which they link in turn to entrenched interests that were at best sceptical of a model that challenged many existing assumptions 'about the role and power of management, the primacy of financial capital as a resource for the firm, and the role that human capital should play' (ibid.: 145).

We would argue that constraints such as this are generic in capitalist organizations. Constraints do not mean that people cannot overcome them, but they equally mean that the idea that organizations will learn simply because some key people in them think that they should will generally be an unrealistic one. The tacit knowledge owned by workers is not only a resource for the firm but it is also a means of resistance to managerial definitions of what the firm is about and what workers should do in consequence.

Conclusions

Three main lessons can be highlighted. They cover how one thinks about stories of success and failure, the politics of organizations, and the ways in which existing structures and assumptions may be challenged.

First, we have seen the value of reconstructing the logic of the situation and also, in relation to groupthink, the problems of doing so. Examples and precedents are used frequently in daily life and are also a common educational device. One rule in thinking about them is to ask whether they make intelligible what is otherwise obscure (as with Box 8.6) without imposing a single narrative or reading history backwards. By reading backwards, we mean starting with an outcome and then seeking explanations for an event as though the causal factors necessarily led to the given result. A second rule therefore is to ask in respect of a given case why factor X appeared to lead to event Y, that is what mechanisms are at work. A third rule is to seek other cases where X is present and ask whether it always produces Y or whether Y arises only when other conditions are also present. The account of Honda illustrates the kinds of causal analysis that can be developed.

Second, we have analysed structures of decision-making in terms, not of individual preferences or social–psychological processes, but in the light of the political interests that individuals and groups pursue. The Taurus example illustrated this most clearly. It is reasonable to ask at this point, however, how far such results are true of any complex decision-making system or whether they say anything specifically about capitalism. We would argue that some aspects are indeed the product of complexity and competing interests groups, and to that extent are a reflection of any modern social organization. But there are two additional themes that place such organizations in their wider context.

- There are differences between countries, as the discussion of Honda and learning suggests: it is not necessarily the case that individual self-serving will be the dominant motivation. There are thus different approaches to an issue, and some of these reflect assumptions that are embedded in one society rather than another, a point developed in Chapter 9. Organizational functioning is shaped by the kind of capitalist society in which it is embedded.
- Some pressures on decision-making are driven by markets, as we also saw in Chapter 7. Taurus, for example, reflected a fear of loss of business to other stock exchanges, while financial imperatives also underlay actions in the Tenerife air disaster. The pressures exerted by capitalist markets impose particular sorts of demands and contribute to decision-making in certain ways, for example to introduce changes because competitors are moving in a particular way.

Finally, we have seen a few examples, as at Shoreham, where organizational routines and logics can be challenged. Overt and formal challenges are not a central theme of this chapter, but the possibility of less direct questioning has been implicit throughout. Organizations certainly have formal hierarchies and informal procedures and assumptions. But these are not unbending or all-powerful. Formal rules can often be challenged in their own terms, for example where one rule contradicts another. And procedures and assumptions are socially constructed and are thus open to revision. Cases such as Taurus and Honda illustrate how assumptions and organizational myths can change. There is space for people to shape such myths. This chapter has shown how myths work and develop; with this information people can question existing assumptions. We now consider how such organizational processes are located in and shaped by wider processes, namely, the functioning of markets.

9

How Are Markets Constructed?

The market is perhaps the core institution of capitalism. It is the means through which goods and services are exchanged and prices are determined. The language of supply and demand is universal, and the proposition that markets ensure the efficient allocation of resources has become almost an axiom. For our purposes there are two linked issues. First, how far and in what sense are markets efficient and what are the implications for work experience within firms? The argument is that markets are constructed rather than existing naturally and that a drive towards efficiency cannot be assumed. This is the concern of this chapter. Second, the argument that the capitalist market has an increasingly global character is addressed in Chapter 10.

The importance of this first question is illustrated by major developments in the largest, and, many would say, most fully marketized, capitalist economy, the USA. The high-profile collapse of the energy company Enron in 2001 sparked major debate about corporate malpractice. Less spectacular but equally important developments had been in train for at least the preceding twenty years. They included sharply widening income distribution (a trend observed in some other countries but, with the exception of the UK, on nothing like the same scale) and massive restructuring exercises by many firms so that experience of job loss, insecurity, and pressure to work long hours became widespread (Lazonick and O'Sullivan 2000). Were corporate scandals merely extreme and unrepresentative events? And was restructuring just part of the cost of economic change as new industries supersede old ones? On the first question, we follow many commentators in seeing scandals as particularly sharp illustrations of much wider trends in modern US capitalism towards unrestrained self-interest.

The answer to the second question is more complex. It is true that change is a constant feature of capitalism, for capitalism is a system based above all on accumulation and dynamism. Critics of capitalism in general, and of specific episodes of restructuring in particular, sometimes suggest that the costs of change can be avoided. Our argument, by contrast, is that some costs are inevitable. As against the hypothesis of efficient markets, however, it is not the case that every case of restructuring was the result of efficiency. Such a view neglects changes in the choices made by large firms—in the terms of Lazonick and O'Sullivan (2000) a shift of strategy from 'retain [profits] and re-invest' to 'downsize and distribute'. Markets are institutions of power, there is no necessary drive towards efficiency, and there is no one best way to construct capitalist markets. Political considerations are often important, and issues of escalation and the creation of beliefs (as discussed in Chapter 8) are often salient. In short, market processes are neither inevitable nor natural.

To develop these themes we first outline some basic and surprising facts about how (certain) markets work. Second, we examine the evolution of the market for corporate control in the USA. This leads, third, to the location of scandals and restructuring within this new market context. The effects of market restructuring on work are summarized next. The final two sections turn to models of capitalism as practised in other countries, the key theme being that markets can be structured in very different ways. Finally, we draw together conclusions in relation to debates about different approaches to corporate governance.

How Do Markets Work?

At first sight, the answer to this question is obvious: 'through the intersection of the forces of supply and demand' is the solution that would be offered not only by any first-year economics student but also by many managers and politicians. Yet the fact that such a conclusion is a commonplace illustrates the power of a particular way of thinking about the world which begs many questions. From the standpoint of economics as a discipline, one would need to ask what conditions need to hold before 'supply and demand' offers a meaningful solution. We quoted Joseph Stiglitz in Chapter 1, whose observation about perfect information points to one such condition. In the absence of perfect information, markets may fail to function according to the 'laws' of supply and demand.

The common image of a market is of spot trading for a homogeneous product such as corn, so that the price reflects how much of it is there in a market and how much is in demand.

- Yet, first, how do people judge the quality of particular batches of corn? In the absence of perfect knowledge by buyers and sellers as to the nature of goods on offer, there will be no uniform price.
- Second, why buy corn today when it may be cheaper tomorrow? The spot price will interact with a futures price, which will (as discussed

below) depend on assumptions as to what the state of supply and demand will be and also on time preference (how important is corn today to me as compared to corn tomorrow?)

- Third, what happens when there is no system of a large number of buyers and sellers acting as independent individuals and instead there are small numbers of firms?
- A fourth question, asked more by sociologists than economists, concerns the social conditions that must exist for a market to function: How can I trust that the supplier of corn is its rightful owner, and what legal underpinnings exist to ensure that contracts are honoured?
- Finally (in this less than exhaustive list), what determines which goods are produced and offered for sale? That is, a model of supply and demand says nothing about how goods are produced, other than assuming that, when there is a demand, 'signals' are sent out and people respond, but how do they learn what is demanded, how do they organize the production of goods, and how do they try to control the market? If they make a certain product, will they not wish to control its sale rather than rely on the uncertainties of a spot market?

These questions have arisen in economics from at least the time of Adam Smith, who famously asserted that any group of producers will be concerned, not to accept the dictates of 'the market' passively, but to engage in what he termed a conspiracy to control the market. They have recently returned to centre stage. A good example is a work subtitled 'a natural history of markets' (McMillan 2002). As it points out, economics used to be curiously silent on this fundamental issue. 'The [conventional] supply-and-demand diagram . . . is a bloodless account of exchange. . . . It tells us what prices can do, but is silent on how they are set. Supply and demand bypasses questions of how buyers and sellers get together, what other dealings they have, how buyers evaluate what they are buying, and how agreements are enforced' (McMillan 2002: 8). The book's central message is that markets work but do not do so automatically, and that different markets need designing according to their specific needs. It also makes many points that we also stress, notably that large firms do not take market signals as given.

One key example is the well-known dispute about drugs to combat AIDS, wherein developing countries accused the major pharmaceuticals companies of charging excessive prices, while the companies argued that the prices reflected the huge costs of research and development. McMillan argues that in some ways the companies were right: they were operating according to the rules of the market as it was designed, investing in drugs that would sell in developed countries. This included developing expensive AIDS treatments that were out of reach in the countries most seriously affected by the disease. The companies also gave little attention to treatments for major tropical diseases such as malaria.

Yet the drug companies 'actively try to shape' market rules, lobbying governments fiercely, to the tune of $167 million in the US presidential election of 2000, more than any other industry (McMillan 2002: 32). The reason is that they need their patents protecting through laws on intellectual property, and intellectual property 'could not exist without the state'. These laws, he goes on, 'represent an uneasy compromise between the needs of the innovator and the needs of the state' (p. 34). The terms of the compromise can be altered, and he gives examples of how some countries, including India and South Africa, overrode existing intellectual property rights in order to reduce the costs of AIDS drugs. In his view, the benefits of doing this exceeded the costs.

It is thus no longer adequate to caricature economics as assuming that markets work smoothly. Yet there is a large remaining issue. McMillan, and other authors of the same stamp such as Kay (2003), say nothing about the tradition of the sociology of markets as discussed in this chapter. If we wish to understand markets as social and political structures, then direct engagement between approaches would seem useful. We offer here, and in Chapter 10, some effort on these lines. The aim is to complement the analysis offered by writers such as McMillan through greater emphasis on the social shaping of markets. Economists tend to underestimate the ways in which market processes are embedded in institutional arrangements and structures of power. The structuring of power analysed in Chapter 6 and the kinds of behaviour discussed in Chapter 8 are hard to grasp within an economics perspective.

A useful way to approach such questions is to recognize that there is no such thing as 'the' market. Different markets are constituted with different rules and assumptions (Callon 1998). For example, when is failure to disclose facts about a product normally accepted negotiating practice, when is it slightly dubious, and when is it illicit? Different answers will be given in different contexts. Another point is that markets are socially constructed. Callon gives the example of the creation in part of France of a 'perfect' market for strawberries, where buyers and sellers interacted in close to ideal conditions. This market did not exist in nature but was consciously created by a group of people who, among other things, built a warehouse for storage and the setting of prices, created an inventory system to track quantities and prices, and established a trading ring in which buyers and sellers traded without being able to see each other (so that tacit collusion was prevented). This was one particular market, with rules that were socially generated through identifiable processes, and not an autonomous or natural entity. Box 9.1 gives further instances, from cases where 'pure' markets should be most developed.

The works just discussed are compatible with the view of economists such as McMillan, though they also delve more deeply into the ways in which markets are embedded in social relations. The idea that markets are structures of power, in which interest group concerns can and do override any tendency towards efficiency, also needs making central. We now address this issue.

Box 9.1 Market opportunism

Abolafia (1996) conducted an ethnographic investigation of different sorts of markets. He chose financial markets, where the principles of economic rationality should be most clearly expressed. In one case, bond markets, he found unconstrained opportunism. Here all kinds of self-interested practice were accepted as part of the rules of the game. They included giving false information to clients and 'front running' (learning that a client wants a bond, buying it up, and then selling it on at a higher price). Yet such practices reflected particular conditions rather than being inherent in markets. The conditions here included the facts that, in this context, aggressive traders make the highest profits and that bond traders deal with clients at a distance, usually by phone and through intermediaries. In contrast, Abolafia found, markets such as that of the New York Stock Exchange have much more centralized trading between people who know each other and who have group norms of behaviour. Markets fluctuate between opportunism and restraint according to conditions. (The discussion in Chapter 5 of workers' fiddles has strong parallels.) Abolafia lists four constraints on opportunism:

- the strength and efficiency of reputational networks (so that where one's reputation is important for future relationships, opportunism will be limited);
- the distribution of power among stakeholders;
- institutional rules; and
- the threat and reality of legal sanctions.

A later study of trades in the UK of fixed income and equity products found that knowledge was necessarily tacit and based on 'flair'. Though traders on some occasions represented markets as purely rational economic institutions, they also underlined the importance of instinct rather than carefully calculated objective economic decision-making (Willman et al. 2001).

Corporate Control in the USA and Britain: From Managerial Capitalism to Shareholder Value

Enron and other scandals reflected the extent to which shareholder value had become established as the fundamental principle of US capitalism. The USA is normally taken to be the country with the economy run on most purely capitalist lines. Yet shareholder value has not existed throughout US history and it is a product of a distinct historical process.

A conventional starting point is that firms pursue efficiency. The alternative view is expressed by Fligstein (1990: 302):

[M]anagers rarely known what is economically efficient. They have a sense of controlling a market or market share, and to some degree can control costs. But the driving force for managers... is to preserve their organizations and further their individual and collective interests.

This neatly reverses the usual economic assumption. Efficiency may be an outcome if firms are in the long run forced to behave in efficient ways or fail. But, says Fligstein (1990: 300), to treat what in fact emerges as being necessarily efficient is to read 'history backwards' (a point with parallels in relation to Honda and learning: see Chapter 8). As for the choices as opposed to their possible results, there is, first, no particular reason why efficiency should be perceived: how are the relevant signals sent and interpreted? Second, and even more importantly, 'efficiency' is not something that an economic agent will necessarily seek if it also means cutting costs and engaging in an effort to change existing ways of working. The idea of increasing market share or controlling a market through price agreements or other means is likely to speak directly to managers, whereas efficiency in this sense is something that may be imposed on them rather than being an incentive that is welcomed. Firms try to control competition rather than responding naturally to its alleged dictates.

Four main conceptions of corporate control can be distinguished (Fligstein 1990: 12–16):

- the direct control of competitors through predatory pricing, cartels, or monopoly;
- the integration and stabilization of the production process, leading to oligopolistic conditions; this is a 'manufacturing' strategy;
- the finding and keeping of markets through a 'marketing' strategy; and
- the financial conception based on the measurement of performance in each line of business, with merger and divestment being a key tool.

These conceptions played dominant roles in the USA at different periods, with the last coming to prominence between 1945 and 1970 (Fligstein 1990: 289–94). The conglomerate firms that came to dominate much of industry had poor profits, albeit rapid growth. Mergers persisted, despite their limited efficiency properties, because they encouraged growth, which was a goal not least because managers running large firms were paid more than those in small firms, and because financial intermediaries such as banks themselves made profits from funding the mergers.

An unanticipated challenge to the financial conception in the USA emerged in the 1980s and became dominant in the following decade. Fligstein (2001: 147–56) argues that the financial conception faced a crisis as it was felt to fail to promote profitability, the causes of the crisis being growing foreign competition and an economic background of slow growth, high inflation, and low profits. (For more on crises, see Chapter 10.)

Changing conceptions of corporate control reflected two sets of processes. The first were problems being faced by large firms as economic performance worsened and competition from overseas grew. The second set reflected responses to these problems. The first part of the set was 'a group of American financial economists [who] developed . . . agency theory' (O'Sullivan 2000: 7). As outlined in Box 9.2, this theory treats shareholders as principals who employ managers as their agents. The market mechanism had failed to discipline managers, because large firms could in effect control the market, so that the solution was an active takeover system, or a market for corporate control. Agency theory was widely proclaimed as much more than an academic approach by one of its leading advocates Jensen (1989), who argued that active takeover markets and devices such as leveraged buyouts would promote efficiency and productivity.

The triumph of agency theory was secured by the second set of influences, the rise of institutional investors notably pension funds and life insurance companies. Table 9.1 shows figures for the USA. Shareholdings are dominated by institutions. Not only do households own less than half of corporate stock in the USA but such holdings are also small and dispersed whereas unit trusts and pension funds hold significant amounts of the stock of particular companies and can thus exert leverage over the management. A further encouragement to the hostile takeover was a move by investment banks into active trading from underwriting (O'Sullivan 2000: 162). Institutional investors took a much more active interest in the share price than did private investors, and firms began to pursue shareholder value almost exclusively.

Box 9.2 Five models of corporate governance

Keasey et al. (1997: 3–11) lay out four competing models of corporate governance:

1. The 'dominant' Principal–Agent (P–A) model argues that markets for capital, managerial skills, and corporate control constrain managerial discretion. It is assumed that, in the absence of such control by or on behalf of the principal (the shareholders), the agents (senior managers) will pursue their own agenda, which may embrace raising their own salaries or becoming lazy and inefficient.

2. The myopic markets model agrees with the P–A model that the aim is to maximize shareholder value, but suggests that markets tend to undervalue long-term returns. But there is little evidence that long-term issues are in fact neglected; for example, research and development expenditure, an indicator of long-term orientation, is not disliked by markets.

3. Abuse of executive power: companies are dominated by boards of directors that pursue their own interests, and some managerial pay rises are out of control.

4. The stakeholder model is the 'most fundamental' challenge to the P–A model. It argues that stakeholders other than shareholders, notably customers and employees, have interests in firms. The efficiency case for the model has two strands: firms that develop ethical and trust-based relations with stakeholders secure mutually beneficial long-term relationships; and countries such as Japan and Germany, both of which have extensive stakeholder involvement, are widely seen as successful models. As Keasey et al. note, it is obvious that the first point is no challenge to the P–A model, for if efficiency benefits exist then, *ex hypothesi*, an efficient market will recognize them and value firms accordingly. The second point raises wider issues about competing models of capitalism discussed below.

Models 2 and 3 simply point to some possible imperfections in the market for control and are thus empirical qualifications to Model 1. The whole point of growing attention to active markets for control, moreover, is that many analysts think that these imperfections can be eliminated or at least minimized. The fourth model is as much normative as it is analytical: its proponents argue that capitalism *should* become more caring and that firms should be driven by concerns other than shareholder value (most clearly, Hutton 1995, 2002). We try to distinguish these two elements.

A fifth model is that of O'Sullivan (2000: 4). She terms it the organizational control theory: a system of governance requires 'financial commitment, organizational integration, and insider control'. These three terms refer, respectively, to the provision of finance to support investment, the development of organizational structures and routines to permit the deployment of the resources, and control of these structures by managers within the firm. It is in effect the analytical basis of Model 4, and is also pursued below.

TABLE 9.1 Ownership of corporate stock in the USA (per cent)

	Households	Private pension funds	Public pension funds	Mutual funds	Other
1946	93.0	0.3	0	1.5	5.2
1997	42.7	13.8	10.2	16.2	17.1

Source: Abbreviated from O'Sullivan (2000: 156).

TABLE 9.2 Equity holdings in the UK (per cent)

	Individuals	Institutions	Companies and banks	Other
1963	54.0	29.0	6.4	10.6
1993	17.7	61.2	2.1	19.0

Source: Abbreviated from Short and Keasey (1997: 19). Institutions include pension funds and insurance companies.

In the UK, developments broadly similar to those in the USA took place. As shown in Table 9.2, institutions achieved an even more dominant position than in the USA. Hostile takeovers also became commonplace (Hutton 2002: 225–6).

The influence of finance capital on the operation of the firms in which financial intermediaries invest is often direct. Carleton et al. (1998) investigated the links between a leading US insurance and pension fund and the firms in which it held shares, demonstrating frequent private negotiations and clear instances in which behaviour was changed. Similarly, Mintz and Schwartz (1990) identify two mechanisms. First, there are direct interventions: they report that between 1977 and 1981 there were interventions by financial firms in the internal affairs of 5 per cent of the largest US companies. Second, stockholding in major firms and the coordinated buying and selling of stock influence behaviour and establish norms of conduct. A loser in one such event, whose attempt to take over another firm was frustrated by the intervention of financial institutions, ruefully commented, 'I always knew there was an Establishment... I just used to think that I was part of it' (Mintz and Schwartz 1990: 210). (These instances illustrate the exercise of Faces 1 and 2 of power, merging into Face 3 power, in the terms of Chapter 6).

If the market for corporate control works, then its core device, the takeover, should deliver benefits to the firms concerned. Moreover,

Box 9.3 Takeovers or makeovers?

O'Sullivan (2000: 168–71) summarizes the US evidence on the benefits of take-overs:

1. It is true that shareholders in target firms make sizeable gains around the time of takeover announcements.
2. Shareholders of acquiring companies, however, see their wealth does not change or decrease.
3. If takeover is a device to discipline poor managers, taken-over firms should perform badly prior to acquisition and well subsequently. There is little evidence of this.
4. Some gains to shareholders are not efficiency gains but transfers from other groups, a classic case being lower wages and pension entitlements for employees (see further Box 9.9, below).

As she comments, moreover, to equate efficiency with the wealth of share-holders is a common but highly questionable assumption.

As for the UK, the country's system, says the experienced financial journalist Plender (2003: 118), is the 'most takeover-friendly in the world'. Plender sum-marizes the experience of the chemicals giant ICI, perhaps the country's leading manufacturing firm. The conglomerate firm Hanson began buying shares in the late 1980s, which was widely seen as a prelude to a hostile takeover bid. Though the threat was seen off, the event deeply affected ICI managers, who felt that a more market-oriented strategy was needed and who were concerned that reli-ance on traditional bulk chemicals put the firm in low-growth sectors that were also subject to highly cyclical demand. They thus proceeded to split the company into two new entities, Zeneca specializing in pharmaceuticals, and the remaining ICI. The latter then engaged in a massive wave of divestments and takeovers with the aim of making it less subject to economic fluctuations, but the result was a smaller firm that was in fact more economically vulnerable. Zeneca meanwhile merged with the Swedish firm Astra. Market-driven restructuring did not yield meaningful long-term efficiency.

agency theory also claimed that there would be system-wide efficiency gains. The evidence summarized in Box 9.3 suggests otherwise.

One natural expectation of agency theory is that the agents (senior managers) will be rewarded in line with corporate performance and that job tenures will shorten as a result of markets for corporate control. It is certainly the case that pay rose sharply. One of the most notable trends is that in 1965 the pay of the average chief executive officer in the USA was 44 times that of the average worker; by 1998, this number had risen to a staggering 419 (O'Sullivan 2000: 200). Yet in the UK there was little evidence that the presence of institutional investors influenced the pay–performance link or the risk of dismissal (Cosh and Hughes 1997), while overall many studies have failed to find clear links between CEO pay and the performance of their firms (Mayer 1997). As one review puts it, 'the dominant theme emerging from the empirical analysis of the remuneration–performance relationship is that the link is relatively weak' (Bruce and Buck 1997: 97). One study showed that CEO pay was influenced, not by performance or by the size of firms, but by social comparisons, that is the pay of other managers in similarly sized firms (O'Reilly et al. 1988).

This last study points to a central weakness in agency theory and other models of rational choice. They assume that 'principals' are motivated solely by a desire to ensure that their agents pursue the principals' goals. But, first, these are people who constantly interact with each other and who, research has consistently shown, are parts of closely connected social networks (Scott 1997). They will tend to share assumptions as to what is reasonable. It has, for example, become a commonplace that remuneration committees that are supposed to monitor the pay of senior directors and establish performance targets in fact comprise small groups of people who operate with the same assumptions. Second, what does monitoring the behaviour of agents really mean? Modern corporations are large and complex, and as noted above managers may have only a very broad idea of what they are trying to do. The concept of shareholder value tried to cut through these issues by setting the share price as the single measure of performance. But raising the share price can be achieved in many ways, some of which are not sustainable in the long term (as illustrated by the discussion below of scandals that broke as a result of such practices). Similarly, there are great uncertainties as to whether a particular takeover will work, and if so over what timescale. In practice, principals usually become involved only in crises, and at other times leave their agents relatively free (Short and Keasey 1997; Mayer 1997). As the cases of scandals again show most clearly, problems can be allowed to emerge until it is too late.

The conception of corporate control discussed above assumes that firms are the sole property of their shareholders and that shareholder value is the only criterion of success. Yet as one of the founding scholars of the ownership and control debate, Berle, recognized, purchasers of stock are not in fact placing their savings at the disposal of a company but are simply betting on the performance of the share price (in the preface to Berle and Means 1968, quoted in O'Sullivan 2000: 48). This is a profound insight that the reader surprised by it may wish to contemplate further. Other 'stakeholders' have arguably placed more of their economic interests in the hands of their firm, notably employees who may have firm-specific skills with limited value to other firms and whose future pension rights are also tied to the firm's performance.

Before proceeding, we should underline the limits of the stakeholder view, which is sometimes presented as the desirable, and as noted in Box 9.2, by some writers as the most radical, alternative to the market-driven shareholder view. As an empirical account of how US or UK corporate governance in fact works, it is simply false. Its argument is that stakeholders such as employees were able to gain recognition as corporate 'insiders' Yet, as O'Sullivan (2000: Ch. 4) points out, it confuses specific gains such as pension rights with the idea that employees and their unions were part of the governance structure: the gains were part of the post-war settlement between capital and labour, and they did not entail rights of participation. On the contrary, US firms were alarmed at the famous demand by the auto workers' leader, Walther Reuther, in 1945 that they 'open the books' to unions, and went out of their way to exclude unions from any 'insider' role (Rubinstein and Kochan 2001: 13).

If we consider stakeholder capitalism as a normative model, how would it work? It would entail deciding who the stakeholders are with respect to certain decisions (local communities when a new facility is proposed, employees in relation to pension plans, employees and communities in addressing environmental issues, and so on) and devising means for their involvement. And what would such involvement in fact mean? Would it imply information and consultation or more active rights of co-decision? How would differences of view be resolved? This is not to say that caring capitalism is undesirable, but simply to argue that pointing to other stakeholders will not resolve the tensions inherent in any capitalist enterprise.

In O'Sullivan's terms, neither approach says anything about the origins of innovation, that is, how in a dynamic sense one can move forward from a given system. In our terms, the two approaches take for granted a capitalist system and argue about the distribution of rewards. Any conception of capitalism as a system that structures interests in certain ways, privileges some viewpoints, and imposes requirements on states is absent. Stakeholder theory similarly does not ask how stakeholder interests are shaped and defined by capitalism, and it lacks any material grasp of the economy.

Option Pricing, Financial Instruments, and Corporate Scandals

The developments outlined above were brought into sharp focus by the scandals at companies such as Enron and WorldCom. The Enron case broke in 2001. Yet it was heralded by earlier events, in two ways.

The first aspect is deep and long-standing evidence on corporate crime. At the start of Chapter 7 we cited Box's (1983) analysis of industrial death rates. This was part of a much larger catalogue of corporate wrongdoing. He cites for example the well-known US case in 1961 of price-fixing in the heavy electrical industry. (The case is summarized, along with nine others, by Punch 1996: 95–104.) In this case, senior executives of major companies including General Electric and Westinghouse deliberately and systematically broke laws (the Sherman Antitrust Act of 1890) against price-fixing. As Box (1983: 48) tartly points out, this was the first time that any corporate officials were imprisoned under the Sherman Act, and they numbered only seven defendants who received terms of thirty days; trade union officials had routinely been prosecuted under the Act for many years. Box estimates that financial losses due to corporate crime far exceed those due to theft. Both he and Punch argue that illegal activity is encouraged by a set of factors including the weakness of deterrence and an emphasis on goal attainment (profits) regardless of means. In Punch's (1996: 223) words, 'when the reward system is strongly geared to the quarterly report . . . this may encourage . . . considerable guile in generating figures that enhance one's rewards'. Recent developments have heightened this structure of incentives.

The second aspect of the context concerns changes in the functioning of markets. The abstruse world of financial economics and futures markets reached public attention with the collapse in 1998 of the 'hedge fund' Long-Term Capital Management (LTCM). This case throws important light on how markets are regulated and more fundamentally on the use and misuse of the economic theory of markets. To understand these points, we need first to explain hedge funds and how they came to prominence (Plender 2003: 59–66). The story of LTCM is told engagingly by Lowenstein (2001).

Hedge funds engage in arbitrage. The textbook example is foreign exchange dealing. Consider the ratios between dollars, yen, and euros. If the three (dollar:euro, dollar:yen and yen:euro) are not in perfect alignment, it will be possible to make a profit by exchanging euros into dollars, dollars into yen, and yen back to euros. Arbitrage seems here to be a simple way of making markets work. It becomes more complicated when applied to futures markets. Arbitrage here is in effect a bet on how prices will change in relation to each other; the arbitrageur is not concerned with whether average prices go up or down, only in whether the price of one item changes more quickly than that of another. An arbitrageur may at the same time sell Treasury bills and buy bills futures (that is, an agreement to buy at some specified point in the future). If futures prices rise more (or fall less) than current prices, then the arbitrageur gains. Note finally that the gains to any individual trade will be very small, so that to make any amount of money very large amounts of cash have to be placed in the buying and selling sides of the scales.

Now, arbitrage is a long-recognized practice. It grew in significance as a result of two developments. First, markets emerged in derivatives, which are assets derived from an underlying 'real' economic asset. Traders began to deal in more and more exotic products, notably in futures markets for financial assets. The founders of LTCM were pioneers of derivatives trading. Second, the pricing of derivatives was revolutionized by the work of the economists Black, Merton, and Scholes, who cut the knot that had tied earlier efforts to deal with the issue. The formula is usually called the Black–Scholes model. (Note that Merton is the son of the celebrated sociologist Robert K. Merton: economics was literally here the child of sociology, whereas, for example through the social embeddedness of markets, it is more generally figuratively so.) The knot was the calculation of a correct premium for the risk attached to an asset. The 'solution' was to treat price changes as following the law of large numbers, so that any distribution of prices will follow a normal (strictly, log-normal) curve. Any individual price follows a 'random walk' but the collection of these random events is predictable. As is commonly pointed out, the direct precursor of this idea is that of the ways in which the molecules of oil would spread when the oil is poured on water: we cannot predict the behaviour of any one molecule, but because they follow the law of large numbers we can predict their overall distribution (Eatwell and Taylor 2000: 103). These authors add the neat put-down that the Black–Scholes formula is itself a 'profitable piece of arbitrage—from Einstein's famous 1905 paper on Brownian motion to financial economics seventy years later'. But the arbitrage was not solely from physics. The economist Louis Bachelier proposed a 'random walk' explanation of prices in 1900, but was ignored and his work was not taken up until the 1960s. (We are grateful to Donald MacKenzie for drawing Bachelier to our attention.)

In the Black–Scholes model, the existing stock market price of the asset already reflects risk, with risky stock trading for a lower price than an otherwise less risky one. A hypothetical portfolio can then be created in which changes in prices are balanced by changes in the value of options, with the portfolio changing as prices change, so that a new quantity of options is held (Stix 1998). The other key concept is volatility, which is the amount of the typical change in prices; the prices of some goods change more rapidly (i.e. they are more volatile) than those of others. But the volatility of any given security is assumed to be constant because past prices in the market have already taken into account and adjusted for its underlying riskiness.

The genius of LTCM was to translate abstruse financial mathematics into a practical method of arbitrage. The Black–Scholes model allowed its traders to calculate when a given derivative was trading outside its normal range, as reflected by its volatility. This defined a strategy for buying and selling, and for some time it was highly successful. The pinnacle of official recognition came with the award in 1997 of the Nobel Prize for economics to Merton and Scholes (Black having died earlier). But by 1998, LTCM was in ruins after its debts mounted. Because it had borrowed huge amounts of money its collapse threatened the whole of the financial system. A rescue package funded by leading banks and coordinated by the Federal Reserve Bank of New York was put in place, but the firm's independent operations were over.

A particular but important lesson lies in Plender's comment (2003) that the rescue was the first time in which a central bank had helped a hedge fund in distress. Such rescues of private institutions, based on the 'lender of last resort' principle, were designed to support a whole regime. The price to the commercial banks was that they played by very clearly defined rules of the game. Hedge funds did not play by these rules, and might have been expected to be left to the laws of the market. But LTCM had been allowed to grow so large that its collapse threatened many other firms. Though some if its partners lost a great deal, they did not become penniless and some recommenced trading; according to Lowenstein (2001) the main losers were the firm's employees. The case might well be cited by laid-off car or steel workers who lose their jobs because of 'the market'.

Why, though, did the Black–Scholes model fail to live up to expectations? The key reason is that the model is not an exact account of options prices. Price movements are concentrated further towards the extremes than the assumption of random changes allows (a fact that was already underlined by other financial theorists even before LTCM took off: Lowenstein 2001: 70–2). The reason, say Eatwell and Taylor (2000: 12–16), resides in a fundamental feature of markets of this kind. Financial markets turn on convention, or what Keynes called beauty contests in a very specific sense: newspaper competitions in the 1930s required contestants to evaluate the beauty of women in photographs not on the basis of their own opinion but by guessing what the average preference of other contestants would be. Similarly, the price of a financial asset turns on average opinion as to what average opinion will be. Instability is heightened, these authors go on, by three other processes. These are:

- asymmetric information;
- moral hazard (an economists' term meaning an incentive to take risks in the knowledge that the potential costs will be covered, for example if a central bank always bails out lending banks that get into difficulties, an eventuality that applied in the LTCM case: Blackburn 2002); and
- systemic risk (the externalization of costs from a party undertaking a risk to some other group).

As Lowenstein (2001: 69) puts it, the Black–Scholes formula was seductive, not because it was wrong, but because it was nearly right. It represented how markets would operate under ideal conditions, and as long as real markets approximated to those conditions then the formula worked. But even financial markets, which must be the closest approximation to pure markets with traders acting as economic men (and most of them were indeed men), are influenced by beliefs, norms, and expectations that cannot be modelled mathematically.

These points tend to treat markets either as timeless (beauty contests occur all the time) or as subject to exogenous cyclical change. A 'historical sociology of a financial derivates exchange' helps us move further. The argument is summarized in Box 9.4. Note the key points that the Black–Scholes model changed behaviour rather than simply modelling it and that the model worked only at a given period; for both reasons it was thus not a universally true economic law but a historically contingent product.

Lest it be thought that these conclusions are those of unorthodox or maverick economists, consider one study co-authored by Lawrence Summers, who has held senior positions in the US Treasury and World Bank (Cutler et al. 1989: 9). The study examined patterns of stock returns, which it related to numerous indicators of macroeconomic events. The expectation would be that returns should reflect these fundamentals, but it was hard to explain 'as much as a half' of the variation. These authors speculate that this may be due to two factors: changes in average assessments of given facts (which is in effect the beauty contest effect); or the possibility that small shocks tend to have large effects. Such ideas seem to be efforts to grope towards the fact that markets are socially constructed and that, to

Box 9.4 Constructing a market

MacKenzie and Millo (2003) studied the Chicago Board Options Exchange, which was opened in 1973 to trade options (the right, but not the obligation, to purchase a commodity at a future date). Options became an extraordinarily important market, and also created (or more precisely, as the authors show, reflected) a whole academic discipline of options pricing.

- Their first point is the simplest and in some ways the most notable. For many years, even financial experts saw derivatives trading as a form of gambling because there was no underlying asset that was being bought and sold. Yet as time proceeded during the latter half of the twentieth century exactly the opposite position was established, that derivatives trading assisted efficient markets and was thus positively desirable.
- Second, the market could never have come into existence had it depended on the pure self-interested actors of economic theory, for such actors are unable to pursue collective interests. The market arose because there was a relatively self-contained group capable of imposing moral sanctions on its members and hence limiting free-riding.
- Third, the 'breakthrough' in options pricing was the Black–Scholes model. But the key point was that this model did not passively describe an under-lying market logic. On the contrary, markets at the time behaved in quite different ways, and the model reflected 'performativity': the markets came to perform what the theory determined.
- Finally, the 1987 crash highlighted a key limitation of the model. It was possible to run the model 'backwards', that is using observed option prices to infer the volatility of stock. The model states that this implied volatility is independent of the strike price of an asset, which was the case for some time. But ever since 1987 there has been a distinct skew in the relationship between volatility and price, so that the model is not an accurate representation.

cite a study that asked investors what they in fact did in various crises, people react 'to each other with heightened attention and emotion' and fall back on 'intuitive models' (Shiller 1990: 58).

Economics tends to stop with where these models may come from. One interesting effort to ground behaviour in a model of social interaction is laid out in Box 9.5.

If we turn to Enron, the firm is an extreme example of changing corporate behaviour. As Blackburn (2002) points out, it was created through a merger of two natural gas pipeline companies in 1987 and might have been expected to have made solid profits in a slow-changing utilities market. In fact, it made money by trading in energy futures.

Box 9.5 Butterflies, ants, firms, and economic development

The critique of economic theory underpinning this chapter can be pursued in the work of Ormerod (1998). His reference to butterflies is intended to highlight that societies, like organisms, adapt and learn, rather than working like machines. In particular, the behaviour of individuals is affected by the actions of others. The ants come in because of entomologists' experiments with the insects. Two piles of food were placed at equal distance from a nest. One might expect ants to visit each pile randomly. Each ant would tend to return to the source of food located originally, but overall half would go to one pile and half to the other. But there is a third factor, that ants provide information to each other in the form of chemical signals about food location, and each ant may switch behaviour in the light of this information. Models of ant colonies then show that, even in this very simple world, the proportion visiting one food pile or the other fluctuates without settling to an equilibrium level.

Economic activity, says Ormerod, displays parallels with the ant model. People can stick with their own previous choices, change of their own volition, or switch in the light of what others do. Actors thus follow simple rules of behaviour, which are entirely rational. But their interactions make forecasting impossible. Conventional economics seeks a model of the representative consumer and assumes that all consumers behave in the same way. But when there are interactions the system does not behave like a single consumer.

He then turns to economic growth. Growth is a fundamental feature of capitalism. Yet two things happened in economics. First this 'defining characteristic of capitalism . . . was not a matter of concern in mainstream economic theory for the best part of a century' (Ormerod 1998: 151). Second, when the issue was taken up, conventional economics expected a convergence of wealth across economies. This was because technology was assumed to be freely available and because of a core assumption, that of constant or diminishing returns to scale. Countries with a low stock of capital will thus grow relatively fast. Yet it is well established that growth rates have not converged. The most recent effort to reflect this is New Endogenous Growth Theory, associated with Robert Lucas and Paul Roemer. 'Endogenous' means that sources of growth occur within the system rather than being assumed, as in previous neo-classical theory, to arise only from technical change that existed entirely outside the economic system. The sources can include learning triggered by capital accumulation and investment in human capital. Coates (2000: 268) identifies two key lessons, that growth rates can differ permanently between economies (or, perhaps better, at least not converge) and that state policy can help to influence what happens in a given case. For Ormerod, the new theory is consistent with his model of adaptation and learning. He then goes on to discuss the individual firm as a core economic institution and to show that the rise of large firms can be 'explained' in terms of learning and the accumulation of knowledge.

Plender's (2003: 161) conclusion is apt: the company was 'doing what everyone else in corporate America was doing, only more so'. What the firm was doing was to focus exclusively on the share price, with financial reports being manipulated to hide losses and inflate profits. Enron's behaviour was particularly blatant in that it published a now notorious statement of its values, claiming to practise integrity and trust, while consciously manipulating its results, and its chief executive encouraged employees to buy shares while selling his own. A further feature is the role of market analysts who failed to spot warning signs notably 'related party transactions', which are transactions with associated companies. The point of these is that Enron had a highly complex network of firms trading with each other, so that it was able to manipulate reported profits. According to Plender, the analysts' failings reflected a conflict of interest, in that their companies made a great deal of money from fees and were thus constrained from blowing the whistle. We would add that under-lying such economic motivations are the belief systems discussed in relation to escalation. It was (probably) not that analysts consciously saw error and did not report it, but rather that they were not inclined to see error and that a battery of assumptions grew up unchallenged. It is a feature of corporate collapses that, after the event, the warning signs seem clear and inquests begin. The process of escalation helps us grasp how markets swing so sharply in their valuation of companies — a process that financial economics addresses in terms of beauty contests while not exploring the social processes through which real contests, as distinct from newspaper competitions, develop.

Effects of Market Restructuring in the USA

There are now substantial debates on the effects of the developments discussed above on income distribution and living standards. The following discussion highlights some pertinent trends in the USA, makes some links with the foregoing evidence, and addresses how people have responded to restructuring. Salient facts under the first head are listed in Box 9.6. Although the US economy has generated jobs, the costs in terms of inequality and the types of new jobs available are substantial.

There is also widespread evidence that substantial parts of the costs of restructuring are borne by employees and communities, with the gains if any being taken elsewhere (Box 9.7). It does not follow that all restructuring is unnecessary or inefficient, but it is clear that there are more losers than is often thought and that, as the models of trust-based capitalism suggest, it is possible to moderate the effects to a significant extent.

How Are Markets Constructed?

Box 9.6 Restructuring of the US labour market

- The earnings of non-supervisory workers fell in real terms by about 15 per cent in the twenty years after 1973; and in 1990 US workers on average worked 163 hours a year longer than in 1970 (Coates 2000: 25).
- Wage inequality in the USA is higher than in other industrialized countries and has increased. Households in the bottom fifth of the income distribution received 3.6 per cent of aggregate income in 1998, down from 4.3 per cent twenty years earlier (Lazonick and O' Sullivan 2002: 1).
- As against the view that the minimum wage affects only youth pay, 75 per cent of those paid at or below the minimum in 1993 were adults, and 36 per cent of those affected by a rise in the minimum in 1989 were the sole wage earners of their families (Gordon 1996: 216).
- The poorest 10 per cent of Americans are worse off in absolute terms than the equivalent group in Europe and Japan (though the poorest Britons are poorer than the poorest Americans); and the likelihood of exiting poverty in any one year is, images of a land of opportunity notwithstanding, lower than in other countries (Hutton 2002: 149, 152).
- US unemployment is significantly underestimated because of the high rate of imprisonment, especially of young men. The incarceration rate per 100,000 is 306 for whites and 1,947 for blacks, as against 116 in Canada, 93 in the UK, 91 in Australia, 80 in Germany, and 36 in Japan. Adjusting unemployment rates accordingly add about 0.3 percentage points in most countries, but raises the 1995 US rate from 5.6 per cent to 7.5 per cent (on a par with Germany) (Western and Beckett 1999: 1036–41).

Box 9.7 Paying for restructuring

- When the airline TWA was taken over in 1985, all the post-takeover improvements in performance were only equal in value to the concessions in terms of pay and benefits made by trade unions at the time of the takeover. In takeovers generally, 27 per cent of the stock price premium that results is the direct result of savings through lay-offs (Cappelli 1999: 79).
- Local communities eager to attract inward investment engage in bidding wars. The national average bid is about $4,000 per job per year for the life of a plant. In 1992, Omaha (Nebraska) and Spartanburg (South Carolina) competed for a prestigious new BMW plant, expecting high wages and good jobs. When the plant went to the latter, it was estimated that tax breaks and other concessions amounted to half the value of the plant. Wages were no higher than those of other firms in the area (Craypo 1997: 14).

As to the consequences of change, a reasonable starting position was that people who had lost their jobs felt resentful and powerless. As Smith (2001: 8) puts it:

[W]orkers have become engaged with new, flexible and participative types of work reform even when faced by glaring reminders that secure employment has become elusive or uncertain.... Why don't workers [therefore] collectively band together [against employers' agendas that do not] advance workers' interests or goals?

A series of studies helps to provide an answer. An influential analysis of workers who were laid off from GM's auto plant in Linden (New Jersey) found that, though they had lost in terms of job security and earnings, they welcomed the independence that new work, often based on self-employment, gave them (Milkman 1997). It should be stressed that GM's programme of lay-offs involved relatively generous resettlement packages that may have made its ex-workers' experience atypical.

Batt (1996) studied telecommunications workers, and explicitly identifies contradictions faced by managers. One of these is key in the present context: the fact that top managers were judged on shareholder returns whereas middle managers were assessed against customer satisfaction. This points to obvious tensions within managerial ranks, as top managers pursuing one goal strive to influence the behaviour of others with different objectives. A survey of lower and middle-ranking managers found a mixed picture of dissatisfaction with career opportunities and with senior managers' consideration towards employees, combined with substantial job satisfaction and a willingness to work harder for the company. The data did not permit a clear explanation, but it is reasonable to argue that managers recognized the need for some change and accepted it.

Dudley (1994) by contrast catalogues the destruction of collective working-class traditions in Kenosha (Wisconsin), which may possibly reflect the workers' isolation from alternative sources of employment or a greater sense of shock or both.

Smith herself studied three groups: photocopy workers with temporarily secure employment contracts; timber workers who were about to lose traditional secure employment; and assembly and office workers with temporary employment contracts. She argues (echoing the discussion of risk in Chapter 7) that each was shaped by interactions between three processes, of *uncertainty*, *risk*, and *opportunity*. For example, the first group not only had low skills and low wages but also low risks because they worked for a core employer while they were also able to take some opportunities from an employee involvement programme. The woodworkers' opportunities, in the shape of a similar programme, were limited by the uncertainties and risks of a programme that was about plant survival and that called on the workers to undertake many of the associated risks.

Smith (2001: 170) concludes that collective challenges to uncertainty have been 'minimized' by a series of 'fracturing forces' that further divide US workers. These forces stem from the way in which markets are structured and also from the meaning systems that workers develop as they are led to cooperate with some changes and to tolerate others. It is the dynamics of US markets that underpin these conclusions.

Alternative Models of Capitalism

Numerous writers have sought alternatives to the Anglo-American model of market capitalism. The three most commonly discussed countries are Germany, Japan, and Sweden, for all three have variants of stakeholder involvement in firms and have for substantial periods combined economic growth with low inflation and low unemployment. We will follow most commentators in leaving Sweden to one side because of its small size and its distinctive institutional structure (see Coates 2000: 94–101, 239–44, for a cogent analysis of this case). There has been lengthy and heated debate on four issues: how each case in fact operates, its historical origins, how sustainable it is in the long run, and what implications if any it has for other systems of governance. Each issue is itself complex. In relation to a system's operation, for example, attention has focused variously on relations within firms (including skill formation, managerial organization, and systems of employee representation), links between firms and their environment (including national education systems and systems of corporate governance), and the role of the state in promoting economic development. Finally, analysis is often conflated with prescription, as writers aim not only to find the 'secret' of a country's apparent success but also to argue either that that country offers lessons of good practice to others or that, whether or not the lessons are welcome, its capitalist system is competitively superior to other systems and will eventually dominate them.

One model posits a three-stage development of capitalism through proprietorial, managerial, and 'collective' forms, as summarized in Box 9.8 (Lazonick 1991, 2002). The leading examples of each are the UK up to the middle of the nineteenth century, the USA up to the 1970s, and Japan thereafter. These stages, it should be stressed, are not peculiar to Lazonick, for the idea that Japanese capitalism was superseding the USA

Box 9.8 Three stages of capitalism

Proprietorial	Large number of small firms; little separation of ownership and control; main line of division is between top managers exercising general direction of the firm and all other employees. Based on craft skills and informal knowledge. Represented by early Industrial Revolution firms in the UK.
Managerial	Reflects growth of large firms, separation of ownership and control. Main division is between general managers plus specialist middle managers, on the one hand, and 'operatives' (who would probably include routine clerical workers) on the other. Narrow skill base, sharp distinction between managers and semi-skilled operatives. Reflects rise of giant multidivisional firms in the USA, 1900–70.
Collective	Large firms with shared community of interest, integration of workers into the enterprise, operatives included within the firm, drive for market share not short-term performance. Broad skill base, significant training. Exemplified by large Japanese firms from 1945.

Sources: Lazonick (1991: 24–44; 2002).

became a standard view, as Japanese imports invaded core US industries from the 1980s and as armies of scholars sought the essence of the Japanese system. Lazonick is one of the more interesting analysts, however, since he offers a historically informed and critical view — as opposed to many short-sighted efforts to find in Japan a solution to the USA's industrial ills — that he explicitly relates, moreover, to the theories of capitalism of Karl Marx and Joseph Schumpeter and thus aims to ground in some deeper analysis of capitalist systems.

Though this typology looks simple, it and many like it are efforts to characterize highly complex social structures and, moreover, to offer explanations for their origins and development. Japan as a country with a specific history and traditions can never reflect completely the idealized model of collective capitalism. The analytical question is not whether a complete picture is painted but whether the necessary abstractions of a model misrepresent the underlying reality.

Before developing some critical themes, some key contributions of writers such as Lazonick should be stressed. First, it is evidently the case that types of economy other than the Anglo-American have thrived for substantial periods and indeed outperformed the USA and the UK on standard measures such as the rate of growth of GDP. Second, it follows that market capitalism is not the only way of organizing an economy. Third, countries like Japan seem to invert or ignore economic logics that are taken for granted in the USA and the UK. A key example is the managerial labour market in large firms. Japanese managers will typically expect to remain with a single firm throughout their careers and can also expect to move upwards through a clear promotion system. It is also the case that pay differentials are much narrower than they are in the USA. How, then, is the principal–agent problem resolved, given that the stick of job loss and the carrot of pay for performance are either absent or weak? We summarize below some answers to this specific question, but for the present its purpose is to signal that assumptions about economic incentives do not necessarily travel between countries. Fourth, there is substantial evidence to sustain the idea that 'stakeholder' systems do indeed work.

Varieties of Capitalism

Japan and Germany have some similarities here. Their structures of corporate governance constrain the market for corporate control. In the case of Japan, as Coates (2000: 178–82) presents and evaluates the evidence, large industrial concerns are linked through interlocking reciprocal share-ownership, shares of banks are themselves owned by the industrial groups that are the banks' main customers, networks extend into a large group of supplier firms, the threat of takeover is low, and the establishment of market share could be privileged over short-term profit maximization. In the case of Germany, an outstanding fact is how few joint-stock companies with extensive share trading there are; the number in the early 1990s was about 660, compared to 6,300 in the USA and 2,300 in the UK (Clarke and Bostock 1997: 235). Banks also have close relationships with industrial concerns, a picture that remains broadly true despite some qualifications (Coates 2000:173–7).

The extent to which Germany and Japan continue to differ from Anglo-Saxon models is illustrated in Tables 9.3 and 9.4. The first underlines the role of banks and the financial sector in the first two countries and the role of pension and investment funds in the latter. The second points to the limited extent of a market for corporate control in Germany and Japan.

The differences are also marked. Germany has a formal two-tier system of supervisory and management boards. The role of the former is to oversee the latter. As is well known, they contain worker representatives as well as representatives of banks, while as discussed in Chapter 6 the

TABLE 9.3 Ownership of listed companies, 2000 (per cent)

	Germany	Japan	USA
Banks	8	19	—
Non-financial and insurance firms	45	33	4
Pension funds	—	4	26
Investment firms	5	4	22
Individuals	16	26	41

Source: Abbreviated from Jackson (2003: 275); other holdings omitted, hence columns do not add to 100.

TABLE 9.4 Market indicators in four countries

	Germany	Japan	USA	UK
Stock market capitalization (% GDP), 1999	68	104	181	201
Bank sector assets as % total financial system, 1995	74	64	<25	*c*.25

Source: Abbreviated from Jackson (2003: 279).

works council system gives workers and their representatives legally prescribed rights of co-determination or consultation, depending on the specific issue. Supervisory boards become involved in matters of detail only when the company is in difficulties; for example, in 1993 Metallge-sellschaft, the country's fourteenth largest conglomerate, made substantial losses on trading in oil futures on the New York futures market, and the entire senior management team was dismissed (Doremus et al. 1998: 34–5). Japan lacks any such formal recognition of employees as stakeholders, and arguments about employees as stakeholders would need to turn on a broader view that sees the firm as a community with decision-making being consensual rather than being based on the authority of top managers as would be the case in the USA (see Lincoln and Kalleberg 1990).

The advantages of such governance systems do not mean, however, that 'stakeholders' have all been given equal rights. A fundamental problem with stakeholder models as analytical devices is that they imply that recognizing the existence of stakeholders and operating in ways other than those of pure market capitalism is equivalent to treating stakeholders as equals. (As *normative* devices, they may in fact help to point up the fact that many stakeholders are treated as no more than junior partners.) The point is clearest in relation to Japan. A mass of evidence contrasts with the picture painted by Lazonick. The skill base is not in fact broad, with most studies equating Japanese lean production with very narrow skills and limited worker autonomy (Appelbaum and Batt 1994). And the costs to workers of an unrelenting work pace and long hours are widely documented (e.g. Williams et al. 1994).

The picture in relation to Germany is more complex. Up to the 1970s, it was conventional among UK radicals to underline the limitations of the system from a worker's point of view: co-determination does not mean equal power on supervisory boards, where even in the most extreme cases the chair, who is a shareholder nominee, has the casting vote; and at workplace level works councils have no right to strike and are thus limited in many key areas to persuasion and argument. It is also true that 'the system' is less all-pervasive than is sometimes thought: the works council system covers only about half of companies, and overseas firms that so wish are able to ignore most of it, a key example being McDonald's (Donnelly 2000; Royle 2000). As Thelen and Kume (2003) argue, there are two competing forces in Germany and Japan: towards cost-cutting and neo-liberalism, but also towards increasing employer needs for predictability at workplace level. These forces have encouraged divisions among employers, with large employers who are wedded to traditional systems retaining the core elements of those systems while smaller and newer firms that cannot afford its costs tending to defect from it.

These facts also suggest that the system may be less distinct from shareholder capitalism than is sometimes thought. The conventional economic expectation would be that decision-making is slower and more likely to take account of concerns other than efficiency than would be the case without co-determination. Yet, as O'Sullivan (2000: 234–57) points out, supervisory boards meet rarely while the powers of managing boards are strong, with the law expressly requiring them to run the firm under their own responsibility, consulting the supervisory board only on major questions. It seems clear that German, and Japanese, systems continue to function without facing agency problems, or at least problems any greater than in the USA or the UK. This does not, however, mean that the they have been pushed from a capitalist path; they pursue capitalist goals in distinct ways.

This point leads to three further questions, how they manage to constrain agency problems, how far they have been or might be emulated elsewhere, and whether they represent the future of capitalism.

On the first question, much of the debate touches on the concept of culture. It has been surprisingly common for scholars to 'read history backwards' by starting from Japanese economic success and then search-ing for a clue in the country's history and, often, religion. A large amount of this can be dismissed. If there is a uniform Japanese culture, why does it appear only in certain industries, for in some sectors, most notably agri-culture, productivity is notoriously low? What exactly is it about some supposed cultural trait that leads people to design car factories in certain specific ways (and how do we explain the fact that some of the key principles such as total quality management were imported from the USA)? And how can culture explain the conscious strategy of the state to promote economic development? Most critics are properly wary of the term 'culture'. But it has one value: economic agents are embedded in a normative order. Japan has a normative order different in character from that of the USA, and 'culture' may be a reasonable summary term.

As to how the culture works, we may return to the issue of managers and how they are led to work conscientiously in the absence of US sticks and carrots. Sanctions and incentives take on different forms. An import-ant sanction for managers in the large core firms is fear of the loss of the job. Dismissal is rare but not unknown, and the consequences, in view of the prestige attached to working in core firms, are severe. A more likely threat derives from the ways in which the celebrated 'jobs for life' system works: part of the system entails assigning managers aged in their mid-fifties to a firm's smaller associated companies, while another part involves temporary transfers during downturns. The least favoured man-agers are the most likely to suffer such fates. A less severe sanction is slow promotion. Though Japan is often characterized as stressing seniority and though career progression is the norm, it is not the case that progression is automatic. On the contrary, personal merit evaluations are widespread and, it would seem from comparisons with UK firms (Storey et al. 1997), relatively systematic and purposive. The other side of this coin is that relatively rapid promotion is a strong incentive. The Japanese system is not one without individual motivation, but rather links individual striv-ing to a sense of commitment to group norms (see Box 9.9).

As to the second question concerning emulation elsewhere, a central theme since the 1980s has been the extent of the borrowing of Japanese production systems. But it has been notable that systems of corporate governance have not been emulated. One reason is that they are relatively strongly embedded in their context: the principles of lean production have been shown to be transferable, but Japanese corporate governance rests on the strong networks of the *keiretsu* and linkages with banks, arrangements that are not exportable in the same way.

Box 9.9 Seniority and performance in Japan

Western accounts of Japan often turn on the idea that payment is based on a mix of rigid seniority-based pay and smaller performance bonuses. Yet the Japanese term translated as seniority, *nenko-joretsu*, really means seniority and achievement, while *noryotushuji* means 'rewarding ability', not performance in the Anglo-Saxon sense of meeting set targets. The traditional system was not locked into promotion on fixed seniority principles, it included assessments of individual achievements, and it continues to function.

Source: Dore (2000: 107).

A second argument is that Japanese and German 'coordinated market economies' (CMEs) are relatively good at incremental innovation, because of their integrated training systems that encourage the progressive improvement of existing systems, but worse at radical innovation because the systems discourage risk-taking; the 'liberal market economies' (LMEs) of the USA and the UK are by contrast better at radical innovation (Hall and Soskice 2001: 38–44). Evidence offered in support is that German patents are concentrated in mechanical engineering and transport, and US ones in biotechnology and semiconductors. Though the difference between these two countries is striking in this measure, several questions arise.

1. Is the difference replicated across other economies falling into the two analytical categories?
2. How can one explain innovations that do not fall into the expected categories?
3. Some features of the coordinated economies, notably their long-term perspective, surely allow risk-taking and tolerate initial failures.
4. Patterns of innovation vary between industries, and it would be relevant to examine differences between 'radical' and 'incremental' cases (assuming that they could be clearly distinguished other than in *ex ante* fashion) within one sector between countries.

The contrasting approaches to innovation in CMEs and LMEs are presumably intended as broad characterizations rather than robust distinctions, and the many possible influences on a firm's innovative activity would also need to be recognized. Seen in this light, the argument is reasonable, and it draws attention to important features of CMEs, namely, that they are not high-performing in all sectors and hence the idea that they can supersede other systems is implausible.

Third, as the expert on Japan, Dore, points out, 'in modern societies, trust comes expensive; expensive, particularly, in terms of managerial effort and abstention from privilege' (Dore 1985: 217; quoted in Coates 2000: 58). Some writers argue that trust is a cheap alternative to monitoring, since it does not entail the costs of surveillance and contract enforcement. But it has to be created and sustained; it does not exist freely in the air of CMEs. Note also that Dore stresses not just time and effort but also abstention from privilege, which would include relatively low levels of managerial pay but perhaps more importantly the acceptance that authority has to be shared and that the 'obvious' solutions to problems in terms of divestments and lay-offs are seen as extreme rather than normal. Such costs mean that CMEs may work with a particular balance of trust and conventional command-and-control, and that they do not necessarily dominate other systems.

A final, and central, point concerns the place of a production system within capitalism as a whole (Coates 2000). It is correct to say that the USA replaced Britain as the dominant economic force in the world. As discussed in more detail in Chapter 10, this included hegemony in the global economic order with the dollar becoming the benchmark for all other currencies and the world effectively running on a dollar standard. Neither Japan nor Germany has achieved such dominance. Despite the challenges to the ways in which US firms produced goods, the US economy remains the largest and most powerful, and the USA has set out to shape the global economic order to meet its own needs.

This point leads neatly to the theme of sustainability of CME approaches. Supporters of liberal markets have revelled in the difficulties faced by leading CMEs during the 1990s. In Germany, these took the form of slowing economic growth and rising unemployment, and they were widely attributed to excessive pay costs and rigid labour market institutions. In Japan, economic slowdown was associated with corruption scandals, and there was a significant shift of production towards lower-wage Asian economies. As Coates (2000: 238) argues, corruption was not an accident, but was a predictable consequence of a system of close and often secretive relationships between firms and governments.

The clearest analysis of CME economies argues that they are not evolving towards a shareholder system. They are adopting aspects of it while retaining traditional features, so that 'hybrid' models are emerging. These are likely to mean growing internal differentiation. We noted above that some German firms retain established employee representation systems while others act outside it. A second line of differentiation is between domestically oriented firms, which are likely to continue to rely on bank-based approaches, and internationally oriented sectors, where a capital market model is more prominent (Vitols 2003).

Conclusions: Competing Logics, not Competing Models

The idea that state intervention interferes with market processes is now taken for granted. Yet there is no such thing as a free market, so that the issue is not whether or not regulation should exist but its form. We have seen that markets have been reconstituted by large firms. It is true that such firms may oppose what they see as burdensome regulation. It is also true that regulations may be genuinely burdensome. But the first fact does not necessarily entail the second. The problem with the predominance of market thinking is that firms may not only oppose regulation out of narrow and conscious self-interest, but also take it for granted that regulation is indeed intrusive. There is then the danger of the self-fulfilling prophesy. Persuading firms to think differently, and to think about *types* of regulation rather than more or less of it, may be a lengthy task. But it is nonetheless the case that different regulatory models are possible.

A 'hyper development' of capital markets has, together with a shift away from hierarchical organizational forms towards looser networks, created problems for existing theories of organizations (Davis and McAdam 2000). Two of the theories are pertinent here. The economics of the market for corporate control neglects political action such as a 1990 law in Pennsylvania banning hostile takeovers. And conventional class theory, which would put owners and managers in the same, dominant, class no longer applies because hostile takeovers and the rise of pension funds have fragmented the unity of the class. The solution for Davis and McAdam is to see contemporary economic action as akin to social movements. They draw here on a large body of writing on social movements (for an introduction, see Cohen and Kennedy 2000: 287–302). Social movements are informal organizations usually oriented around a specific issue such as the environment. Social movement theory has tried to capture the conditions that lead groups to mobilize and that permit them to sustain their existence. The point for Davis and McAdam is that economic action is like social movement behaviour in being more or less episodic and more or less coordinated.

There are several useful ideas here. First, economic models can be challenged politically. Whether or not a law in a single state is a good example is a moot point, for much evidence (e.g. Craypo 1997) suggests that states find themselves competing against each other for jobs and investment. But the general point is clear, as exemplified by efforts to tighten regulatory frameworks in the wake of the Enron scandal. Second, the way in which US capitalism works was overturned by the rise of hostile takeovers, leveraged buyouts, junk bonds, and much else. This may have discomforted some, arguably unimaginative, views of class that saw a ruling class as a homogeneous group. Yet more subtle views see classes as constantly being formed and re-formed as capitalism develops (Katznelson 1986). Fragmentation within ruling groups has been common (Strinati 1979). Third, the idea of episodes and fashions is counter to the view that markets are rationally driven equilibrating mechanisms, though again this is not distinctive to the current period, for it is well established that takeovers have emerged in waves, and it is surely beyond doubt that some organizational forms have always developed as a result of fashion. In the well-known analysis of DiMaggio and Powell (1983), organizations display 'isomorphism', and one process leading to it is copying from other organizations (mimesis, hence mimetic isomorphism). The social movement model stresses that corporate behaviour is the result of common assumptions and languages, which can embed certain processes for a time but then be disrupted by external forces.

The analogy of social movements needs grounding, however, in a view of capitalism as a mode of production. We have seen that US capitalism has moved through at least five models of corporate control. Each has arisen as weaknesses in its predecessor have emerged, and each has its contradictions. The core contradiction of the most recent model is that it promotes an extreme focus on short-term financial return and thus permits scandals to emerge. It also leads to a particular structuring of the market in terms of winners and losers, and is thus open to challenge from the losers or from those driven by ideas of social justice. The clearest historical parallel is the age of 'robber barons' in the late nineteenth century, which led to reaction in the so-called Progressive Era when the excesses of large corporations were curtailed.

It is not, then, the case that there is a fixed US, or neoliberal, model. Models have evolved in which different elements of capitalist organization have been stressed at different times. Models of corporate control are not logically complete systems. As we have seen, the market for corporate control emerged for particular historical reasons and it contained contradictory elements. It placed relative weight on management through performance controls and monitoring, but could not dispense with a degree of trust (given the costs and uncertainties of monitoring). By contrast, Japanese and German systems were stronger on trust but this was not a free-floating resource as created through the histories of the two countries. In these cases, there have been more recent shifts towards Anglo-Saxon systems as the contradictions of trust-based capitalism came to the surface.

Nor is it the case that current US approaches are doomed to fail. The limitation of O'Sullivan's analysis is the tendency to stress failure of innovation. Yet US capitalism enjoyed something of a resurgence after 1990. It is true that the resurgence was weakly based, depending on the continued ability of the USA to run trade deficits and on productivity improvement that turned on downsizing and work intensification rather than more progressive developments (Brenner 1998; Coates 2000: 248). Yet the fact that such developments were possible indicates the several ways in which capitalism can continue to accumulate capital. And, though we would not go as far as Hall and Soskice in relation to genuine innovation, the role of biotechnology and IT firms should not be wholly discounted. US capitalism has its dynamic elements, and given the economy's still dominant place in global capitalism (see Chapter 10) the opportunities to pursue particular developmental paths are greater than in more constrained economic systems.

10

How Is Globalization Affecting Work?

The term 'globalization', scarcely heard before the mid-1980s, is now so commonplace that one might ask what can usefully be said. Not only has the term become an everyday one, but there is now a substantial set of books or parts of books that add the phrases 'the myth of' or 'and its discontents'. Studies under the first heading dispute the extent and significance of the process while those under the second signal that the process is contested and produces winners and losers. Discussion of globalization also embraces a wide array of analytical debates about the world economic and political order. Our purpose is to focus on the links between work organizations and the global context, with two main themes.

First, globalization is not an inevitable force but is an organized project, and we address how particular organized interests have promoted their own conceptions of the process. There are two linked sub-themes here.

- First, the reader addressing the process from the perspective of organizations may find it useful to have a discussion of some elements of the international economy and the organizations designed to regulate it. Bodies such as the World Trade Organization (WTO) have come into prominence ever since the protests at a meeting of that body in Seattle in 1999. But where do such organizations come from and what do they do? As it happens, moreover, the WTO has been seen as the villain of the piece, even though several observers argue that it is more democratic in process and people-friendly in outcome than several other international bodies such as the International Monetary Fund (IMF). What, then, is the link between globalization and organizations designed to manage the world economy?
- Second, we analyse globalization as a contested process. This is scarcely a new approach, but we hope to draw together some strands from diverse sources and to relate the idea of a contested process to the themes of contradiction and tension that run through this book.

The second theme embraces the implications of globalization for concrete work experience. This book is about working life, but it is also about the influences on concrete work experience. We thus need to show what we mean about linkages and connections, bearing in mind that making such connections is difficult for many reasons. One associated purpose is to explain why it is so hard, and what we do and do not currently know.

We take globalization to be a process of increasing economic integration of national economic systems that is driven mainly by three groups of organizations, transnational bodies such as the WTO, nation states, and Multinational Companies. This is what Sklair (2002) reasonably insists on calling capitalist globalization, for one could welcome the breaking down of national barriers without accepting the distinctive forms of globalization in train recently. In the words of the leading 'antiglobalizer' Klein (2002: 46), 'what I am talking about . . . is corporatization'; in other words, 'antiglobalizers' are often in favour of global action on issues such as the environment, and what they oppose is a specific form of globalization. To argue that there is such a thing as capitalist globalization is to argue, first, that the three processes identified by Sklair are linked; second, that the links are not just accidental; and, third, that their joint operation is shaped (albeit, not determined) by the evolution of capitalism as a system.

This chapter begins with an attempt to sift from the many debates on globalization a reasonably clear picture of what it means to say that the world economy is globalizing. We then consider briefly some effects attributed to globalization. The third section discusses the main organizations involved in the globalization process, while the fourth looks at the political processes shaping global trade. Finally, we turn to implications for work.

Globalization: Myth and Reality

We are concerned here only with economic issues, that is the degree to which the world economy is becoming increasingly interlinked and the ease with which capital and labour are globally mobile. Questions of whether consumption patterns are converging and culture is being homogenized are excluded. Three positions have been identified, the hyperglobalist, the sceptical, and the transformationist (Held et al. 1999: 2–10) . They are summarized in Table 10.1.

Hyperglobalists such as Ohmae (1995) argued that globalization was driven by inevitable forces and hence that the state was being 'hollowed out'. Yet such sweeping assertions have been dismissed by scholars such as Held et al. on two sets of grounds. Not only is empirical evidence for alleged trends much less clear and unidirectional than claimed, but finding a tendency and asserting its inevitability is also theoretically unsatisfactory because there is no demonstration of the causes of the trend or discussion of counter-influences.

TABLE 10.1 Schools of thought on globalization

	Hyperglobalism	Scepticism	Transformation
Drivers of process	Capitalism and technology	States and markets	Forces of modernity
Power of national governments	Reduced	Reinforced	Reconstituted
Key historical trends	Global civilization	Regional blocs	(Indeterminate)

Source: Abbreviated from Held et al. (1999: 10).

Extreme sceptics argue by contrast that the extent of globalization is exaggerated and that the world economy was as open in 1914 as it is today. It may readily be agreed that there was an opening of the world economy up to 1914, that the process went into sharp reverse with the rise of protectionism and depression in the 1920s and 1930s, and that on some indicators the degree of openness is barely greater than before the First World War. Looking at world trade, its growth is at first sight impressive. On one set of figures it comprised 6 per cent of world GDP in 1953 and 17 per cent by 1996; but most of this increase occurred in the 1970s, with stabilization thereafter, rather than a steady rise. Moreover, the figure was 14 per cent in 1914 (Fligstein 2001: 196). It is also true that, if globalization is a process, it has a long way to go before it is complete. In the USA, for example, 90 per cent of consumption consists of US-produced goods and services; since the rest of the world accounts for 75 per cent of global production, in a fully globalized economy the figure for home consumption in the USA would need to fall from 90 to 25 per cent (Eichengreen 2002b: 1).

'Transformation' writers make claims including the following:

- National states lose their independent influence and are driven by global competition to deregulate their markets and to reduce social protections (e.g. Gray 1998: 78).
- MNCs can play countries off against each other to find the economic regime most suitable to them (Beck 2000b: 4).

We address specific evidence on such questions below. But it should be stressed at the outset that it is as unclear as it is with the hyper-globalizers just what processes are at work. To label historical processes as the rise of modernity is to say little about their distinctiveness and to merge national states, global organizations, and MNCs into a jumble. The theory explaining why 'globalization' produces the claimed results is weak. As Goldthorpe (2001) points out, the theory apparently adopted is that of conventional economic trade theory (the Hecksher–Ohlin theory) in which countries concentrate where their comparative advantage is greatest. In a closed world economy, some factors of production can earn more than they would under open competition and national states can use the closure of the economic order to make policy choices. An open economy is expected to wash away these sources of national difference. And yet the theory operates only on a range of assumptions; some of these were considered in Chapter 9, while others are discussed below. In short, to assert that there is a natural drive towards a certain kind of global economy is, ironically, to ape conventional economics in a way that the 'transformationists' would otherwise reject.

This is an area in which it is easy to light on apparently convincing numbers. However, the detailed figures suggest that trade is more salient than in the past, a case made in particular by Bordo et al. (1999). They make three main points about trade, as detailed in Box 10.1. They also argue that the underlying processes have been different. In the late nineteenth century, declining transport costs provided a powerful engine for economic integration. In the current period, the drivers are reductions in tariff and other barriers. To point out that trends have similarities is not a very cogent account of the underlying processes.

Box 10.1 Globalization and trade

1. Aggregate figures disguise the importance of examining *tradable goods*. A substantial part of any economy comprises services that are necessarily consumed locally, such as those of restaurants or barbers' shops, as well as government activities. The tradable sector (agriculture, mining, and manufacturing) has roughly halved as a proportion of GDP since 1914. A constant share of world GDP that is traded would thus mean that the proportion of tradable goods traded internationally has doubled. In the USA, for example, exports comprised 20 per cent of tradable production in the late nineteenth century and 40 per cent a hundred years later.
2. Services were little traded in 1900 but are now increasingly international in scope.
3. Foreign direct investment (FDI) by MNCs has grown, for example in the USA tripling in relation to GDP between 1914 and 1996. Moreover, early FDI was in sectors such as mining and petroleum and it often entailed simply portfolio investment, whereas by 2000 the emphasis had switched to manufacturing and services, and it increasingly entailed operational control.

Source: Bordo et al. (1999: 6–12).

Patterns of trade also remain concentrated. It is routinely noted that the bulk of trade continues to be between the developed countries. Some regions such as Latin America have even had a weakening position in the world economy, while much of the growth of trade comes from a small number of Asian countries. There are two points to be made here. First, the exclusion of some parts of the world, notably much of Africa, from the global economy, and the weakening of global integration of others, means that globalization is not a smooth or inevitable process. It is a project that could in principle be reversed. Second, however, the success of the project seems substantial. According to Held et al. (1999: 165) the proportion of the world's population living in countries with broadly open trade policies rose from about a quarter in the 1960s to over a half by the 1990s. The accession of China to the WTO pushed this process further (Legrain 2002: 16).

If we turn to capital mobility, the extent to which world financial markets have been globalized is staggering. Restrictions on international capital movements were lifted by most large industrialized countries between 1973 and 1990. Foreign exchange trading *each day* was in 1973 twice the total of annual world trade; by 1995, this ratio had reached seventy (Eatwell and Taylor 2000: 3-4). Cross-border transactions in bonds and equities grew even more rapidly (Table 10.2).

In relation to the role of MNCs and their FDI, two views are widely stated. The first stresses the size and power of MNCs. Commonly cited figures are that there are over 35,000 MNCs with sales equivalent to almost one-third of total world output (Cohen and Kennedy 2000: 132). Yet some otherwise careful scholars can go wrong at this point. Cohen and Kennedy (2000: 123) state that, 'of the 100 most important economic units in the world today, half are nation states and half are TNCs [Transnational corporations]'. On Sklair's (2002: 36-7) figures, thirty-five of the fifty largest economic organizations are MNCs. Yet this does not compare like with like. Cohen and Kennedy compare corporate sales with

TABLE 10.2 Cross-border transactions in bonds and equities (as % of GDP)

	USA	Germany	Japan
1980	9	7	8
1998	230	334	91

Source: Ferguson (2001: 281).

countries' GDP, while Sklair relates sales to government revenues from taxation and other sources. But sales represent total income. The relevant comparison with GDP is the value added of companies, that is, sales minus the cost of inputs. Using this comparison, the economic journalist Legrain (2002: 140) finds that only two of the top fifty economic units are MNCs, with the largest having value added around the same as the GDP of Chile (whereas Sklair ranks the biggest MNC along with a country the size of France).

As Legrain goes on to point out, moreover, inferences from size to power are at best very inaccurate; his word is 'fatuous'. Even large firms compete with others and have to persuade customers to buy their products. States impose taxes and regulations on firms. There is also evidence that concentration in globalizing industries is falling not rising (Legrain 2002: 144).

Yet MNCs remain influential, if less brutally powerful than critics imply. In the past the typical MNC was, he argues, moving overseas in the pursuit of markets or natural resources, whereas there is now much closer integration of production chains and a greater tendency for research and development to move beyond the home country (Dunning 2000). One indicator is that substantial amounts of trade are conducted *within* MNCs. The proportions of trade so conducted are necessarily hard to establish but the figures given by Gilpin (2002: 169) are similar to other estimates: in 1994 intrafirm trade accounted for one-third of US exports and two-fifths of imports, while half of US–Japan trade occurred within firms.

The empirical picture is thus mixed. MNCs have not become uniquely footloose, for the bulk of their operations are generally located in home countries or nearby. And much of their operation is international rather than truly global; witness the concentration of FDI in developed countries. And yet scepticism is too extreme a view. Gilpin (2002: 160–70) also stresses the *qualitative* shift in MNC practice, from export of goods from home countries to integrated supply chains and the growth of corporate alliances.

This evidence, together with the examples of the extent of MNC influence on local economies given in Chapter 9, suggests the following. MNCs' development does mark a move towards a global economy. Their contribution to this economy is global, rather than only international, to the extent that MNCs organize themselves with declining reference to national boundaries (for example, designing products for sale across borders, or using product divisions rather than national subsidiaries as their primary sub-unit). Yet such trends remain limited in extent, are most obvious in certain sectors and may not generalize to other sectors, and are counteracted by continuing national characteristics (including modes of regulation and patterns of consumer preferences). MNCs themselves, moreover, will often be in competition with each other and have to adjust to different national regimes. They are part of an uncertain and contested dynamic.

The central, and simple, point is that globalization is not a single process and that the term is a shorthand for a series of developments that need have no underlying logic or direction. Methodologically, some arguments commit the error of historicism, the identification of some trend and the assumption that it will continue and that it has its own law of motion rather than simply being a current of events. This is not to say that globalization is a myth. The world economy has been transformed in significant ways, some by design and some as the largely unintended result of particular sets of choices.

Contests over Effects of Globalization

The effects of these choices have been as hotly debated as their causes. It has for example become a commonly repeated fact that poverty has increased. Stiglitz (2002: 5), for example, stresses 'dire poverty' in the Third World, citing figures showing a rise of 100 million people between 1990 and 1998 living on less than $2 a day, despite an annual increase in world income of 2.5 per cent a year. More radical critics of globalization such as Sklair (2002: 48–53) argue that there has been a growing polarization between rich and poor, and that such rising inequality is a feature of many developed countries as well.

Clear examples of the kinds of arguments offered are given in Box 10.2. There is agreement on at least some of the key facts, but profound disagreement as to how far they can be attributed to globalization and what the solutions might be. Note that acceptance of rising inequality need not imply rejection of a globalization project, and may even underpin it.

Recent studies of income inequality in fact come to a clear conclusion (Bourguignon and Morrisson 2002; Sala-i-Martin 2002; Firebaugh and Goesling 2004). The key focus is global income inequality (GII), meaning the distribution of income across the world population. Central findings are as follows:

- GII became more even in the period from 1970 to 1998.
- It is true that differences remain stark. On the figures of Firebaugh and Goesling, average income in rich regions in 1998 was twenty times that in poor regions, compared to a ration of nine times in 1900 and three times in 1800.

Box 10.2 Does a global free market improve conditions in developing countries?

Yes

- There is currently no global free market, with restrictions being particularly strong in agriculture and cheap manufactured goods. Bangladeshi exports to the USA faced tariffs of about 16 per cent of their value, whereas the figure for French exports was 1 per cent.
- The world economy is distorted by the system of trade barriers, plus extensive farm subsidies in developed countries (the subsidy to each cow in the EU is equivalent to the income of the average African worker).
- Involvement in the world economy has promoted growth and the reduction of poverty in many Asian countries including India and Vietnam; the exclusion of much of Africa from the world economy has by contrast contributed to continued poverty.

No

- The current regime of world trade has heightened poverty and inequality in the poorest regions of the world, especially Latin America and Africa.
- The theory of comparative advantage tends to legitimize the existing balance, whereby developed countries focus on high-value goods. The relative prices of goods from different countries are determined by political rather than economic factors. Developing countries would be stuck producing low-wage goods with little chance of economic development.
- The solution lies in reforming interventionist and protectionist development models.

Comment

Both sides agree on the faults of the current regime. But for the 'yes' view it is a distortion of true markets; for the 'no' view it is a representation of how markets work. The 'no' view may give insufficient attention to the possibilities of trade liberalization; the 'yes' view sees the process as unduly simple.

It is true that the current system is nothing like 'free' trade. But does it follow that a totally free market (whatever that might mean: see Chapter 9) would be the solution? Would resources flow as expected, what about the dislocations of those now disadvantaged, and what of the 'externalities' (e.g. agricultural land in developed countries that might be abandoned)? Debate needs to focus on what *kinds* of regulation are needed, both to define the ways in which markets work and to act to stimulate development. Development is a dynamic process that static models of comparative advantage cannot address.

Source: 'Yes' and 'no' arguments summarized from articles by Paul Munro and Richard Peet in *Royal Society of Arts Journal* (April 2004: 16–17).

- The key proximate driver of increased equality is growing equality between countries, notably growing income in large poor countries, in particular China. Thus growth in China reduces GII, even though inequality within that country is also rising.
- The main driver of equality is not IT but the spread of traditional industrial processes. Claims that inequality is an essential element of the IT revolution are false.

These studies also indicate reasons why the myth of rising inequality prevails. Key reasons include confusion over: trends within a country and that trend's overall effect (as in the case of China); terminology (GII is not the same as income equality in every country in the world); and analysis between nations and people (most poor nations have had less than average growth rates, but most poor people are in large countries that have grown fast).

There is also a series of questions as to the broader significance that can be attached to this particular evidence. Rather than treat capitalism as hero or villain, it makes more sense to examine its mechanisms. There is no single force of globalization; rather, there is a set of dynamics embracing MNCs, nation states, and global institutions. As the economic journalist Wolf (2004) — author of a long series of considered pieces in the *Financial Times* generally from a position favouring free market solutions — notes, there are forces of divergence, for example some histories of economic growth and some of failure, as well as convergence.

The Global Economy and the IMF

As noted in Chapter 1, financial crises are endemic to capitalism. We now consider why, and look at the implications for a system that is global in its reach.

Kindleberger (1978) identified twenty-nine significant cases from the eighteenth century to the mid-1970s and argued that Keynesian and monetarist analyses are incomplete because they neglect the 'instability of expectations, speculation and credit'. There tends, says Kindleberger, to be a cycle of boom and panic following the process listed in Box 10.3. Some of the underlying reasons for this instability are laid out by Eatwell and Taylor as discussed in Chapter 9. It does not of course follow that crises are inevitable. Kindleberger stresses that markets generally function, and are overwhelmed only when particular sets of events are put in motion. (One might recall the discussion of escalation in Chapter 8.) He also notes that at some periods institutions existed to control crises, so that in the nineteenth century the UK had acted as an international lender of last resort and thus stabilized the financial system; in his view, the Great Crash of 1929 was due in part to Britain's inability to perform this role and the unwillingness of the USA to take it on.

Box 10.3 The cycle of manias, panics, and crashes

1. Some exogenous shock triggers a boom, which is further fed by bank credit [because banks see the possibility of profits when they lend to businesses that are themselves booming].
2. Price increases generate a sense of euphoria and of ever increasing prosperity.
3. Prices eventually level off and 'distress' (the inability of some firm to meet its commitments) ensues.
4. This acts as a signal or trigger to reassess expectations.
5. As a result a panic begins.

Source: Kindleberger (1978: 6).

The main institutions of the global economic system are the IMF, the World Bank, and the WTO. How do they regulate the world economy? The first two were created at the landmark conference held at Bretton Woods, New Hampshire, in 1944. The third originated at the same conference, but it was originally called the General Agreement on Tariffs and Trade (GATT), becoming the WTO in 1995. The task of the IMF was to manage the system of fixed exchange rates that was initiated at Bretton Woods, offering support to countries whose rates were under pressure. The Bank was to provide funds for longer-term development, while GATT was used to seek reductions in tariff barriers and to promote free trade. (The British economist Keynes who was a key figure at Bretton Woods remarked that the system was fine, but what was called a Fund was in fact a bank, and the Bank was in fact a fund — which is a good way of thinking about the roles of the respective institutions.)

The Bretton Woods system was a means of managing instability that worked remarkably effectively from 1945 until the adoption of floating exchange rates by the USA in 1971. The system was, not, however, without its contradictions. It was never the product of disinterested rationality but reflected at the outset US domination of the world economy, with the dollar being the new international currency (rather than a wholly new currency as proposed by Keynes) (Hutton 2002: 186). The system meant that the USA could pay for imported goods with dollars but was also constrained to maintain convertibility between dollars and gold. This situation could not continue indefinitely, and increasing drains of gold reserves led the USA to cancel convertibility. In effect, a new system was forced on the world economy. As Strange (1998: 5–7) puts it, the Bretton Woods system did not 'collapse' through an inevitable process but was brought to an end by US decisions.

The end of Bretton Woods did not spell the demise of the influence of the IMF. On the contrary, a model of markets and how they should function became stronger. A significant and remarkably little emphasized crisis even occurred in 1976, when the UK, one of the key architects of Bretton Woods, was subject to IMF pressure. The story is told in Box 10.4.

The subsequent period of floating exchange rates and free capital movements has increased the globalization of the financial system in that crises in one country become more readily transferred to others. 'When the Thai baht collapsed on July 2, 1997', says Stiglitz (2002: 89) in opening his analysis of the East Asian crisis, 'no one knew that this was the beginning of the greatest economic crisis since the Great Depression'. The effects of the crisis were severe, with GDP in Thailand falling in 1998

Box 10.4 Global dominance, the IMF, and the UK economic crisis of 1976

In 1976, for the first time, the economic policy of a major industrialized country was determined by the IMF. The UK crisis of that year was described by leading US officials as 'cosmic' and the 'greatest single threat to the Western world' (the Secretary of State and the National Security Advisor respectively, as quoted by Helleiner 1994: 128–9). The country was facing one of its periodic balance of payments crises, exacerbated by high inflation. The Labour Government, elected in 1974, was struggling to manage the economy through a mixture of conventional Keynesian demand management and an incomes policy. In addition it was Labour Party policy, as adopted at the party conference, to pursue an Alternative Economic Strategy of nationalization of key sectors of the economy and exchange controls. One can readily see how US observers saw the situation as potentially highly threatening to the retention of Britain within a Keynesian orthodoxy (see the 'logic of the situation': Box 8.5). The government secured a loan of £5 billion from the Bank of International Settlements and central banks but only on US insistence that it be repaid in six months. This condition further reduced confidence in the value of sterling and encouraged the adoption of deflationary economic policies (Panitch and Leys 2001: 116). This event pushed the government away from Keynesian demand management towards monetarism (control of the money supply and counter-inflation policies). This was the unwitting thin edge of the substantial monetarist wedge used three years later by the Thatcher Conservative government to break apart the remains of the Keynesian consensus.

by 11 per cent, while the figure in Indonesia was 13 per cent. As to causes, Stiglitz highlights capital and financial market liberalization that were encouraged by IMF policies or what he calls elsewhere the 'Washington consensus'. This term refers to a belief in free markets and sound money, as held by leaders in the IMF and investment bankers, as well as the US government (Sklair 2002: 85). The point therefore is that 'the market' is not an asocial force but takes its identity from political and economic decisions. Had IMF policies been different and had Western governments not pursued a new economic orthodoxy, the market would have worked differently.

As to the roots of IMF behaviour, Stiglitz (2002: 130) argues that there was no overt conspiracy to undermine East Asian countries but instead IMF actions reflected 'the interests and ideology of the Western financial community'. Here and at other points he hints at an explanation that would be familiar to anyone aware of theories of power and the state. These theories have shown that the state does not (necessarily) follow the direct dictates of its capitalist masters, for reasons including divisions among the capitalist class, the fact that capitalists may not in fact have any clear idea of what they want, and the need for the state to have 'relative autonomy' if it is to be accepted as a legitimate actor representing national interest and not the naked will of the ruling class (Offe and Ronge 1982; Block 1980; Edwards 1986: 146–54). Stiglitz seems to be groping towards such a view from the starting point of relatively conventional economics. This is one example of the difficulty, discussed in Chapter 9, that economists have in connecting with social and political theories. Yet his conclusion is reasonable if scarcely developed: interest groups operate according to rules and assumptions that come to be accepted as natural and that in this case have their basis in neo-classical economics, but their exercise of power is more subtle than notions of conspiracy or careful self-interested strategy can comprehend.

The Regulation of Global Trade

We may take the example of telecommunications and begin with the story of the industry's globalization as perceived by Hutton (2002: 200–7), which he presents as a prime example of Americanization. Though he observes that 'it is hard to argue that there was any blueprint', he soon argues that as early as 1962 'the US had been alert' to how satellite technology would allow its companies to dominate the information and communication industries. GATT and then the WTO were pressurized to 'accommodate the US's unilateral ambitions'. The result was the deregulation of telecommunications that produced 'an orgy of takeovers' which in turn produced overcapacity and huge debts as firms concentrated on takeovers rather than the development of communications infrastructure.

A more nuanced account is provided by Comor (1998) in his study of the Digital Broadcasting Satellite (DBS). Between 1962 and 1984, he argues, DBS was seen as rather marginal. Importantly, though the USA was indeed active in the field, such activity tended to cut across the interests of existing corporations, notably AT&T, so that the state was not directly in the control of such capital. Domestic liberalization started with the breaking up of AT&T in 1982, and it began to be realized that competition in the USA would work only if this model was exported. Opening the US market to overseas suppliers meant, in the US view, granting access to firms that were protected in their home markets. This in turn led to pressures to deregulate other markets, which was the 'unintentional' result of domestic liberalization (Comor 1998: 193).

Hutton exaggerates the extent of a considered US plan. It is also difficult in his account to explain why any such plan created what he himself calls a 'fiasco'. The essence of capitalism is that it is not a directed system but one based on markets and uncertainty. States can try to steer it in various ways but there are unintended consequences in their doing so. New instabilities emerge, and there are major losers even in the corporate sector that is supposedly the beneficiary of state action, the key case in telecoms being WorldCom. It would, however, be wrong to argue that there is no dynamic at all in the system and that events can be analysed satisfactorily in terms of the immediate and conscious choices made at certain times. As Comor and Stiglitz both suggest, there was a set of assumptions upon which policymakers drew. A liberal capitalist economy, rather than some other regulatory approach, became an increasingly dominant model from the 1980s. Globalization had not only a capitalist character, but a liberal capitalist one based on ideas of deregulation, privatization, and shareholder value. This was in turn the result of the way in which the Bretton Woods system unravelled.

Turning to GATT, it was run by a small executive council with decisions being made by weighted votes that favoured the developed countries; the WTO by contrast has a council comprising all members of the organization (Comor 1998: 110–11). Ironically, growing protests have occurred at the same time as the organization has become more democratic. Gilpin (2002: 112) concludes that

[T]he achievements of the trading system during the past half century have been remarkable.... [T]ariffs in industrialized countries [are] less than 6 per cent on average (one-tenth of what they were in the 1940s). . . . The number of GATT/WTO members has increased from 23 to 132 in the late 1990s. [But] trade liberalization and globalization . . . conflict more frequently with powerful local interests and popular beliefs. . . . [T]he clash between the forces of globalization and those of trade protection continues to threaten the global trading system.

Desai (2002: 311) similarly remarks that the structure of the WTO 'is the most egalitarian of any of the international institutions — one country, one vote', whereas the IMF in particular was dominated by the developed countries especially the USA.

A less sanguine view emphasizes the limits to trade liberalization. Developing economies, particularly the poorest, have weak manufacturing sectors and thus cannot readily enter the markets of developed countries. Africa had only 2.1 per cent of world exports in 1995, a fall (contrary of course to any simple globalization story) from 5.9 per cent in 1980 (Fligstein 2001: 199). Protections against agricultural imports remain substantial across the developed economies. The sectors that have been opened to trade have, moreover, reflected political pressure rather than some inevitable processes. For example, the opening of national telecommunications markets to global firms reflected US pressure between 1985 and 1996, culminating in the opening of seventy markets to international, often US, firms (Hutton 2002: 203).

A striking fact concerns the 'terms of trade' between advanced and developing countries, that is the relative prices of their products. Sklair (2002: 17), for example, shows that the dollar prices of basic commodities fell between 1980 and 2000. Robusta coffee, for example, traded at $4.50 in 1980 and 90 cents in 2000. Such trends cannot, moreover, be explained away in terms of supply and demand, for tariff barriers in developed countries discriminate against Third World agricultural products. Helleiner (1994) provides a cogent and closely argued analysis of why the neo-liberal project of the Washington consensus was more readily pursued in relation to finance than to trade. His analysis is summarized in Box 10.5.

Whether markets alone are the answer is strongly contested, but it is reasonable to conclude that an increase in free trade may tend, other things being equal, to benefit poor countries, and to the extent that globalization may be beneficial. Yet 'other things' are rarely equal. Would a reduction in tariff barriers help Third World agricultural producers? The answer depends on the politics of the countries in question (i.e. how incomes are taxed and land is distributed, and if agriculture became more profitable there might be conflicts over access to land), on the behaviour of companies

---

Box 10.5 Why was finance globalized while trade remained restricted?

1. Money is mobile and fungible, which reduces collective action problems as compared to trade, for goods do not have these properties and it is much harder to agree on product definitions and quality standards.
2. Central bankers as a group shared a 'world view' and a common project for avoiding crises.
3. The USA, UK and Japan had 'hegemonic interests' in finance but not trade: the USA had a central role in the world finance system but a declining presence in world trade; the UK remained locked into global financial management after its hegemonic period; and Japan's rising power and external assets led it to seek smooth bilateral relations, especially with the USA.
4. Neo-liberal theories are easy to articulate in relation to finance, in part because the financial system does not impinge directly on any particular social group, whereas trade policies affect specific sectors very directly.

Source: Helleiner (1994: 18).

(i.e. Western firms might well increase their existing controls of the supply chains of key products), and on much else. As ever, it is the politics of the process and not the process itself that is critical, and it is the fear that globalization is driven by developed countries, rather than the principle, that underlies many concerns about the process. The example given in Box 10.6 illustrates how a free market and neo-liberal project is also shaped by particular economic interests.

Box 10.6 Tripping up on TRIPs

TRIPs are the Trade-Related aspects of Intellectual Property agreement within the WTO. This obscure topic illustrates the ways in which a global project can be defined. What TRIPs do is to give to the owner of intellectual property a twenty-year monopoly over its use. The rationale was to recognize the rights of inventors and to promote economic development, but there was little empirical support for the latter proposition. TRIPs originated in the demands of twelve large US firms, that established the Intellectual Property Committee in 1986, which then won changes in domestic law and US support in the WTO. US trade negotiators, concerned at a lack of national competitiveness, saw intellectual property as an area in which they could fight back. Intellectual property pirates were readily blamed, and firms claimed extensive damage from a lack of protection, though these claims were 'wildly exaggerated'.

Source: Sell (2000: 97).

How can we understand the role of states at national level and of supranational regulatory bodies such as the WTO? An early view argued that the power of transnational firms was leading to a 'hollowing out' of the state and an inability to pursue projects requiring high levels of taxation. A more adequate view is 'the myth of the powerless state' as laid out in particular by Weiss (1997, 1998): it is easy to exaggerate the power of the state in the past, and hence the extent of weakening; not all states pursue a neo-liberal agenda; that agenda is driven by some states rather than being a free-floating tendency; state capacities vary, so that in countries such as Japan and Germany there is the organizational ability to steer economic transformation; and globalization does not produce a uniform response by states. Globalization is not only an organized process, but also one that necessarily has different conceptions and dimensions, so that its nature is inherently contested. The general point is made well by Woods (2000: 2–3):

> [S]trong states have not only influenced the nature and pace of globalization but, equally, have controlled their own integration into the world economy. Their sovereignty may well be qualitatively changing, but it is surely not being eroded.

Earlier theories of the state, seen here as a national actor, continue to have some relevance. A reasonable conclusion from these often arcane discussions emerged from the work of Offe and Ronge (1982), who argued that the state does not pursue the interests of particular capitalists, for there are plenty of examples of states acting against the explicit wishes of capitalists and of divisions within the ranks of capital. Instead, it protects a set of rules and processes that define how a capitalist economy works. This formulation allows one to say why a state is necessary, for the role cannot be performed by capitalists themselves. It also allows for the rules to evolve in unplanned directions, and for them to reflect in part the interests of groups other than capitalists, for if the rules are clearly biased they will lack legitimacy. Offe's other work also stressed the two, inherently contradictory, roles of the state, to promote accumulation and development, and to sustain the legitimacy of the capitalist order.

One implication of this argument has subsequently become apparent. As initially stated, it said that the logic of accumulation needed tempering with legitimation, as in the development of a welfare state. But subsequent neo-liberal attacks on the size of the state and the alleged inefficiency of state enterprises suggested that accumulation logics also have legitimatory arguments on which to draw. The 'Washington consensus' reflects a belief system as well as economics. The need for a degree of legitimacy remains a fundamental constraint in capitalism, but the bases of legitimacy can be more broadly based than writers like Offe anticipated.

Globalization and Work in Organizations

We have seen that globalization creates resources for multinational actors. Previous chapters have analysed in detail how work is changing, and one influence is that of the global economy. Much of the discussion of globalization and work remains, however, abstract in that it ignores the concrete links between the two.

A 'strong' globalization thesis would expect that increasing openness of any given economy to world trade will have consequences for its social organization. A 'race to the bottom' would encourage a reduced expenditure by the state on welfare programmes; it could also heighten pressures towards inequality *within* the economy, because the least skilled will be most subject to global competition and may thus lose out compared to the more skilled. It would also expect a growing convergence *between* countries. Yet there is little evidence to support such expectations. Garrett (2000), for example, shows that, across the OECD countries at least, openness to trade did not reduce government expenditures and that convergence was largely absent. Various indicators of political relations within a country, notably trade union power and the strength of political parties of the left, continue to influence patterns of distribution. The implication is that forces within a country have not been swamped by the imperatives of globalization.

The resilience of distinct national capitalist systems is a lasting theme of many accounts. To put the matter sharply, consider the discussion of careers in Chapter 4. What, one might ask, is happening to management careers in the light of global forces? Is it the case, for example, that national systems are being eroded and replaced with a standard model? The question might be posed of Japan in particular, for the country has long had a distinctive system of managerial careers marked by long employment in a single firm, highly structured career paths, and 'lifetime employment' (at least for male managers in large firms) (Storey et al. 1997). Will it not be the case that globalization promotes restructuring and job losses, particularly when Japan has been rocked by scandals and its image of an economic miracle tarnished? Yet Dore (2000) finds the traditional employment system largely unchanged.

The question of course is why. Answers might include the fact that Japanese exposure to inward FDI remains remarkably small (Dunning 2000) and that the employment system itself continues to deliver benefits to the firms that use it. This does not mean that in other countries similar forces will operate. It points to the key lesson, that globalization is mediated by some forces and possibly counteracted by others. The only meaningful answer to the question of whether globalization is affecting career structures may be, 'it depends, for it varies between countries and sectors of the economy'. It may be possible to go further to illustrate what kinds of countries experience an effect and why, but in the present state of knowledge this may be difficult.

A second key example concerns the ways in which gender and race are mobilized as an economic resource for companies. Recent feminist theories have begun to analyse how gender is embedded in the restructuring of global production. This has two linked aspects. Local gender relations are a resource for transnational corporations to pay women low wages and to feminize work. At the same time, immigration of women from poor to richer countries provides a cheap source of labour that frees members of the global elite from domestic tasks such as cleaning and child care (Acker 2004).

One estimate is that between a third and a half of families in the Philippines are sustained by remittances from overseas by migrants, many of whom are women working in domestic service and similar occupations in the developed economies (Parreñas 2003: 39). Similarly, evidence about poor working conditions of Third World workers producing such items as shoes and clothing for MNCs is now commonplace. One feature is worth underlining, however. Much of this production takes place in export processing zones, where MNCs are often granted tax concessions and where workers' legal rights may be restricted. Klein (2000: 202–9) offers an account of the zone of Cavite, located in the town of Rosario in the Philippines. About 50,000 workers are employed in over 200 factories. According to Klein, working conditions are poor, rights to a minimum wage and trade union membership are in effect ignored, and firms receive generous tax concessions. It is not, then, the case that MNCs have simply entered countries where labour is cheap. They have been attracted by states that have set up such zones, and state decisions shaped the way in which the economy was integrated into the global system. (A more balanced view of MNCs and labour in developing countries is developed below.)

It is also the case that workers are not necessarily powerless. Reviewing recent literature, Gille and Ó Riain (2002) note that there may be resistance, and also make the more subtle point that women drawn into factories as a result of global production chains may reap some benefits since they can use the income and independence of this work to escape from patriarchy in the family. Wolf's (1992) detailed ethnography in Indonesia pointed to this effect. Yet it also argued that it is not universal: in Taiwan, family structures were stronger, and young women working in capitalist factories remained largely subordinated at home. Wolf also made the important point that workers' integration into capitalist production is shaped by prior experience. Ong (1987), studying workers in Malaysia, had found that a significant source of resistance to the demands of disciplined work was possession by spirits: workers coped with an alien system by interpreting it in terms of 'traditional' spirits, one effect being that they could be hard for a rationally minded capitalist to manage. Yet in Indonesia the workers, previously inured to hard work in agriculture and having few positive expectations of factory labour, displayed no such responses.

Yet this point illustrates the problems of going further. There have been numerous exposés of global corporations, but it is often far from clear how far the practices described (where they reflect detailed evidence and not mere anecdote) could be attributed to globalization rather than to long-standing tendencies to exploit workers where conditions permit. What is true in one country (e.g. the position of female workers in Taiwan) may not be true in another. Economic sectors will also differ substantially. Low-skill manufacturing may be open to relatively intense exploitation, whereas in other sectors workers may have more skills to shape the work process. There will also be differences between countries, with modes of integration into the global economy varying considerably.

Ethnographies are an essential tool to grasp how globalization is affecting work experience. Without close analysis of concrete experience, there is the danger that analysts will assume that globalization is having certain effects. Yet, as Thompson (2003) notes, it is important to seek a multi-level analysis within case studies, so that the nature of global-level and corporate strategies can be discerned and their linkages with workplace behaviour addressed. We would add that it is also crucial that ethnographies be connected with each other. Wolf, for example, pointed to possible contrasts between Taiwan and Indonesia in the ways in which family structure mediates globalization. Study in countries that vary on this dimension while sharing other similarities with these two cases are needed to extend and test this hypothesis.

These are demanding criteria, and it is not surprising that information is at present patchy. It is too early to state with confidence what the effects of globalization on work experience have been, but we can make some progress first by illustrating some connections and second by indicating the variables that may be involved.

A first illustration of connections is that of the clothing industry (Box 10.7). Globalization did not eliminate the industry in developed countries, but instead contributed to its reconstitution, influenced by trade arrangements such as the Multi-Fibre Agreement. That said, studies of the industry generally report substantial shifts of jobs to developing countries, while in sectors such as steel some developed economies have retained jobs. The reasons for this contrast might be pursued. Consider, for example, studies of these two industries in the same book. On clothing, Taplin and Winterton (2002: 277) conclude that enterprises in high-wage economies 'have to address the same imperatives' resulting from low-cost competition. On steel, Bacon and Blyton (2002) underline an absence of direct effects of globalization on work conditions. In some respects, skills and training were found to improve though workloads increased and job security declined; moreover, particular aspects of globalization such as ownership change could benefit workers while others had more costs. These accounts do not provide explanations for the contrast but they are likely to turn on factors including: the height of barriers to entry; the size and power of companies, with steel firms being large and influential, whereas small firms predominate in clothing; the power of trade unions; and local political influence (for large steel plants are symbols of traditional jobs that are readily identified, while small clothing factories are relatively invisible).

As for developing countries, it is not the case that the end of the Multi-Fibre Agreement in 2004 will necessarily ease their integration into the global economy. Bangladesh, for example, is heavily dependent on the clothing and knitwear sector, which generates 76 per cent of the country's export earnings. It has suffered rapidly fluctuating demand as various countries compete for trade. In addition, the country's 'advantage' of low wages is offset by the weak integration of its supply chain and dependence for raw materials on other countries (Ward et al. 2004).

A second illustration is a study of work experience, which is particularly interesting because it makes the links with global forces more directly than do many studies of this kind (Box 10.8). In this case, workers with high levels of education and skill did not feel threatened by globalization, for their skills were valuable and transferable. They nonetheless expressed criticism of the contradictions of global management, which appeared here in a tension between managing at a distance and achieving coordination.

By 'the variables that may be involved', we mean analytical categories that may enable us to make sense of the complex interplay between globalization and work. These categories do not in the present state of

Box 10.7 Combined and uneven development in the clothing industry

Trade rules and protectionism

Why did producers switch from cotton to synthetic materials in the 1960s and 1970s? Schwartz (1994: 290–2) stresses the role of tariff systems, as opposed to some technological imperative. Of world production, synthetics accounted for 22 per cent in 1960 and 51 per cent twenty years later, while in Taiwan there was a massive switch, from 6 to 78 per cent. This reflected a growth of cotton imports to the USA in the 1950s, which led to 'voluntary' restrictions of these imports (under the 1962 Long-Term Agreement, which was the price of acceptance by Congress of tariff cuts), which meant in turn that exporting countries were encouraged to switch to synthetics. Exports from newly industrializing countries exploded during the 1960s, which generated a further agreement covering all fibres. European producers then became concerned at the diversion of exports to their markets, and in 1973 the much more extensive and restrictive Multi-Fibre Agreement was reached (according to Gilpin 2002: 81, the 'most notorious' example of protectionism).

The Los Angeles clothing industry

Low-wage and low-skill jobs do not always leave developed economies. Bonacich and Appelbaum (2000) demonstrate that employment in the Los Angeles clothing industry grew by 40 per cent between 1979 and 1997, when it accounted for one-fifth of all manufacturing jobs in the city. These trends reflected three things; the need for producers to be close to the market; the place of the city as a cultural centre; and geographical concentration that generated benefits of networks linking firms together (Bonacich and Appelbaum 2000: 10, 32–8). The industry was also, however, connected to a global production system (imports constituting 57 per cent of US consumption of clothing), and of the Los Angeles firms many had offshore production facilities, increasingly in Mexico. As for work conditions in Los Angeles, a Department of Labor investigation found that, of the legal firms in the industry (i.e. leaving to one side the unknown number of illegal producers), only 39 per cent were in full compliance with wage and hours laws. The authors document low wages and the extensive use of home-workers and conclude that 'there appears to be no internal dynamic that leads away from the low-wage (sweatshop) low road' (Bonacich and Appelbaum 2000: 258).

Implications

The developed countries have defined the shape of world trade, which does not reflect the free flow of 'natural' forces. Protectionism up to the 1970s continued into the 2000s, for example with US restrictions on steel imports. Patterns of global production not only undermine established systems in developed countries but also generate new niches in which low-wage producers continue to survive.

Box 10.8 Working in a global corporation

Ó Riain (2000) studied what could well stand as an exemplar of the networked global production system: the Irish software development team of a US multi-national, which also outsourced graphics and helpdesk functions to independent contractors. Work was managed at a distance rather than directly, the key process being pressure to meet deadlines and the resultant intensification of time use. High wages were paid in return, and notably independent contractors were paid more than permanent employees, with the former arrangement being preferred by the workers. But there was also very high job mobility, which questioned the long-term sustainability of this system. There were also internal tensions, for management at a distance meant that the system was poorly coordinated and controlled. The work team 'does not resist the global in and of itself but contests how the global should operate, showing disdain for the mismanagement of the global by the remote managers' (Ó Riain 2000: 187).

knowledge provide anything like a complete map, but they help us to think about the connections. The test of them is whether they can be applied to areas other than those in which they were originally developed: do they help one to think about the relevant processes? We think that they do.

Looking specifically at MNCs and their links with globalization on one hand and national employment systems on the other, Ferner and Quintanilla (2002: 249, emphasis in original) offer the following insightful conclusion:

[T]he subtle distinctions and complexities of interaction . . . appear not as the frills, but as an inherent part of the 'texture' of global capitalism: the globalization dynamic is *intrinsically* played out through the medium of interacting, internally heterogeneous, nationally rooted MNCs, seeking to draw their international competitive advantage from the distinctive and variegated institutional configurations, including systems of employment relations, in which they are embedded.

The development of global capitalism is thus seen as a negotiated process. MNCs are themselves varied in nature, they draw on particular parts of their home country national contexts rather than simply being the 'bearers' of US or German features, and they interact with host country institutions in similar, varied, ways. These authors' emphasis on the inherent nature of these processes is also important: the environment is necessarily uncertain and shifting, and globalization is a process involving actors with different strategies.

To take one recent study from many, Biggart and Guillén (1999) examine the auto industry, an interesting case given that it is often seen as prototypically global and thus as likely to exhibit standard features across the globe. These authors study four countries and show that their positions within the world industry differed. For example, South Korea's core organizational form, the *chaebol*, comprises closely linked familial groups with strong internal ties but a limited willingness to cooperate with other groups. This was appropriate for mass production and auto assembly but was less fitted for components manufacture. These four cases offer analytical generalizations about linkages between national business systems and production in the auto industry, which can in principle be applied to other countries and other industries.

A framework that helps to address these issues is summarized in Box 10.9. It argues that global forces enter the regulation of labour through three 'logics', and that the strength of each logic varies with a set of five conditions. Where, therefore, the logic of competition is strong, by reason of the state of these five conditions, globalization's effects are likely to be particularly powerful.

Box 10.9 Logics of action and globalization

Frenkel and Kuruvilla (2002) argue that there are three logics shaping the regulation of labour within a national context. These are the logics of:

- industrial peace (important for social and political stability);
- competition (the logic most directly linked to globalization though not necessarily dependent on that process); and
- employment and income security (which includes unemployment insurance and standard of hours of work and safety, and which is important because of the need for social order and legitimacy).

These authors analyse the operation of the logics in four developing countries. They argue that in three of them (China, Malaysia, and the Philippines) the logic of competition has been dominant; in addition, in China the other two logics have been growing in influence whereas in the Philippines by contrast they remain weak. In the fourth case, India, industrial peace has been traditionally strong while employment and income security have also been important. They explain variation in the strength of the logics in terms of 'economic development strategies, the intensity of globalization, government responsiveness to worker expectations, labor market characteristics, and unions' strength' (Frenkel and Kuravilla 2002: 388).

Implicit in the idea of logics is an argument developed in the present book, namely, that capitalism contains inherently contradictory principles. The first and the third logics reflect the principle of order and legitimacy, while the second reflects that of accumulation. Globalization adds a new twist to the tensions between these principles. A country pursuing global integration cannot for long neglect issues of the employment and income security of its citizens, for fear of two things: popular protest and also the unwillingness of firms to invest if the logic of industrial peace is not pursued, and such a pursuit will entail attention to social order.

The idea of legitimacy can be taken further, conveniently pursuing a different analysis by Frenkel, this time of global labour standards as exemplified by two Adidas sub-contractors in China (Frenkel and Scott 2002). The argument here is that acceptance of standards is promoted by three factors: consumer pressure and demands for ethical investment; producers' own wish to avoid a race to the bottom; and policymakers' desire for continued support for the world trading system. The second and third merit brief comment. Under the second, the concept of 'taking wages out of competition' is a long-established one, the benefit to employers being that a floor is placed under wage competition and undercutting pressure from cheaper producers is eliminated. The same logic is likely to operate at global level, as large producers seek means to restrict entry to their markets. As for the third factor, (what passes for) free trade is always open to challenge, and national policymakers, like firms, find themselves balancing competing pressures around legitimation and accumulation.

Related work (Moran 2002: 24–5, 35–43, 90–1) develops this theme:

- Conditions encouraging the maximization of worker oppression are quite limited. (We can see these as constraints on the pursuit of a competition logic, that are in effect internal to that logic.) First, as labour markets in developing countries emerge, alternative forms of employment will arise and an exploitation strategy will be less able to attract workers. Second, to meet international product standards calls for capable workers.
- In countries including the Philippines conditions in export processing zones have improved. FDI has shifted from poverty-stricken countries to competitive labour markets offering skilled workers.
- Corporate codes of conduct have been developed; for example, 85 per cent of large US firms have social responsibility guidelines though they are less common in firms from countries including Japan and France.

A further logic, therefore, is that of the insertion of a production chain in the global system. Legitimatory pressures on firms constrain their freedom, even in an economy such as China. Some of these pressures may be consistent with their own preferences (as with the 'race to the bottom' argument), so that it is not a matter of external forces making firms do what they would otherwise avoid. Complying with labour standards can be a competitive advantage for some firms, so that the various logics interact with each other. Globalization is indeed a contested process.

Conclusions

Conclusions may be presented through the eyes of our questioning observer. First, one can see that globalization is not a uniform process and nor is it inevitable. Recent developments in the global economy reflect conscious choices. If one thinks of a globalizing elite it is clear that its view of the process is not one of a shift towards a global end state in the sense of the removal of all barriers and regulations; different parts of the elite have different interests and these will be shaped by tensions between competing logics. Trade has remained restricted, and the ways in which the global economy have been opened up reflect a project in which particular interests have sought openness in some respects and not others. The observer can thus challenge simpler views.

Second, because globalization is contested, there are numerous ways in which active questioning can be undertaken. Until very recently, debate was highly polarized, with critics tending to adopt extreme positions. These positions have been criticized for ignoring positive aspects of globalization, for coming close to old-style protectionism, and for an incoherence of argument. Though such criticisms have a point logically, a certain degree of emotive protest can be a powerful force. Would global environmental issues be so much in the public eye were it not for highly charged protests? That said, there is a range of critical positions that can be taken. Thus it is feasible to argue that reform is possible and that, as with large apparel firms and labour standards, genuine progress can be made. Writers such as McMillan (2002) and Wolf (2004) do not argue simply that markets work but instead stress the role of institutions in making them work. The development of regulatory regimes may thus be feasible. More radical views are also possible. The point of analysis such as that offered here is not to say which view is preferable, but to point to the tools of thought that are available. Key tools include the different logics of globalization and the ways in which contradictions offer space for action.

Third, if the observer became a manager in an MNC, he or she should be prepared to expect to manage through degrees of uncertainty. Frenkel and Scott (2002) report that Adidas had, in each of the two plants owned by sub-contract firms, about twenty of its own engineers. These people are likely to face a number of tensions between, for example, the letter of the Adidas code of conduct and day-to-day realities in which the principles have to be applied, and between working with local managers while pursuing corporate agendas. Where do their loyalties lie? The only answer is that they have to draw on principles and standards to try to reach reasonable judgements. Moran (2002: 97) argues for the role of voluntary standards:

[N]ame-and-shame techniques that rely on common-sense standards and that place the burden of proof on the firms to show that its plants or suppliers are living up to the firm's own guidelines [are more likely to produce results] than a process that depends on dispute-settlement panels and appellate tribunals.

This may be to take voluntary approaches too far. Firms respond to external pressures, and voluntary action needs a wider framework of rules within which to work. The negotiation of competing logics will remain a complex task. Globalization arguably increases this complexity. Chapter 11 looks at some current debates on balancing different demands in the light of ethical standards.

11

What Are the Opportunities and Responsibilities of Organizational Life?

Two major issues shape current debates on organizations. The first is structural: are changes in the world economy associated with globalization leading to the convergence of national systems of capitalism around a free market model, and is there an emerging model of jobs in firms that results from this model? The second relates to a set of social responsibilities in the light of structural changes. These include two areas of major debate: corporate social responsibility (CSR), which refers to the duties of organizations to customers, employees and others; and ethics, which gives particular attention to the responsibilities of individuals. One key example in relation to ethics is the phenomenon of the whistle-blower: a person who exposes in public the unethical practices of the organization for which he or she works. The whistle-blower has become a clearly recognized category, with substantial books being written on it.

In this concluding chapter we address some issues of ethics on the basis of the previous chapters. In line with our approach as a whole, we do not see ethics as independent of the forces of capitalist competition or suppose that an ethical approach is a wholly new one that can transform organizations fundamentally. This is the reason why we have not written a free-standing chapter on the theme but prefer to relate ethical questions to the foregoing evidence on how organizations behave: having seen how organizations work, we can now draw some conclusions about how individuals might respond. We retain this specific focus, and do not set out to discuss ethical theories and debates in detail.

Capitalist Futures

In his introduction to a volume on changing organizational forms in international perspective, the sociologist DiMaggio lists six reasons why capitalism has survived (2001: 11–12). These reasons, he suggests, are offered by a range of scholars, who have often been influenced by Marxist writings while themselves not subscribing to a Marxist view. They are:

1. The military subjection of the world led to the ability to pay higher wages than would otherwise be feasible to workers in the core capitalist countries.
2. Monopoly capitalism generated rents that were also shared with workers.
3. This system also allowed management to focus on labour peace and stability instead of a sole emphasis on profit.
4. Bureaucratic systems provided job security.
5. Marginal workers were used as shock absorbers.
6. The state acted as a manager of the system.

According to DiMaggio, there are three challenges to this synthesis: the reassertion of shareholder control, attacks on social accords between capital and labour, and the growth of interfirm alliances.

The list of six factors is a useful compilation, as is the critique of those analysts (both Marxist and non-Marxist) who saw large monopolistic firms as the apotheosis of capitalism. Yet the three challenges should not really be seen as undermining any sensible materially grounded (or Marxist if that label is preferred) view of capitalism as a dynamic system. It is true that the permanency of the social systems of the 1945–80 period was often exaggerated and that the decline of these systems was not predicted. It is also true that the decline reflected particular historical contingencies and not some inexorable law. As we saw in Chapter 9, the concept of shareholder value grew up in the USA as a result of weaknesses in previous models of corporate control, external challenges, and the presence of economic theories that both justified and helped to generate a different model of market behaviour. Similarly, Chapter 10 discussed the ways in which actors on the global stage defined economic management in particular terms. Yet the assertion of shareholder value and an attack on a truce with labour is surely a reflection of the underlying logic of capitalism rather than a denial of it.

The growth of interfirm alliances and networks, together with the 'knowledge economy' and much else, is of a different order. An assertive and profit-oriented capitalism would be expected to destroy all forms of social accord, and there have of course been tendencies in that direction, notably the weakening of trade unions and a rise in wage inequality in many countries, the growth of contingent employment and job insecurity, and clear evidence of stress and work intensification (Lapido et al. 2003). Yet the liberal market model has not swept away that of coordinated market economies. Even in the liberal economies, the pure market model has gone alongside trends that seem to conflict with it. These include growing emphasis on trust relationships between organizations, on employee discretion and responsibility within them, and on new ways of governing organizations and of managing their social responsibilities.

There are two explanations of this apparent contradiction. First, within the capitalist organization of work itself, the use of skilled and responsible labour is a natural strategy to build on the possibilities of technologically advanced systems. Asserting a goal of profit does not mean that the only route to that goal is that of work intensification. Second, there are, as we saw in Chapter 10, competing logics. Firms cannot neglect the needs for labour cooperation, and as noted in Chapter 9 these needs may intensify with increasing competition and an emphasis on lean production systems. Other logics include those of relations with states, consumers, and environmental and other interest groups. The future of capitalism is shaped by a continuing and uncertain negotiation of competing principles.

Within this negotiation, there has been growing interest in questions of governance. The fundamental point about this issue is that, if shareholder value were a transparent goal there would be no need to debate governance, for the appropriate approach, technical questions apart, would be clear. The debate reflects the fact that there is necessarily uncertainty in decision-making and that alternatives are rarely clear in advance. In addition, the lack of attention to the role of employees in matters of governance is increasingly remarked. As discussed in Chapter 6, debates on 'empowerment' have tended to focus on schemes devised at the top of organizations and directed at giving employees a degree of discretion within pre-defined systems. At the same time, and disconnected from these debates, social responsibility has also come into prominence. There may now be some possibility to connect these two strands.

Corporate Social Responsibility: Business Issues

CSR became a major focus during the 1990s. Its core meaning is that firms have responsibilities other than those of maximizing shareholder value, including duties to the environment and to 'stakeholders' affected by their operations. It has certainly not become universal, so that an account of the 'new corporate cultures', for example, manages without reference to it (Deal and Kennedy 2000). But it has become a very popular theme in large firms, with such concepts as sustainable development and corporate ethical standards becoming commonplace. Many such firms sign up to the UN Global Compact and have detailed ethical statements on their websites.

The development of a CSR rhetoric is neatly illustrated by EU policy. The EU Commission published a green paper on the subject in 2001 and a Council resolution of 2003 stressed not only the 'external aspects of CSR' but also 'the internal aspects such as health and safety at work and management of human resources' (quoted in Barnard et al. 2004).

The issues around CSR are also increasingly familiar. Critics from the political left ask questions such as the following. Is it anything more than window dressing? Is it a subtle (or not-so-subtle) reputational device, whereby firms practising CSR aim to define the competitive terrain in ways that suit them (because they have the resources to sustain it) and that make life harder for competitors? And does it cut any ice within the firms themselves? Equally obvious points from more conventional business circles suggest that CSR may be adopted by firms because of external pressure, with the result that costs increase and they are diverted from the core economic tasks of any business. Sceptics from both camps might also point to the growing together of former opponents. When environmental issues were first forced onto the corporate agenda, organizations such as Greenpeace were seen as radical social movements operating to challenge corporations whereas there is now increasing dialogue, and some firms use environmental organizations to monitor their CSR achievements.

Our purpose is not to assess debates on CSR in detail but rather to use the debates to illustrate some more general and abiding features of organizational practice. One key illustration is the relationship with financial performance. Critics of CSR argue that its practice will worsen a firm's financial performance. The conventional business case is that it diverts firms from their proper activities, while 'left' critics would say that, if the triple bottom line is to mean anything, it must imply that values other than profit are given weight, so that again financial performance should suffer. Yet a meta-analysis of extant research found fifty-two studies (itself an indicator of the popularity of CSR) and concluded that social and financial performance are positively correlated (at a level of $r = 0.36$) and mutually reinforcing (Orlitzky et al. 2003). But it plainly does not follow that CSR is in the interests of all firms:

- Firms using it may have captured some competitive advantage, and if more firms follow they may find no similar advantage, or they may dilute the advantage gained by the early movers.
- It is not clear what kinds of firms gain from CSR (i.e. where the link with performance is greater than average) and what kinds may see no gains or even losses; a correlation of 0.36 can mask massive variation around the average.

- Has it been shown that there is a specific mechanism linking CSR to performance, for example through changes in the behaviour of managers? If not, then just where the value lies is very uncertain, and an association should not be taken as evidence of causality.

One possible argument is that CSR is not just about balancing different (fixed) objectives but about finding different ways to attain those objectives. The explanation for the positive association would then be that such new ways to pursue profit also mean that social and environmental aims are met.

This is a potentially appealing view, particularly to critics of currently existing capitalism: present arrangements are not the only feasible ones. It is also plausible in the specific context of CSR: firms can bring into their decision-making the demands of various stakeholders and can reach solutions different from those that might otherwise have been made. Yet this outcome may be less impressive than it seems at first sight:

- If one starts with a 'hard' model of decision-making, the assumption is that there is a rational best choice that is then altered when new parameters are included. Yet most decision-making is much less certain than this, in which case the inclusion of CSR may not make as much difference as might appear, and it may simply reflect a language of alternative ways of formulating a policy rather than something strong and free-standing.
- One test is clear evidence that under otherwise equivalent conditions CSR leads to one set of choices rather than another. Such evidence is hard to provide. Examples of firms using CSR certainly suggest that some new lines of choice have been made, but might these have been made in any event?
- If a firm is a profit-maximizer, and if CSR is compatible with profits, then why were the relevant decisions not made anyway? It may be that CSR acts to remove some barriers to 'optimal' choices, rather than directly improving performance.

Corporate Social Responsibility: Beyond the Stakeholder View

The issue of 'alternatives to capitalism' is neatly brought into focus by Block (1990). He points out that conventional arguments about the logic of the market had a close replica in leftish models based on the idea that capitalism is characterized by a contradiction between the demands of accumulation and legitimation. These models, developed in the 1970s, argued that overconcentration on accumulation would lead people to question the benefits that capitalism was giving them and hence make demands for health and welfare spending and other actions aimed at producing consent (legitimation). By the same token, however, an excess of attention to social welfare might create an accumulation crisis, which as a matter of logic should imply the reassertion of market disciplines favoured by conventional thought. (Block sees a strong parallel here. We would, however, give the left view the credit for stressing the balancing of contradictory forces, whereas the logic of the market is always dominant in conventional thinking).

The orthodox left resolution of this issue was to argue that capitalism is self-destructive and that a shift towards socialist principles would emerge. In the absence of this, the question then becomes that of how market societies work. We have reviewed in Chapters 9 and 10 several examples of different ways of running such societies, notably the evidence on varieties of capitalism. We also saw that regulation was not opposed to markets. It is not the case that markets are self-regulating or that external regulation interferes with them. On the contrary, they need regulations to exist at all, and some forms of regulation stimulate their functioning. We also saw that societies contain several different 'logics' that are in tension with each other, with a market logic being only one of several. Finally, a market logic establishes only broad principles that can be realized in various ways. In particular, interest groups such as large companies may claim that what they want is a natural product of the needs of the market, but it is often the case that those needs can be expressed in different ways and that what any particular group of firms want is not at all the same thing as what an 'efficient' market might produce. Firms shape rules in their own image, and can interfere with, as much as promote, approaches that lead to the efficiency of an economy as a whole.

One way in which firms shape rules turns on the language of stakeholders. It is apparently attractive to argue that CSR means the addition of stakeholders, including employees, customers, local communities, and so on, to shareholders, and that the making of decisions then reflects the concerns of these different interest groups. But to take this view is to limit analysis to the first face of power as discussed in Chapter 6 (perhaps with a touch of the second face): decision-making is seen as the overt making of choices unhindered by the ability of some groups to shape the agenda and to exert tacit forms of influence. Some 'stakeholder' language is very limited because it implies that the balancing of different stakeholder concerns is a technical matter. Express concerns may not in fact be compatible, and the surfacing of these concerns and not others is likely to reflect processes of legitimation and social definition. As argued below, this is not to dismiss CSR, but it is to suggest that bland stakeholder language should invite some deeper questions.

A developed critical view on CSR is provided by Sklair and summarized in Box 11.1. This clearly advances from debates as to whether CSR is or is not mere propaganda. Sklair shows that it is part of an ideological (as we defined the term in Chapter 1) agenda and that it can shape the terms of debate.

An analysis in terms of hegemony and forms of domination can be extremely valuable. As we saw in Chapter 6, power is often exercised in hidden ways, and it is the case that processes of legitimation help to establish what is acceptable and what is not. There is always the possibility in organizations to manipulate information and symbols to define certain behaviour as acceptable and hence to define the rules of the game. The dangers and limitations are, however, significant:

- There is often a very implied criticism, to the effect that the creation of meaning is in some way improper. Using labels such as hegemony can suggest a criticism that is not in fact carried through.
- We noted in Chapter 5 that Armstrong and Baron (1998) ask the question that academics tend to duck: what is wrong with firms laying down their own expectations? It is inevitable that arguments develop around certain courses of action, and a historical reconstruction of how CSR, for example, came into existence is perfectly sensible. But unless some concrete alternative is suggested, which would be preferable in identifiable ways, it is not clear what the analytical, as distinct from the historical, implication is. What might Shell managers do as the result of the deconstruction of their behaviour?
- Establishing that processes of legitimation and hegemony occur does not help us explain when they are most likely to occur. Nor does it identify the different kinds of processes involved or what they mean: is it the case that all forms of the construction of meaning are essentially the same, or are some processes more self-serving and more properly subject to criticism than others?

Sklair's key argument, that firms such as Shell have been able to define the terms of a debate and have sought to render necessarily contested issues into relatively bland forms that are amenable to measurement and management, is well taken. The language of CSR can take very difficult issues that involve political judgements and imply that there are solutions that can then be pursued through conventional management processes.

Box 11.1 A critique of CSR

Sklair (2001) reviews MNC activity in such areas as community development, the health and safety of consumers and employees, and the environment. He gives detailed examples of the practices of major companies including Procter & Gamble, RTZ, and the then BP Amoco (a merger of the two firms in 1998, now known simply as BP). Central points made are the following:

- Why do large firms engage in community service projects that deflect resources from the pursuit of profit? 'The answer . . . is that the boundary between business (especially globalizing business) and everyday life has been progressively blurred as capitalism has globalized' (Sklair 2001: 180).
- What should we make of claims to global citizenship? Sklair analyses the example of the 'Profits and Principles' that Shell produced in 1998. This is a key example since Shell had been at the forefront of criticism and then produced a substantial and detailed document that contained significant self-criticism. Its key question is whether profits and principles are in conflict. Sklair's reading is that 'while this highly reflexive Report is full of invitations . . . and concrete opportunities . . . for all the stakeholders to let the company know what they think, it answers the question and provides soft closure on the issue. . . . The issue is closed, but the process of persuasion, testing, measuring, matching actions to promises, matching policies to principles, is open and ongoing for all stakeholders' (Sklair 2001: 190).

  (The Shell website contains substantial updates of the 1998 report, including accounts of community and health work. When accessed on 1 March 2004, it also contained the statement by the chairman that, 'sustainable development is good for business, and business is good for sustainable development', which may or may not be a conscious reflection of the often-criticized statement that what was good for General Motors was good for the USA. The fact that the chairman was soon forced to resign is taken up below).

- Big business 'successfully recruited much of the global environmental movement in the 1990s to the cause of "sustainable" global consumerist capitalism. This achievement is an object lesson in how dominant classes incorporate potential enemies into what Gramsci called new historical blocs. Historical blocs are fluid amalgamations of forces that coagulate into social movements to deal with specific historical conjunctures' (Sklair 2001: 206). (We introduced some of Gramsci's core ideas in Chapter 1. Note here Sklair's argument that economic and ideological forces combined to establish a new definition of social reality: a materially driven social construction).

But in doing so the firms concerned have not simply pursued their own interests. They have had to change behaviour, and to some extent their actions may secure common as well as sectional interests. Environmental issues are debated in ways that are quite different from those of the past. The creation of a new historical bloc does not mean that everything in it is subordinate to its dominant member. If this were so, the value of the bloc would crumble and ideology would be exposed as mere propaganda.

One empirical study addresses the meanings of CSR in organizations in the UK (Barnard et al. 2003, 2004). The management of working time (which as we saw in Chapters 2 and 3 is a key issue) is the focus. The link here is the following: working time was regulated by a European Directive of 1993; such regulation was justified as a health and safety measure; and these measures are defined as being part of CSR. Key conclusions were that such links were rarely made in practice, that CSR was seen either as an external issue or as window dressing, and that regulation of working time was seen as an interference with firms' otherwise efficient use of labour. The last point is key. Though some actors recognized that existing practices were in fact inefficient (e.g. in generating stress, inducing absence from work as an escape mechanism, and in underpinning the use of overtime to resolve labour shortages, rather than organizing work more effectively), the ideology to which they adhered meant that the efficiency-inducing potentials of regulation were not attained. It may take more effort to allow the general rhetoric of CSR's benefits to secure desired changes in concrete practice, such as the management of working time.

It is not, then, the case that everything on the CSR agenda is to be dismissed. It is true that some firms have rendered it into a managerially acceptable form, with performance measures for environmental standards and ethical business along with those for sales and profit. But this is scarcely surprising, and it does set up expectations against which firms can be judged. If they themselves subscribe to certain objectives, then a clear test is whether they meet them, whereas with standards imposed from outside there is bound to be debate as to whether they are the right ones and whether firms can in fact be held accountable against them. As we saw in Chapter 10, moreover, issues such as child labour and human rights have led at least some firms to amend their behaviour in distinct ways and to recognize that they need to impose requirements on their suppliers as well as on themselves. Whether or not such behaviour is 'really' self-interested, in establishing brand reputation and maintaining consumer loyalty, will never be decisively answerable, for we cannot know what the alternative might have been and nor does it make much sense to try to establish singular fundamental objectives in what are necessarily multifaceted decisions.

CSR is thus best seen as one among several contradictory forces that firms need to manage. Its 'triple bottom line' cannot provide a solution to corporate dilemmas, for how are the elements to be weighed against each other? Indeed, it heightens the dilemmas in adding such objectives as sustainable development to an already long list. It is a contested and contestable set of concepts. Firms may wish to establish conceptual closure, and some of this wish may be sensible: to leave debate open would invite criticism that CSR was simply vague, and to make the concepts mean something to managers not accustomed to its language does require specific tools and techniques. But closure need not be complete, and solutions raise new sets of questions. This point was brought into sharp relief in early 2004, when one of the leaders of CSR, Shell, admitted that it had exaggerated the size of its 'proven' oil reserves, the firm had to delay producing its annual report, and there were suggestions that some managers had knowingly made false claims about the reserves. Using the language of CSR does not enable a firm to establish total ideological closure. But we would also argue against an absolutist argument to the effect that nothing changes or that all firms are the same. Shell and firms like it established rules for their own conduct that recognized their responsibilities and that set out to change the behaviour of their managers. The fact that they can never be wholly successful does not mean that they have simply failed.

Our questioning observer is thus armed with a set of measures against which a firm's CSR claims can be assessed:

- Is the external rhetoric matched by detailed internal standards covering relevant issues? What are relevant will depend on the firm and where it does business. If, for example, it operates in countries where bribery is common, it can be expected to have a policy on bribes. Oil or mining companies operating in regions of ecological importance need environmental standards more than do other firms.
- Are the internal standards enforced, notably through reward and PMSs?
- Is the policy responsive to new concerns? Does it evolve? And does it have a place for employee voice?
- Is there evidence that potential disasters and escalations in decision-making have been addressed, or is the culture in practice simply reactive?
- Are standards meaningfully imposed on suppliers, and is there evidence that suppliers with whom employees interact engage in more than lip service?

The observer himself or herself should also have some tools with which to think about his or her own behaviour in relation to themes such as CSR. If he or she works in a firm with a social responsibility statement he or she might ask whether it offers any useful guidance in how to balance different expectations? Does it, for example, suggest how a conflict between production demands and safety, or between profits and the environment, can be addressed? Does it offer training on such questions? Is the context one in which concerns can be raised and debated, or is closed? Do PMSs explicitly address social responsibility issues? And are employees able to draw on sources of ideas from outside the firm? In relation to the last question, we are thinking of the degree to which CSR is presented as a tool kit designed from above, or alternatively as a set of less certain principles, and the degree to which employees are treated as citizens who are able to bring in their own ideas, rather than primarily as corporate subjects.

In terms of one's own behaviour, the key lesson is that CSR is a language that can be used in various ways, and even turned upon itself. It certainly defines the world, but not totally, and individuals can to a degree alter it. But on the basis of what principles? Here we need to consider questions of ethics.

Business Ethics

The interest in CSR is one part of a wider interest in business ethics, a subject that has seen substantial growth recently. In the wake of various corporate scandals, the need for ethical standards is widely stated. Estimates suggest that around 80 per cent of large firms have statements of ethical principles. Yet attempts to develop such principles go back at least as far as the Greek philosophers, and ethical issues long impinged on business, for example in defining the boundaries between legitimate business behaviour, sharp practice, and unambiguously illegitimate actions. And there are examples throughout the history of capitalism of entrepreneurs who have set out to conduct business according to philanthropic principles. The current interest is simply the latest reflection of established concerns. Jackall (1988: 4–5), for example, attributes interest in the 1980s to 'the Watergate crisis and its spillover into business' together with 'a series of corporate and governmental scandals'. We can easily replace the references with more recent scandals and ask what is new.

We should also note that the issues are unavoidable. One well-known argument appears to state the opposite: Milton Friedman is celebrated for his robust defence of the view that firms are there to focus on profits, not engage in ethical debate, and yet he stressed the need to conform not only to the letter of the law but also to ethical custom (Barry 1998: 7). Customs are, however, variable and socially generated, and much harder to identify than legal standards. They are also likely to contain mutually contradictory expectations. Any firm following Friedman's approach will have to take some view as to what the prevailing customs say and what parts of them are to be followed.

Some commentators also argue that it is not the case that unethical behaviour has become more common; it is, rather, that there is more media, public, and pressure group concern. This is a very uncritical view that neglects the key lessons of studies of crime and deviance. First, there is no reliable historical information on rates of behaviour. Second, and more fundamentally, what is deemed to be ethical or criminal is shaped by processes of social definition, so that what is acceptable in one time and place is seen as unethical or even illegal in another. Hence one key way into the issue of ethics is to assess what people in fact do.

Jackall (1988: 6), for example, focuses on 'moral rules-in-use fashioned within the personal and structural constraints of one's organization'. This study, based on interviews with managers and close observation in three US firms (in the textiles, chemicals, and public relations sectors) identifies some of the key constraints faced by managers. They include the following:

- *Avoiding responsibility*. Senior managers would push responsibility onto others; in the words of a 'high-level executive', 'a lot of bosses don't give explicit directions. They just give a statement of objectives, and then they can criticize subordinates who fail to meet their goals' (Jackall 1988: 20). A blame culture was common.
- *Social uncertainty*. Decisions could be changed suddenly, and maintaining the goodwill of superiors was crucial. Promotion was based on reputation and perceived loyalty rather than any more objective skills. Fear and anxiety were the result.
- *A sense of isolation from and distrust by the rest of society*. Managers felt that their contribution to economic progress was not understood and that the public often took a simplistic view of problems. For example, a scare about the potentially carcinogenic properties of a food product neglected the small size of the risk and the fact that the product had other benefits (in this case, reducing the dangers of botulism).

Jackall's conclusion is bleak: 'the real meaning of work...becomes keeping one's eye on the main chance' and managers help to create and sustain 'a society where morality becomes indistinguishable from the quest for one's own survival and advantage' (Jackall 1988: 202, 204).

Yet this seems to be to identify a tendency in modern society and treat it as the sole determinant of behaviour. One of Jackall's other key points is a lack of fixity of expectations, which means that people have the space to make choices. Jackall also mentions sources of ethical standards, such as a belief in producing goods of value to society and a strong commitment to the satisfactions of helping to make a production facility function. And if people behaved literally as he suggests there would be no moral order at all. Some sense of the limits to behaviour is provided by the work of the celebrated criminologist Clinard (1983) who turned his attention to corporate ethics. He interviewed sixty-four retired managers from large industrial firms in the USA. Reported pressures were not as widespread as might have been expected: a fifth, for example, reported pressures to show profits and control costs. And only one in ten said that such pressure led to an encouragement to violate their own ethical standards.

What, then, are the pressures towards ethical behaviour in business? The most obvious ones are the combined effects of regulatory bodies and pressure groups; Clinard found that managers stress government regulation. Further evidence here is summarized in Box 11.2. Then there are the internal standards, which are increasingly common, that firms themselves adopt. These will be more influential the more that they are formal and the more that they set specific standards for performance which are monitored and enforced. Demands from worker representatives and the threat of whistle blowers are further sources of checks on malfeasance. Disciplinary action against rule-breakers might be a further control. As Fisse and Braithwaite (1993: 9) argue, however, such sanction appears to be used rarely, and this is the 'dark side of corporate self-regulation about which little is known by outsiders'. Finally, the values that people themselves espouse will help to shape the moral climate of the workplace.

The limits of the view that people are self-serving agents, and hence that the only way of inducing desired behaviour is to affect the balance of costs and benefits of certain actions, are demonstrated by Hirschman (1985). People have abilities including those of self-evaluation, self-reflection and the expression of voice, and interests in membership of groups. Values are not fixed, and, for example, the propensity of a company to pollute the environment can be changed through norms as well as through the price system.

We need to elaborate on the last point. As just indicated, and as emphasized throughout this book, values are not fixed things that are imported into organizations. Organizations create their own codes of conduct; the 'fiddles' discussed in Chapter 5 exist, not because the people practising them are individually disposed to fiddle, but because of the

Box 11.2 Is correction always better than punishment?

Braithwaite (2002) argues that in the sphere of business regulation an approach based on rewarding desirable behaviour may not work as it does in other spheres of life. A key reason, reflecting the discussion in Chapter 5, turns on 'creative compliance': where businesses are rewarded for meeting certain targets they can achieve, the impression but not the substance of the target. Braithwaite's research included US care homes rewarded on the number of patients in an activity programme; they met the targets by wheeling sleeping patients into the activity room and counting them as participating. Underpinning this practice is the difference between regulations and a market. In a market, customers who are duped can walk away, but government inspectors cannot simply close unsatisfactory workplaces to focus on others, and they are subject to legal challenges to their decisions. Braithwaite argues that incentives can work when rewards are small and incentives to fiddle the figures are limited. Praise and encouragement have also been found to be effective but understudied ways to produce compliance; for example, care homes monitored by inspectors using praise were more likely than others to comply with required standards. In general, sanctions buttressed by praise and reward where appropriate is the favoured approach.

structure of the occupation. Values brought into the organization are important, but how far they shape practice in it, or are even counteracted by an occupational culture, depends on the context.

Cultures, moreover, have varying degrees of strength. Where they are very strong, the individual has little option except to conform or quit. And there are numerous examples, probably more plentiful in fiction than in academic study, of groups with initiation rituals and strict norms of behaviour. But 'culture' is often used in a weaker sense, to refer to situations where forms of behaviour are taken for granted and unquestioned but not in fact explicitly supported. Examples include the cases discussed in Chapter 8, and also some of the more celebrated whistleblowing cases. An example is fraud in the European Commission, which was exposed in 1998 by an assistant auditor who later published his own account (Van Buitenen 2000). He describes a culture of secrecy and of toleration of corruption. But this seems to have been more a matter of tacit acceptance than of direct inducement to engage in corrupt practice. An intermediate position is represented by cases such as Enron, where there was a more explicit culture than in the European Commission, driven above all by a drive for profit and a belief that enormous rewards were available and desirable. In such a context, the steps from aggressive selfserving to malpractice were short and simple.

The conclusion offered by Legge (forthcoming) is a simple and powerful one: ethics are not 'purely situational' but 'absolute ethical codes are resources upon which all organizational stakeholders draw to justify their actions and further their interests'. We would add that actors may not be furthering *only* their own interests. They may also be genuinely improving the way in which an organization works. And even in the absence of such clear positive sum results it is likely that attempts to pursue interests will have unintended consequences that other actors can exploit. For example, the rhetoric of CSR creates opportunities that groups other than its sponsors can turn to their own ends.

Our observer can thus use propositions such as the following to think through the expectations that organizations have of him or her, and he or she of them.

- The norms and values of concrete situations do not totally determine opportunities for action. Norms and values from outside can be deployed to indicate alternatives.
- It is true that some contexts are more powerfully determining than others, and thinking about how strongly they constrain behaviour will help to decide on possible courses of action. Careful consideration of the constraints will suggest what actions are feasible and what are not. In addition, if constraints are to be overcome, alliances may need to be built.
- Essentially, in any situation there is the choice between 'voice' (expressing views that reflect one's own interests, possibly in concert with others) and 'exit' (which may be done quietly, or as part of a conscious decision to blow the whistle while recognizing that whistle-blowing is part of an exit strategy, or as the unintended result of blowing the whistle). Assessing the costs and benefits of different lines of action may help to focus one's thinking.
- Adopting a line of action entails rejecting others. Continually reviewing options may lead to intellectual paralysis, but periodic reviews may have value. PMSs claim to help in this process. Though, as we saw in Chapter 5, they are often driven by other agendas, this fact does not necessarily empty them of all value.

These observations underline the political processes of organizations. We have tried in this book to show how these processes operate and to offer ideas for thinking about them. But these ideas provide no more than a perspective. Applying—and, we hope, questioning—it is a task for action, as people contend with the challenges, both old and new, of organizational life.

REFERENCES

ABOLAFIA, M. Y. (1996). *Making Markets*. Boston, MA: Harvard University Press.

ACKER, J. (1990). 'Hierarchies, Jobs, Bodies: A Theory of Gendered Organizations', *Gender and Society*, 4: 139–58.

—— (2004). 'Gender, Capitalism and Globalization', *Critical Sociology*, 30: 17–41.

ACKROYD, S., and THOMPSON, P. (1999). *Organizational Misbehaviour*. London: Sage.

ADAM, A. and GREEN, E. (1998). 'Gender, Agency and Location and the New Information Society', in B. Loader (ed.), *Cyberspace Divide*. London: Routledge.

ADAMS, G. B., and BALFOUR, D. L. (1999). *Unmasking Administrative Evil*. Thousand Oaks: Sage.

ADLER, N. (2002). 'Global Managers: No Longer Men Alone', *International Journal of Human Resource Management*, 13: 743–60.

ADLER, P. S. (2001). 'Market, Hierarchy and Trust', *Organization Science*, 12: 215–34.

ALVESSON, M., and THOMPSON, P. (2004). 'Post-bureaucracy?', in S. Ackroyd, R. Batt, P. Thompson, and P. Tolbert (eds.), *A Handbook of Work and Organisation*. Oxford: Oxford University Press.

ANDERSON, B. (2000). *Doing the Dirty Work: The Global Politics of Domestic Labour*. London: Zed.

APPELBAUM, E., and BATT, R. (1994). *The New American Workplace*. Ithaca: ILR Press.

—— and BERG, P. (1996). 'Financial Market Constraints and Business Strategy in the USA', in J. Michie and J. G. Smith (eds.), *Creating Industrial Capacity*. Oxford: Oxford University Press.

—— BAILEY, T., BERG, P., and KALLEBERG, A. L. (2002). *Shared Work/Value Care: New Norms for Organizing Market Work and Unpaid Care Work*. Washington: Economic Policy Institute.

ARAM, J. D. (1989). 'The Paradox of Interdependent Relations in the Field of Social Issues in Management', *Academy of Management Review*, 14: 266–83.

ARBER, S., and GINN, J. (1995). 'The Mirage of Gender Equality: Occupational Success in the Labour Market and Within Marriage', *British Journal of Sociology*, 46: 21–43.

ARGYRIS, C., and SCHÖN, D. (1978). *Organizational Learning*. Reading, MA: Addison-Wesley.

ARMSTRONG, M., and BARON, A. (1998). *Performance Management*. London: Institute for Personnel and Development.

ARMSTRONG, P., HYMAN, J. D., and GOODMAN, J. F. B. (1981). *Ideology and Shop-Floor Industrial Relations*. London: Croom Helm.

ARMSTRONG, P., MARGINSON, P., EDWARDS, P., and PURCELL, J. (1996). 'Budgetary Control and the Labour Force: Findings from a Survey of Large British Companies', *Management Accounting Research*, 7: 1–23.

ARNESON, R. (1987). 'Meaningful Work and Market Socialism', *Ethics*, 97, 517–45.

ARTHUR, M. B., and ROUSSEAU, D. M. (eds.) (1996). *The Boundaryless Career: A New Employment Principle for a New Organizational Era*. New York: Oxford University Press.

Australian Bureau of Statistics (1998). *Community Services*. Canberra: ABS.

BACH, S. (2000). 'From Performance Appraisal to Performance Management', in S. Bach and K. Sisson (eds.), *Personnel Management*, 3rd edn. Oxford: Blackwell.

BACKETT, K. (1987). 'The Negotiation of Fatherhood', in C. Lewis and M. O'Brien (eds.), *Reassessing Fatherhood: New Observations on Fathers and the Modern Family*. London: Sage.

BACON, N., and BLYTON, P. (2002). 'The Impact of Ownership Change on Industrial Relations, Jobs and Employees' Terms and Conditions', in Y. A. Debrah and I. G. Smith (eds.), *Globalization, Employment and the Workplace*. London: Routledge.

BALDAMUS, W. (1961). *Efficiency and Effort*. London: Tavistock.

BARLOW, G. (1989). 'Deficiencies and the Perpetuation of Power', *Journal of Management Studies*, 26: 493–517.

BARNARD, C., DEAKIN, S., and HOBBS, R. (2003). 'Opting Out of the 48-Hour Week', *Industrial Law Journal*, 32: 223–52.

— — — (2004). 'Reflexive Law, Corporate Social Responsibility and the Evolution of Labour Standards', in O. de Schutter and S. Deakin (eds.), *Social Rights and Market Forces*. Brussels: Bruylant.

BARRY, N. (1998). *Business Ethics*. Basingstoke: Macmillan.

BATSTONE, E., BORASTON, I., and FRENKEL, S. (1977). *Shop Stewards in Action*. Oxford: Blackwell.

— FERNER, A., and TERRY, M. (1983). *Unions on the Board*. Oxford: Blackwell.

BATT, R. (1996). 'From Bureaucracy to Enterprise?', in P. Osterman (ed.), *Broken Ladders*. New York: Oxford University Press.

BAUMAN, Z. (1989). *Modernity and the Holocaust*. Cambridge: Polity.

BAUMOL, W. J., BLINDER, A. S., and WOLFF, E. N. (2003). *Downsizing in America: Reality, Causes and Consequences*. New York: Russell Sage Foundation.

BAZERMAN, M. H., GIULIANO, T., and APPELMAN, A. (1984). 'Escalation of Commitment in Individual and Group Decision Making', *Organizational Behavior and Human Performance*, 33: 141–52.

— LOEWENSTEIN, G., and MOORE, D. A. (2002). 'Why Good Accountants Do Bad Audits', *Harvard Business Review*, 80: 96–102.

BECK, U. (1992). *Risk Society: Towards a New Modernity*. London: Sage.

— (2000*a*). *The Brave New World of Work*. Cambridge: Polity.

— (2000*b*). *What Is Globalization?* Cambridge: Polity.

— and BECK-GERNSHEIM, E. (1995). *The Normal Chaos of Love*. Cambridge: Polity Press.

BECKER, B. E., HUSELID, M. A., and ULRICH, D. (2001). *The HR Scorecard*. Boston: Harvard Business School Press.

BEER, M., and RUH, R. A. (1976). 'Employee Growth through Performance Management', *Harvard Business Review*, 54: 59–66.

BEHREND, H. (1959). 'Financial Incentives as the Expression of a System of Beliefs', *British Journal of Sociology*, 10: 137–47.

BÉLANGER, J., and BJÖRKMAN, T. (1999). 'The ABB Attempt to Reinvent the Multi-national Corporation', in J. Bélanger, C. Berggren, T. Björkman, and C. Kohler (eds.), *Being Local Worldwide: ABB and the Challenge of Global Management*. Ithaca and London: Cornell University Press.

BELL, D. (1996). *The Cultural Contradictions of Capitalism*, rev. edn. New York: Basic.

BENNETT, H. S. (1969). *Life on the English Manor*. Cambridge: Cambridge University Press.

BERGER, P. L., and LUCKMANN, T. (1967). *The Social Construction of Reality*. Harmondsworth: Penguin.

BERLE, A. A., and MEANS, G. C. (1968). *The Modern Corporation and Private Property*, 4th edn. New York: Harcourt, Brace and World.

BEVAN, S., and THOMPSON, M. (1992). *Merit Pay, Performance Appraisal and Attitudes to Women's Work,* Report 234. Brighton: Institute for Manpower Studies.

BIANCHI, S. M., MELISSA, A., MILKIE, L. C., and ROBINSON, J. P. (2000). 'Is Anyone Doing the Housework? Trends in the Gender Division of Household Labor', *Social Forces*, 79: 191–228.

BIGGART, N. W., and GUILLÉN, M. F. (1999). 'Developing Difference', *American Sociological Review*, 64: 722–47.

BILLING, Y. D., and ALVESSON, M. (2000). 'Questioning the Notion of Feminine Leadership: A Critical Perspective on the Gender Labeling of Leadership', *Gender, Work and Organization*, 7: 144–57.

BITTMAN, M., ENGLAND, P., SAYER, L., FOLBRE, N., and MATHESON, G. (2003). 'When Does Gender Trump Money? Bargaining and Time in Household Work', *American Journal of Sociology*, 109: 186–214.

— RICE, J., and WAJCMAN, J. (2004). 'Appliances and their Impact: The Ownership of Domestic Technology and Time Spent on Household Work', *British Journal of Sociology*, 55: 401–23.

BLACKBURN, R. (2002). 'The Enron Debacle and the American Crisis', *New Left Review*, 14: 26–52.

BLAIR, M., and KOCHAN, T. (2000). *The New Relationship: Human Capital in the American Corporation*. Washington: Brookings Institution Press.

BLAU, P. M. (1963). *The Dynamics of Bureaucracy*, rev. edn. Chicago: Chicago University Press.

BLOCK, F. (1980). 'Beyond Relative Autonomy', *Socialist Register*, 227–42.

BLOCK, F. (1990). 'Political Choice and the Multiple "Logics" of Capital', in S. Zukin and P. DiMaggio (eds.), *Structures of Capital*. Cambridge: Cambridge University Press.

BOLTON, S. C., and BOYD, C. (2003). 'Trolley Dolly or Skilled Emotion Manager?: Moving on from Hochschild's Managed Heart', *Work, Employment and Society*, 17: 289–308.

BONACICH, E., and APPELBAUM, R. P. (2000). *Behind the Label*. Berkeley: University of California Press.

BORDO, M. D., EICHENGREEN, B., and IRWIN, D. A. (1999). 'Is Globalization Today Really Different Than Globalization a Hundred Years Ago?', National Bureau of Economic Research Working Paper 7195, June.

BOSCH, G. (1999). 'Working Time: Tendencies and Emerging Issues', *International Labour Review*, 138: 131–49.

BOTTOMORE, T., and RUBEL, M. (1963). *Karl Marx: Selected Writings and Social Philosophy*. Harmondsworth: Penguin.

BOURGUIGNON, F., and MORRISSON, C. (2002). 'Inequality among World Citizens', *American Economic Review*, 92: 327–44.

BOWLES, M., and COATES, G. (1993). 'Image and Substance: the Management of Performance as Rhetoric or Reality?' *Personnel Review*, 22: 3–21.

BOX, S. (1983). *Power, Crime and Mystification*. London: Routledge.

BRADLEY, H. (1999). *Gender and Power in the Workplace*. Basingstoke: Macmillan.

BRAITHWAITE, J. (2002). 'Rewards and Regulation', *Journal of Law and Society*, 29: 12–26.

BRANNEN, J., and MOSS, P. (1991). *Managing Mothers: Dual Earner Households After Maternity Leave*. London: Unwin Hyman.

—— LEWIS, S., NILSEN, A., and SMITHSON, J. (eds.) (2002). *Young Europeans, Work and Family: Futures in Transition*. London: Routledge.

BRANNEN, P., BATSTONE, E., and FATCHETT, D. (1976). *The Worker Directors: A Sociology of Participation*. London: Hutchinson.

BRAVERMAN, H. (1974). *Labor and Monopoly Capital: The Degradation of Work in the Twentieth Century*. New York: Monthly Review Press.

BRENNER, R. (1998). 'Uneven Development and the Long Downturn', *New Left Review*, 229: 1–265.

British Social Attitudes Survey (1992). *Ninth Report*. Aldershot: Dartmouth Publishing.

BROWN, P. (1995). 'Cultural Capital and Social Exclusion: Some Observations on Recent Trends in Education, Employment and the Labour Market', *Work, Employment and Society*, 9: 29–51.

BROWN, W. (1973). *Piecework Bargaining*. London: Heinemann.

—— MARGINSON, P., and WALSH, J. (2003). 'The Management of Pay as the Influence of Collective Bargaining Diminishes', in P. Edwards (ed.), *Industrial Relations*, 2nd edn. Oxford: Blackwell.

BRUCE, A., and BUCK, T. (1997). 'Executive Reward and Corporate Governance', in K. Keasey, S. Thompson and M. Wright (eds.), *Corporate Governance*. Oxford: Oxford University Press.

BUCHAN, N. R., CROSON, R. T. A., and DAWES, R. M. (2002). 'Swift Neighbors and Persistent Strangers', *American Journal of Sociology*, 108: 168–206.

BUDIG, M. J. and ENGLAND, P. (2001). 'The Wage Penalty for Motherhood', *American Sociological Review*, 66: 204–25.

BURAWOY, M. (1979). *Manufacturing Consent*. Chicago: University of Chicago Press.

— (1985). *The Politics of Production*. London: Verso.

BURCHELL, B. (2002). 'Flexibility and the reorganisation of work', in B. Burchell, D. Ladipo, and Wilkinson, F. (eds.), *Job Insecurity and Work Intensification*. London: Routledge.

CALLON, M. (ed.) (1998). 'Introduction', *The Laws of the Markets*. Oxford: Blackwell.

CAPPELLI, P. (1999). *The New Deal at Work*. Boston: Harvard Business School Press.

CARLETON, W. T., NELSON, J. M., and WEISBACH, M. S. (1998). 'The Influence of Institutions on Corporate Governance through Private Negotiations', *Journal of Finance*, 53: 1335–62.

CASEY, C. (1995). *Work, Self and Society*. London: Routledge.

CASTELLS, M. (1996). *The Rise of the Network Society*. Oxford: Blackwell.

— (2001). *The Internet Galaxy*. Oxford: Oxford University Press.

CBI (Confederation of British Industry) TUC (Trades Union Congress) (2001). *Submission to the Productivity Initiative*, October. London: CBI and TUC. Available at *www.tuc.org.uk/economy*

CEC (Commission for the European Communities) (1997). *Partnership for a New Organisation of Work*. Bulletin of the European Communities, Supplement 4/97. Luxembourg: Office for the Official Publications of the European Communities.

CHENG, C. (ed.) (1996). *Masculinities in Organizations*. London: Sage.

CLARKBERG, M., and MOEN, P. (2001). 'Understanding the Time-Squeeze: Married Couples' Preferred and Actual Work-Hour Strategies', *American Behavioral Scientist*, 44: 1115–35.

CLARKE, L. (1999). *Mission Improbable*. Chicago: University of Chicago Press.

CLARKE, T., and BOSTOCK, R. (1997). 'Governance in Germany', in K. Keasey, S. Thompson, and M. Wright (eds.), *Corporate Governance*. Oxford: Oxford University Press.

CLINARD, M. B. (1983). *Corporate Ethics and Crime*. Beverley Hills: Sage.

COATES, D. (2000). *Models of Capitalism*. Cambridge: Polity Press.

COCKBURN, C. (1983). *Brothers: Male Dominance and Technological Change*. London: Pluto Press.

— (1991). *In the Way of Women: Men's Resistance to Sex Equality in Organizations*. London: Macmillan.

COHEN, G. A. (1978). *Karl Marx's Theory of History*. Oxford: Clarendon.

COHEN, L., and MALLON, M. (1999). 'The Transition from Organizational Employment to Portfolio Working: Perceptions of "Boundarylessness"', *Work, Employment and Society*, 13: 329–52.

COHEN, M. D., MARCH, J. G., and OLSEN, J. P. (1972). 'A Garbage Can Model of Organizational Choice', *Administrative Science Quarterly*, 17: 1–25.

COHEN, R., and KENNEDY, P. (2000). *Global Sociology*. Basingstoke: Palgrave.

COHEN, S. (2001). *States of Denial*. Cambridge: Polity Press.

COLLINSON, D. L. (1999). 'Surviving the Rigs', *Organization Studies*, 20: 579–600.

COLLINSON, D., KNIGHTS, D., and COLLINSON, M. (1990). *Managing to Discriminate*. London: Routledge.

COLLOM, E. (2003). 'Two Classes and One Vision?', *Work and Occupations*, 30: 62–96.

COMOR, E. A. (1998). *Communication, Commerce and Power*. Macmillan: Basingstoke.

COSH, A., and HUGHES, A. (1997). 'The Changing Anatomy of Corporate Control and the Market for Executives in the UK', in S. Deakin and A. Hughes (eds.), *Enterprise and Community*. Oxford: Blackwell.

COWAN, R. S. (1979). 'From Virginia Dare to Virginia Slims: Women and Technology in American Life', *Technology and Culture*, 20: 51–63.

COWTON, C. J., and DOPSON, S. (2002). 'Foucault's Prison? Management in an Automotive Distributor', *Management Accounting Research*, 13: 191–213.

CRAYPO, C. (1997). 'The Impact of Changing Corporate Strategies on Communities, Unions and Workers in the United States of America', *Journal of Law and Society*, 24: 10–25.

CROMPTON, R., and HARRIS, F. (1998). 'Gender Relations and Employment: The Impact of Occupation', *Work, Employment and Society*, 12: 297–315.

— and SANDERSON, K. (1990). *Gendered Jobs and Social Change*. London: Unwin Hyman.

CROUCH, C. (1999). *Social Change in Western Europe*. Oxford: Oxford University Press.

CULLY, M., WOODLAND, S., O'REILLY, A., and DIX, G. (1999). *Britain at Work*. London: Routledge.

CURRAN, M. (1988). 'Gender and Recruitment: People and Places in the Labour Market', *Work, Employment and Society*, 2: 335–51.

CURRIE, W. (1997). 'Computerising the Stock Exchange', *New Technology, Work and Employment*, 12: 75–83.

CUTLER, D. M., POTERBA, J. M., and SUMMERS, L. H. (1989). 'What Moves Stock Prices?', *Journal of Portfolio Management*, 15: 4–12.

DAVIS, G. F., and MCADAM, D. (2000). 'Corporations, Classes and Social Movements after Managerialism', *Research in Organizational Behavior*, 22: 193–236.

DEAL, T., and KENNEDY, A. (2000). *The New Corporate Cultures*. London: Texere.

DESAI, M. (2002). *Marx's Revenge*. London: Verso.

DEX, S. (1987). *Women's Occupational Mobility: A Lifetime Perspective*. London: Macmillan.

DEX, S. and SMITH, C. (2002). *The Nature and Pattern of Family-Friendly Employment Policies in Britain*. Bristol: The Policy Press.

DIAMOND, T. (1992). *Making Gray Gold: Narratives of Nursing Home Care*. Chicago: University of Chicago Press.

DICKENS, L. (1999). 'Beyond the Business Case: a Three-Pronged Approach to Equality Action', *Human Resource Management Journal*, 9: 9–20.

DiMAGGIO, P. (ed.) (2001). 'Introduction: Making Sense of the Contemporary Firm and Prefiguring its Future', *The Twenty-First Century Firm*. Princeton: Princeton University Press.

—— and POWELL, W. (1983). 'The Iron Cage Revisited', *American Sociological Review*, 48: 147–60.

DOBBIN, F., and BOYCHUK, T. (1999). 'National Employment Systems and Job Autonomy', *Organization Studies*, 20: 257–91.

DONNELLY, S. (2000). 'The Public Interest and the Company in Germany', in J. Parkinson, A. Gamble and G. Kelly, (eds.), *The Political Economy of the Company*. Oxford: Hart.

DORE, R. (1985). 'Authority or Benevolence', *Government and Opposition*, 20: 196–217.

—— (2000). *Stock Market Capitalism*. Oxford: Oxford University Press.

DOREMUS, P. N., KELLER, W. W., PAULY, L. W., and REICH, S. (1998). *The Myth of the Global Corporation*. Princeton: Princeton University Press.

DOWNES, D., and ROCK, P. (2003). *Understanding Deviance*, 4th edn. Oxford: Oxford University Press.

DRUMMOND, H. (1996a). *Escalation in Decision-Making*. Oxford: Oxford University Press.

—— (1996b). 'The Politics of Risk', *Journal of Information Technology*, 11: 347–57.

—— (1998). 'Is Escalation Always Irrational?' *Organization Studies*, 19: 911–29.

DU GAY, P. (1996). *Consumption and Identity at Work*. London: Sage.

DUDLEY, K. M. (1994). *The End of the Line*. Chicago: University of Chicago Press.

DUNNING, J. H. (2000). 'Globalization and the New Geography of FDI', in N. Woods, (ed.), *The Political Economy of Globalization*. Basingstoke: Macmillan.

EAGLY, A., MAKHIJANI, M., and KLONSKY, B. (1992). 'Gender and the Evaluation of Leaders: A Meta-Analysis', *Psychological Bulletin*, 111: 3–22.

EATWELL, J. and TAYLOR, L. (2000). *Global Finance at Risk*. Cambridge: Polity Press.

Economist, The (2001). 'A Survey of the Near Future', 3 November.

EDMONDSON, A. C. (1996). 'Learning from Mistakes is Easier Said than Done', *Journal of Applied Behavioral Science*, 32: 5–28.

EDWARDS, P. K. (1986). *Conflict at Work*. Oxford: Blackwell.

—— (ed.) (2003). 'The Employment Relationship and the Field of Industrial Relations', in *Industrial Relations*, 2nd edn. Oxford: Blackwell.

EDWARDS, P. K., and COLLINSON, M. (2002). 'Empowerment and Managerial Labor Strategies', *Work and Occupations*, 29: 271–90.

—— and SCULLION, H. (1982). *The Social Organization of Industrial Conflict*. Oxford: Blackwell.

—— and WHITSTON, C. (1994). 'Disciplinary Practice', *Work, Employment and Society*, 8: 317–38.

—— —— and REES, C. (1998). 'The Determinants of Employee Responses to Total Quality Management', *Organization Studies*, 19: 450–75.

—— FERNER, A., and SISSON, K. (1996). 'The Conditions for International Human Resource Management', *International Journal of Human Resource Management*, 7: 20–40.

—— GEARY, J., and SISSON, K. (2002). 'New Forms of Work Organization in the Workplace', in J. Belanger, A. Giles, and G. Murray (eds.), *Work and Employment Relations in the High-Performance Workplace*. London: Continuum.

EEF (Engineering Employers' Federation)/CIPD (Chartered Institute of Personnel and Development) (2003). *Maximising Employee Potential and Business Performance*. London: EEF/CIPD. Available at www.cipd.co.uk/surveys

EHRENREICH, B. (2001). *Nickel and Dimed: On (Not) Getting by in America*. New York: Metropolitan.

—— and HOCHSCHILD, A. (eds.) (2003). *Global Women: Nannies, Maids and Sex Workers in the New Economy*. New York: Metropolitan.

EICHENGREEN, B. E. (2001). *Capitalizing on Globalization*. Asian Development Bank, Economics and Research Department Working Papers, 1.

—— (2002*a*). *Financial Crises and What to Do About Them*. Oxford: Oxford University Press.

—— (2002*b*). *Capitalizing on Globalization*. Asian Development Bank, Economics and Research Department Working Papers, 1.

ELLIOTT, A. (2002). 'Beck's Sociology of Risk', *Sociology*, 36: 293–315.

ENDO, K. (1994). '*Satei* (Personal Assessment) and Interworker Conflict in Japan', *Industrial Relations*, 33: 70–82.

ENGLAND, P. (1992). *Comparable Worth: Theories and Evidence*. New York: Aldine de Gruyter.

EPSTEIN, C. F. and KALLEBERG, A. (eds.) (2004). *Fighting for Time: Shifting Boundaries of Work and Social Life*. New York: Russell Sage Foundation.

Equal Opportunities Commission (2002). *Women and Men in Britain*. Manchester: EOC.

EVANS, S., and HUDSON, M. (1994). 'From Collective Bargaining to "Personal" Contracts', *Industrial Relations Journal*, 25: 305–14.

EVETTS, J. (1996). *Gender and Career in Science and Engineering*. London: Taylor and Francis.

FAGAN, C. (2001). 'Time, Money and the Gender Order: Work Orientations and Working-Time Preferences in Britain', *Gender, Work and Organizations*, 8: 239–66.

FAGENSON, E. (ed.) (1993). *Women in Management: Trends, Issues, and Challenges in Managerial Diversity*. Newbury Park: Sage.

FELSTEAD, A., GALLIE, D., and GREEN, F. (2002). *Work Skills in Britain, 1986–2001* Nottingham: DfES Publications.

—— JEWSON, N., PHIZACKLEA, A., and WALTERS, S. (2002). 'The Option to Work at Home', *New Technology, Work and Employment*, 17: 204–23.

FENTON-O'CREEVY, M. (1995). 'Empowerment', in N. Nicholson (ed.), *Blackwell Encyclopedic Dictionary of Organizational Behavior*. Oxford: Blackwell.

—— (2001). 'Employee Involvement and the Middle Manager', *Human Resource Management Journal*, 11: 24–40.

FERGUSON, N. (2001). *The Cash Nexus*. London: Allen Lane.

FERNER, A. (1985). 'Political Constraints and Management Strategies', *British Journal of Industrial Relations*, 22: 47–70.

—— and QUINTANILLA, J. (2002). 'Between Globalization and Capitalist Variety', *European Journal of Industrial Relations*, 8: 243–50.

FIREBAUGH, G., and GOESLING, B. (2004). 'Accounting for Recent Declines in Global Income Inequality', *American Journal of Sociology*, 110: 283–312.

FISSE, B., and BRAITHWAITE, J. (1993). *Corporations, Crime and Accountability*. Cambridge: Cambridge University Press.

FLETCHER, C. (1999). 'The Implications of Research on Gender Differences in Self-Assessment and 360 Degree Appraisal', *Human Resource Management Journal*, 9: 39–47.

FLIGSTEIN, N. (1990). *The Transformation of Corporate Control*. Cambridge, MA: Harvard University Press.

—— (2001). *The Architecture of Markets*. Princeton: Princeton University Press.

—— and SHIN, T. (2004). 'The Shareholder Value Society: A Review of the Changes in Working Conditions and Inequality in the United States, 1976–2000', in K. Neckerman (ed.), *Social Inequality*. New York: Russell Sage Foundation.

FOX, A. (1985). *History and Heritage*. London: Allen and Unwin.

FRANZWAY, S. (2003). 'You Need to Care. The Work of Care Between Home and Market', Paper presented for The Australian Sociological Association Annual Conference, UNE, Armidale, Australia.

FRASER, N. (1997). 'After the Family Wage: A Postindustrial Thought Experiment', in Swedish Council for Planning and Coordination of Research, *Crossing Borders: Gender and Citizenship in Transition*. SCPCR: Stockholm.

FREEMAN, R. B., and MEDOFF, J. L. (1984). *What Do Unions Do?* New York: Basic.

—— and ROGERS, J. (1999). *What Workers Want*. Ithaca: Cornell University Press.

FREGE, C. M. (2002). 'A Critical Assessment of the Theoretical and Empirical Research on Works Councils', *British Journal of Industrial Relations*, 40: 221–48.

FRENCH, J. R. P., and RAVEN, B. H. (1959). 'The Social Bases of Power', in D. Cartwright (ed.), *Studies in Social Power*. Ann Arbor: University of Michigan Press.

FRENKEL, S. J., and KURUVILLA, S. (2002). 'Logics of Action, Globalization, and Changing Employment Relations in China, India, Malaysia and the Philippines', *Industrial and Labor Relations Review*, 55: 387–412.

FRENKEL, S. J., and SCOTT, D. (2002). 'Compliance, Collaboration and Codes of Practice', *California Management Review*, 45: 29–49.

FULLER, S. R., and ALDAG, R. J. (1998). 'Organizational Tonypandy: Lesson from a Quarter Century of the Groupthink Phenomenon', *Organizational Behavior and Human Decision Processes*, 73: 163–84.

GALINSKY, E. (1999). *Ask the Children: What America's Children Really Think About Working Parents*. New York: William Morrow.

—— and BOND, J., (1998). *The 1998 Business Work-Life Study: A Sourcebook*. New York: Families and Work Institute.

GALLIE, D. (1996). 'Skill, Gender and the Quality of Employment', in R. Crompton, D. Gallie, and K. Purcell (eds.), *Changing Forms of Employment*. London: Routledge.

—— FELSTEAD, A., and GREEN, F. (2001). 'Employer Policies and Organizational Commitment in Britain, 1992–97', *Journal of Management Studies*, 38: 1081–101.

—— WHITE, M., CHENG, Y., and TOMLINSON, M. (1998). *Restructuring the Employment Relationship*. Oxford: Oxford University Press.

GARRETT, G. (2000). 'Shrinking States?' in N. Woods, (ed.), *The Political Economy of Globalization*. Basingstoke: Macmillan.

GERSHUNY, J. (2000). *Changing Times: Work and Leisure in Postindustrial Society*. Oxford: Oxford University Press.

—— and ROBINSON, J. P. (1988). 'Historical Changes in the Household Division of Labour', *Demography*, 25: 537–52.

—— GODWIN, M., and JONES, S. (1994). 'The Domestic Labour Revolution: A Process of Lagged Adaption?' in M. Anderson, F. Bechhofer, and J. Gershuny (eds.), *The Social and Political Economy of the Household*. Oxford: Oxford University Press.

GHERARDI, S. (1995). *Gender, Symbolism and Organizational Cultures*. London: Sage.

GIDDENS, A. (1977). *Studies in Social and Political Theory*. London: Hutchinson.

—— (1990). *The Consequences of Modernity*. Cambridge: Polity Press.

—— (1991). *Modernity and Self-Identity: Self and Society in the Late Modern Age*. Stanford: Stanford University Press.

—— (1992). *The Transformation of Intimacy*. Cambridge: Polity Press.

—— (1999). *Runaway World*. Reith Lectures. London: BBC. Available at *www. news. bbc.co.uk/ hi/English/static/events/reith_99*

GILLE, Z., and Ó RIAIN, S. (2002). 'Global Ethnography', *Annual Review of Sociology*, 28: 271–95.

GILPIN, R. (2002). *The Challenge of Global Capitalism*, rev. edn. Princeton: Princeton University Press.

GIMPL, M. L., and DAKIN, S. R. (1984). 'Management and Magic', *California Management Review*, 27: 125–37.

GIROUARD, M. (1980). *Life in the English Country House; A Social and Architectural History*. Harmondsworth: Penguin.

GLASS, J., and ESTES, S. (1997). 'The Family Responsive Workplace', *Annual Review of Sociology*, 23: 289–313.

GLASSNER, B. (1999). *The Culture of Fear*. New York: Basic.

Global Information Network (2002). *U.S. Women: Number of Women in Top Corporate Jobs Rises*. New York: Global Information Network.

GOLDSCHMIDT-CLERMONT, L. (1991). *Economic Management of Non-Market Household Production: Relating Purposes and Valuation Methodologies*, World Employment Programme Research Working Paper No. 174. Geneva: ILO.

GOLDTHORPE, J. H. (2001). 'Globalization and Social Class', Vortrag 9, Mannheimer Zentrum für Europäische Sozialforschung.

GOOS, M., and MANNING, A. (2003). 'McJobs and MacJobs: The Growing Polarisation of Jobs in the UK' in R. Dickens, P. Gregg, and J. Wadsworth (eds.), *The*

Labour Market Under New Labour: The State of Working Britain. New York: Palgrave Macmillan.

GORDON, D. (1996). *Fat and Mean: The Corporate Squeeze of Working Americans and the Myth of Managerial Downsizing*. New York: The Free Press.

GOULDNER, A. W. (1954). *Patterns of Industrial Bureaucracy*. New York: The Free Press.

GRAMSCI, A. (1971). 'Selections from the Prison Notebooks', in Q. Hoare and G. Nowell Smith (eds.), *Selections from the Prison Notebooks of Antonio Gramsci*. London: Lawrence and Wishart.

GRANT, R., LIPPARINI, A., LORENZONI, G., and ROMANELLI, E. (2003). 'Who needs multinationals? Lessons from Open-Source Software' in J. Birkinshaw, S. Ghoshal, C. Markides, J. Stopford, and G. Yip (eds.), *The Future of the Multinational Company*. London: Wiley.

GRATTON, L., HOPE-HAILEY, V., STILES, P., and TRUSS, C. (1999). *Strategic Human Resource Management: Rhetoric and Human Reality*. Oxford: Oxford University Press.

GRAY, J. (1998). *False Dawn*. London: Granta.

GREEN, F. (2001). 'It's Been A Hard Day's Night: The Concentration and Intensification of Work in Late Twentieth-Century Britain', *British Journal of Industrial Relations*, 39: 53–80.

—— (2003). 'The Demands of Work', in R. Dickens, P. Gregg, and J. Wadsworth (eds.), *The Labour Market Under New Labour: The State of Working Britain*. New York: Palgrave MacMillan.

GREGSON, N., and LOWE, M. (1993). 'Renegotiating the Domestic Division of Labour? A Study of Dual Career Households in North East and South East England', *Sociological Review*, 41: 475–505.

GRIMSHAW, D., BEYNON, H., RUBERY, R., and WARD, K. (2002). 'The Restructuring of Career Paths in Large Service Sector Organizations: "Delayering", Upskilling and Polarisation', *Sociological Review*, 3: 89–115.

—— WARD, K., RUBERY, R., and BEYNON, H. (2001). 'Organisations and the Transformation of the Internal Labour Market', *Work, Employment and Society*, 15: 25–54.

GRINT, K. (1993). 'What's Wrong with Performance Appraisals?' *Human Resource Management Journal*, 3: 61–77.

GRUNBERG, L. (1986). 'Workplace Relations in the Economic Crisis', *Sociology*, 20: 503–30.

—— (1991). 'The Plywood Co-operatives', in R. Russell and V. Rus (eds.), *International Handbook of Participation in Organizations*: Vol 2, *Ownership and Participation*. Oxford: Oxford University Press.

HALFORD, S., SAVAGE, M., and WITZ, A. (1997). *Gender, Careers and Organisations*. London: Macmillan.

HALL, A. (1993). 'The Corporate Construction of Occupational Health and Safety', *Canadian Journal of Sociology*, 18: 1–20.

HALL, P. A., and SOSKICE, D. (eds.) (2001). 'An Introduction to Varieties of Capitalism', in *Varieties of Capitalism*. Oxford: Oxford University Press.

HANDY, C. (1995). *The Empty Raincoat*. London: Arrow.

HARDIN, G. (1968). 'The Tragedy of the Commons', *Science*, 162: 1243–8.

HARDY, C., and LEIBA-O'SULLIVAN, S. (1998). 'The Power Behind Empowerment', *Human Relations*, 51: 451–83.

HARKNESS, S. (2003). 'The Household Division of Labour: Changes in Families' Allocation of Paid and Unpaid Work, 1992–2002', in R. Dickens, P. Gregg, and J. Wadsworth (eds.), *The Labour Market Under New Labour*. Basingstoke: Palgrave.

HEALY, G. (1997). 'The Industrial Relations of Appraisal', *Industrial Relations Journal*, 28: 206–20.

HEARN, J., and PARKIN, W. (1987). *Sex at Work: The Power and Paradox of Organization Sexuality*. Brighton: Wheatsheaf Books.

—, SHEPPARD, D., TANCRED-SHERIFF, P., and BURRELL, G. (eds.) (1989). *The Sexuality of Organization*. London: Sage.

HECKMAN, J., LYONS, T., and TODD, P. (2000). 'Understanding Black–White Differentials, 1960–1990', *American Economic Review*, 90: 344–9.

HECKSCHER, C. (1995). *White Collar Blues: Management Loyalties in an Age of Corporate Restructuring*. New York: Basic Books.

HEERY, E., and SALMON, J. (eds.) (2000). 'The Insecurity Thesis', in *The Insecure Workforce*. London: Routledge.

HELD, D., McGREW, A., GOLDBLATT, D., and PERRATON, J. (1999). *Global Transformations*. Cambridge: Polity Press.

HELGESON, P. (1990). *The Female Advantage*. Sage: London.

HELLEINER, E. (1994). *States and the Re-Emergence of Global Finance*. Ithaca: Cornell University Press.

HELLER, F., PUSIĆ, E., STRAUSS, G., and WILPERT, B. (1998). *Organizational Participation*. Oxford: Oxford University Press.

HERTZBERG, F. (1966). *Work and the Nature of Man*. New York: Staples Press.

HEWLETT, S. (2002). *Creating a Life: Professional Women and the Quest for Children*. New York: Talk Miramax.

HIRSCHMAN, A. O. (1982). 'Rival Interpretations of Market Society', *Journal of Economic Literature*, 20: 1463–84.

— (1985). 'Against Parsimony', *Economics and Philosophy*, 1: 7–21.

HOBBS, P., and JEFFERIS, K. (1990). 'So How Many Co-operatives Are There?', in G. Jenkins and M. Poole (eds.), *New Forms of Ownership*. London: Routledge.

HOCHSCHILD, A. (1983). *The Managed Heart: Commercialization of Human Feeling*. Berkeley: University of California Press.

— (1997). *The Time Bind*. New York: Metropolitan Books.

HODSON, R. (2001). *Dignity at Work*. Cambridge: Cambridge University Press.

HOPWOOD, A. G. (1973). *An Accounting System and Managerial Behaviour*. Farnborough: Saxon House.

HOSKIN, K., and MACVE, R. (1994). 'Writing, Examining, Disciplining', in A. G. Hopwood and P. Miller (eds.), *Accounting as Social and Institutional Practice*. Cambridge: Cambridge University Press.

Hotchkiss, J., and Moore, R. (1999). 'On the Evidence of a Working Spouse Penalty in the Managerial Labor Market', *Industrial and Labor Relations Review*, 52: 410–23.

Howell, D. (1991). 'Railway Safety and Labour Unrest', in C. Wrigley and J. Shepherd (eds.), *On the Move*. London: Hambledon.

Hsiung, P. (1996). *Living Rooms as Factories: Class, Gender and the Satellite Factory System in Taiwan*. Philadelphia: Temple University Press.

Hudson, M. (2002). 'Flexibility and the Reorganisation of Work' in B. Burchell, D. Ladipo, and F. Wilkinson (eds.), *Job Insecurity and Work Intensification*. London: Routledge.

Humphreys, M., and Brown, A. D. (2002). 'Narratives of Organizational Identity and Identification', *Organization Studies*, 23: 421–47.

Humphries, J. (1977). 'Class Struggle and the Persistence of the Working Class Family', *Cambridge Journal of Economics*, 1: 241–58.

Hutton, W. (1995). *The State We're In*. London: Jonathan Cape.

—— (2002). *The World We're In*. London: Little Brown.

Hyman, R. (1987). 'Strategy or Structure', *Work, Employment and Society*, 1: 25–56.

Industrial Relations Services (2002). *Employment Review*, Issue 766, UK.

Ironmonger, J. (2004). 'Bringing up Bobby and Betty: The Inputs and Outputs of Childcare Time', in N. Folbre and M. Bittman (eds.), *Family Time: The Social Organisation of Care*. New York: Routledge.

Jackall, R. (1988). *Moral Mazes: the World of Corporate Managers*. New York: Oxford University Press.

Jackson, G. (2003). 'Corporate Governance in Germany and Japan', in K. Yamamura and W. Streeck (eds.), *The End of Diversity?* Ithaca: Cornell University Press.

Jacobi, O., Keller, B., and Müller-Jentsch, W. (1998). 'Germany', in A. Ferner and R. Hyman (eds.), *Changing Industrial Relations in Europe*. Oxford: Blackwell.

Jacobs, J., and Gerson, K. (2004). *The Time Divide: Work, Family, and Gender Inequality*. Cambridge, MA: Harvard University Press.

Jacoby, S. M. (1997). *Modern Manors*. Princeton: Princeton University Press.

—— (1999). 'Are Career Jobs Headed for Extinction?', *California Management Review*, 42: 123–45.

Janis, I. L. (1982). *Groupthink*. Boston: Houghton Mifflin.

Jarvie, I. C. (1972). *Concepts and Society*. London: Routledge and Kegan Paul.

Jenkins, R. (1986). *Racism and Recruitment*. Cambridge: Cambridge University Press.

Jensen, M. C. (1989). 'Eclipse of the Public Corporation', *Harvard Business Review*, 67: 61–74.

Kalleberg, A., Reskin, B., and Hudson, K. (2000). 'Bad Jobs in America: Standard and Nonstandard Employment Relations and Job Quality in the United States', *American Sociological Review*, 65: 256–78.

Kanter, R. M. (1977). *Men and Women of the Corporation*. New York: Basic.

—— (1989). *When Giants Learn to Dance: Mastering the Challenge of Strategy, Management, and Careers in the 1990's*. New York: Simon and Schuster.

KATZNELSON, I. (1986). 'Working-Class Formation', in I. Katznelson and A. R. Zolberg (eds.), *Working-Class Formation*. Princeton: Princeton University Press.

KAY, J. (2003). *The Truth about Markets*. London: Allen Lane.

KEASEY, K., THOMPSON, S., and WRIGHT, M. (1997). 'Introduction', in K. Keasey, S. Thompson and M. Wright (eds.), *Corporate Governance*. Oxford: Oxford University Press.

KERFOOT, D., and KNIGHTS, D. (1996). 'The Best is Yet to Come?: The quest for Embodiment in Managerial Work', in D. Collinson and J. Hearn (eds.), *Men as Managers*. London: Sage.

KESSLER, I. (2000). 'Remuneration Systems', in S. Bach and K. Sisson (eds.), *Personnel Management*, 3rd edn. Oxford: Blackwell.

—— and PURCELL, J. (1992). 'Performance-Related Pay: Objectives and Application', *Human Resource Management Journal*, 2(3): 34–59.

KINDLEBERGER, C. P. (1978). *Manias, Panics and Crashes*. New York: Basic.

KINNIE, N., PURCELL, J., and HUTCHINSON, S. (2000). 'Managing the Employment Relationship in Telephone Call Centres', in K. Purcell (ed.), *Changing Boundaries in Employment*. Bristol: Bristol Academic.

KLEIN, N. (2000). *No Logo*. London: Flamingo.

—— (2002). 'Interview', *Feminist Review*, 70: 46–56.

KNIGHTS, D., and WILLMOTT, H. (1999). *Management Lives*. London: Sage.

KOCHAN, T. A., SMITH, M., WELLS, J. C., and REBITZER, J. B. (1994). 'Human Resource Strategies and Contingent Workers', *Human Resource Management*, 33: 55–77.

KORCZYNSKI, M. (2002). *Human Resource Management in Service Work*. London: Palgrave.

KORTEN, D. C. (1995). *When Corporations Rule the World*. West Hartford, CT.: Kumarian.

KRAMER, R. M. (1998). 'Revisiting the Bay of Pigs and Vietnam Decisions 25 Years Later', *Organizational Behavior and Human Decision Processes*, 73: 236–71.

KUNDA, G. (1992). *Engineering Culture: Control and Commitment in a High-Tech Corporation*. Philadelphia: Temple University Press.

—— and VAN MAANEN, J. (1999). 'Changing Scripts at Work: Managers and Professionals', *Annals of the American Academy of Political and Social Science*, 561: 64–80.

LA VALLE, I., ARTHUR, S., MILLWARD, C., SCOTT, J., and CLAYDEN, M. (2002). *Happy Families? Atypical Work and it's Influence on Family Life*. Bristol: Policy Press.

LADIPO, D. (2000). 'The Demise of Organizational Loyalty', in K. Purcell (ed.), *Changing Boundaries of Employment*. Bristol: Bristol Academic.

—— MANKELOW, R., and BURCHELL, B. (2003). 'Working Like a Dog, Sick as a Dog: Job Intensification in the Late Twentieth Century', in B. Buchell, S. Deakin, J. Michie and J. Rubery (eds.), *Systems of Production: Markets, Organisations and Performance*. London: Routledge.

LAPIERRE D., and MORO J., (2003). *Five Past Midnight in Bhopal*, London: Scribner.

LAZONICK W. (1991). *Business Organization and the Myth of the Market Economy*. Cambridge: Cambridge University Press.

LAZONICK W. (2002). 'Organizational Learning and International Competition', in W. Lazonick and M. O'Sullivan (eds.), *Corporate Governance and Sustainable Prosperity*. Basingstoke: Palgrave.

—— and O'SULLIVAN, M. (2000). 'Maximizing Shareholder Value', *Economy and Society*, 29: 13–35.

—— —— (2002). 'Introduction', in W. Lazonick and M. O'Sullivan (eds.), *Corporate Governance and Sustainable Prosperity*. Basingstoke: Palgrave.

LEGGE, K. (2000). 'Personnel Management in the "Lean Organization" ', in S. Bach and K. Sisson (eds.) *Personnel Management: A Comprehensive Guide to Theory and Practice*. Oxford: Blackwell.

—— (forthcoming). 'Ethics and Work', in M. Korczynski, R. Hodson, and P. Edwards (eds.), *Social Theories and Work*. Oxford: Oxford University Press.

LEGRAIN, P. (2002). *Open World*. London: Abacus.

LEIDNER, R. (1993). *Fast Food, Fast Talk: Service Work and the Routinization of Everyday Life*. Berkeley: University of California Press.

LIFF, S. (2003). 'The Industrial Relations of a Diverse Workforce', in P. Edwards (ed.), *Industrial Relations*, 2nd edn. Oxford: Blackwell.

—— and WAJCMAN, J. (1996). ' "Sameness" and "Difference" Revisited: Which Way Forward for Equal Opportunities Initiatives?' *Journal of Management Studies* 33: 79–94.

LINCOLN, J. R., and KALLEBERG, A. L. (1990). *Culture, Control and Commitment*. Cambridge: Cambridge University Press.

LITTLER, C., WIESNER, R., and DUNFORD, R. (2003). 'The Dynamics of Delayering: Changing Management Structures in Three Countries', *Journal of Management Studies*, 40: 225–54.

LOWENSTEIN, R. (2001). *When Genius Failed: The Rise and Fall of Long-Term Capital Management*. London: Fourth Estate.

LUKES, S. (1974). *Power*. London: Macmillan.

—— (2005). *Power: A Radical View*, 2nd edn. Basingstoke: Palgrave.

LUPTON, T. (1963). *On the Shop Floor*. Oxford: Pergamon.

McCAFFREY, D. P., Faerman, S. R., and Hart, D. W. (1995). 'The Appeal and Difficulties of Participative Systems', *Organization Science*, 6: 603–27.

McDOWELL, L. (1997). *Capital Culture: Gender at Work in the City*. Oxford: Blackwell.

McGOVERN, P, Hope-Hailey, V., and Stiles, P. (1998). 'The Managerial Career after Downsizing: Case Studies from the "Leading Edge" ', *Work, Employment & Society*, 12: 457–77.

McGOVERN, P., SMEATON, D., and HILL, S. (2004). 'Bad Jobs in Britain', *Work and Occupations*, 31: 225–49.

McGREGOR, D. (1957). 'An Uneasy Look at Performance Appraisal', *Harvard Business Review*, 35: 89–94.

—— (1960). *The Human Side of Enterprise*. New York: McGraw-Hill.

McINTOSH, I., and BRODERICK, J. (1996). 'Neither One Thing nor the Other: Compulsory Competitive Tendering and Southburgh Cleaning Services', *Work, Employment and Society*, 10: 413–30.

MacKenzie, D. (1990). *Inventing Accuracy*. Cambridge, MA: MIT Press.

—— (1996). *Knowing Machines*. Cambridge, MA: MIT Press.

—— and Millo, Y. (2003). 'Constructing a Market, Performing Theory', *American Journal of Sociology*, 109: 107–45.

—— and Wajcman, J. (1999). *The Social Shaping of Technology: Second Edition*. Buckingham: Open University Press.

McMillan, J. (2002). *Reinventing the Bazaar*. New York: Norton.

Machin, S. (2003). 'Wage Inequality Since 1975', in R. Dickens, P. Gregg, and J. Wadsworth (eds.), *The Labour Market Under New Labour: The State of Working Britain*. Basingstoke: Palgrave.

Mair, A. (1999). 'Learning from Honda', *Journal of Management Studies*, 36: 25–44.

Marchington, M., and Wilkinson, A. (2000). 'Direct Participation', in S. Bach and K. Sisson (eds.), *Personnel Management*, 3rd edn. Oxford: Blackwell.

Marginson, P. (2000). 'The Euro Company and Euro Industrial Relations', *European Journal of Industrial Relations*, 6: 9–34.

Mars, G. (1982). *Cheats at Work*. London: Counterpoint.

Martin, B., and Wajcman, J. (2004). 'Markets, Contingency and Preferences: Contemporary Managers' Narrative Identities', *Sociological Review*, 52: 239–63.

Maslow, A. (1943). 'A Theory of Human Motivation', *Psychological Review*, 50: 370–96.

Mayer, C. (1997). 'Corporate Governance, Competition and Performance', in S. Deakin and A. Hughes (eds.), *Enterprise and Community*. Oxford: Blackwell.

Merchant, K. A. (1990). 'The Effects of Financial Controls on Data Manipulation and Management Myopia', *Accounting, Organizations and Society*, 15: 297–313.

Milkman, R. (1997). *Farewell to the Factory*. Berkeley: University of California Press.

Miller, E., and Hatcher, J. (1978). *Medieval England*. London: Longman.

Mills, A., and Tancred, P. (1992). *Gendering Organizational Analysis*. London: Sage.

Mills, C. W. (1953). *White Collar: The American Middle Classes*. New York: Oxford University Press.

Mintz, B., and Schwartz, M. (1990). 'Capital Flows and the Process of Financial Hegemony', in S. Zukin and P. DiMaggio (eds.), *Structures of Capital*. Cambridge: Cambridge University Press.

Mintzberg, H., Ahlstrand, B., and Lamperl, J. (1998). *Strategy Safari*. New York: Prentice Hall.

Modell, S. (2001). 'Performance Measurement and Institutional Processes', *Management Accounting Research*, 12: 437–64.

Modood, T., Nazroo, R., Lakey, J., Nazroo, J., Smith, P., Virdee, S., and Beishon, S. (eds.) (1997). *Ethnic Minorities in Britain: Diversity and Disadvantage*. London: Policy Studies Institute.

Moran, T. H. (2002). *Beyond Sweatshops*. Washington, DC: Brookings.

Mueller, F., and Purcell, J. (1992). 'The Europeanisation of Manufacturing and the Decentralisation of Bargaining', *International Journal of Human Resource Management*, 3: 15–34.

NEUMARK, D. (2000). *On the Job: Is Long-Term Employment a Thing of the Past?* New York: Russell Sage Foundation.

NEWELL, H (2000). 'Managing Careers' in S. Bach and K. Sisson (eds.), *Personnel Management*, 3rd edn. Oxford: Blackwell.

NEWTON, T., and FINDLAY, P. (1996). 'Playing God? The Performance of Appraisal', *Human Resource Management Journal*, 6: 42–58.

NHS Women's Unit (1994). *Top Managers. Creative Career paths in the National Health Service*, Report No. 1, London.

NICHOLS, T. (1975). 'The Sociology of Accidents and the Social Production of Industrial Injury', in G. Eslans, G. Salaman, and M-A. Speakman (eds.), *People and Work*. Edinburgh: Holmes McDougall.

—— (1997). *The Sociology of Industrial Injury*. London: Mansell.

NOLAN, P., and SLATER, G. (2003). 'The Labour Market', in P. Edwards (ed.), *Industrial Relations*, 2nd edn. Oxford: Blackwell.

—— and WOOD, S. (2003). 'Mapping the Future of Work', *British Journal of Industrial Relations*, 41: 165–74.

NONAKA, I., and TAKEUCHI, H. (1995). *The Knowledge-Creating Company*. New York: Oxford University Press.

NOON, M., and BLYTON, P. (2002). *The Realities of Work,* 2nd edn. Basingstoke: Palgrave.

NOVEK, J., YASSI, A., and SPIEGEL, J. (1990). 'Mechanization, the Labour Process and Injury Risk in the Canadian Meat Packing Industry', *International Journal of Health Services*, 20: 281–96.

Ó RIAIN, S. (2000). 'Networking for a Living', in M. Burawoy, J. Blum, S. George, Z. Gille, T. Gowan, L. Haney, M. Klawiter, S. Lopez, S. Ó Riain, and M. Thayer, *Global Ethnography: Forces, Connections, and Imaginations in a Postmodern World*. Berkeley: University of California Press.

O'REILLY, C., MAIN, B., and CRYSTAL, G. (1988). 'CEO Compensation as Tournament and Social Comparison: a Tale of Two Theories', *Administrative Science Quarterly*, 33: 257–74.

O'SULLIVAN, M. A. (2000). *Contests for Corporate Control*. Oxford: Oxford University Press.

OECD (2002). *Babies and Bosses: Reconciling Work and Family Life, Vol. 1, Australia, Denmark and the Netherlands*. Paris: OECD.

OFFE, C., and RONGE, V. (1982). 'Theses on the Theory of the State', in A. Giddens and D. Held, (eds.), *Classes, Power and Conflict*. London: Macmillan.

OGDEN, S. G. (1995). 'Transforming Frameworks of Accountability: The Case of Water Privatization', *Accounting, Organizations and Society*, 20: 193–218.

OHMAE, K. (1995). *The End of the Nation State*. New York: Free Press.

ONG, A. (1987). *Spirits of Resistance and Capitalist Discipline*. Albany: SUNY Press.

ORLITZKY, M., SCHMIDT, F. L., and RYNES, S. L. (2003). 'Corporate Social and Financial Performance', *Organization Studies*, 24: 403–41.

ORMEROD, P. (1998). *Butterfly Economics*. London: Faber and Faber.

ORWELL, G. (1954). *1984*. Harmondsworth: Penguin.

OSTERMAN, P. (1994). 'How Common is Workplace Transformation and Who Adopts It?', *Industrial and Labor Relations Review*, 47: 173–88.

—— (1999). *Securing Prosperity*. Princeton, NJ: Princeton University Press.

PAGE ARNOT, R. (1953). *The Miners*. London: George Allen and Unwin.

PAHL, J., and PAHL, R. (1971). *Managers and Their Wives: A Study of Career and Family Relationship in the Middle Class*. London: Penguin.

PALMER, T. (2004). *Results of the First Flexible Working Employee Survey*. DTI Employment Relations Occasional Papers, London.

PANITCH, L., and LEYS, C. (2001). *The End of Parliamentary Socialism*, 2nd edn. London: Verso.

PARREÑAS, R. S. (2003). 'The Care Crisis in the Philippines', in B. Ehrenreich and A. R. Hochschild (eds.), *Global Women*. New York: Henry Holt.

PASCALE, R. T. (1984). 'Perspectives on Strategy', *California Management Review*, 26: 47–72.

PATEMAN, C. (1988). *The Sexual Contract*. Cambridge: Polity Press.

PERES, L. F., and ROBSON, K. (1999). 'Ritual Legitimation, De-Coupling and the Budgetary Process', *Management Accounting Research*, 10: 383–408.

PERROW, C. (1999). *Normal Accidents*, 2nd edn. Princeton: Princeton University Press.

PETERS, T., and WATERMAN, R. H. (1982). *In Search of Excellence*. New York: Harper and Row.

PLENDER, J. (2003). *Going Off the Rails*. Chichester: Wiley.

POCOCK, B. (2003). *The Work/Life Collision*. Sydney: The Federation Press.

POLLERT, A. (1981). *Girls, Wives, Factory Lives*. London: Macmillan.

POWELL, G. (1993). *Women and Men in Management*. Newbury Park: Sage.

POWELL, W. (2001). 'The Capitalist Firm in the Twenty-first Century: Emerging Patterns in Western Enterprise', in P. DiMaggio (ed.), *The Twenty-First Century Firm: Changing Economic Organization in International Perspective*. Princeton: Princeton University Press.

POWER, M. (1997). *The Audit Society*. Oxford: Oxford University Press.

PRESSER, H. (2003). *Working in a 24/7 Economy: Challenges for American Families*. New York: Russell Sage Foundation.

PRESSER, H. (2000). 'Nonstandard Work Schedules and Marital Instability', *Journal of Marriage and Family*, 62: 93–110.

PricewaterhouseCoopers, (1999). *International Student Survey: Summary Findings Report*. London: PWC.

PUNCH, M. (1996). *Dirty Business*. London: Sage.

QUAID, M. (1993). 'Job Evaluation as Institutional Myth', *Journal of Management Studies*, 30: 239–60.

RADIN, M. (1996). *Contested Commodities*. Cambridge, MA.: Harvard University Press.

RAKE, K. (ed.) (2000). *Women's Incomes over the Lifetime: A Report to the Women's Unit*. London: Cabinet Office.

RAPOPORT, R., and BAILYN, L. (1996). *Relinking Life and Work: Toward a Better Future.* New York: Ford Foundation.

REBITZER, J. B. (1995). 'Job Safety and Contract Workers in the Petroleum Industry', *Industrial Relations*, 34: 40–57.

RESKIN, B., and McBRIER, D. (2000). 'Why Not Ascription? Organizations' Employment of Male and Female Managers', *American Sociological Review*, 65: 210–33.

RIESMAN, D. (1950). *The Lonely Crowd*. New Haven: Yale University Press.

ROBERTS, K. H. (1990). 'Some Characteristics of One Type of High Reliability Organization', *Organization Science*, 1: 160–76.

ROBINSON, J., and GODBEY, G. (1997). *Time for Life: The Surprising Ways Americans Use Their Time*. University Park: Penn State University Press.

ROSE, M. (2003). 'Good Deal, Bad Deal? Job Satisfaction in Occupations', *Work, Employment and Society*, 17: 503–30.

ROSENER, J. (1990). 'Ways Women Lead', *Harvard Business Review*, 68: 119–26.

ROSENTHAL, P., HILL, S., and PECCEI, R. (1997). 'Checking Out Service', *Work, Employment and Society*, 11: 481–504.

ROSS, J., and STAW, B. M. (1993). 'Organizational Escalation and Exit', *Academy of Management Journal*, 36: 701–32.

ROUSSEAU, D. M. (1995). *Psychological Contracts in Organizations: Understanding Written and Unwritten Agreements*. Thousand Oaks: Sage.

ROY, D. (1954). 'Efficiency and "the Fix" ', *American Journal of Sociology*, 60: 255–66.

ROYLE, T. (2000). *Working for McDonald's in Europe*. London: Routledge.

RUBERY, J. (1995). 'Performance Related Pay and the Prospects for Gender Pay Equity', *Journal of Management Studies*, 32: 637–54.

RUBINSTEIN, S. A., and KOCHAN, T. A. (2001). *Learning from Saturn*. Ithaca : ILR Press.

RUNCIMAN, W. G. (1999). *The Social Animal*. London: Fontana.

SAGAN, S. D. (1993). *The Limits of Safety*. Princeton: Princeton University Press.

SALA-I-MARTIN, X. (2002). 'The World Distribution of Income', National Bureau of Economic Research, Working Paper 8933, May.

SASS, R. (2000). 'The Dark Side of Taiwan's Globalization Success Story', *International Journal of Health Services*, 30: 699–716.

SAVAGE, M. (2000). *Class Analysis and Social Transformation*. Buckingham: Open University Press.

—— and WITZ, A. (1992). *Gender and Bureaucracy*. Oxford: Blackwell.

SCASE, R., and GOFFEE, R. (1989). *Reluctant Managers: Their Work and Lifestyles*. London: Unwin Hyman.

SCHLOSSER, E. (2002). *Fast Food Nation*. New York: Perennial.

SCHOR, J. (1991). *The Overworked American*. New York: Basic Books.

SCHWARTZ, F. (1992). *Breaking with Tradition: Women and Work, the New Facts of Life*. New York: Time Warner.

SCHWARTZ, H. M. (1994). *States versus Markets*. New York: St. Martin's.

SCOTT, J. (1997). *Corporate Business and Capitalist Classes*. Oxford: Oxford University Press.

SELL, S. K. (2000). 'Structures, Agents and Institutions', in R. A. Higgott, G. R. D. Underhill, and A. Bieler, (eds.), *Non-State Actors and Authority in the Global System*. London: Routledge.

SENNETT, R. (1998). *The Corrosion of Character: The Personal Consequences of Work in the New Capitalism*. New York: W.W. Norton.

SHILLER, R. J. (1990). 'Speculative Prices and Population Models', *Journal of Economic Perspectives*, 4: 55–65.

SHORT, H., and KEASEY, K. (1997). 'Institutional Shareholders and Corporate Governance in the UK', in K. Keasey, S. Thompson, and M. Wright (eds.), *Corporate Governance*. Oxford: Oxford University Press.

SISSON, K., and MARGINSON, P. (2003). 'Management: Systems, Structures and Strategy', in P. Edwards (ed.), *Industrial Relations:* 2nd edn. Oxford: Blackwell.

SKLAIR, L. (2001). *The Transnational Capitalist Class*. Oxford: Blackwell.

—— (2002). *Globalization: Capitalism and Its Alternatives*. Oxford: Oxford University Press.

SMITH, V. (2001). *Crossing the Great Divide: Worker Risk and Opportunity in the New Economy*. Ithaca: ILR Press.

SMITH-DOERR, L. (2004). *Women's Work: Gender Equality vs. Hierarchy in the Life Sciences*. Boulder: Lynne Rienner Publishers.

STAW, B. M. (1976). 'Knee-deep in the Big Muddy', *Organizational Behavior and Human Processes*, 16: 27–44.

STEVENS, J., BROWN, J., and LEE, C. (2004). *The Second Work-Life Balance Study: Results from the Employees' Survey*, DTI Employment Relations Research Series 27. London: DTI.

STIGLITZ, J. E. (2002). *Globalization and Its Discontents*. London: Allen Lane.

STILES, P., GRATTON, L., TRUSS, C., HOPE-HAILEY, V., and McGOVERN, P. (1997). 'Performance Management and the Psychological Contract', *Human Resource Management Journal*, 7: 57–66.

STIX, G. (1998). 'A Calculus of Risk', *Scientific American*, 278: 70–5.

STOREY, J., EDWARDS, P., and SISSON, K. (1997). *Managers in the Making: Careers, Development and Control in Corporate Britain and Japan*. London: Sage.

STRANGE, S. (1998). *Mad Money*. Manchester: Manchester University Press.

STREECK, W. (1987). 'The Uncertainties of Management and the Management of Uncertainty', *Work, Employment and Society*, 1: 281–308.

STRINATI, D. (1979). 'Capitalism, the State and Industrial Relations', in C. Crouch (ed.), *State and Economy in Contemporary Capitalism*. London: Croom Helm.

TAPLIN, I. M., and WINTERTON, J. (2002). 'Responses to Globalized Production', in Y. A. Debrah and I. G. Smith (eds.), *Globalization, Employment and the Workplace*. London: Routledge.

TAYLOR, P., HYMAN, J., MULVAY, G., and BAIN, P. (2002). 'Work Organization, Control and the Experience of Work in Call Centres', *Work, Employment and Society*, 16: 133–50.

TAYLOR, R. (2002). *The Future of Work-Life Balance*, ESRC Future of Work Programme Series. Swindon: ESRC.

THELEN, K., and KUME, I. (2003). 'The Future of Nationally Embedded Capitalism', in K. Yamamuru and W. Streeck (eds.), *The End of Diversity*. Ithaca: Cornell University Press.

THOMPSON, L. (1991). 'Family Work: Women's Sense of Fairness', *Journal of Family Issues*, 12: 186–96.

THOMPSON, P. (1989). *The Nature of Work*, 2nd edn. London: Macmillan.

—— (2003). 'Disconnected Capitalism', *Work, Employment and Society*, 17: 359–78.

—— and McHUGH, D. (2002). *Work Organisations*, 3rd edn. Basingstoke: Palgrave.

——, WARHURST, C., and CALLAGHAN, G. (2001). 'Ignorant Theory and Knowledge-able Workers: Interrogating the Connections between Knowledge, Skills and Services', *Journal of Management Studies*, 38: 923–42.

TILLY, C. (2001). 'Welcome to the Seventeenth Century', in P. DiMaggio (ed.), *The Twenty-First-Century Firm*. Princeton: Princeton University Press.

TOWNLEY, B. (1996). 'Accounting in Detail', *Critical Perspectives in Accounting*, 7: 565–84.

—— (1999). 'Practical Reason and Performance Appraisal', *Journal of Management Studies*, 36: 287–306.

TOYNBEE, P. (2003). *Hard Work: Life in Low-Pay Britain*. London: Bloomsbury Publishing.

TRIST, E., and BAMFORTH, K. W. (1951). 'Some Social and Psychological Consequences of the Long-Wall Method of Coal-Getting', *Human Relations*, 4: 3–38.

TURNER, A. (1996). 'Link Pay to Performance and We'll Stay on Track', *People Management*, 8 February.

TURNER, B. A. (1976). 'The Organizational and Interorganizational Development of Disasters', *Administrative Science Quarterly*, 21: 378–97.

TURNER, M. E., and PRATKANIS, A. R. (1998). 'Twenty-Five Years of Groupthink Theory and Research', *Organizational Behavior and Human Decision Processes*, 73: 105–15.

VALLAS, S. P. (2003). 'Why Team Work Fails', *American Sociological Review*, 68: 223–50.

—— and BECK, J. P. (1996). 'The Transformation of Work Revisited', *Social Problems*, 43: 339–61.

VAN BUITENEN, P. (2000). *Blowing the Whistle*. London: Politico's.

VAUGHAN, D. (1996). *The Challenger Launch Decision*. Chicago: University of Chicago Press.

—— (1999). 'The Dark Side of Organizations', *Annual Review of Sociology*, 25: 271–305.

VINKENBURG, C. J., JANSON, P. G., and KOOPMAN, P. L. (2000). 'Feminine Leadership—A Review of Gender Differences in Managerial Behaviour and Effectiveness' in M. J. Davidson and R. J. Burke (eds.), *Women in Management: Current Research Issues. Volume II*. London: Sage.

VITOLS, S. (2003). 'From Banks to Markets', in K. Yamamuru and W. Streeck, (eds.), *The End of Diversity?* Ithaca: Cornell University Press.

VUCKOVIC, N. (1999). 'Fast Relief: Buying Time with Medications', *Medical Anthropological Quarterly*, 13: 51–68.

WADSWORTH, J. (2003). 'The Labour Market Performance of Ethnic Minorities in the Recovery', in R. Dickens, P. Gregg, and J. Wadsworth (eds.), *The Labour Market Under New Labour: The State of Working Britain*. New York: Palgrave Macmillan.

WAJCMAN, J. (1991). *Feminism Confronts Technology*. Cambridge: Polity Press.

—— (1998). *Managing Like a Man: Women and Men in Corporate Management*. Cambridge: Polity Press.

—— (2004). *Technofeminism*. Cambridge: Polity Press.

—— and MARTIN, B. (2001). 'My Company or My Career: Managerial Achievement and Loyalty', *British Journal of Sociology*, 52: 559–78.

WALBY, S. (1997). *Gender Transformations*. London: Routledge.

WALDFOGEL, J. (1997). 'The Effects of Children on Women's Wages', *American Sociological Review*, 62: 209–17.

WALTON, R. E. (1985). 'From Control to Commitment in the Workplace', *Harvard Business Review*, 53: 77–84.

WARD, K., RAHMAN, F., SAIFUL ISLAM, A. K. M., and AKHTER, R. (2004). 'The Effects of Global Economic Restructuring on Urban Women's Work and Income-Generating Strategies in Dhaka, Bangladesh', *Critical Sociology*, 30: 63–102.

WEICK, K. E. (1993). 'The Vulnerable System', in K. H. Roberts (ed.), *New Challenges to Understanding Organizations*. New York: Macmillan.

WEISS, L. (1997). 'Globalization and the Myth of the Powerless State', *New Left Review*, 225: 3–28.

—— (1998). *The Myth of the Powerless State*. Cambridge: Polity Press.

WELCH, J. (1993). 'Jack Welch's Lessons for Success', *Fortune*, 25 January, 68–72.

WEST, C. and ZIMMERMAN, D. (1987). 'Doing Gender', *Gender and Society*, 1: 125–51.

WESTERN, B., and BECKETT, K. (1999). 'How Unregulated is the US Labor Market?', *American Journal of Sociology*, 104: 1030–60.

WEVER, K. (1995). *Negotiating Competitiveness*. Boston: Harvard Business School Press.

WHEEN, F. (1999). *Karl Marx*. London: Fourth Estate.

WHITE, M., HILL, S., MCGOVERN, P., MILLS, C., and SMEATON, D. (2003). 'High-Performance Management Practices, Working Hours and Work-Life Balance', *British Journal of Industrial Relations*, 41: 175–95.

WHITLEY, R. (1999). *Divergent Capitalisms*. Oxford: Oxford University Press.

WHYTE, W. F., and WHYTE, K. K. (1988). *Making Mondragón*. Ithaca: ILR Press.

WHYTE, W. H. (1956). *The Organization Man*. New York: Simon and Schuster.

WILKINSON, A. (1998). 'Empowerment', in M. Poole and M. Warner (eds.), *The IEBM Handbook of Human Resource Management*. London: International Thomson.

WILLIAMS, K., HASLAM, C., JOHAL, S., and WILLIAMS, J. (1994). *Cars*. Providence: Berghahn.

WILLMAN, P., FENTON-O'CREEVEY, M. P., NICHOLSON, N., and SOANE, E. (2001). 'Knowing the Risks: Theory and Practice in Financial Market Trading', *Human Relations*, 54: 887–910.

WILSON, F., and THOMPSON, P. (2001). 'Sexual Harassment as an Exercise of Power', *Gender, Work and Organization*, 8: 61–83.

WINNER, L. (1999). 'Do Artifacts Have Politics?' in D. MacKenzie and J. Wajcman (eds.), *The Social Shaping of Technology: Second Edition*. Buckingham: Open University Press.

WIRTH, L. (2001). *Breaking Through the Glass: Women in Management*. Geneva: ILO.

WITTE, J. F. (1980). *Democracy, Authority and Alienation in Work*. Chicago: University of Chicago Press.

WOKUTCH, R. E., and VANSANDT, C. V. (2000). 'National Styles of Worker Protection in the US and Japan', *Law and Policy*, 22: 369–84.

WOLF, D. L. (1992). *Factory Daughters*. Berkeley: University of California Press.

WOLF, M. (2004). 'We Need More Globalization, but We Will Only Get It if We Have Better States', *Financial Times*, 10 May.

WOODS, N. (ed.) (2000). 'The Political Economy of Globalization', in *The Political Economy of Globalization*. Basingstoke: Macmillan.

WORRALL, L., and COOPER, C. (2001). *The Quality of Working Life: The 2000 Survey of Managers' Experiences*. London: Institute of Management.

—— CAMPBELL, F. K., and COOPER, C. L. (2000). 'The New Reality for UK Managers', *Work, Employment and Society*, 14: 647–68.

YEANDLE, S., WIGFIELD, A., CROMPTON, R., and DENNETT, J. (2002). *Employed Carers and Family-Friendly Employment Policies*. Bristol: Policy Press.

INDEX

Note: Entries in **bold** refer to text boxes.

Index